Hanging by a Promise

The author with Dr. Oswald Bayer in March 2012.

Hanging by a Promise
The Hidden God in the Theology of Oswald Bayer

Joshua C. Miller

Foreword by
Steven D. Paulson

☙PICKWICK *Publications* • Eugene, Oregon

HANGING BY A PROMISE
The Hidden God in the Theology of Oswald Bayer

Copyright © 2015 Joshua C. Miller. All rights reserved. Except for brief quotations in critical publications or reviews, no part of this book may be reproduced in any manner without prior written permission from the publisher. Write: Permissions. Wipf and Stock Publishers, 199 W. 8th Ave., Suite 3, Eugene, OR 97401.

Pickwick Publications
An Imprint of Wipf and Stock Publishers
199 W. 8th Ave., Suite 3
Eugene, OR 97401

www.wipfandstock.com

ISBN 13: 978-1-62564-195-3

Cataloguing-in-Publication data:

Miller, Joshua C.

    Hanging by a promise : the hidden God in the theology of Oswald Bayer / Joshua C. Miller ; foreword by Stephen D. Paulson.

    xx + 354 p. ; 23 cm. Includes bibliographical references and indexes.

    ISBN 13: 978-1-62564-195-3

    1. Bayer, Oswald. 2. Theology. 3. Luther, Martin, 1483–1546. I. Paulson, Stephen D. II. Title.

BT30 G3 M56 2015

Manufactured in the USA   02/12/2015

All Scripture quoted from the New Revised Standard Version of the Bible. New Revised Standard Version Bible, copyright 1989, Division of Christian Education of the National Council of the Churches of Christ in the United States of America. Used by permission. All rights reserved.

To my wife, Katie

Contents

Foreword by Steven D. Paulson | ix
Preface | xiii
Acknowledgments | xv
Abbreviations | xvii

1 Introduction | 1
2 The Hidden God in the Theology of Martin Luther | 13
3 The Reception of Luther's Doctrine of the Hidden God in the Modern German Protestant Theological Tradition | 41
4 Bayer's Approach to Theology | 115
5 Bayer's Theology of Justification by the Promise | 147
6 The Hidden God in Bayer's Approach to Theology | 173
7 The Hidden God and Bayer's Doctrine of Justification | 209
8 Bayer's Interpretation of Luther on the Hidden God | 257
9 Review, Assessment, and Possibilities | 303

Bibliography | 331
Name Index | 347
Subject Index | 349
Scripture Index | 353

Foreword

THIS EXCELLENT BOOK BY Joshua Miller serves a dual purpose. It introduces you to Oswald Bayer, one of the most important theologians of our age, and immerses you in the thorny, disruptive discussion of God's hiddenness. Bringing these two together in an investigation of Bayer's teaching of the hidden God is itself a revelation. Most modern theology is premised on a bewitching denial of God hiding, or at least a severe curtailing of divine hiddenness. Bayer has broken that spell. It is also the case that Germany has long enjoyed Professor Bayer's work, and a flood of recent translations into English have now opened his work to a wider audience. Yet English speakers have needed an introduction to his work and life, which this book amply supplies. Dr. Miller is an erudite scholar who makes Bayer's considerable body of work accessible and shows its import for current theological study.

Bayer's fascinating theology began with his doctoral dissertation, *Promissio*, which established a fresh approach to Luther's breakthrough—Luther became Lutheran when he heard that the promise-word of absolution (I absolve you) accomplishes what it says: it actually forgives sinners. This set the nature of a promise at the center of theology, and made it possible to understand the importance and content of preaching for the evangelical cause. A promise that divinely creates what it says grasps the essential work of theology, justification by faith alone, that makes the proper distinction between two divine words, law and gospel. This was a Copernican revolution in theology, and continues to be, since the person receiving God's word was defined by that speaking God (*deus dicens*) rather than defining God by the thinking human subject (faith seeking understanding).

Therein lies the importance of God's several ways of hiding, since God not only gives the promise that makes faith—hidden under the sign of his opposite—but is also the very one who proceeds to contradict his own promise. So along with the two ways of God encountering us through law and gospel there is a third irreconcilable confrontation apart from preaching altogether where God hides as unpreached. God unpreached is no less a real encounter than when God speaks to you. At the very least this makes God infinitely more interesting than the bulk of recent attempts to make the subjective, abstract speculations of thinking, feeling or doing the be-all and end-all of theology. More significantly, Bayer is among the very few who are willing to address what happens when God becomes the very enemy of a believer. Ever since Martin Luther took up the matter of what it meant for God to be the very one who attacks and tries the believer, *Anfechtung*, people have run for cover in some theory that disallows this attack. Moreover, Bayer is willing to address Luther's profound biblical, and worldly, observation that God comes to oppose God, not only in the faith of the believer, but in Himself. There is a great divine duel in the cross of Christ that leaves most theologians running for their lives. Barth is simply the most famous of those who warned against entering this discussion of God's hiddenness as God against God as Luther did, rather than simply treating God hidden in the sign of his opposite. Too dangerous, they say! All sorts of bad things can be said about God unpreached that would lead people to flee rather than seek God. But for this very reason, no one comes close to Bayer's thrilling descriptions of Jacob wrestling with God at the Jabbok, or Job in the middle of his lawsuit against God, to say nothing of Bayer's exegetical work in the Psalms of lament.

Dr. Miller not only explains what Bayer is saying with these biblical texts, but also illuminates why Bayer's departure from pedestrian theodicy is so liberating. Imagine working with a theology that not only accepts as data, or experience, the word of God in the law that kills and the gospel that gives life, but also the profound spiritual attack of God hidden outside any preached word at all. But we have it in Bayer, and it means he approaches the most disruptive theological questions squarely: Why does God chose some and not others? And Why is there evil? Predestination and theodicy are the inescapable trials of theology. When one does not distinguish between a God hidden outside his preached word and God hidden under the sign of his opposite in the preached word, these two questions leave one with excruciating decisions between impossible alternatives: God is all powerful and allows evil; or God is not all powerful, and so cannot help but allow evil. Of course the solution to such dualisms is always some attempt at a free will or the teaching that "faith" is a human potential to enact the word, rather than the word that makes faith. No wonder people abandon theology when it comes to this kind of choice. Bayer is much more interesting than such a dismal science. Instead of an imaginary subjectivity that is active while the word lies dormant (in need of someone to think it, or believe it, or to do it), God himself is recognized as most active precisely in addressing creation. Creation is thus built upon God's language, and the word of God is the most active thing of life. Creatures, especially humans, are passive, not in the sense of never doing or thinking themselves, but in the fundament sense of hearing or undergoing the address of God—suffering the language of God. God speaks; humans hear.

Because of these active, divine words, Bayer respects the details of language, and so stretches far beyond typical theology with his rhetorical explorations of linguistic genres. This openness, in turn, allows him to draw from sources often considered beneath systematic theology and speculative thought, such as hymns and catechism and everyday human speech. Bayer has thus stepped beyond the barrier between continental idealism and analytical philosophy of language, but more so into the developments beyond words as mere propositions and assertions to speech acts like we find in J. L. Austin's *How to Do Things with Words*. Although Austin could not recognize the theological difference between a divine and human word, and so their intersection, Bayer nevertheless uses Austin as a way of helping to describe what it means for humans to have active words and a language that precedes thought and will. But Bayer's main interest philosophically is not Austin, but the "magus of the North," J. G. Hamann, who replaced Kant's dualistic, active form of enlightenment with a radical enlightenment in which life is passive at its root—a suffering or undergoing of the address of God. This is what it means to say that language precedes thought because it is God's divine speech that creates anything out of nothing. This creation is not a onetime act, but a daily matter—moment by moment—God speaking creation continually by means of that very creation. Not only is the word active, but instead of thinking of word as a subjective thing meant for pure reason, the divine word is bodily word (*leibliches Wort*) that comes to us by creation for creation. For this reason Bayer can tell the story of Christ healing the deaf mute with such verve: "*Ephphatha*"! ("Be opened!") is not a word for subjective speculation, but a new creation which the deaf undergo by means of a word put in an earthly thing.

All of theology, therefore is a kind of experience, but not that of Schleiermacher's absolute dependency. It is the suffering of hearing. So, the words of God become the total occupation of theology which are especially addressed in the work of interpreting Scripture. The exegesis is not treating the words as if they needed animation, or application, or "relevance" for the current situation. Instead, the words of Scripture, law and gospel, are addressed to us for the purpose of proclaiming the promise of forgiveness to the ungodly, while we are yet ungodly. In other words, the shape of theology (and so Christian life) is the three-fold experience of meditation (meditation) on the text of Scripture, prayer (oratio) that suffers these words as God's own address to us, and the uncontrollable matter of God's hiddenness that attacks the very promise made to you and makes God the enemy of the believer (tentatio).

This is truly theology "the Lutheran way," and no one in our time does it better than Oswald Bayer. Unpacking this considerable work with its depth of riches is not easy. Comparing it to other theologies, offering perspective and critique, and faithfully laying out the argument is no simple matter either. Yet Dr. Miller's book accomplishes that work and more. It will inspire you to explore the work of Oswald Bayer. Then it will ruin the common monistic theologies of thought, deed, or feeling by opening you to the theology that takes God's hiddenness seriously. Such fractures in life and thought are not easy, but indeed they will be very rewarding in the end, as will your pilgrimage into this book

Steven Paulson
Professor of Systematic Theology
Luther Seminary, St. Paul

Preface

IN ONE OF HIS greatest known works, *The Bondage of the Will*, the sixteenth-century reformer Martin Luther sets forth his teaching on the hidden God. In this teaching, Luther articulates that God's existence and will revealed in Jesus Christ are to be distinguished from God's existence and will hidden outside of Christ. Whereas in Christ through the Word God reveals God's self as a God of grace, mercy, and love, God hidden outside of revelation exists as a God of wrath, who wills the death and damnation of sinners and wills all things that come to pass.[1] Although this doctrine of Luther's was somewhat neglected by his successors, it was rediscovered by Theodosius Harnack and has been taken up, discussed, and interpreted by scholars and theologians in the modern German Protestant theological tradition ever since.

One of the contemporary theologians from this tradition who addresses and utilizes Luther's doctrine of the hidden God is Oswald Bayer. A prominent voice within contemporary confessional Lutheran theology, Bayer interacts with Luther's doctrine of the hidden God in conjunction with his own approach to doing theology as a Lutheran and his contemporary articulation of the reformer's theology of justification by faith in Christ alone through the preached Word of the gospel.

In this work I examine the place of Luther's understanding of the hiddenness of God in the Lutheran theology of Bayer. I introduce Oswald Bayer as a Luther scholar and a Lutheran systematic theologian, sketch the theme of hiddenness in Bayer's thought, and explore how Luther understands the hiddenness of God and how this understanding has been assessed and interpreted in the German Protestant theological tradition, from T. Harnack to Eberhard Jüngel. I highlight how Oswald Bayer is unique amongst

---

1. Luther, *BOW*, 169–71; *De servo arbitrio*, WA 18:684–86.

modern German Protestant theologians in that he actually seeks to reclaim and utilize Luther's doctrine of the hidden God in his own theology.

I then move on to investigate how Bayer defines and uses divine hiddenness in his own Lutheran theology. I explore how exactly Bayer's theology is "Lutheran" in terms of how he approaches the doing of theology through his interpretation of Luther concerning the mode, method, data, and central subject of theology, as well as how Bayer inherits and adopts Luther's view of hiddenness and inherits and reacts to the tradition's treatment of Luther's teaching, how divine hiddenness functions within Bayer's theology, and how his view of hiddenness compares to Luther's view of it and the modern German Protestant tradition's interpretation of Luther on hiddenness. Finally, I conclude by evaluating Bayer's use of divine hiddenness and relate how Bayer's Lutheran theology with its view of God's hiddenness might be used constructively by Lutheran theologians today.

Acknowledgments

I WOULD LIKE TO express my appreciation to the many people whose help and encouragement helped to make this publication possible. Firstly, I would like to thank my Ph.D. thesis committee, including my advisor Steven Paulson, and my readers, Amy Marga and Mark Tranvik. These three have all been teachers and mentors to me, helping to shape the way I think theologically and how best to express my thoughts, especially with regard to the theme of God's hiddenness. Secondly, I would like to thank Robert Kolb, whose intricate reading of and comments on my work as well as his friendly conversation here helped to refine my arguments, claims, and conclusions. Thirdly, I would like to thank my Pastor and friend, Thomas Trapp, whose work translating Oswald Bayer's *Martin Luther's Theology* sparked and fueled my interest in Bayer's theology. Fourthly, I would like to thank my friend and colleague, Adam Morton, who has spent many hours discussing Bayer's theology as well as systematic and historical theology in general and who has helped me nuance many of my thoughts. Fifthly, I would like to thank my young sons Martin, Peter, and Thomas whose patience and humor with me during this endeavor have not been in vain. Sixthly, I would like to express my sincere thanks and love to my wife, partner, friend, and critic, Katie. She has given and continues to give me more support than I could ever retell, from countless conversations on the topics addressed in this work, to rearranging our lives to make the writing of it possible, to laborious proofreading and giving critical suggestions on the text. Finally, I would like to express my heartfelt gratitude to Oswald Bayer whose continued gracious and generous conversation has brought me the greatest joy in the midst of the experience that is the doing of theology. Thank you all.

Abbreviations

Ap	Philip Melanchthon, *Apology of the Augsburg Confession* (1531). Translated by Charles Arand. In *BC*
BC	*The Book of Concord: The Confessions of the Evangelical Lutheran Church*. Edited by Robert Kolb and Timothy J. Wengert. Translated by Charles Arand, et al.
BOW	Martin Luther, *The Bondage of the Will* (1525). Translated by J. I. Packer and O. R. Johnston. Grand Rapids: Revell, 2000
BSLK	*Die Bekenntnisschriften der evangelisch-lutherischen Kirche*, 2. Auflage. Edited by Horst Georg Pöhlmann. Gütersloh: Mohn, 1987
CA	*The Augsburg Confession* (1530). Translated by Eric Gritsch. In *BC*
CD	Karl Barth, *Church Dogmatics*. Translated and edited by Geoffrey W. Bromiley and T. F. Torrance. Edinburgh: T & T Clark, 1936–69; rev. ed., 1975; reprinted 2004.
CR	*Corpus Reformatorum. Philippi Melanchthonis Opera*. Halle: C. A. Schwetschke et Fillium, 1834–1860
Dogmatics	Emil Brunner. *Dogmatics*. Translated by Olive Wyon. Philadelphia: Westminster, 1950-1962
EG	*Evangelisches Gesangbuch*. Ausgabe für die Evangelsich-Lutherischen Kirchen in Bayern und Thüringen. Munich: Evangelischer Presseverband für Bayern; Weimar: Wartburg
ELW	*Evangelical Lutheran Worship*. Minneapolis: Augsburg Fortress, 2006

Excerpts	*Excerpts from the Writings of Philip Melanchthon.* Selected and translated by Michael Rogness. Howard Lake, MN.
ET	English translation
FC	*Formula of Concord.* Translated by Robert Kolb. In *BC.*
FC,Ep	*Epitome of the Formula of Concord*
FC,SD	*Solid Declaration of the Formula of Concord*
Freedom	Martin Luther, *The Freedom of a Christian.* Translated by Mark D. Tranvik. Minneapolis: Fortress, 2008
GD	Karl Barth, *The Göttingen Dogmatics: Instruction in the Christian Religion, Volume I.* Translated by Geoffrey W. Bromiley. Edited by Hannelotte Reiffen. Grand Rapids: Eerdmans, 1991
IJST	*International Journal of Systematic Theology*
JBT	*Jahrbuch für Biblische Theologie*
JR 1	Albrecht Ritschl, *A Critical History of the Christian Doctrine of Justification and Reconciliation.* Translated by John S. Black. Edinburgh: Edmonston & Douglas, 1872
JR 3	Albrecht Ritschl, *The Christian Doctrine of Justification and Reconciliation: The Positive Development of the Doctrine.* Translated by H. R. Mackintosh and A. B. Macaulay. Edinburgh: T&T Clark, 1900
K&D	*Kirche und Dogma*
Loci (1521)	*The Loci Communes of Philip Melanchthon* (1521). Translated by Charles Leander Hill. Eugene, OR: Wipf & Stock, 2005
Loci (1543)	*Loci Communes* (1543). Translated by J. A. O. Preus. St. Louis: Concordia, 1994
Loci (1555)	*Loci Communes* (1555). Translated and edited by Clyde L. Manschreck. Oxford: Oxford University Press, 1965
LQ	*Lutheran Quarterly*
LSB	*Lutheran Service Book.* St. Louis: Concordia, 2006
LW	*Luther's Works.* Edited by Jaroslav Pelikan and Helmut T. Lehmann. 56 Vols. St. Louis and Philadelphia, 1955–

NZSTh	*Neue Zeitschrift für Systematische Theologie und Religionsphilosophie*
Römerbrief	Karl Barth, *The Epistle to the Romans*. Translated by Edwyn C. Hoskyns. Oxford: Oxford University Press, 1968
SA	*Smalkald Articles*. Translated by William Russell. In *BC*
SJT	*Scottish Journal of Theology*
StA	*Studienausgabe—Melanchthons Werke*. Edited by Robert Stupperich. Gütersloh: Mohn, 1952–
TE	*Theological Essays II*. Translated by Arnold Neufeldt-Fast and J. B. Webster. Edited by J. B. Webster. Edinburgh: T. & T. Clark, 1995
WA	*D. Martin Luthers Werke*. Kritische Gesamtausgabe (Weimarer Ausgabe). Weimar: Herman Böhlaus Nachfolger, 1883–
WA TR	*D. Martin Luthers Werke, Tischreden*. Kritische Gesamtausgabe (Weimarer Ausgabe, Tischreden). Weimar: Herman Böhlaus Nachfolger, 1883–
ZThK	*Zeitschrift für Theologie und Kirche*

1

Introduction

IF THERE IS ONE theologian in particular whose works Lutheran theologians in America should read today, it is Oswald Bayer. Bayer has contributed greatly to the pursuit of Luther scholarship, to scholarship on the eighteenth-century philosopher and linguist Johann Georg Hamann, and to systematic theology.[1] These contributions have brought to light new perspectives and insights to theological, philosophical, and linguistic circles both in and outside of Europe. Bayer's doctoral dissertation, entitled *Promissio*, presents Martin Luther's understanding of God's justifying Word of promise in the gospel of Christ as seen particularly in the reformer's teaching regarding Holy Communion in *The Babylonian Captivity of the Church* (1520) as the essential theological core of the reformational movement.[2] In his work, *Martin Luthers Theologie: Eine Vergegenwärtigung*, Bayer has provided a comprehensive commentary on Luther's theology from the standpoint of God's justifying promise as its center.[3] In his works, *Zeitgenosse im Widerspruch: Johann Georg Hamann als radikaler Aufklärer* and *Vernunft ist Sprache: Hamanns Metakritik Kants*, Bayer has opened a new discussion in contemporary circles of linguistic philosophy and the philosophy of religion regarding the person, work, and thought of the long-neglected Enlightenment figure Hamann.[4]

---

1. Mattes, *The Role of Justification in Contemporary Theology*, 145.

2. Bayer, *Promissio*, "Vorwort," 11–13, 225–29ff. Helmer, "The Subject of Theology in the Thought of Oswald Bayer," 22–24.

3. Bayer, *Martin Luthers Theologie*, 49; ET *Martin Luther's Theology: A Contemporary Interpretation*, 53–54.

4. Betz, "Enlightenment Revisited," 291. Bayer, *Vernunft ist Sprache*, xii.

As a systematic theologian rooted firmly within the Lutheran tradition, Bayer has offered his own uniquely Lutheran approaches to the discussion of theological hermeneutics, theological methodology, the doctrine of creation, the doctrine of sanctification, theological ethics, and sacramentology.[5] Bayer's greatest contribution to contemporary theology, however, lies in his project of doing systematic theology as a Lutheran from the standpoint of God's justifying promise as the "basis and boundary" and only true subject of all theology.[6] This focus on the foundational nature of justification in theology uniquely positions Bayer amongst others in contemporary theology as one who approaches the theme of divine hiddenness uniquely from the standpoint of God's justification of the sinner in Jesus Christ.

Oswald Bayer's Life

Oswald Bayer was born on September 30, 1939, in Nagold, Württemberg, Germany, where he was baptized the following day.[7] His father was killed in June 1941, in Lithuania during the initial phases of Operation Barbarossa, the invasion of the Soviet Union by the Third Reich. Bayer was then raised by his mother and maternal grandfather.[8] In his formative years, Bayer greatly enjoyed being out in nature, cycling, and painting.[9] In 1966, he married Eva Hennig, with whom he had two children, Bettina and Joachim.[10] He studied theology at the Rheinische Friedrich-Wilhelms Universität in Bonn in the Bundesland of Nordrhein-Westfalen, at the Eberhard Karls Universität in Tübingen in the Bundesland of Baden-Württemberg, and at the Waldensian Faculty in Rome. He also spent time studying philosophy at the Ruprecht-Karls Universität in Heidelberg. He became a Doctor of Theology, graduating from Bonn in 1970 and having completed *Promissio* as his dissertation and habilitation under the theologian and Luther scholar Ernst Bizer and having also studied under Ernst Käsemann.[11] After serving

---

5. Mattes, *The Role of Justification in Contemporary Theology*, 145. Silcock and Mattes, "Editors' Introduction," in *Theology the Lutheran Way*, by Bayer, xvi–xvii.

6. Bayer, *Justification as the Basis and Boundary of Theology*, 274, 187; *Leibliches Wort*, 20, 34. Helmer, "The Subject of Theology in the Thought of Oswald Bayer," 25.

7. Bayer, *Zeitgenosse im Widerspruch*, 2. Bayer, "Selbstdarstellung," 305.

8. Ibid.

9. Ibid.

10. Author's personal conversation with Oswald Bayer, Luther Seminary, St. Paul, MN (March 24, 2012).

11. Bayer, *Promissio*, 11. Bayer "Selbstdarstellung," 303. Email exchanges with

his vicariate in the Evangelical Church of Württemberg, Bayer served as a parish pastor of that same Church in Täbingen, Baden-Württemberg from 1972–1974. During the same time, Bayer served as an assistant professor (*Privatdozent*) at Tübingen, before teaching as a full professor of systematic theology at the Ruhr-Universität in Bochum from 1974 to 1979 and then back at Tübingen as a full professor of systematic theology from 1979 to 2005.[12] In 1993, Eva Bayer died and Bayer later remarried to Athina Lexutt.[13] In 2005, he retired from Tübingen and became a professor emeritus.[14] In 2009, a Festschrift was published in Bayer's honor on the occasion of his seventieth birthday. It was edited by Johannes von Lüpke and Edgar Thaidigsmann and was composed by theologians and scholars including Otto Hermann Pesch, Gerhard Sauter, Martin Seils, Notger Slenczka, Johannes von Lüpke, Peter Stuhlmacher, Volker Stümke, and Jürgen Moltmann. It was funded jointly by the Evangelischen Kirche in Deutschland (EKD), the Vereinigten Evangelisch-Lutherische Kirche Deutschlands (VELKD), the Selbständige Evangelisch-Lutherischen Kirche in Deutschland (SELK), and the Luther-Akademie in Sondehausen-Ratzeburg, and was titled *Denkraum Katechismus*.[15] Bayer lives with his wife Athina in Hennef, near Bonn, and continues to be active today in writing articles, preaching, and giving guest lectures throughout the Lutheran world.[16]

Bayer's Major Works

As was noted above, Bayer's writings include works on Luther's theology, the philosophy of Hamann, and on Lutheran systematic theology. His Luther scholarship includes both *Promissio* and *Martin Luthers Theologie: Eine Vergegenwärtigung*. Beginning in *Promissio*, Bayer approaches Luther's theology as centered on the doctrine of justification. Bayer understands the reformer to teach a view of this doctrine in which God's declaration of the sinner's righteousness in Christ by faith happens through an active Word

---

Oswald Bayer (summer, 2014).

12. Bayer, *Was ist Das—Theologie?*, back cover. Bayer, *Umstrittene Freiheit*, iii–v. Bayer, "Selbstdarstellung," 301, 307.

13. Author's personal conversation with Oswald Bayer, Luther Seminary, St. Paul, MN (March 24, 2012).

14. O'Donovan, "Preface," in *Freedom in Response*, by Oswald Bayer, v.

15. von Lüpke and Thaidsmann, ed., *Denkraum Katechismus*, v–x.

16. Author's personal conversation with Oswald Bayer, Luther Seminary, St. Paul, MN (March 24, 2012).

of God, which brings the human into a right relationship with God.[17] In *Promissio*, Bayer traces the development of Luther's understanding of justification through the active Word of God's promise, beginning in Luther's early *Lectures on the Psalms* (1513-1515)[18] and his *Lectures on Romans* (1515-1516).[19] Bayer then moves through the encounter with Cardinal Cajetan in Augsburg in October of 1518 (to which Bayer attaches special significance),[20] up to *The Babylonian Captivity of the Church* (1520) in which Luther gave the classic articulation of his understanding of justification by God's promise.[21]

In the later of these two works, *Martin Luthers Theologie*, Bayer also explores how it is that Luther does theology. He explains Luther's perspective of theology as a matter of "experiential wisdom," which grips every Christian.[22] Bayer then further describes how for Luther, the method of such experiential theology consist of a three-fold rule practiced by the theologian of *oratio* (prayer), *meditatio* (meditation), and *tentatio* (agonizing struggle).[23] After establishing how it is that Luther does theology, Bayer turns to address Luther's doctrine of justification. In doing this he demonstrates how for Luther justification by God through faith in Jesus Christ forms both the center of Luther's theology and the demarcation for what constitutes the only true subject of theology: the sinning human and the justifying God in Christ.[24] Following his argument in *Promissio* in briefer form, he also sets forth how it is that he understands Luther to be articulating his doctrine of justification as occurring by the divine act of the divine Word of God's promise in Jesus Christ.[25] Throughout the remainder of this work, Bayer then deals with other important themes in Luther's theology—including the distinction between the law and the gospel, the nature of Scripture, God's work in creation, the bondage of the will, and the hiddenness of God—and relates them to Luther's doctrine of justification, a content which serves as the center and at the same time as the boundary of the subject matter of the-

---

17. Bayer, *Promissio*, 11-13, 225-29ff. Bayer, *Martin Luthers Theologie*, 34-38, 46-53; Bayer, *Martin Luther's Theology*, 37-42, 50-58.

18. Bayer, *Promissio*, 17ff.

19. Ibid., 32ff, especially 115-28.

20. Ibid., 182, 191, 194-97. Cf. Bayer, "What is Evangelical?," 4-7; Bayer, *Zugesagte Gegenwart*, 25-29 Bayer explains that it is in his debate with Cajetan that Luther first realizes how the *promissio* of God is the norming factor in Christian theology.

21. Bayer *Promissio*, 161-63, 204-25. Bayer, "Selbstdarstellung," 302-3.

22. Bayer, *Martin Luthers Theologie*, 29; Bayer, *Martin Luther's Theology*, 31.

23. Bayer, *Martin Luthers Theologie*, 30-34; Bayer, *Martin Luther's Theology*, 32-37.

24. Bayer, *Martin Luthers Theologie*, 34-38; Bayer, *Martin Luther's Theology*, 38-42.

25. Bayer, *Martin Luthers Theologie*, 46-53; Bayer, *Martin Luther's Theology*, 50-58.

ology. In doing this, Bayer demonstrates how all of these themes flow from and relate to the overall subject matter of Luther's theology, the justification of the sinner by God's active word of promise in the gospel of Christ.[26]

These two works of Luther scholarship offer the community of Luther studies a new approach to the theology of the sixteenth-century reformer. The bedrock of this approach is Bayer's observation concerning the significance of Luther's teaching concerning the active Word of God's promise. Bayer sees this teaching as constituting the content of Luther's doctrine of justification. Furthermore, he understands Luther as treating this particular doctrine of justification as the center and boundary of the subject matter of theology. Although other Luther scholars before Bayer, particularly Gerhard Ebeling and Ernst Bizer, identify God's active Word of promise as important for Luther,[27] no one had made such a detailed study of Luther's idea of God's active promise. Nor has there been until Bayer a concerted attempt to understand this teaching as forming the center of Luther's entire theological project. Bayer's two works of Luther scholarship thus stand as original contributions to the overall field of Luther studies.

Like his works on Luther's theology and its service to the discipline of Luther studies, Bayer's scholarship on Hamann constitutes an original and important contribution to the study of the history of philosophy. Moreover, Bayer's reading and use of Hamann's thought informs his reading and use of Luther as well as his own approach to theology. Bayer's works on Hamann include *Zeitgenosse im Widerspruch*, *Vernunft ist Sprache*, and *Kreuz und Kritik: Johann Georg Hamanns Letztes Blatt, Text und Interpretation*, as well as several important articles in scholarly journals and essays in anthologies.

26. Bayer, *Martin Luthers Theologie*, 53–60, 62–83, 87–159, 160–76, 177–92; Bayer, *Martin Luther's Theology*, 58–66, 68–92, 95–176, 177–95, 196–213.

27. In his studies on Luther, Ebeling relates how this theme was important for the development of Luther's thought in its early period from the *Lectures on Psalms* to the confrontation with Cardinal Cajetan and *The Babylonian Captivity of the Church*. Luther, *The Babylonian Captivity of the Church* (1520), *LW* 36:38–45; *De captivitate Babylonica ecclesiae*, WA 6:513–19. Ebeling, *Luther*, 71–73. Ebeling, *Lutherstudien*, Band I, 34, 257, 267–78, 294–95, 298–99. Ebeling appropriates Luther's idea of the active Word of God in his own hermeneutical approach to theology and proclamation as Word-event. Ebeling, *Lutherstudien*, Band I, 318–19, 322, 331–32. Bayer's *Doktorvater*, Ernst Bizer, comes close to something like Bayer's understanding of God's justifying promise in his own work on Luther's theology. According to Bizer, Luther's evangelical breakthrough occurred as the young reformer began to understand God's righteousness in connection with God's Word as the means of grace. Like Bayer, Bizer even connects this new theme in Luther to the important encounter with Cardinal Cajetan. Yet, Bizer does not articulate Bayer's view of the justifying promise in Luther's early theology. Cf. Bizer, *Fides ex auditu*, 170–73. Schaeffer, *Createdness and Ethics*, 103–4. Bayer acknowledges his own debt and gratitude to both Ebeling and Bizer in this regard in the forward of *Promissio*. Bayer, *Promissio*, 8.

In the first of these works, *Zeitgenosse im Widerspruch*, Bayer addresses the life and thought of Hamann from the standpoint of the philosopher's own era, describing his thought systematically on its own terms but also comparatively by putting Hamann's thought side by side with the thought of other philosophers of the eighteenth and early nineteenth centuries. Such thinkers include Johann Gottfried Herder, Hermann Samuel Reimarus, Gotthold Ephraim Lessing, and the most significant figure of the German Enlightenment, Immanuel Kant.[28] In *Zeitgenosse im Widerspruch*, Bayer presents Hamann as a radical figure within the German Enlightenment (*radikaler Aufklärer*) who is at odds with the general thrust of the philosophy of his time, yet as one who truly exists and function as a person of his time. According to Bayer, Hamann is not the father of modern irrationalism but a radical Enlightenment figure who takes Enlightenment criticism further that his contemporaries and critiques their own philosophy.[29] In chapters seven and nine of this work, Bayer relates how Hamann articulates a focused critique (*Metakritik*) of Kant's Enlightenment epistemology.[30]

In his work, *Vernunft ist Sprache*, Bayer expands his treatment of Hamann's critique of Kant from two chapters into an entire book. Here Bayer shows how Hamann questions the most basic presupposition that Kant assumes in his Enlightenment epistemology, one consequently passed on by Kant to the entire German Enlightenment and its modern theological posterity. That presupposition is that reason is present, intact, and active within the human consciousness to analyze the data of the empirical world. For Hamann, says Bayer, the phenomenon of language precedes that of thought or reason.[31] Though Hamann does address this empirically in terms of human development, he argues first and foremost from the standpoint of Christian theology. Language is not just the phenomenon of humans putting together sounds and syllables. Even before the use of language amongst humans, language was and is a phenomenon of the divine; it is God's own Word, whereby God created and sustains the world. Bayer demonstrates how Hamann describes God as creating the universe through language. The world of nature itself and human reason are built upon and dependent upon

---

28. Bayer, *Zeitgenosse im Widerspruch*, 108ff., 125ff, 138ff, 151ff, 179ff; Bayer, *A Contemporary in Dissent*, 87ff, 104ff, 117ff, 128ff, 156ff. Personal conversation with Mark Mattes.

29. Bayer, *Zeitgenosse im Widerspruch*, 9–10; Bayer, *A Contemporary in Dissent*, xi–xii.

30. Bayer, *Zeitgenosse im Widerspruch*, 138ff, 179ff; Bayer, *A Contemporary in Dissent*, 117ff, 156ff.

31. Bayer, *Zeitgenosse im Widerspruch*, 187; Bayer *A Contemporary in Dissent*, 164–65. Cf. Hamann, *Sämtliche Werke*, 3:231, 240.

the language of God, says Hamann. Without language, there is no reason, no world, no reality![32]

In the third of his major works on Hamann, *Kreuz und Kritik*, Bayer and co-author Christian Knudsen present a restored text of and a commentary on Hamann's last writing. Bayer and Knudsen say that in this last writing Hamann presents his entire philosophy *in nuce*. More specifically, in their commentary Bayer and Knudsen address how Hamann describes human existence as consisting of passive suffering of what happens in life (*passio*) in stark contrast to Kant's understanding of human life as defined by action (*actio*). In contrast to Kant's focus on moral *actio*, Hamann focuses on *passio* as the goal of humanity and the trajectory of religion. It is not that Hamann saw no place for human action, even moral action, say Bayer and Knudsen, but such action flows from and is part of a larger overall picture of suffering as that which characterizes human existence.[33] Bayer and Knudsen show how Hamann sees God as the author of humanity and human existence as suffering (or undergoing) the language of God. For Hamann, the human being is not essentially an actor who reasons and wills his or her own moral destiny but is one who undergoes being addressed by God.[34]

In these three works concerning Hamann, and in articles and essays that reflect particular aspects of these works, Bayer brings to the fore a long-neglected figure in the history of German philosophy. Bayer presents Hamann as a figure who stands out in the Enlightenment as a critic of one of the basic assumptions of the Enlightenment, and with these works, Bayer has opened up a new space for discussing Hamann and his thought. In this way, Bayer has contributed greatly not only to the field of theology but also to that of philosophy.[35]

Bayer's contribution to Lutheran systematic theology is two-fold. On the one hand, he has written several works dealing with particular themes in Lutheran theology. The most important of these works include *Autorität und Kritik*, in which Bayer deals with theological hermeneutics; *Gott als Autor*, in which he addresses both theological hermeneutics and the doctrine of God; *Schöpfung als Anrede*, in which he addresses both the doctrine of creation and the doctrine of revelation; *Freiheit als Antwort*, translated into

---

32. Bayer, *Vernunft ist Sprache*, 4. Bayer, *Zeitgenosse im Widerspruch*, 219-21; Bayer, *A Contemporary in Dissent*, 197-200. Hamann, *Briefwechsel*, 5:95.

33. Bayer, *Zeitgenosse im Widerspruch*, 185; Bayer, *A Contemporary in Dissent*, 162. Hamann, *Letztes Blatt*, in *Kreuz und Kritik*, by Bayer and Knudsen, 54-55. Bayer and Knudsen, *Kreuz und Kritik*, 103-6, 110-11.

34. Mattes, *The Role of Justification in Contemporary Theology*, 150. "God as Author of My Life History," 437ff; "Wer bin ich?," in *Gott als Autor*, 21-40.

35. Betz, "Enlightenment Revisited," 291.

English as *Freedom in Response* by Jeffrey F. Cayzer, in which he approaches ethics from the perspective of Lutheran theology centered in God's promise; and *Zugesagte Gegenwart*, in which Bayer addresses a variety of theological themes including the doctrine of God and the Trinity, the doctrine of justification, the doctrine of revelation, the nature of humanity, and even homiletics. On the other hand, Bayer's contribution to Lutheran systematic theology lies in the fact that he offers his theology with its center of his interpretation of Luther's doctrine of justification as programmatic for the future of Lutheran theology. His works *Theologie*, *Leibliches Wort*, and *Aus Glauben Leben* are particularly oriented towards this constructive theological task. While all of Bayer's systematic works contribute towards the goal of this constructive theology, in his volumes that address specific theological themes—these three works mentioned immediately above—Bayer lays out his theology as an alternative, uniquely Lutheran way of doing theology over and against the modern approaches to theology taken in the German Protestant theological tradition. These works are all available at least in part in English. While the late Geoffrey Bromiley translated the entirety of *Aus Glauben Leben* into English under the title *Living by Faith*, only the most significant portions of *Theologie* and *Leibliches Wort* for constructive, systematic theology have been translated.[36] In these works especially, as well as in his work of Luther scholarship, *Martin Luthers Theologie*—which has great significance for his constructive, systematic theology as well as for Luther studies—he delineates his way of doing theology, his view that justification constitutes the subject matter of theology, and his understanding of justification through God's active promise.

Focus of This Book

In his systematic works, Bayer understands justification to be the center of theology. For Bayer, justification is not simply one point of doctrine amongst many, nor is it an interior private experience of the individual, nor

36. The former of these works, *Theologie*, has been translated into English and edited by the Australian Lutheran theologian Jeffrey Silcock and the American Lutheran theologian Mark Mattes. Silcock and Mattes have edited out some of Bayer's interaction with the German theological tradition, but they have retained the most important constructive, systematic pieces of this work under the title *Theology the Lutheran Way*. Only a portion of the latter of these two works, *Leibliches Wort*, has been translated into English. Christine Helmer, who has also translated many essays and articles by Bayer as well as contributing her own thoughts as secondary material on Bayer's theology, has translated the second chapter of this work, entitled "Rechtfertigung: Grund und Grenze der Theologie," literally as "Justification as the Basis and Boundary of Theology." This translation was published as an article in the fifteenth volume of *Lutheran Quarterly*.

is it one way amongst many that may be used to describe human salvation. Instead, says Bayer, justification is the framework of both all discourse on God and of human existence itself.[37] Far from being a narrow or minimalistic outlook on reality, justification has both depth and breadth for Bayer. It is the heading for the depths of theology and it is the key that opens the door to the breadth of life.[38] Justification "embraces the totality" of all reality ("*Es geht dabei ums Ganze*").[39] Throughout all of his systematic works, Bayer approaches all of the themes and topics of systematic theology from the perspective of justification, and this is how he understands his theology as particularly Lutheran. One of these themes is the hiddenness of God. Bayer's adoption of this theme from Luther, his interpretation of it, and its place in his Lutheran systematic theology centered on and defined by justification is the theme of this book. I have not chosen this theme arbitrarily as merely one theme out of many in Bayer's theology that in some way relates to the doctrine of justification. Instead, I have chosen to write on this theme because Bayer's articulation of the doctrine of the hidden God is so particularly defined by his uniquely Lutheran approach to doing theology and by his particular understanding of justification through God's active Word of promise. Although some authors have noted the theme of the hidden God within Bayer's theology, I intend to make a more in-depth study of Bayer's reception and interpretation of Luther's understanding of the hidden God as well as his use of it in his own Lutheran systematic theology.

Summary of Secondary Scholarship

A handful of theologians have provided some limited scholarship on the topic of the hidden God in Bayer's theology. Mark Mattes, Reinhard Hutter, Hans Schaeffer, Trygve Wyller, Gerhard Sauter, Thomas Reinhuber, Klaas Zwanepol, Paul Hinlicky, and Christine Helmer have all at least mentioned Bayer's view of God's hiddenness in their discussions of Bayer's overall theology.[40] None of these authors undertake a detailed study of Bayer's understanding of divine hiddenness, yet they do merit some mention, especially

---

37. Bayer, "Preface to the English Edition," in *Living by Faith*, xiv. This preface is not contained in the German original, *Aus Glauben Leben*.

38. Ibid.; Bayer, *Aus Glauben Leben*, 21; Bayer, *Living by Faith*, 9. Bayer, *Leibliches Wort*, 19–20; ET "Justification as the Basis and Boundary of Theology," 273–274.

39. Bayer, *Aus Glauben Leben*, 21; Bayer, *Living by Faith*, 9.

40. See the literature review in my original PhD thesis, Miller, "The Hidden God in the Lutheran Theology of Oswald Bayer," 13–25 for a more comprehensive treatment of these authors as they address Bayer's doctrine of the hidden God.

since the field of secondary material on Bayer's theology is still relatively small compared to other contemporary German Protestant theologians.

While each of these scholars, except Sauter, note something of the importance and nature of divine hiddenness in Bayer's theology,[41] none of them deal extensively with the topic as it features in Bayer's thought. Hutter recognizes the presence of divine hiddenness in Bayer's theology, but he does not go beyond this recognition into any description.[42] Reinhuber implicitly recognizes and understands how Bayer understands the hiddenness of God outside of revelation by adopting and utilizing it in his own theological work, but he does not describe or discuss Bayer's view on its own terms.[43]

Helmer, Mattes, Schaeffer, Wyller, Zwanepol, and Hinlicky differ from these other two scholars in that they directly address, to some extent, how hiddenness appears in Bayer's theology, but even these treatments of the subject are brief and mostly tangential. Although her treatment of divine hiddenness in Bayer's theology is direct and relates well how Bayer identifies hiddenness as one of the data of theology through which God addresses human beings and as the contradiction of the promise, Helmer discussion of the subject in Bayer's thought is very brief due to the summary nature of her major article on his theology.[44] Similarly, while Mattes also recognizes that Bayer employs hiddenness as one of the ways in which God addresses humans and commends Bayer for integrating into his theology, he does not explore at any length how Bayer utilizes hiddenness in his theology. Furthermore, though his book addresses Bayer's theology as a theology of justification, Mattes does not discuss the important link between justification and hiddenness drawn by Bayer.[45] Schaeffer and Wyller both identify this important connection. Yet, Schaeffer does so only in service to the narrow task of relating Bayer's doctrine of creation in his overview of Bayer's theology, and he does not go beyond simply identifying this connection.[46] Wyller does something similar when he mentions the link between God's justifying promise and the work of the hidden God in Bayer's theology only with

---

41. Although he mentions the hiddenness of God in passing—particularly decrying how the Erlangen theologians Paul Althaus and Werner Elert misinterpreted its importance in theology—Sauter does not elucidate what place the subject has in Bayer's theology. Cf. Sauter, "Katechismus-Grammatik: Katechismusunterricht als Pendant des Theologiestudiums," in *Denkraum Katechismus*, 23–26.

42. Hutter, *Suffering Divine Things*, 71.

43. Reinhuber, *Kämpfender Glaube*, 114–15.

44. Helmer, "The Subject of Theology in the Thought of Oswald Bayer," 35.

45. Mattes, *The Role of Justification in Contemporary Theology*, 149, 158, 168–69.

46. Schaeffer, *Createdness and Ethics*, 105.

reference to evil in the world and disharmony in creation as forms of the hidden God's work.[47] While Zwanepol discusses Bayer's use of hiddenness, he does so very briefly. Moreover, he interacts with Bayer's understanding of hiddenness primarily from the standpoint of an "overarching gospel," such as one finds in the theologies of Barth and Jüngel.[48]

Hinlicky's treatment of Bayer on the hidden God is far too brief and serves as a straw man for the author's own polemic, so that the critique offered there needs to be corrected.[49] I will enter briefly into such critique in this work. Similarly to Hinlicky, in her essay, "Does Luther Have a 'Waxen Nose'?," Helmer does not satisfactorily describe Bayer's view of hiddenness, its overall function in Bayer's theology, or its relationship to Luther's own view of hiddenness.[50] Thus, it becomes apparent from the small amount of secondary material on the subject, that the theme of the hidden God in Oswald Bayer's theology remains an area of contemporary theology to be explored.

Trajectory of This Book

Oswald Bayer is a significant voice in German theology today and has much to offer to scholarship outside of Germany as well. His contributions to the areas of Luther studies, the study of the thought of Hamann, and the area of Lutheran systematic theology have been noted above. My focus concerns the last of these three areas. Bayer's presents contemporary Lutheranism with a unique approach to theology from the standpoint of God's justification through God's active Word of promise as the center, basis, and boundary of theology. In this context, Bayer's adoption, interpretation, and utilization of Luther's understanding of the hidden God appear as distinctive precisely because his view of God's hiddenness is defined by and works in concert with his central teaching concerning justification through God's active Word of promise.

I will examine the place of Martin Luther's understanding of the hiddenness of God in the Lutheran theology of Oswald Bayer. I will first relate how Luther understands the hiddenness of God and how this understanding has been assessed and interpreted in the German Protestant theological tradition. I will then investigate how Bayer uses divine hiddenness in his own Lutheran theology. This will include exploring how exactly Bayer's

47. Wyller, *Glaube und Autonome Welt*, 122–25.
48. Zwanepol, "Zur Diskussion um Gottes Verborgenheit," 53–55, 56–58, 59.
49. Hinlicky, *Luther and the Beloved Community*, 360–63, 367–70.
50. Helmer, "Does Luther Have a 'Waxen Nose'?" 27–29, 209 n9.

theology is "Lutheran," as well as how he inherits and adopts Luther's view of hiddenness and inherits and reacts to the tradition's treatment of Luther's teaching. I will then turn to how divine hiddenness functions within Bayer's own theology, which is centered in the teaching concerning God's justification through God's Word of promise, and how his view of hiddenness compares to Luther's view of it. Finally, I will conclude with my own evaluation of Bayer's use of divine hiddenness, including relating how Bayer's Lutheran theology with its view of God's hiddenness might be used constructively by Lutheran theologians today.

2

The Hidden God in the Theology of Martin Luther

IN TAKING UP THE theme of the hidden God, Bayer operates within a particular trajectory in theology formed by the sixteenth-century reformer Martin Luther. In order to understand how Bayer functions both as an interpreter of Luther's theology and as a Lutheran theologian concerning the reformer's doctrine of the hidden God, it is first necessary to recognize Luther's own teaching on this doctrine and observe how it functions in his theology. Through his own original statement of the doctrine of the hidden God, Luther set down a teaching that would be read and interpreted in various ways by those coming after him in the German Protestant theological tradition, including Oswald Bayer.

There are two kinds of divine hiddenness that Martin Luther addresses in his theological works. Luther speaks both of a hiddenness of God within revelation and a hiddenness of God outside of revelation. The first of these two kinds of hiddenness is exemplified in Luther's theology by the almighty and eternal God's being hidden under the sign of God's opposite, hidden under the signs of suffering and death. Luther describes this hiddenness as taking place particularly in the cross of Jesus Christ, and Luther addresses it as such in his *Heidelberg Disputation* (1518). Luther identifies the second of these two kinds of hiddenness as God's existence outside of revelation, God's hiddenness in God's self. Luther introduces and discusses this kind of divine hiddenness in his treatise against Erasmus of Rotterdam, *The Bondage of the Will* (1525), in which Luther also refers to this kind of hiddenness as "God not preached" and God hidden in himself [God's self].[1]

---

1. Although Luther uses the term "himself" with reference to God, I have here used

Two Kinds of Divine Hiddenness

Bayer's discussion of the hiddenness of God is concerned primarily with God's hiddenness outside of revelation. I therefore will discuss God's hiddenness in revelation only briefly and will discuss chiefly God's hiddenness outside of revelation. I will explore Luther's teaching concerning this hiddenness of the unpreached God presented in its classic setting of Luther's arguments in *The Bondage of the Will* and further explicated in some of his later works. Then I will demonstrate how this teaching relates to other key themes in Luther's theology.

The Hiddenness of God in Revelation

The classic text where Luther speaks of God's hiddenness within revelation is the *Heidelberg Disputation*, in which he discusses God's hiddenness in the revelation in the cross of Jesus Christ. The cross of Christ—which Luther maintains should serve as the paradigm for all theology—constitutes a revelation of God hidden under the sign of its opposite. In the cross, God is revealed in Christ as a God of life and salvation, hidden under the sign of suffering and death. Luther pits this theology of the cross against what he identifies as a triumphalistic theology of glory in the theology of medieval scholasticism.[2] The hiddenness of God in the cross is a revealed hiddenness of God that encounters humans as divine mercy and forgiveness in Jesus Christ.[3]

Yet such hiddenness in revelation is not the only kind of divine hiddenness in Luther's theology. There is also the hiddenness of God outside of revelation, in God's self, which is something other than just God's hiddenness

---

"God's self" due to its common usage in theological discourse today.

2. Luther, *Heidelberg Disputation* (1518), LW 31:40–41; *Disputatio Heidelbergae*, WA 1:354–55. Paul Althaus, *The Theology of Martin Luther*, 276–77. Hans-Martin Barth, *Die Theologie Martin Luthers*, 210–11; ET *Theology of Martin Luther*, 107-108.

3. Such a theology, says Luther, stands in stark contrast to any notion of human striving for salvation by the use of reason and obeying the law through the use of free will. Luther posits that these two ways of doing theology—the theology of the cross and the theology of glory—are embodied by two different kinds of theologians who each approach God differently. Whereas the theologian of glory seeks to find "the invisible things of God" clearly by the use of human reason, the theologian of the cross recognizes God as God is revealed hidden under suffering, death, and the cross. While the theologian of glory seeks to please God and gain righteousness by obeying the law "with the aid of natural precepts" by the power of "free will," the theologian of the cross relies passively upon the work of God's grace in the cross of Christ, since it is not the active doer but the passive believer who truly pleases God. Theses 19–20, 25–27, LW 31:40; WA 1:354.

under the sign of God's opposite. This hiddenness of God in God's self is a hiddenness outside of all revelation, a hiddenness of God outside of Jesus Christ, a hiddenness of God in which God cannot be found as merciful and forgiving. It is a divine hiddenness of wrath and damnation.[4] In contrast to God hidden in God's self, God exists for sinners revealed in Jesus Christ as a God of love and mercy.

The Hiddenness of God outside of Revelation

Martin Luther first introduces the hiddenness of God outside of revelation in his important treatise *The Bondage of the Will*. In this writing, Luther makes the astonishing statement that God wills the death of the sinner and at the same time, in Christ, does not will the death of the sinner. This dual will of God characterizes the distinction between God as God exists hidden in God's self outside of revelation and God as God is revealed in the gospel of Jesus Christ. Luther identifies this distinction as "God preached" and "God not preached." This important distinction, says Luther, must be made when one speaks of the activity of God's will.[5]

Luther's Doctrine of the Hidden God in His Theological Writings

Luther gives his first and fullest statement of his doctrine of the hiddenness of God outside of revelation in *The Bondage of the Will* (1525). Here Luther couches the doctrine in his discussion of the difference between the law and the gospel as part of his argument against Erasmus concerning the enslaved and passive nature of the human will before God in salvation. This is not, however, the only place in his theological writings where Luther addresses this doctrine. Although he does not fully restate his doctrine in later works, he does give further reflections on and clarifications of the theme of the hidden, unpreached God in his subsequent *Lectures on Jonah* (1525–1526), *Lectures on Isaiah* (1527–1530) and *Lectures on Genesis* (1535–1545). From Luther's teaching on the hiddenness of the unpreached God in *The Bondage of the Will* and these later biblical lectures, there emerges a unified picture of Luther's understanding of the hiddenness of God outside of revelation that can be juxtaposed with other key themes in his theology.

---

4. BOW, 169–71; WA 18:684–86. Althaus, *Martin Luther's Theology*, 277–79.
5. BOW, 169–71; WA 18:684–686. Hans-Martin Barth, *Die Theologie Martin Luthers*, 200.

The Bondage of the Will (1525)

Luther first articulated his notion of the unpreached God's hiddenness outside of revelation in *The Bondage of the Will*, a work that scholars of Luther's theology have described as being perhaps the most significant and the most theologically comprehensive of all of the reformer's writings. In a correspondence with his fellow evangelical theologian Wolfgang Capito, Luther himself described this treatise as one of the only two of his works that deserve to survive him.[6] In this work, Luther defended his reformational theology against Erasmus of Rotterdam who was one of the foremost scholars of Luther's day. Erasmus had composed his own *Diatribe* against Luther's theological belief that God in Christ alone is the one who decides the sinful human's destiny and that the sinner is merely a passive object of God's saving activity. The human, Erasmus asserted, is not passive or determined before God but truly possesses freedom of the will.[7] The importance of Luther's response in *The Bondage of the Will* should not be underestimated, considering that in this treatise he publicly defended his theology from the attack of such a learned and revered scholar as Erasmus.[8] Furthermore, Luther himself regarded the theological argument concerning the bound will as absolutely central to the entire evangelical theological enterprise, identifying this theological locus in the close of his treatise as "the hinge on which all turns" (*cardinem rerum*) and "the vital spot" (*ipsum iugulum*).[9]

Since *The Bondage of the Will* is deemed to be of such primary importance as a source of Luther's theology, Luther's description of God's hiddenness outside of revelation given in this treatise should serve as the basic explication of this notion of divine hiddenness. In setting forth Luther's understanding in this treatise of this hiddenness of God, it is important to take into account how it functions in Luther's broader argument against Erasmus. In this treatise Luther articulates his notion of God's hiddenness in God's self in response to Erasmus' use of Ezekiel 18:23 and 33:11 in support of the humanist's view of "free will." This concept of divine hiddenness parallels God's activity in the law as Luther describes it in this same treatise

---

6. Schwarzwäller, *Theologia crucis*, 9. Packer and Johnston, "Historical and Theological Introduction: in *BOW*, 40. Kolb, *Bound Choice, Election, and Wittenberg Theological Method*, 15. Kaufmann, "Luther und Erasmus," in *Luther Handbuch*, ed. Beutel, 145.

7. Erasmus, *On the Free Will: A Diatribe or Discourse*, 37–40.

8. Nestingen, "Introduction: Luther and Erasmus on the Bondage of the Will," in *The Captivation of the Will*, by Forde, 1. Cf. Kaufmann, "Luther und Erasmus," 149–52.

9. *BOW*, 319; WA 18:786.

and could also be seen as possibly being connected to Luther's explanation of the three lights at the end of this treatise.

Luther's articulation of his notion of God's hiddenness in God's self is set amidst the reformer's critique of Erasmus' use of passages from the Old Testament in support of the Dutch humanist's theological belief in the ability of the "free will" of the human to work with God in striving to live a moral life.[10] In his *Diatribe*, Erasmus uses both Old Testament texts in which God commands God's people to do something or to suffer divine punishment instead (Dt. 30:11–19, Is. 1:19–20) and Old Testament texts in which God offers salvation to God's people through repentance (Joel 2:12, Jonah 3:8, Is. 46:8, Jer. 26:3–4, Ez. 18:31, 18:23/33:11). Erasmus appeals to this group of proof texts as evidence that the Scriptures support the idea that such a thing as "free will" exists by means of which the human can please God by fulfilling God's commands.[11]

Luther rejects Erasmus' use of these Old Testaments texts in order to support such a notion of "free will" on the grounds that Erasmus does not properly distinguish between which of these texts are functioning as law (i.e. as a command from God) and which are functioning as gospel (i.e. promising salvation).[12] The law's work, says Luther, is actually to destroy the sinful human's claim to have a "free will" with which one can please God through obedience. The work of the gospel, on the other hand, is to save the sinner whose false perception of "free will" and self-confidence has been obliterated by the work of the law.[13] According to Luther, Erasmus misuses both the texts of law and the texts of gospel. The law is no proof for "free will," says Luther, because obligation is not proof of ability. The work of the law's obligation is to destroy the illusion of ability within the sinner.[14] Nor is the gospel any proof for ability, says Luther, for the gospel promises salvation to those who have been exposed to the reality of their own helplessness and wretchedness and to the futility of their self-confidence through the work of the law in order that they may be saved by Christ apart from their own will and efforts.[15] Luther's articulation of his teaching about God hidden outside of revelation and the distinction between God preached and unpreached comes in the midst of this discussion of the respective works of the law and the gospel upon the sinner. Luther argues that Erasmus' theology fails

---

10. Erasmus, 41; Kaufmann, "Luther und Erasmus," 149–50.
11. Erasmus, 54–57.
12. *BOW*, 163; WA 18:680.
13. *BOW*, 162, 165, 287–88; WA 18:679–81, 766–67.
14. *BOW*, 157, 160, 162; WA 18:676, 679–80.
15. *BOW*, 162, 165; WA 18:679–81.

to make the proper distinction between these two works and in so doing misconstrues both.

Luther focuses particularly on Erasmus' misuse of Ezekiel 18:23 and 33:11: "I desire not the death of the wicked."[16] When treating this passage and using it in support of his position on "free will," says Luther, Erasmus neglects to distinguish between God preached and God not preached. That is, Erasmus does not distinguish between God as God is proclaimed in the promise of salvation in the gospel of Jesus Christ and God as God is hidden in God's self.[17] It is true, says Luther, that God does not will the death of the sinner as God exists in revelation, as God is revealed in Jesus Christ through the Word. Yet, says Luther, God is not bound to exist in revelation alone but also exists above and beyond revelation, hidden in God's self. While God as God is preached and revealed in Christ through the Word does not desire the death of the sinner, God unpreached and hidden outside of revelation, does desire the death and damnation of the sinner. There are, thus, two wills of God. There is the will of God revealed in which God wills the life and salvation of the sinner, and there is the will of God hidden in God's self wherein God wills the death and damnation of the sinner. Luther emphasizes that God hidden in God's self and the hidden will of God are not to be speculated about by the sinner. Instead, the sinner has to do only with God revealed in Jesus Christ through the Word, who wills and promises the sinner's life and salvation.[18]

From a close look at the reformer's use of the distinction between God unpreached and God preached in his argument against Erasmus' view of "free will," one can observe that this distinction runs parallel to the distinction between the law and the gospel and that the will of the unpreached God is identifiable with God's work in the law. In *The Bondage of the Will*, Luther specifies that the work of God in the law entails the death and damnation of the sinner, in order that the sinner may be made alive through the work of God in the gospel.[19] This mirrors Luther's claim, articulated in the same treatise, that the unpreached God wills the death and damnation of the sinner, though the preached God wills the sinner's life and salvation.[20] In view of these similarities it is not unreasonable to state that Luther here describes the hidden God's wrath and willing of the destruction of the sinner as a work congruous to the work of God in the law.

16. *BOW*, 157, 163–65; WA 18:676, 680–82.
17. *BOW*, 169–71; WA 18:684–86.
18. *BOW*, 169–71; WA 18:684–86.
19. *BOW*, 151, 161–65, 171–89; WA 18:673, 679–81, 686–99.
20. *BOW*, 169–171; WA 18:684–86.

Yet while Luther somewhat equates this aspect of the will of the hidden God with God's work in the law, Luther by no means exhaustively defines the hidden God in terms of the law. For Luther says in *The Bondage of the Will* that the hidden God works and wills "all things," even "evil."[21] This idea that the hidden God brings about everything that comes to pass reflects Luther's earlier statements in his argument against Erasmus regarding God's immutable will, namely, that it causes to come to pass all things.[22] Though the description of the hidden God's wrath and God's willing the destruction of the sinner parallels the work of God through the law, there are many evil things that happen in the world, and if the hidden God's will encompasses "all things," this leaves Luther's understanding of the hidden God open for some interpretation and development.

Luther's understanding in *The Bondage of the Will* of God's hiddenness in God's self may also be connected to his teaching concerning the three lights at the conclusion of this treatise. The three lights identified by Luther are the light of nature (unaided human reason), the light of grace (the Christian's view of the world in Christ), and the light of glory (a future eschatological knowledge). Luther uses these three lights to explain the problem of affliction (what would later become known as the problem of evil or theodicy). While it is impossible to comprehend why the righteous should be afflicted by the light of nature, one can comprehend this by the light of grace. Nevertheless, says Luther, not even the light of grace can explain why God damns sinners who are bound to sin, for this can only be understood in the eschatological light of glory.[23]

Luther's doctrine of the hidden God emerges from its context in *The Bondage of the Will* as it is shaped by Luther's overall argument against Erasmus' view of free will, wherein it parallels the reformer's teaching on the condemning work of God in the law and may be connected also to his teaching on the three lights. In this treatise, Luther argues that God's existence is not bound to revelation, but that God also exists hidden in God's self. Luther contrasts God hidden in God's self (God unpreached) with God as God is revealed and preached in Jesus Christ through the Word. Against Erasmus' claim that God wills only the salvation of the sinner, Luther claims that it is true that God revealed [God preached] wills the life and salvation of the sinner but that God hidden in God's self wills the death and damnation of the sinner as well as all things. Luther here completely forbids speculation into the inner-workings of the hidden God with God's hidden

---

21. *BOW*, 170; *WA* 685.
22. *BOW*, 80; *WA* 615.
23. *BOW*, 317; *WA* 18:785.

will of wrath and condemnation; yet one can note that Luther's description of the killing and damning will of God hidden in God's self parallels at least to some extent his definition of the killing and damning work of God in the law, and, as a development of Luther's understanding of hiddenness, one might then make a connection in *The Bondage of the Will* between this concept of divine hiddenness and the three lights motif at the conclusion of this treatise. Though the account of the hiddenness of God outside of revelation given in this treatise is the fullest and most classic treatment that Luther gives to this doctrine, it is not an exhaustive treatment. The important aspect of the natural knowledge of God as the hiddenness of God is left to be treated by the reformer in his *Lectures on Jonah* (1525-1526), while the theme of the human's experience of the hidden God through trials (or *Anfechtung*) is left to be treated by the reformer later in his *Lectures on Isaiah* and his *Lectures on Genesis*.

Lectures on Jonah (1525-1526)

Luther's *Lectures on Jonah* were composed and published around the same time as his great treatise, *The Bondage of the Will*. Some of the same concerns present in his argumentation against Erasmus also appear in these lectures. One such concern is the hiddenness of the unpreached God of wrath. In these lectures, Luther continues this theme, first articulated in *The Bondage of the Will*, that God hidden outside of Christ is a God of wrath who damns sinners while God in Christ is a God of grace, mercy, and love. In particular, Luther here further clarifies how it is that the hidden God is known by humans. The hidden God is known experientially as a God of wrath by all humans through the natural order.

Luther begins his description of the human knowledge of the hidden of God in his *Lectures on Jonah*, in his commentary of Jonah 1:5. In this verse, the author of Jonah states that the sailors who had taken Jonah on board their vessel were afraid and called out each to their own gods. Luther uses this verse as a springboard into his understanding of how humans experience the hidden God through the natural order.

According to Luther, all humans know something of God, but they do not truly know God. All humans through nature and reason are able to know that God, as something superior to all things, exists. This knowledge is innate within every human being, says Luther, though some attempt to cover it up with the lie of atheism.[24] Yet, says Luther, this knowledge appre-

---

24. Luther, *Lectures on Jonah* (1526), *LW* 19:53-54; Luther, *Der Prophet Jona ausgelegt*, WA 19:205-6.

hended through experience of the natural order and innate reason does not lead to a true knowledge of God and confession of faith in God but, instead, leads humans to idolatry. This is because human reason is too weak a means by which to comprehend God in all God's fullness of glory and grace. Reason may know that there is a God, says Luther, but it does not know the true God nor does it know that God wills to know the human.[25] The best that reason can do is to make a god fashioned according to the human's own desires and illusions or to find the devil instead of the true God. Either way, reason cannot truly know the true God.[26] Moreover, whether the idolatrous human is worshiping god(s) made in the human's own image or the devil, they ultimately are serving the devil, since it is he and not God who is active in their false belief.[27]

While Luther states that the knowledge of God through nature and reason is not a true knowledge of God, he maintains that there is some real experience of God in nature. Luther goes on to comment further on the particular situation of the sailors and the prophet Jonah. Luther says that the sailors and Jonah were experiencing God's wrath through the fierce storm that came upon the ship. Though the sailors may not have been able to identify this as such, Jonah knew that this was God's wrath and told them to deal with him accordingly, since he had brought the wrath of God upon them.[28] Luther then universalizes this argument concerning God's wrath towards the human sinner. Through conscience, all of nature and all creatures show God's anger of wrath against sin.[29] Thus it is with the God of nature, says Luther, through nature humans experience the God of wrath, raging against sinners, actively seeking their death and destruction. While believers, like Jonah, know more fully than unbelievers that this is the work of the wrath of the Almighty God, unbelievers at least know that some divine force is behind this work, causing trouble for them and truly do experience the wrath of the hidden God.[30]

This is the same work of the hidden, unpreached God that Luther describes in *The Bondage of the Will*. This work of God's wrath is done, says Luther, in order that the sinner who is the object of such wrath might be saved by the revealed God of the promise in Jesus Christ.[31] Here Luther

25. *LW* 19:54–55; WA 19:206.
26. *LW* 19:55; WA 19:206–7.
27. *LW* 19:56–57; WA 19:207–8.
28. *LW* 19:66–67; WA 19:217–18.
29. *LW* 19:75; WA 19:226.
30. *LW* 19:56, 66–67; WA 19:208.
31. *LW* 19:17; WA 13:249

states that the only escape from the hidden God experienced and to some extent known in nature and the conscience is through the revealed God in Jesus Christ, who alone constitutes in himself the only place where God can be known by humans as a God of grace, mercy, and love through the promise of God.[32] Christ, reiterates Luther, is the sinner's mercy seat, the only place where the sinner can look upon God as God truly is and find mercy and grace.[33] It is to this God alone that the sinner must flee when confronted by the wrath of God experienced through a natural knowledge of God. The sinner must believe firmly, praying to God to save, hold "God against God," to the promise of God's mercy in Christ against the wrath of the hidden God.[34]

Throughout the remaining portions of the book of Jonah, wherein the prophet is thrown overboard, then is saved from drowning by the great fish sent by God, and prays his psalm of penitence for sin and thanksgiving for salvation to God, Luther describes Jonah's lot as a personal example of experiencing God's wrath and the turn from such wrath to the revealed God. Through the storm, nature itself becomes the means by which Jonah experiences the wrath of God.[35] Jonah had been fleeing God's Word and had experienced God's wrath through the natural order, but then Jonah flees from what he knows to be God's wrath to the mercy of God, by prayer and entreaty to the revealed God of the Word.[36] It is clear that, in this passage, Luther understands the wrath of the hidden God to be killing and damning Jonah in order to raise him up and save him, in order to overcome Jonah's resistance. The hidden God causes the waves of death to come over Jonah so that the prophet thinks himself already killed by God's wrath.[37] Moreover, Luther describes the inside of the fish wherein Jonah finds himself "the belly of death" and as the realm of the departed and devils who await the final judgment and condemnation to hell.[38] It is only when Jonah has reached this pit of death that he can call out to God's mercy. Luther thus identifies the wrath of the hidden God as God's work of damnation, which drives the sinner to utter in desperation what Luther identifies as "the cry from the depths" to God's mercy. This cry, says Luther, is one that proceeds from

---

32. *LW* 19:17, 80; WA 13:249, WA 19:230.
33. *LW* 19:80; WA 19:230.
34. *LW* 19:17, 72; WA 13:249, WA 19:222–23.
35. *LW* 19:18, 76; WA 13:250, 19:226–27.
36. *LW* 19:72; WA 19:222–23.
37. Ibid.
38. *LW* 19:74; WA 19:224–25.

death and damnation to the grace of the revealed God in Christ against the wrath of the hidden God.[39]

In his *Lectures on Jonah*, Luther's understanding of the hiddenness of God outside of revelation appears to reflect the same teaching as he articulates in *The Bondage of the Will*, but in these lectures, he also clarifies that the sinner experiences God hidden outside of Christ in terms of the "natural knowledge" of God that comes through reason and the experience of nature. Though Luther repeats here that the hidden God is ultimately unknowable and is the God of wrath, he adds here that the hidden God and this God's wrath are experienced through nature. While Luther here affirms that the hidden God wills the death and damnation of the sinner as he does in *The Bondage of the Will*, he is clearer in these lectures that such death and damnation is worked for the sake of salvation. Furthermore, while in *The Bondage of the Will* Luther states that humans can only truly know God as God is revealed in Jesus Christ through the Word, in the *Lectures on Jonah*, Luther develops this into the idea that humans actually should flee from the hidden God of wrath to the revealed God of mercy and grace in Jesus Christ through calling out to the revealed God of the promise from the depths.

There is one final observation to make regarding how Luther presents his doctrine of the hidden God in his *Lectures on Jonah*. Here, for the first time, Luther associates the hidden God with the devil. In describing how the human's natural knowledge of the hidden God is a perverted knowledge of God, Luther goes beyond simply saying that the natural knowledge of God is not a true knowledge of God or that the hidden God is ultimately incomprehensible to saying that worshiping God according to the natural knowledge of the hidden God is worshiping the devil. As will be demonstrated below, Luther later identifies the hidden God with the devil by saying that the two are indistinguishable. This and the trials and existential agonizing struggle of *Anfechtung* sent by the hidden God are addressed by Luther in his subsequent *Lectures on Isaiah* and *Lectures on Genesis*.

Lectures on Isaiah (1527–1530)

Luther describes God's hiddenness in God's self in his *Lectures on Isaiah* in much the same way as he does in *The Bondage of the Will*. The lectures were given by Luther at the University of Wittenberg over a span of nearly four years, though they were interrupted twice. In them, when he speaks of God's hiddenness the reformer does not directly say that he is specifically

---

39. *LW* 19:74, 78–80; *WA* 19:224–25, 229–31.

addressing God hidden in God's self.[40] Nevertheless, it is apparent from what Luther says in these lectures that the divine hiddenness about which he speaks here is identical to God's hiddenness in God's self as he also describes it in *The Bondage of the Will*. In these lectures, Luther describes God's hiddenness as incomprehensible and as being related to the alien work of God whereby God sends trials in order to drive sinners to despair of their own efforts and to find God revealed in the Word.

The first aspect of God's hiddenness in God's self discussed by Luther in his *Lectures on Isaiah* is the incomprehensibility of the hidden God and of God's hidden will. In dealing with Isaiah 45:15 ("Truly, you are a God who hides himself"), Luther explains that the hiddenness of God entails a work of God characterized by incomprehensible strangeness.[41] The secret work of the hidden God, says Luther, is veiled from human comprehension or understanding. The sinner thinks that since he or she sees nothing that, in fact, God is not at work. Yet, God is at work with God's own plans that God puts into place despite the fact that the sinner does not perceive them. The sinner does not comprehend the work of God's will because God actively hides it from the sinner.[42] This understanding of the incomprehensibility of the will of the hidden God reflects how Luther describes the hiddenness of God in God's self and the hidden will of God in *The Bondage of the Will*. In this earlier treatise, Luther argues that human understanding cannot and should not attempt to probe into the existence and will of the hidden God. It is enough, Luther says, to know that such a God with such an incomprehensible will exists, to silently reverence this God, and to know the revealed God in Jesus Christ.[43]

The second aspect of the hiddenness of God in God's self that Luther discusses in the *Lectures on Isaiah* is how the hidden God works through trials to drive sinners to faith in the revealed God. This aspect of divine hiddenness may be seen as a development or further explication in the reformer's understanding of the hidden God, since Luther does not address it in his description of divine hiddenness in *The Bondage of the Will*. The notion of God sending trials (*Anfechtungen*) upon the believer, whereby he or she would be driven to despair of his or her own efforts and to trust God's gracious Word in the gospel of Christ became prominent in Luther's

---

40. Cf. Hilton Oswald, "Introduction to Volume 17," *LW* 17:ix–x.

41. Isa 45:15 (NRSV). Luther, *Lectures on Isaiah* (1527–1530), *LW* 17:131; Luther, *Vorlesung über Jesaja*, WA 31–2:364.

42. *LW* 17:131–132; WA 31–2:364.

43. *BOW*, 169–171; WA 18:684–86.

theological works after *The Bondage of the Will*.[44] Yet, it is not as if the concept of such a work of God was new in Luther's theology, for such was the content of Luther's description of the work of God in the law, which the reformer identified as early as 1518 in his *Heidelberg Disputation*.[45] There is, however, beginning in the *Lectures on Isaiah* a clearer venue for this alien work of God through trials sent from God to believers.

In his commentary on Isaiah 57:17 ("... I struck them, I hid and was angry..."), Luther explains that the hidden God hides in his wrath by sending trials on all sinners but that different sinners react differently to such trials.[46] Some sinners, like David, react in faith and repentance and "run to the Lord." Others, like Ahab and the papists react by running "to their own judgment and their own righteousness and their own merits." Luther thus sees the work of the hidden God as a purifying work that separates these two types of people.[47]

Luther describes the hidden God's use of trials more in depth in other places within his commentary on Isaiah, including his handling of chapters one, twenty-eight, and forty-one. In his commentary on chapter twenty-eight, Luther describes this work of the hidden God as God's "alien work." This work is distinct from God's "proper work" of saving sinners, says Luther, but God's alien work is necessary for God's proper work to take place. Sinners are so proud in themselves and confident in their own righteousness that they must first be brought low and humbled through trials. Only once their pride and confidence in works is destroyed by God's alien work are they driven to the Word where God operates God's proper work upon them and saves them.[48] Foreshadowing how he describes the work of the hidden God in chapter fifty-seven of Isaiah, Luther here states that the alien work of God is a dividing work which separates between those who respond to trials in faith and those who remain in their sin.[49] In his commentary on Isaiah 1 Luther says that God chastises sinners not in order to utterly destroy them but in order to raise them up. Through trials, God's alien work refines sinners that they might be opened to the proper work of

44. Cf. Luther, *Vorrede zum ersten Band der deutschen Schriften Luthers* (1539) WA 50:660.

45. Theses 23–28, *LW* 41; WA 1:354. *Explanation to the Theses* (1518), *LW* 41:62–63; WA 1:369.

46. Isa 57:17 (nrsv). *LW* 17:278–279; WA 31-2:476.

47. Ibid.

48. *LW* 16:233–235; WA 31-2:168–169. Cf. "For the Lord will rise up as on Mount Perazim, he will rage as in the valley of Gibeon to do his deed—strange is his deed!—and to do his work—alien is his work!" Isa 28:21 (nrsv).

49. *LW* 16:234; WA 31-2:168–69.

God.⁵⁰ In his commentary on chapter twenty-eight Luther states that God even subjects believers to trials through God's alien work in order to divide faith from self-righteousness in them. Through God's alien work, God operates on both believers and unbelievers, killing the flesh in order to bring the spirit to life.⁵¹

While the parallel may not be precise, this explanation of the alien work of God in Luther's *Lectures on Isaiah* bears a very close resemblance to his description in *The Bondage of the Will* of both the will of God hidden in God's self and the work of God in the law. Like his description in *The Bondage of the Will* of the work willed and accomplished by the hidden God through the law, in his *Lectures on Isaiah*, Luther describes the alien work of the hidden God as consisting of God's humbling and killing of the sinner in order to raise the sinner to life.⁵² In *The Bondage of the Will*, Luther describes this as taking place through the law's condemnation of the sinner; in the *Lectures on Isaiah*, he describes it as taking place through the trials that God sends in order to continually deprive the sinner of confidence in himself or herself and drive him or her to the Word. Although Luther adds here in the *Lectures on Isaiah* that God also sends trials to believers in order to continually deprive them of their self-righteousness and drive them to the Word, in both of these writings, the reformer teaches that the hidden God kills in order to make alive.

Lectures on Genesis (1535–1545)

In this exegetical work, Luther further nuances his doctrine of the hidden God through his commentary on God's dealings with the patriarchs of Israel. The importance of the *Lectures on Genesis* for the understanding of Luther's doctrine of the hidden God should not be underestimated. Although Luther warns his students in these lectures against attempting to speculate about the will of the hidden God, he does not abrogate the view of the hiddenness of God that he delineates in *The Bondage of the Will*.

Luther's decade-long teaching of the book of Genesis constitutes some of the reformer's last theological work. At the conclusion of these lectures, Luther expressed that he was completely exhausted from this work and prayed that God would soon grant him a peaceful last hour.⁵³ In these lec-

---

50. *LW* 16:24; WA 31-2:16–17.

51. *LW* 16:234–35; WA 31-2:168–69. *LW* 17:49–50; WA 31-2:298–99.

52. BOW, 151, 161–165, 169–89; WA 18:673, 679–81, 684–99. *LW* 16:234–35; WA 31-32:168–69. *LW* 17:49–50, 131–132; WA 31-2:298–99, 364.

53. Pelikan, "Introduction to Volume 8," *LW* 8:ix.

tures, Luther addresses a variety of theological subjects that arise from the text of the first book of the Pentateuch. One of these subjects is the hiddenness of God in God's self, which Luther discusses in his treatment of the narratives surrounding Abraham, Isaac, Jacob, and Joseph.

Some scholars do not approach the *Lectures on Genesis* or do so only with hesitation because these lectures were gathered and published by some of Luther's students from their own notes rather than being published by the reformer himself or being published at least from his notes.[54] There are other scholars, however, who have not shied away from taking up these lectures for inquiry and discussion.[55] Since Bayer falls into the latter category and uses these lectures heavily in his treatment of Luther's view of the hidden God, and since in these lectures Luther only further clarifies and illustrates this view, they will be dealt with here in so far as they contain Luther's teaching on the hidden God.

The hiddenness of God that Luther addresses in the *Lectures on Genesis* is the hiddenness of God in God's self, as may be seen from the reformer's description of the hiddenness of God in his commentary on Genesis 26, which records Abraham's deceitful dealing with Abimelech and failure to trust God's promise. Here Luther reaffirms the distinction between God hidden in himself and God revealed in Jesus Christ. Luther's description in this passage of the hidden God and the hidden work of God frames the basic thrust of his discussion of the hiddenness of God in God's self throughout the *Lectures on Genesis*. Luther here delineates three aspects to his teaching concerning the hiddenness of God in God's self. The hidden God is complete incomprehensible to the sinner. The hidden God brings trials upon the sinner in order to drive him or her to God in Jesus Christ where they may be saved. The sinner can only truly find salvation in the revealed God through the promise of God in Jesus Christ and that this promise should be held up against the God hidden in God's self.[56]

God hidden in God's self, says Luther, is completely incomprehensible to the sinner. God simply cannot and will not be found and understood by the sinner outside of God's revelation, thus God actively hides from the sinner in God's self. In these lectures, Luther centers his discussion of the hiddenness of God in God's self on the existential question of whether or not

---

54. Steinmetz, *Luther in Context*, 156. Oberman, *Luther: Man between God and the Devil*, 166–167.

55. E.g. Maxfield, *Luther's Lectures on Genesis and the Formation of Evangelical Identity*, 1ff. Schwanke, *Creatio ex nihilo*, 17ff. Asendorf, *Lectura in Biblia: Luthers Genesisvorlesung (1535–1545)*, 65–67ff.

56. Luther, *Lectures on Genesis (1535–1545)*, LW 5:43–50; Luther, *Vorlesung über 1.Mose*, WA 43:458–63.

one is predestined. Here Luther argues that one can never know one's status according to God's decree in predestination by speculating about that decree. The divine decree of predestination lies outside the realm of God's revelation in the incarnation of God in Christ and in the Word and Sacraments, for predestination is the decree of God hidden in God's self. The workings of God in God's self cannot be probed by the inquiring human mind.[57] There can be no profit in speculating about this hidden God, says Luther. Believers must abide in God's revelation through Christ in God's Word. Otherwise, they will fall into utter despair, for the enticement to speculate concerning the hidden God is a temptation to unbelief from Satan.[58]

At this juncture, it important to note that Luther's prohibition against speculation about the will of the hidden God in predestination is not a rejection of his doctrine of the hidden God although some scholars hold and different view.[59] The idea that Luther changed his view could be based on his words concerning predestination in the fifth volume of the *Lectures on Genesis*:

> From an unrevealed God I will become a revealed God. Nevertheless, I will remain the same God. I will be made flesh, or send my Son. He shall die from your sins and rise again from the dead . . . For 'he who sees me,' says Christ, 'also sees the Father himself.' If you listen to him, are baptized in his name, and love his Word, then you are certainly predestined and are certain of your salvation . . ."
>
> "If you believe in the revealed God and accept his Word, he will gradually also reveal the hidden God, for "he who sees me has seen the Father . . . if you cling to the revealed God with a firm faith, so that your heart is so minded that you will not lose Christ even if you are deprived of everything, then you are most assuredly predestined, and you will understand the hidden God."[60]

---

57. *LW* 5:42-50; *WA* 43:457-63.

58. *LW* 5:45; *WA* 43:459-60. Luther, *Lectures on Genesis* (1535-1545), *LW* 3:138; Luther, *Vorlesung über 1.Mose* (1535-1545); *WA* 42:464.

59. Kolb, *Bound Choice, Election, and Wittenberg Theological Method*, 37. Robert Kolb argues that Luther goes back, at least in part, on his doctrine of the hidden God as he articulated it in *The Bondage of the Will*. At the very least, Kolb holds that in the *Lectures on Genesis* Luther "rejects any discordance between [the] hidden God and [the] revealed God even though the hidden God lies far beyond human grasp."

60. *LW* 5:45-46; *WA* 43:459-460. Kolb, *Bound Choice, Election, and Wittenberg Theological Method*, 37-38.

It is my contention that these words of Luther here must be understood from the context of Luther's prohibition of speculating about the hidden God's decrees in double predestination and not taken to be a general abrogation of his overall doctrine of the hidden God or as a statement that there is no discordance between the hidden and revealed God. Instead of going back on his doctrine of the hidden God, Luther is here arguing what he has all along: that God's revelation in Christ through the Word and Sacraments is the only place where God can be grasped. As to Luther's statement that the hidden God will become revealed to the believer, this should not be understood ontologically but, rather, eschatologically. The words, "cling to," "faith," and "most assuredly," constitute the language of promise, of God's promise in the gospel of Jesus Christ. They communicate God's promise in Christ precisely because they are contradicted by the experienced reality of the hostile hidden God; they communicate the revealed God's promise in spite of the work of the hidden God in Anfechtung: "even if you are deprived of everything."[61] In this context Luther's statement that the hidden God will become a revealed God should not be understood to mean that Luther is going back on his previous doctrine of the hidden God but as an eschatological qualification of it similar to the one that he makes in his teaching on "the three lights" at the conclusion of *The Bondage of the Will*. In the context of the language of promise, Luther should be understood here as giving a reminder of the eschatological hope of God revealed in the gospel of Christ over and against the hiddenness of God.[62] Luther thus does not here, in the *Lectures on Genesis*, resolve the tension and contradiction between the hidden God and the revealed God, but, rather, merely reiterates his earlier teaching that the hidden God's will in double predestination is incomprehensible but that God is revealed as a God of grace and mercy in the promise of election given in the gospel of Jesus Christ through the Word and Sacraments.

Luther states that God hidden in God's self is completely incomprehensible to the sinner, but he also describes the work of the hidden God as something which one can at least recognize through experience. This work of the hidden God consists of God's sending trials against the sinner, in order that he or she may give up on his or her own efforts at righteousness and speculations concerning the hidden God and cling instead to the promise of the revealed God in Jesus Christ.[63] In these trials, says Luther, God

61. LW 5:46; WA 43:460. Hans-Martin Barth, *Die Theologie Martin Luthers*, 200, 211–12.

62. LW 5:45–46; WA 43:459–60. Kolb, *Bound Choice, Election, and Wittenberg Theological Method*, 37–38.

63. LW 5:49; WA 43:462. LW 6:151; WA 44:112–13.

hides from the sinner as a God who is against the sinner in way that starkly contrasts with God's giving of God's self in the revelation of the promise of Christ.[64]

Whereas in *The Bondage of the Will* and the *Lectures on Isaiah* Luther merely describes the work of the hidden God, in his *Lectures on Genesis* he gives a vivid illustration of this work. This illustration, which Luther presents in his commentary on Genesis 32, consists of God's wrestling with Jacob at the banks of the Jabbok. Even Jacob, the direct recipient of God's promise, was not immune to trials. Rather, because of his receiving the promise, Jacob became the object for the work of the hidden God. In fact, Luther depicts the hidden God as pouncing upon Jacob at the Jabbok and attacking him not only physically but also with words, words aimed at causing Jacob to doubt God's promise.[65] This, says Luther, is the work of the hidden God. The hidden God comes in trials to assault the believer's faith in the promise itself, the promise of God's salvation not only through sin, death, and the devil but also directly through God's own wrath.[66] Yet, in the midst of this assault of the hidden God, the believer must cling to God revealed in the promise all the more, just as Jacob clung to God in the midst of his wrestling, demanding "I will not let you go; bless me!"[67] Like Jacob who refused to yield to the assault of the hidden God, the believer must remain resolute and even talk back to the hidden God: "Lord God, you have promised this in your Word. Therefore, you will not change your promise. I have been baptized; I have been absolved!"[68]

In the midst of this assault on faith in the promise, God hidden in God's self hides "as the worst devil," says Luther, in order to drive the sinner away from their trust in themselves and away from speculating about God hidden in God's self, driving them to belief, to grasping God revealed in Christ through the gospel's Word of promise.[69] God only hides in this way in order to mortify the old self and to make alive the new self through the gift of the promise of the revealed God in Jesus Christ.[70] As God hidden in God's self thus fought with Jacob at the banks of the Jabbok and later sent fierce trials upon his son, Joseph, in order that God might be found by them in the

64. *LW* 6:259; *WA* 44:192.
65. *LW* 6:135; *WA* 44:100–101. Steinmetz, *Luther in Context*, 162.
66. *LW* 6:135–136, 139; *WA* 44:100–101, 103–4.
67. *LW* 6:139–40; *WA* 44:103–4.
68. *LW* 6:141; *WA* 44:105.
69. Luther, *Lectures on Genesis* (1535–1545), *LW* 7:175–76; Luther, *Vorlesung über 1.Mose*, *WA* 44:428–29.
70. *LW* 6:354; *WA* 44:264–65.

revelation of God's promise, so too, says Luther, does the hidden God send trials upon believers in order to drive them continually away from trust in their own efforts and to faith in the revealed God in Christ through the promise given through Word and Sacrament. Thus, says Luther, the believer is the participatory witness to God against God: the hidden God against the revealed God of the promise of the gospel in Christ, and the revealed God of that promise overcoming the wrath of the hidden God who assaults faith in the promise.[71]

God does not leave the sinner in the damnation which God has brought upon them. Instead, says Luther, God brings them down to hell only in order to raise them up again.[72] In these lectures, Luther clearly communicates that the ultimate purpose of the work of God hidden in God's self is the salvation of the sinner by God revealed in Christ through the Word and Sacraments. God may be incomprehensible and even against the sinner as God is in God's self, but God is graspable by human faith as God is revealed in Christ through the Word and Sacraments. Through these means, says Luther, God presents God's self as a faithful and trustworthy God, a God bound to the promise.[73]

The human sinner must leave alone God hidden in God's self and this God's hidden decrees, says Luther, and take hold of the revealed God in Christ who comes to the sinner in Word and Sacrament. The revealed God of promise must be so grasped by the sinner through these means, precisely in face of the work of God hidden in God's self.[74] Luther even argues that the believer must hold up the promise of the revealed God against the incomprehensible and hostile God hidden in God's self. The believer must fight against the hidden God, claiming the power and faithfulness of the revealed God in Jesus Christ against the hidden God's incomprehensibility and wrath. The believer must cry out against the hidden God, "I am baptized!" The believer must cling to the words of Christ's absolution given for the forgiveness of sins. The believer must set the pledge of the revealed God in the body and blood of Jesus Christ in the face of the hidden God who kills, destroys, and damns.[75] The promise of the revealed God is the only hope of

---

71. *LW* 6:145–51; WA 44:108–13. Luther, *Lectures on Genesis* (1535–1545), *LW* 8:3–10; Luther, *Vorlesung über 1.Mose*, WA 44:582–87. Cf. Steinmetz, *Luther in Context*, 156–68. Hans-Martin Barth, *Die Theologie Martin Luthers*, 210–12.

72. *LW* 6:151; WA 44:113.

73. *LW* 5:49; WA 43:462.

74. *LW* 5:47, 49–50; WA 43:460–61, 462–63. *LW* 6:398; WA 44:297–98.

75. *LW* 5:46–50; WA 43:460–63. *LW* 6:259, 354, 398; WA 44:192, 264–65, 297–98.

the believer against the work of God hidden in God's self, and it is indeed what the work of God hidden in God's self pushes the believer towards.[76]

Luther's explanation in his *Lectures on Genesis* of the hiddenness of God in God's self bears an overall similarity to his articulation of this same concept in *The Bondage of the Will*, yet Luther's teaching on this concept in these lectures also has its own distinctive features. Luther's assertion that God hidden in God's self and the hidden work of God are both incomprehensible may be found in both of these writings of the reformer.[77] Similarly, Luther's description in the *Lectures on Genesis* of the work of God hidden in God's self closely parallels his description of this same work in his earlier treatise written against Erasmus. Both in the *Lectures on Genesis* and in *The Bondage of the Will*, Luther describes the work of God hidden in God's self driving the sinner to despair of his or her own efforts at righteousness and to cling to God revealed in Jesus Christ.[78] Furthermore, in both the *Lectures on Genesis* and in *The Bondage of the Will*, Luther presents God's revelation in Christ through the Word as the only place where the sinner can truly know God.[79]

Although Luther describes the hiddenness of God outside of revelation similarly in both his *Lectures on Genesis* and *The Bondage of the Will*, he explains it more in depth in the *Lectures on Genesis*. In *The Bondage of the Will*, Luther states that the God hidden in God's self and this God's hidden will are incomprehensible, but in the *Lectures on Genesis*, he locates such divine incomprehensibility more overtly within the issue of divine predestination than he does in his treatise of 1525.[80] Similarly, Luther goes deeper into the discussion of the hidden God's work of damning the sinner in order to save him or her in the *Lectures on Genesis* than he does in *The Bondage of the Will*, identifying this work as taking place within the trials God sends upon the sinner.[81] Finally, Luther goes further in his *Lectures on Genesis* than in *The Bondage of the Will* concerning his assertion that God is to be found by the sinner only as God reveals God's self in Christ through the Word and Sacraments. Through his use of the vivid illustration of the work of the hidden God as existential struggle between the human and God through the narrative of God's wrestling with Jacob at the banks of the Jabbok, Luther argues that the promise of the revealed God in Christ must be

---

76. *LW* 6:151, 398; *WA* 44:112–13, 297–98.
77. *LW* 5:42–50; *WA* 43:457–63. *BOW*, 169–71; *WA* 18:684–86.
78. *BOW*, 151, 161–65, 169–89; *WA* 18:673, 679–81, 684–99.
79. *LW* 5:46–47, 49; *WA* 43:460–461, 462. *BOW*, 170–71; *WA* 18:685–86.
80. *LW* 5:43–50; *WA* 43:458–63.
81. *LW* 5:49; *WA* 43:462. *LW* 6:151; *WA* 44:112–13.

held up by the believer against God hidden in God's self and emphasizes the promise not only in the Word but also in the Sacraments.[82]

A Unified Picture of the Hidden God in Luther's Works

A certain unified picture of Luther's understanding of God's hiddenness in God's self may be discerned from the reformer's discussion of this theme in *The Bondage of the Will*, the *Lectures on Jonah*, the *Lectures on Isaiah*, and the *Lectures on Genesis*. In these four writings, Luther teaches that God hidden in God's self and this God's hidden work are incomprehensible, that God hidden in God's self kills and damns sinners in order that they may be raised to life and saved by God revealed, and that God revealed in Christ through the Word is the only way in which one can know God. Luther's explanation of God's hiddenness in God's self in his treatise written against Erasmus in 1525 serves as the foundation for a unified view of this teaching. The reformer's articulations of this teaching in his *Lectures on Jonah*, his *Lectures on Isaiah* and his *Lectures on Genesis* then serve as further clarifications of this teaching.

Luther's Doctrine of the Hidden God in Its Systematic-Theological Dimensions

From looking at Luther's teaching concerning the hiddenness of God in God's self as it appears in *The Bondage of the Will* and is further nuanced in the *Lectures on Isaiah* and the *Lectures on Genesis*, one may conclude that this teaching is interconnected with several other important themes in the reformer's theology, including the distinction between law and gospel, God's double decree of predestination, and God's salvation of the bound sinner in Christ through the Word and Sacraments. This teaching is related to, complements, and is clarified by the other important loci of the reformer's thought delineated above.

The Distinction between the Law and Gospel

The first systematic theme of Luther's theology with which the teaching concerning the hiddenness of God in God's self is connected is his teaching concerning the distinction between God's work in the law and God's work in the gospel. As I have already noted above, Luther articulates his teaching

---

82. *LW* 5:46–50; *WA* 43:460–463. *LW* 6:259, 354, 398; *WA* 44:192, 264–65, 297–98.

concerning the distinction between God not preached (God hidden in God's self) and God preached (God revealed in Christ) within his argument concerning the distinction between the law and the gospel. In fact, these two distinctions may be seen as parallel to each other as Luther's statement of the distinction between God preached and God not preached functions as part of an expanded critique of Erasmus' confusion of the law and the gospel in his use of Old Testament texts to support his notion of the free and active will of the sinner in salvation. Amidst his distinctions between texts that function as law and gospel, Luther focuses particularly on Erasmus' use of Ezekiel 18:23 and 33:11: "I desire not the death of the sinner," and here articulates his understanding of God hidden outside of revelation.[83]

Luther's teaching of the hidden God's work of wrath complements and parallels very closely his distinction between the work of the law and the work of the gospel. In his treatise of 1521, *Answer to the HyperChristian, Hyperspiritual, Hyperlearned Book by Goat Emser in Leipzig,* Luther clearly delineates exactly what work God accomplishes in the law and what work God accomplishes in the gospel. Luther argues that the work of the law is to point out to sinners their own helplessness and to condemn them, but that the work of the gospel is give to them salvation through the promise of Jesus Christ.[84] Even as early as 1518 in *The Heidelberg Disputation* and its *Explanation,* Luther states that "the law brings the wrath of God, kills, reviles, accuses, judges, and condemns everything that is not in Christ" but that the grace of God and the love of God accomplish "everything already" for righteousness before God through the "pardon of God" in the gospel.[85] In *The Bondage of the Will,* Luther echoes this definition of the differing works of God in the law and in the gospel, saying that the law only identifies and condemns the sinner's sin, laying him or her bare before God's justice, stripping him or her of the chimera of "free will."[86] Similarly, the reformer maintains that the unpreached God holds only wrath for the sinner and actively wills the sinner's death.[87] The gospel, on the other hand, gives the

---

83. *BOW* 169–171; WA 18:684–86.

84. Luther, *Answer to the HyperChristian, Hyperspiritual, and Hyperlearned Book by Goat Emser in Leipzig—Including Some Thoughts Regarding His Companion, the Fool Murner* (1521), *LW* 39:182–83; Luther, *Auf das überchristlich, übergeistlich und überkünstlich Buch Bocks Emsers zu Leipzig Antwort. Darin auch Murnarrs seines Gesellen gedacht wird,* WA 7:653–55.

85. Theses 23–28, *LW* 41; WA 1:354. *Explanation to the Theses* (1518), *LW* 41:62–63; WA 1:369.

86. *BOW* 157, 161–62, 165, 287–88; WA 18:676, 679, 681, 766–67.

87. *BOW* 169–71; WA 18:684–86.

sinner the promise of new life, saving him or her.[88] Likewise, the preached God does not will the death of the sinner but wills the sinner's life and salvation instead.[89]

Furthermore, in other writings, such as in *Against the Heavenly Prophets* (1525) and the *Antinomian Disputations* (1537–1540) Luther states that the condemning law of God is, to some extent, immanent in the natural order and within the conscience of the human being. This is not a "natural law" teaching *per se*, especially since Luther argues that little to nothing can actually be known by humans based on "natural" moral law because of the pervasiveness of sin. Yet, Luther does teach that the wrath and condemnation of the law against sinners comes to them through the natural order and through conscience.[90] This parallels his argument in his *Lectures on Jonah* that God effects God's wrath and damnation against human sinners through the natural order.

In terms of a textual analysis of Luther's doctrine of the hidden God in *The Bondage of the Will*, Luther's teaching concerning the distinction between the works of the law and the gospel and his teaching concerning the distinction between God unpreached and God preached function together in *The Bondage of the Will* in a sort of symbiosis. The distinction between the work of the law and the work of the gospel in Luther's theology may be said to be undergirded by the distinction between the unpreached and preached God in that it is the unpreached God who wills through the law and the preached God who wills through the gospel. On the other hand, Luther's teaching concerning the law and the gospel clarifies his teaching concerning the preached and unpreached God. The literary context of Luther's teaching concerning the preached and unpreached God within his argument concerning the distinction between the work of the law and the work of the gospel and the common condemning and saving works accomplished by the law and the gospel and the unpreached and preached God clarify that the teaching concerning the preached and unpreached God is a furtherance and outworking of his teaching regarding the distinction between the work of the law and the work of the gospel. The unpreached God is the God of the law who wills the condemnation and destruction, and the preached God is the God of the gospel who wills the life and salvation of the sinner.

---

88. *BOW* 163, 166–67, 289; *WA* 18:680, 682–83, 676.

89. *BOW* 169, 171; *WA* 18:684, 686.

90. Luther, *Antinomerdisputation* (1537–1540), *WA* 39, I:361, 508–9, 515–17. Luther, *Against the Heavenly Prophets in the Matter of Images and Sacraments* (1525), *LW* 40:98; Luther, *Wider die himmlischen Propheten, von den Bildern und Sacrament*, *WA* 18:81. Lohse, *Martin Luther's Theology*, 273–74.

God's Double Decree in Predestination

The second theme in Luther's theology which intersects with the reformer's teaching concerning the hiddenness of God in God's self is God's two-fold decree in predestination. According to Luther, the distinction between God hidden in God's self and God revealed in Christ extends to the divine will as well. God, in fact, has two wills. God hidden in God's self wills the death and damnation of the sinner, while God revealed in Christ wills the sinner's life and salvation.[91] Thus, when Luther speaks of the distinction between the hidden and revealed God, one might argue that this distinction itself constitutes a doctrine of double-predestination. Yet Luther does not profess a belief in double-predestination in the same sense that John Calvin and much of Reformed tradition following him does. For Calvin double-predestination means that before the foundation of world, God chose to save certain individuals and to damn certain other individuals as part of his divine plan for the universe.[92] In *The Bondage of the Will*, Luther does not articulate a doctrine of double-predestination in which God decides the eternal destiny of each human from all eternity but posits that God actively damns the sinner and saves the same sinner. God hidden in God's self wills the death and damnation of the sinner, but God revealed in Christ wills the life and salvation of the same sinner.[93]

This view of double-predestination is not relegated to *The Bondage of the Will* but can, in fact, be found in Luther's theological writings as early as the period of 1514–1516 in his *Lectures on Romans*. Here Luther teaches that God damns the sinner through God's alien work—the decree of reprobation—in order to make him or her alive through God's proper work—the decree of election. The reason for this is that the sinner thinks that he or she has "free will" and that he or she can achieve righteousness before God on his or her own. This is not the case, however, and God first damns the sinner through reprobation in order to rob the sinner of his or her well-cherished belief in himself or herself, so that God in Christ may give them life through God's will in election.[94]

This correlation between God's alien and proper works in the two decrees of predestination and the distinction between God hidden in God's self and God revealed in Christ may also be observed in Luther's *Lectures on Isaiah* and his *Lectures on Genesis*. As I have shown above, Luther argues

---

91. *BOW*, 170–71; WA 18:685–86.

92. Calvin, *Articles concerning Predestination*, in *Calvin: Theological Treatises*, 179.

93. *BOW*, 169–71; WA 18:684–86.

94. Luther, *Lectures on Romans* (1515–1516), LW 25:371–72, 375, 377; Luther, *Diui Pauli apostoli ad Romanos Epistola* (1515–1516), WA 56:381–82, 385–87.

in both of these collections of lectures that God hidden in God's self sends trials upon the sinner in order to kill and damn him or her in order to raise him or her to life and save them. Such trials then function as the means through which God accomplishes God's alien work of reprobation in order that God may accomplish God's proper work of salvation in election.[95] On the other hand, Luther teaches in the *Lectures on Genesis* that it is through the revealed God's positive decree in election that the sinner is saved and assured through the promise of God. The promise of the revealed God in Christ given through the Word and Sacraments bestows the true meaning of predestination: God's decree of election unto salvation through Christ.[96]

Like his teaching concerning the distinction between law and gospel, Luther's teaching concerning God's two decrees in predestination parallels his teaching concerning the distinction between God hidden in God's self and God revealed in Jesus Christ. In both his teaching concerning predestination and his teaching concerning God hidden in God's self and God revealed in Christ, Luther argues that God kills in order to make alive and damns in order to save. The will of God hidden in God's self is the will of God enacted in God's alien work of reprobation, and the will of the revealed God is the will enacted through God's proper work of election.

Salvation in Christ through Word and Sacrament

The third—and the most important—theme in Luther's theology that intersects with the reformer's teaching concerning the hiddenness of the unpreached God is that of salvation in Christ alone given as God's promise in Word and Sacrament. In his work *Theologia Crucis*, Klaus Schwarzwäller argues from Luther's 1535 *Lectures on Galatians* that this teaching concerning salvation as God's justification of the sinner in Christ is the focal point around which all of Luther's theology is arranged. Moreover, this article of faith, says Schwarzwäller, is the only proper subject for all of theology according to Luther.[97] Oswald Bayer corroborates Schwarzwäller's understanding here, suggesting that justification functions in Luther's theology as both a center and a protective barrier to guard theology from the entry into it of subject matter foreign to it. Bayer also highlights that for the reformer, justification in Christ alone is not simply one locus among many

---

95. *LW* 16:24, 233–35; *WA* 31.2:16–17, 168–69. *LW* 5:49; *WA* 43:462. *LW* 6:151, 259; *WA* 44:112–13, 192. *LW* 7:175–176; *WA* 44:428–29. *LW* 8:7–9; *WA* 45:584–86.

96. *LW* 5:46–48; *WA* 18:460–62.

97. Schwarzwäller, *Theologia Crucis*, 46–48. Cf. Luther, *Lectures on Galatians* (1535), *LW* 26:276–91; Luther, *In epistulam S. Pauli ad Galata Commentarius*, *WA* 40.1:328.

in theology but the content of all of theology, yet not in a way that limits the subject matter of theology to a simple affirmation of the doctrine of justification but in a way in which all of the loci of theology are defined by this center and boundary.[98] Salvation in Christ alone may be understood as the force of Luther's theology, underlying all his other theological discourse and loci, as a framework within which all of his other theological loci are appropriately articulated and understood.[99]

This teaching about salvation in Christ clarifies the teaching concerning the alien work of God hidden in God's self and the proper work of God revealed in Christ evident through the law and the gospel as well as through the divine decrees of reprobation and election. The central theological locus of salvation in Christ alone, indeed, underlies these two divine works as Luther understands them in *The Bondage of the Will*, the *Lectures on Isaiah*, and the *Lectures on Genesis*. Although these two works are essentially different and distinct from one another, they both have salvation in Christ alone as their ultimate end. God hidden in God's self humbles the sinner who is bound in sin through trials, in order to destroy his or her self-righteousness and false perception of "free will" and to render him or her utterly helpless so that he or she may be saved by the preached God in Christ through the gospel.[100]

In this way, the theological center of salvation in Christ alone clarifies and grounds the teaching concerning God preached and unpreached. The teaching concerning God hidden in God's self and God revealed in Christ, at first glance, might seem to be a venue for theological speculation concerning the necessary willing of the unpreached God. This, however, is not the case. In undergirding this teaching, the central locus of salvation limits the trajectory of the teaching concerning the preached and unpreached God so as to preclude speculation. As the Finnish Luther scholar Lennart Pinomaa identifies, the activity of the God (both unpreached and preached) who necessarily wills everything that comes to pass is "neither indefinite or unknown, but definite and known: God judges and God saves."[101] Pinomaa states that, for Luther, the double-willing of God thus functions as the sole guarantee of salvation.[102] Hence, the damning will of the unpreached God

---

98. Bayer, "Justification: Basis and Boundary of Theology," 273–74; Bayer, *Leibliches Wort*, 19–20.

99 Bayer, *Martin Luther's Theology*, 38; Bayer, *Martin Luthers Theologie*, 35.

100. *BOW*, 100–101, 161–62; 170–71; WA 532–33, 679, 685–86. *LW* 16:233–35; WA 31–2:167–69. *LW* 17:278–79; WA 31.2:475–76. Kaufmann, "Luther und Erasmus," 150–51.

101. Pinomaa, *Faith Victorious: An Introduction to Luther's Theology*, 25.

102. Ibid., 25–26.

has human salvation as its ultimate goal, precisely through the saving will of the preached God in Christ. Ultimately, human salvation is the *telos* towards which both the will of the unpreached God and the will of the preached God ultimately work.

Human salvation as the *telos* of both divine wills relegates the trajectory of these wills to salvation, so that the theologian is barred both from plummeting into complete despair and hatred against God and from taking off into flights of fanciful speculation concerning the works of the divine wills. In fact, Luther expressly forbids such speculation concerning the damning will of the unpreached God, insisting that engaging in speculation concerning the unpreached God will result in the speculator's complete terror and animosity before God. God in God's self is to be "left alone" as the concern of the sinner is only with the preached God in Christ. The preached God in Christ who comes to the sinner in the Word and Sacraments must even be clung to over and against God hidden in God's self.[103] It is salvation, and not speculation, with which the theologian is ultimately concerned, according to Luther, even when dealing with the issue of the hiddenness of God in God's self.[104]

The Hidden God in the Wider Context of Luther's Theology

The hiddenness of God in God's self is not an isolated teaching in Luther's theological writings but one which is interconnected with other important themes in the reformer's thought. In particular, Luther's understanding of God hidden in God's self is interrelated with his teachings concerning the distinction between God's work in the law and God's work in the gospel, God's double decree in predestination, and God's salvation of sinners in Christ alone through the Word and Sacraments.

The picture of God's hiddenness in God's self depicted by Luther in *The Bondage of the Will*, his *Lectures on Jonah*, his *Lectures on Isaiah*, and his *Lectures on Genesis* is one in which God hidden in God's self is incomprehensible to the sinner and wills the damnation of the sinner in order that he or she may be saved by the revealed God in Jesus Christ. The distinction between the will of God hidden in God's self and the will of God revealed in Jesus Christ parallels the distinction between God's work in the law and God's work in the gospel. Furthermore, it also runs alongside the distinction

---

103. *LW* 5:46-50; *WA* 43:460-63. *LW* 6:259, 354, 398; *WA* 44:192, 264-65, 297-98. Hans-Martin Barth, *Die Theologie Martin Luthers*, 200.

104. *BOW*, 170-71; *WA* 18:685-86. *LW* 5:43-50; *WA* 43:458-63. *LW* 6:259, 354, 398; *WA* 44:192, 264-65, 297-98.

between God's alien decree of reprobation and God's proper decree of election. While this explanation of the hidden God's will of wrath does not exhaust the activity of the hidden God, who works good and evil and who wills all things that come to pass, and though Luther leaves the content of the subject of the hidden God open, this alien work of wrath and damnation does stand as a definite activity of the hidden God. In this regard, the hidden God's will of wrath is expressed ultimately for the sake of the sinner's salvation, for God only kills in order to raise up and only damns in order to save. Everything in Luther's theology, even the hiddenness of God in God's self outside of revelation, ultimately returns back to his theology's core: God's salvation of the sinner by faith in Christ alone. This essential observation concerning the relationship between Luther's doctrine of the hidden God and God's salvation of the sinner in Christ as the center of his theology is particularly pertinent to this study, because Oswald Bayer has sought to construct a contemporary Lutheran theology with God's salvation of the sinner by faith in Christ at its center, in which discourse on the hidden God ultimately is defined by this same core of Luther's and Lutheran theology.

3

The Reception of Luther's Doctrine of the Hidden God in the Modern German Protestant Theological Tradition

Between Luther and Theodosius Harnack

ALTHOUGH THE HIDDENNESS OF God outside of revelation is an important teaching within the theology of Martin Luther, his successors hardly even acknowledge it. Though they also saw Christ's salvation of the sinner as central to theology, the generations of Lutheran theologians between Luther and the Enlightenment to greater or lesser extents neglected Luther's doctrine of the hidden God. Neither Melanchthon nor his followers the Philipists acknowledged, interpreted, or developed Luther's understanding of God's hiddenness outside of revelation. Although the Gnesio-Lutherans at least made passing reference to the doctrine, they did not give it the attention due a topic that Luther himself felt was so important to theology. As the doctrine was rejected by the theologians of Lutheran orthodoxy and forgotten by the pietists, it was not to be taken up again until the nineteenth century. Even when taken up again and addressed by thinkers of the modern German Protestant theological tradition, Luther's doctrine of the hidden God was not well received by this tradition in general. Moreover, as the theologians in this theological tradition rejected or interpreted this doctrine, they tended to do so from the standpoint of their own theological orientations and emphases rather than with reference to its true function within Luther's thought with its theological center of God's salvation of the sinner in Christ.

The history of the reception of Luther's doctrine of the hidden God begins with the reformer's colleague and successor, Philip Melanchthon. The concept of divine hiddenness is completely absent from Melanchthon's theology.[1] Instead, Melanchthon expressed reformational teaching through dialectics and Aristotelian systematizing, especially as he was forced to defend the evangelical confession of faith in the face of its sixteenth-century opponents. This methodology of doing theology was passed on to his students the Philipists and the Gnesio-Lutherans who both argued with one another about the freedom or bondage of the will according to this methodology.[2] This methodological shift among Luther's successors perhaps catalyzed the neglect of the doctrine of the hidden God. While Luther understood this doctrine as being central to a description of God's interaction with humans, Melanchthon and the Philipists are silent about it and the Gnesio-Lutherans, including the Concordists—particularly Chemnitz—acknowledge it but interact with it little.

Though there are similarities between aspects of Luther's teaching concerning the hidden God and certain points in Melanchthon's early pedagogical theology, even in this period, Melanchthon never formally addresses the concept of hiddenness itself. In particular, early on, Melanchthon's notion of the natural knowledge of God outside of Christ corresponds to Luther's understanding of the hiddenness of God outside of revelation in that Melanchthon teaches that the human's natural knowledge of God is only one of wrath and that God can only truly be known as a God of grace and mercy in Christ.[3] Furthermore, in agreement with Luther, Melanchthon teaches at this point that the human will is bound and not free and that all things happen by God's all-necessitating predestination.[4] Thus, while Melanchthon may not teach a doctrine of the hidden God *per se*, he at least at

---

1. Rogness, *Melanchthon*, 29-30, 144.

2. Kolb, *Bound Choice, Election, and Wittenberg Theological Method*, 5-6, 71, 75. Croghan, "Melanchthon's *Der Ordinanden Examen* and *Examen Eorum*", 178, 181-82. For a more detailed account of Melanchthon's use of Aristotelian rhetoric in his apologetic theology see Kuropka, *Philipp Melanchthon*, 217-23, 227-33, 239-51, 252-55. Kuropka, "Melanchthon and Aristotle," 20-23.

3. Melanchthon, *Baccalaureate Theses* (1519), in *Melanchthon: Selected Writings*, 17. Melanchthon, *Loci Communes* (1521), 111-17, 171-72. Melanchthon, *Annotationes in Evangelium Ioannis* (1523), in CR 14:1048-49, 1129. Rogness, *Melanchthon*, 15-17.

4. *Loci* (1521), 72-73, 75-77, 86-87. CA 18, in BC, 50-51; BSLK, 73-74. Ap, 3, in BC, 233-35; BSLK, 339-42. Kolb, *Bound Choice, Election, and Wittenberg Theological Method*, 79-80. StA 4:240-42. Cf. Wengert, *Human Freedom, Christian Righteousness*, 98-100.

this early point did not differ with Luther concerning the content of Luther's doctrine of hiddenness.

Any parallels between Melanchthon's theology and Luther's understanding of the hiddenness of God outside of revelation, however, break down in 1532, at which time Melanchthon began to retract his teaching on the bondage of the human will and its inability to effect or participate in human salvation. He began the process of retracting his belief in the bondage of the will in his 1532 *Commentary on Romans* and continued it in his *Examination of Ordination Candidates* (1554), as well as in his revisions of the *Loci Communes* in 1535, 1543, 1555, and 1559.[5] In the theology of these later revisionary works, Melanchthon began to teach that the human will was not completely bound in salvation but that it was actually able to work together with the Word of God and the Holy Spirit. With the retraction of this part of his earlier theology and his new teaching concerning the activity of the will in salvation, any similarity between certain aspects of Melanchthon's earlier theology and Luther's understanding of God's hiddenness outside of revelation collapses, since the entire reason that Luther sees God undertaking God's hidden work is to destroy the idea that humans possess freedom of the will in regard to salvation.[6] Moreover, in advancing his new teaching concerning the ability of the human to cooperate in salvation, Melanchthon denied the notion that God is active through double predestination to reprobate the sinner in order to damn and kill the sinner, on the one hand, and to elect the sinner in order to save and give life to the sinner, on the other hand.[7] He regarded this doctrine of predestination as one of terror and rejected it in his theology.[8] Melanchthon's followers, the Philipists, promulgated Melanchthon's later views on the supposed powers of human free will and his rejections of Luther's view of double predestination, thereby abrogating any agreement between them and Luther concerning the content of the elder reformer's doctrine of the hidden God.[9]

5. Cf. Graybill, *Evangelical Free Will*, 199–223ff.

6. Melanchthon, *Loci Communes* (1543), 42–43. Melanchthon, *Examination of Ordination Candidates* (1554), in *Excerpts from the Writings of Philip Melanchthon*, 48. *Examen Ordinanorum* (1554), in CR 23:15. StA 2:243. CR 21:658. Melanchthon, *Loci Communes* (1555), 58–63. Kolb, *Bound Choice, Election, and Wittenberg Theological Method*, 91–93. Rogness, *Melanchthon*, 126–27. Matz, *Der befreite Mensch*, 151–56.

7 Melanchton, *Loci Communes* (1535), in CR 21:330. Melanchthon, *Commentari in Epistolam Pauli ad Romanos, recens scripti a Philippo Melanthone* (1532), in StA 5:257–58. Manschreck, *Melanchthon*, 296; Kolb, 87. Matz, 157–58, 233–34. Graybill, *Evangelical Free Will*, 205–9, 212–15.

8. Mahlmann, "Die Interpretation von Luthers *De servo arbitrio* bei orthodoxen lutherischen Theologen," 75.

9. Cf. Kolb, *Bound Choice, Election, and Wittenberg Theological Method*, 118–28,

The Gnesio-Lutherans began their theological work at least acknowledging Luther's teaching on the hidden God when it served their arguments for the doctrine of the bound will, which they raised against the Philipists. In particular, Georg Herbst, Cyriacus Spangenberg, and Martin Chemnitz affirmed Luther's distinction between God hidden outside of revelation and God revealed in Christ through the Word.[10] Yet their affirmation of this teaching of Luther's went little beyond simply acknowledging Luther's teaching on the matter. Spangenberg at least attempted to utilize Luther's teaching to support the Gnesio-Lutheran position in the Synergistic Controversy with the Philipists through his preaching on Luther's treatise *The Bondage of the Will*, but in the end, all he did was use this teaching of Luther's as a way to describe God's sovereign rule over all things.[11] As Robert Kolb states in *Bound Choice, Election, and Wittenberg Theological Method*, Herbst and Chemnitz "paused before" Luther's notion of the hidden God, but this notion did not play a significant role in Gnesio-Lutheran theology.[12]

One can observe this pausing in Chemnitz's *Loci Theologici*, where he states that one's understanding of God's existence and nature comes from God's revelation to humanity and not from God's existence outside of revelation. Though Chemnitz does not here refer to Luther's understanding of God's hiddenness or even to the terminology of "hiddenness" itself, it is clearly what Chemnitz assumes. Moreover, his subsequent prohibition against speculation into God outside of revelation shows that Chemnitz is at least in basic agreement with Luther on this element of the reformer's doctrine of the hidden God.[13] Yet, as Theodore Mahlmann highlights, Chem-

---

182-90.

10. Ibid, 144-46.

11. Kolb, *Bound Choice, Election, and Wittenberg Theological Method*, 208-9.

12. Ibid, 146.

13. In chapter three of his "First Locus," Chemnitz states: "*Nos vero in investigande non scrutamur illa arcane essentiae & voluntatis Dei, quae nobis ignota esse voluit: sed ex patefactione ipsius Dei colligimus brevem fummmam quantum nobis in erbo fuo de fua essentiia et voluntate reclavit. Et quia omnium vult Deus ita cognosci & invocavit, sicut se patefecit tenendo est alique description Dei, ad quam mens in invocation se referat.*" [Note: non-standardized spelling is Chemnitz's.] Chemnitz, *Loci Theologici* (1653), 24. Here, the English translation given by J. A. O. Preus suffices: "But in our search for a definition [of the existence of God] we should not look into that secret area of the essence and will of God which he wills that we do not know. Rather we should gain a brief summary from the revelation of God, as far as he in his Word has revealed his essence and his will to us. And because it is an absolute certainty that God wills to be known and invoked in the same way as he has revealed himself, we must cling to any definition of God to which our mind can refer in worship." Chemnitz, *Loci Theologici*, trans. J. A. O. Preus, 57. There may be slight nuances of words used by Chemnitz that differ from those used by Luther in *The Bondage of the Will*, but the general thrust of

nitz also echoes Melanchthon's concern not to blame God for the existence of sin, and it is in this concern, perhaps, that one may observe the beginning of the compromise between Luther's doctrine of the hidden God—complete with double predestination—and Philipist synergism.[14]

By the time of the composition of the *Formula of Concord* (1577), however, even this acknowledgement of Luther's doctrine of the hidden God by the Gnesio-Lutherans had dropped off. Perhaps the Gnesio-Lutherans abandoned speaking of this teaching of Luther's in the context of polemical confrontation with a nascent Reformed theology that taught a doctrine of double predestination in which God makes an individual choice of eternal bliss or eternal damnation for each individual human being before all time. Perhaps it was given up as a concession to the Philipists in the spirit of compromise and Concordia. These both seem to be reasonable conclusions given the rhetoric of the Concordists against Calvinism and double predestination in Article 11, "Concerning the Eternal Predestination and Election of God."[15] In this article, however, the Concordists not only condemn the Reformed view of election but also, albeit implicitly or even unintentionally, reject Luther's understanding of the will and work of the unpreached God hidden outside of revelation when they state that God's predestination applies only to salvation and not to damnation and that the reprobate are damned by their own will and not by God's.[16]

Amongst all of Luther's successors, the Gnesio-Lutherans stand out as the only ones who carried on Luther's doctrine of the hidden God to any extent. Yet even they ultimately gave very little and only indirect attention to this topic in Luther's theology. Furthermore, the Gnesio-Lutherans only related individual aspects of this teaching of Luther's, did not explain the doctrine as a whole, and did not use it significantly in their own theology. Moreover, in the *Formula of Concord* in their defense against Calvinism

---

what Chemnitz is saying mirrors what Luther says concerning knowing God only as God and God's will as revealed in God's Word and not according to God hidden in God's "own nature and majesty." BOW, 170; WA 18:685.

14. Mahlmann, "Die Interpretation von Luthers *De servo arbitrio* bei orthodoxen lutherischen Theologen," 80.

15. Ibid, 80, 84.

16. FC,SD, 11, in BC, 640–42. Schlink, *Theology of the Lutheran Confessions*, 290. If the Concordists merely want to maintain that the true theological meaning to predestination is God's gracious will proclaimed in election, and that there is no room in theology for speculation about God's decrees of double predestination, then they are completely faithful to Luther. As I read the FC, however, I believe that Chemnitz is acquiescing to the Philipists amongst the Concordists, compromising by giving up Luther's understanding of double predestination for the sake of Lutheran theological unity.

and compromise with the Philipists, the Gnesio-Lutherans implicitly but effectively closed the door on the doctrine of the hidden God by rejecting any notion of double predestination and assigning the responsibility of reprobation not to God but to the rejection of God's grace by the individual human will.

Upon coming to the orthodox Lutheran theologians of the seventeenth century, one can find a clear rejection of Luther's understanding of the hiddenness of God in the thought of Johann Gerhard (1582–1637). Though he mentions it only in passing in his discussion of Christian doctrine, Gerhard is clear that he rejects any idea that there is a divided will of God: "We deny with all our might that one should establish a hidden will [of God] not only diverse from the one revealed in the Word but even opposed to it. In fact, we declare that this is wicked and blasphemous."[17] Though Gerhard aims these words against the Reformed understanding of double predestination, they clearly contradict Luther's understanding of the hiddenness of God outside of revelation as well, since the reformer's understanding of such hiddenness clearly constitutes such a distinction between two wills of God, which Gerhard so eagerly rejects.[18]

There is no mention of Luther's doctrine of the hidden God in the theological writings of the Pietists. This is to be expected, as Luther's teaching on the matter complements his doctrine of the bound will, which the Pietist theologians with their theology of conversion and moral transformation either undermined or rejected entirely. For the Pietists, the freedom of the human will is assumed as extant in their theology and is seen by them as being necessary in order for the human to cooperate with (or resist) God's work in conversion (*Wiedergeburt*) and the divine-human synergistic work of holy living.[19] August Hermann Francke does mention *Anfechtung* as something which forms the believer in faith, but he attributes this work to God revealed in Christ as a work of love and not to the hidden God. Indeed, Francke does not recognize the distinction between the hidden and revealed God.[20] By the time of the pietists in the eighteenth century, Luther's doctrine

---

17. Gerhard, *Theological Commonplaces (1625)*, Volume 1, 240–241. Mahlmann, "Die Interpretation von Luthers *De servo arbitrio* bei orthodoxen lutherischen Theologen," 85.

18. Ibid.

19. Stein, "Philip Jakob Spener," in *The Pietist Theologians*, 90–92. Spener, *Der Hochwichtige Articul von der Wiedergeburt* (1696), 121–123, 142–149. Francke, *A Letter to a Friend Concerning the Most Useful Way of Preaching* (1725), 119–20. Francke, *On Christian Perfection* (1690), 114–16.

20. Francke, *Simple Instruction, or How One Should Read Holy Scripture for One's True Edification*, LQ 25 (2011) 379. Cf. Bayer, "Lutheran Pietism, or *Oratio, Meditatio, Tentatio* in August Hermann Francke," 391; Luthersicher Pietismus: *Oratio, Meditatio,*

of the hidden God had thus dropped out of German Lutheran theological discourse entirely.

Throughout the generations following Luther, the reformer's teaching concerning the hiddenness of God was rejected and sidelined. Though one might see in the natural theology of Friedrich Schleiermacher (1768–1834) some understanding of the hiddenness of God outside of revelation, such an idea is inaccurate due to the fact that the notion of actually finding God and building a positive doctrine of God on the universal, general experience of God outside of the special revelation of God in Christ, such as Schleiermacher propounds, runs completely counter to Luther's understanding of the hiddenness of God outside of revelation and his distinction between God hidden and God revealed.[21] There was relatively nothing said concerning Luther's view of the hidden God between Gerhard's rejection of the doctrine in the seventeenth century and the reemergence of the doctrine with the beginnings of modern Luther scholarship in the mid-nineteenth century.

It was, in fact, not until the mid-nineteenth century, when Luther's distinction between God hidden and God revealed was rediscovered after generations of purposeful neglect by the Baltic-German theologian, Theodosius Harnack, that this teaching of Luther's was seriously taken up and interpreted.[22] After Harnack revived Luther's teaching concerning the hidden God, there was an explosion of interaction with this teaching within the modern German Protestant theological tradition. The scholars and theologians who discuss and interpret Luther's doctrine of the hidden God include some of the most important figures in this tradition. Yet there are also some scholars and theologians within this tradition who are not the most eminent figures within the tradition, but who nevertheless have been influential in their work on Luther's and Lutheran theology.

In this chapter, I will follow in semi-chronological order the treatment given to Luther's teaching concerning the hidden God starting with its revival in the scholarship of Theodosius Harnack. Though I will also briefly discuss other thinkers who address the hiddenness of God in revelation, the bulk of my survey will be relegated to addressing those scholars and theologians who deal directly with Luther's understanding of the hiddenness of God outside of revelation. I will address how each of these figures interprets and rejects or utilizes Luther's doctrine of the hidden God by grouping them according to their representative theological sub-tradition

---

Tentatio bei August Herman Francke," Religiöse Erfahrung und wissensachaftliche Theologie, in *Festschrift für Ulrich Köpf zum 70. Geburtstag*, 11–12.

21. Cf. Schleiermacher, *The Christian Faith*, vol. 1, 131–48.
22. Gerrish, "'To the Unknown God," 266.

or school of thought, namely the Ritschlian tradition, the History of Religions School, Erlangen theology, Neo-Orthodoxy, Marburg theology, and Trinitarian Theology.[23]

The Nineteenth Century

Theodosius Harnack

According to Klaus Schwarzwäller, Theodosius Harnack (1816–1889) regarded *De servo arbitrio* as one of Luther's greatest literary achievements.[24] In the first volume of his seminal work, *Luthers Theologie mit besonderer Beziehung auf seine Versöhnungs- und Erlösungslehre*, Harnack presents his commentary on Luther's teaching concerning God hidden and God revealed—a commentary still regarded by scholars as one of the best treatments on the subject—with special emphasis on Luther's notion of God not preached as the God of wrath.[25] In this work, Harnack interprets Luther's teaching concerning God hidden and revealed as two ways in which God relates to humans: through God's Word and outside of God's Word.[26] In God's Word, God is revealed as the God of mercy, grace, and promise in Jesus Christ. Outside of God's Word, God is hidden. It is not that God is completely imperceptible to humans outside of God's Word. Rather, God's merciful promise and gracious will are unknown outside of how God is revealed in God's Word. The God who is not preached is the God who is hidden in God's self outside of God's Word of gracious promise in Jesus Christ; this God is the holy God of majesty who works in all things and who wills only wrath towards humans.[27]

Harnack's overall work on Luther's theology signifies the first attempt to set forth a unified, systematic approach to the thought of the great reformer, and in its day, this work signaled the beginnings of a new interest in the study of Luther's theology.[28] Harnack was also the first major figure

---

23. The division of these thinkers into categories according to centuries is admittedly somewhat arbitrary. While it might be customary to categorize a thinker by the century in which his most significant works were written, I have categorized these thinkers firstly according to their representative schools and the schools according to the century in which they best fit.

24. Schwarzwäller, *Sibboleth:*, 16.

25. Harnack, *Luthers Theologie*, 84–97. Althaus, *The Theology of Martin Luther*, 169.

26. Gerrish, "'To the Unknown God,'" 266.

27. Ibid. Schwarzwäller, *Sibboleth*, 15–16. Harnack, *Luthers Theologie*, 87–89, 93–97.

28. Lohse, *Martin Luther's Theology*, 3. Hillerbrand, "The Legacy of Martin Luther,"

of German Protestant theology in the nineteenth century to address Luther's notion of the hiddenness of the unpreached God of wrath. Although Harnack's theological approach to Luther was not adopted by most other nineteenth-century German theologians (some of whom thought his interpretation of Luther too archaic for their own modern, progressive times), his pioneering work began a wave of interest in Luther's theology in general and the topic of the hiddenness of the unpreached God in particular.[29] Furthermore, in seeking to relate the theology of Luther on its own terms, Harnack gave an overall fair and generous treatment to Luther's doctrine of the hidden God and its place in the reformer's theology.

Harnack's approving treatment of Luther's doctrine of the hidden God was not universally adopted within the broader modern German Protestant tradition. In fact, amongst theologians subsequent to Harnack in the nineteenth century, only Karl Holl followed Harnack in his positive appraisal and essentially correct interpretation of Luther's doctrine of the hidden God. This is due, to some extent, to the fact that other German theologians of this period were biased by their own theological commitments and emphases, which did not allow for the hiddenness of God outside God's Word. These theologians represent the two theological trajectories of the Ritschlians and the History of Religions School. As a whole the Ritschlians, lead by the eminent figure of late-nineteenth century German liberal theology, Albrecht Ritschl, followed a Neo-Kantian path in theology which to a great extent determined their reaction to Luther's doctrine of the hidden God. Otto, from the History of Religions School, on the other hand, demonstrates a definite bias towards his own philosophy of religion in his reception and interpretation of Luther's doctrine of the hidden God. Karl Holl stands out amongst these three theologians in that, despite the fact that he was a Ritschlian and certainly demonstrated a desire to combine Kantianism and Luther's theology with regard to his understanding of justification,[30] he captures something more of Luther's understanding of the hidden God than do Ritschl and the tradition following him or that of Otto.

The Ritschlians

Theodosius Harnack's rediscovery of Luther's doctrine of the hidden God in the mid-nineteenth century set the stage for an ongoing discussion of the teaching within the modern German Protestant theological tradition

---

in *The Cambridge Companion to Martin Luther*, 235.

29. Hillerbrand, "The Legacy of Martin Luther," 235.

30. Paulson, *Lutheran Theology*, 198.

through the nineteenth and twentieth centuries and continuing to today with contemporary theologians in this tradition such as Oswald Bayer. The first theologians to take up this discussion were the Ritschlians, beginning with their namesake, Albrecht Ritschl. Ritschl and the majority of the Ritschlian tradition rejected this teaching of Luther's altogether as a remnant from medieval theology which could not be appropriated by modern theology because it contradicted the idea of God revealed in essence as a God of love in Jesus Christ. If one attempted to describe a God outside this love, it would constitute an arbitrary existence and activity of God which cannot be judged by any standard (*ex lege*).

Albrecht Ritschl

Albrecht Ritschl (1822–1889) is one of the most important figures in modern German theology and the fountainhead of the Ritschlian trajectory in liberal theology. Ritschl represents a turn in German theology away from both pietistic feelings-based thought and orthodox metaphysics-based dogmatics, towards the exploration of theology as a science with scientific methods of analysis.[31] Furthermore, Ritschl was a pioneering historical theologian and scholar of Luther's theology.[32] In his new approach to theology, Ritschl combined a variety of intellectual influences including Schleiermacher's anti-dogmatism, Hegel's anti-pietistic leanings, and the Tübingen Hegelianism of the eminent New Testament scholar, Ferdinand Christian Baur.[33] But the most important influences for the trajectory of his theology were the epistemological philosophy of the Neo-Kantians, especially of Rudolf Hermann Lotze (1817–1881), and the theology of Martin Luther. Ritschl, in fact, filtered his use of Luther's thought through his own Neo-Kantian approach to theology, which ultimately required that he reject Luther's doctrine of the hidden God, turning the idea of God's hiddenness into a mere epistemological limit, which human categories cannot know because of its noumenous nature.[34] This selective combination of Neo-Kantianism and Luther ultimately meant that Ritschl would reject Luther's doctrine of the hidden God on the basis of his own Neo-Kantian influenced understanding of Luther's theology.

Ritschl's epistemology is essentially Neo-Kantian, in that it rejects any notion of metaphysics and seeks instead to establish theology on the basis of

31. Wilson, *Introduction to Modern Theology*, 126–27.
32. Ibid., 127–28.
33. Ibid., 126–27.
34. Ibid., 124–28.

experience's scientific knowledge, which posits limits within which religion can function practically so that morality is the category for understanding the divine. For Ritschl, God is to be known through reality as experienced by the knowing subject rather than in something behind or above that reality.[35] While he appropriates this basic epistemology as his own, Ritschl adds to it that the spiritual realm—the highest form of which is morality—is known only through the natural realm.[36] For Ritschl, this theological epistemology takes the form of a certain kind of correspondence theory regarding God's nature and the nature of the human being flowing from his presupposition of the "given togetherness" of God and humanity. If something is true about God, says Ritschl, then it also can be known in some limited sense by looking at the human being. This epistemology underlies Ritschl's understanding of the doctrine of God, in which Ritschl portrays God as a God of love, revealed in Jesus Christ, who then establishes the ethical Kingdom of God on earth. God's actions are thus perceptible in humans on account of God and humanity's "given togetherness." [37]

Ritschl's concept of God is built not upon metaphysical speculations concerning God as an essence but upon the notion that God has revealed God's self fully and completely who can be experienced in Jesus Christ as a God of love.[38] For Ritschl, God's revelation of love in Christ is manifested through two foci: Christ's redemption of the human as the bringing of freedom from guilt to the individual human and Christ's founding of the ethical Kingdom of God as the corporate *telos* of the human race.[39] It is in the latter of these two facets of revelation, says Ritschl, in which God is ultimately revealed in Christ as a God of love, for the ethical Kingdom of God constitutes

---

35. Ritschl, *Theology and Metaphysics*, 14–25, 161. Wilson, *Introduction to Modern Theology*, 126–127. Neo-Kantian philosophy, in its representation by Rudolf Hermann Lotze, embodied Kant's epistemology which rejected all metaphysics in favor of science (the assessment of observable phenomena) as a basis for pure rational knowledge and viewed morality as the highest form of the knowledge of God. Theology, according to Lotze, should be based on scientific knowledge and teaches the value of the spiritual over the physical, especially the spiritual as realized in the moral. Cf. Kant, *Critique of Pure Reason*, 54–62, 126, 132, 141. Wilson, *Introduction to Modern Theology*, 27–28, 33, 123–25.

36. Wilson, *Introduction to Modern Theology*, 127.

37. Dillenberger, *God Hidden and Revealed*, 12. Paulson, "Analogy and Proclamation," 95. Ritschl, *The Christian Doctrine of Justification and Reconciliation*, 290–291. Lotz, *Ritschl and Luther*, 54.

38. Dillenberger, *God Hidden and Revealed*, 2. Paulson, "Analogy and Proclamation," 95. Mackintosh, *Types of Modern Theology*, 147–48 162–63. JR 3:275–76, 389, 453.

39. Ibid., 13. Dillenberger, *God Hidden and Revealed*, 11.

the highest goal for humanity as well as for God.[40] The love which God embodies is one which is characterized by the lover's selflessly seeking the enrichment of the beloved and by the lover's making the end of the beloved his or her own end.[41] As founder of Christianity and of the Kingdom of God, Christ heralds the beginning of this ethical kingdom through which God's love is realized among humans via the human practice of ethical acts inspired by selfless love.[42] This ethical kingdom of love is the ultimate revelation of God as a God of love and the highest aspiration of both God and the human; it is precisely in this kingdom that the common end of both God and the human bring these two subjects together. Through the realization of the Kingdom of God in the human—beginning with Christ's— practice of selfless acts of love, God is revealed as a God of love.[43]

As H. R. Mackintosh says, Ritschl describes love as the sole character of God as revealed in Christ to such an extent that any notion of God's holiness, God's justice, or God's wrath poured out in the punishment of the wicked is completely absent from his conception of God.[44] Predestination is also discarded by Ritschl, since this doctrine would evidence something within the nature of God other than love.[45] Furthermore, Ritschl sees God's character—that of love—as being perceptible in the morality practiced by humans in his understanding of the Kingdom of God.[46] This leads to Ritschl's concept of the "given togetherness" of God and humanity, which exists in such as way that God and humanity have and work towards the same *telos* (i.e. the ethical realization of the Kingdom of God as the ultimate revelation of God as love) and that what can be said concerning God's nature and activity is in part perceptible in what can be observed in humanity.[47] Such "given togetherness" means that the divine is perceptible in the human, that what is true of God is perceptible in part through humanity.

Ritschl sees Luther's teaching of God revealed as a God of love in Jesus Christ as the heart of the reformer's theology and as his lasting contribution to theology. Yet Ritschl also had to recognize the obvious—that the doctrine

---

40. Ibid. *JR* 3:205–6.

41. *JR* 3:163. Jodock, ed. *Ritschl in Retrospect*, 163.

42. Mackintosh, 158.

43. Jodock, *Ritschl in Retrospect*, 163. Dillenberger, *God Hidden and Revealed*, 11–12; *JR* 3:205–6.

44. Mackintosh, *Types of Modern Theology*, 158–59. Mackintosh further points out that it was this notion of God that Neo-Orthodoxy later attacked.

45. *JR* 3:87, 263–63. Dillenberger, *God Hidden and Revealed* 13.

46. *JR* 3:206.

47. Dillenberger, *God Hidden and Revealed*, 12. Paulson, "Analogy and Proclamation," 95. *JR* 3:205–6, 290–91.

of the hidden God occupies a prominent place in Luther's theology. Ritschl rejects this teaching on the grounds that it presents a view of God as the arbitrary judge who feels wrath against sinners. Ritschl sees these two statements concerning God in Luther's theology as contradictory and mutually exclusive. God cannot be both a God of wrath and a God of love, for the love of God is such that it would invelope wrath.[48] Ritschl is thus selective in his appropriation of Luther's doctrines concerning God. He deliberately confines Luther's teaching concerning God revealed to the God of love in Christ and so discards any teaching of Luther's about God's wrath as irrational and dangerous.

In particular, Ritschl voices his dissent against Theodosius Harnack's approving interpretation of Luther's doctrine of the hidden God in *De servo arbitrio*. As was stated above, Harnack describes a dialectic approach to God's relationship with humanity, in which God reveals God's self to humanity in the revelation of Jesus Christ as a God of love, grace, and mercy, and hides God's self outside of revelation in judgment and wrath towards human sinners.[49] Ritschl rejects Harnack's interpretation of Luther's teaching concerning God preached and God not preached because Harnack approves of the teaching without recognizing and decrying what Ritschl sees as the contradiction between Luther's notions of God revealed as a God of love in Christ and God as a God of wrath outside of revelation. Ultimately, however, Ritschl expresses his anger at Harnack because of the latter's holding to Luther's teaching concerning the unpreached God as a God of wrath.[50]

In addition to chastising Harnack, Ritschl also directly criticizes Luther in his *Geschichtliche Studien zur christlichen Lehre von Gott*. There, Ritschl effectively summarizes Luther's teaching concerning the existence and willing of the preached God, recognizing that Luther is, indeed, positing two ways of God's dealing with humanity through his teaching concerning God preached and God not preached.[51] Ritschl also understands that, for Luther, the unpreached God's willing of the sinner's destruction functions as the necessary precondition of humbling the pride of the sinful human before salvation takes place through the willing of the preached God in Christ. Ritschl further recognizes that Luther maintains that speculation concerning the will of the hidden, unpreached God is absolutely forbidden for the

---

48. *JR* 1:201. Dillenberger, *God Hidden and Revealed*, 9. Paulson, "Analogy and Proclamation," 95.

49. T. Harnack, *Luthers Theologie*, 87–89, 93–97.

50. Ritschl, *Geschichtliche Studien zur christlichen Lehre von Gott*, in *Gesammelte Aufsätze*, , 84. Schwarzwäller, *Sibboleth*, 20. Lotz, *Ritschl and Luther*, 41, 154.

51. Ritschl, *Geschichtliche Studien zur christlichen Lehre von Gott*, 77–78.

theologian.[52] Ritschl, however, asserts that Luther does not remain content to speak of the unpreached God's willing as the precondition for salvation but that the reformer actually embodies a speculative and metaphysical doctrine of God's wrath. Ritschl maintains that with the articulation of such a doctrine of God's wrath, Luther has abandoned his teaching concerning God revealed as love in Christ for a view in which the human must somehow have faith in a God who kills instead of giving life, in a God who hates and wills destruction instead of loving. Luther has abandoned the God of love in Christ for a hateful predestining God who is arbitrariness personified. Such a view of God as the one who wills wrath and the sinner's destruction, says Ritschl, abrogates the reformer's positive teaching concerning God revealed as a God of love in Jesus Christ.[53]

Ritschl slurs Luther's teaching concerning the hiddenness of the unpreached God of wrath as a remnant of the reformer's late-medieval, nominalist theological upbringing. Ritschl equates the two wills of God identified by Luther in *De servo arbitrio* with the two divine wills in nominalist theology, the *voluntas signi* (the outer, expressed will of God) and the *voluntas beneplaciti* (the internal will of God). Ritschl understood the latter of these two wills espoused by nominalism to be an arbitrary will, governed by no external standard but governed by God's inner being alone.[54] Ritschl states that Luther's embodiment of this nominalist distinction between the divine wills is not the whole-hearted embracing of nominalism *per se* but the lingering of a nominalist distinction in Luther's thought. In fact, Ritschl argues that Luther uses this nominalist distinction in *De servo arbitrio* against nominalist Pelagian soteriology, which the reformer sees embodied in Erasmus' theology.[55]

Yet Ritschl is far from sympathetic to Luther concerning the reformer's supposed use of the nominalistic distinction between the two wills of God as a weapon against nominalist Pelagianism. Instead of presenting the God of love in Christ, argues Ritschl, Luther lapses into speculation and the epistemological use of metaphysics characteristic of medieval theology. Instead of focusing solely on the positive understanding of God as love, Luther retreats to an archaic, metaphysical view of a God complete with the concepts of God's retributive justice and predestination. But then Ritschl tries

52. Ibid., 79. Dillenberger, *God Hidden and Revealed*, 4.

53. Ritschl, *Geschichtliche Studien zur christlichen Lehre von Gott*, 80, 84. Dillenberger, *God Hidden and Revealed*, 4–5.

54. Ibid., 6–7. Schwarzwäller, *Sibboleth*, 20. JR 3:271–72. Ritschl, *Geschichtliche Studien zur christlichen Lehre von Gott*, 69–70, 87. Jodock, 161.

55. Ritschl, *Geschichtliche Studien zur christlichen Lehre von Gott*, 67–68, 87. Dillenberger, *God Hidden and Revealed*, 7–8.

to spare Luther for the cause, by positing a split between the "old Luther" [i.e. too medieval] who cannot be followed, and the "new Luther" [i.e. more modern] whom he highly regards on account of the espousal of the positive teaching of God revealed as a God of love revealed in Christ. Luther was seen as beginning well, but lapsing into nominalism's speculative, arbitrary God. What Ritschl did not observe was that Luther had more radically departed from this nominalism than Ritschl could absorb, since the freedom of God in relation to the law takes place in Christ, not outside Him.[56]

For Ritschl, Luther's distinction between God hidden and God revealed simply causes more problems than it solves. Although Luther uses it successfully to combat nominalist Pelagianism, it contradicts Luther's positive doctrine of God revealed as a God of love in Christ, and as such it signifies something medieval still lingering in the reformer's thought that is otherwise beneficial to modern theology. Furthermore, Ritschl rejects Luther's teaching concerning the hiddenness of the unpreached God on the basis that it constitutes a willing of God that cannot be judged by any external standard.

This objection of Ritschl's is rooted in his accusation that Luther's teaching concerning the distinction between God preached and God not preached constitutes an espousal of the nominalist distinction between the *voluntas signi* and the *voluntas beneplaciti*. Ritschl understands the nominalist notion of the *voluntas beneplaciti* to include the idea that God's inner will is arbitrarily dictated, that it is dictated not by standard outside of God but by God's inner being alone.[57] For Ritschl, such *ex lege* arbitrariness is incompatible with the notion of God revealed as a God of love. In Ritschl's thinking, God's will must be able to be held to some standard, even a human standard, on the basis of the "given togetherness" of God and humanity that comes from the revelation of God as love through the mutual goal of God and humanity in the Kingdom of God.[58]

Moreover, Ritschl's epistemology, which is based on this "given togetherness" of God and humanity, cannot fathom the idea of the will of God not being held to a human standard, since in this epistemology things about God are known through their correspondence to similar things reflected in humans. Ritschl's epistemology allows for the understanding of God as love, because through the human realization of the ethical Kingdom of God there is something which exists in humans corresponding to this love. The

---

56. Ibid. Ritschl, *Geschichtliche Studien zur christlichen Lehre von Gott*, 67–68, 87. JR 1:201–2. Jodock, *Ritschl in Retrospect*, 161.

57. Dillenberger, *God Hidden and Revealed*, 7. JR 3:271–72.

58. JR 3:205–6. Dillenberger, *God Hidden and Revealed*, 11–12. Mackintosh, *Types of Modern Theology*, 158.

same cannot be said for Ritschl's epistemology and the notion of the self-determining will of the unpreached God.[59]

For all of his rejection of Luther's notion of the hiddenness of the unpreached God of wrath, Ritschl does see a possibility for the usefulness of this doctrine, if reinterpreted appropriately. Ritschl allows for a revised notion of God's hiddenness outside of revelation based upon the concept of a divine all-working providence, which has more in common with Reformed or scholastic theology than with the thought of Luther. Through providence, God works all things towards God's ultimate aim, the realization of the Kingdom of God. The things which God wills through God's providence for this end may be hidden from humans for a time, only to be revealed later in the complete revelation of God as love in the realization of the Kingdom of God. Such divine hiddenness would, therefore, be hidden outside of revelation only pending a fuller revelation later. Ritschl sees no value in Luther's teaching concerning the hiddenness of the unpreached God as it stands in *De servo arbitrio* unless any notion of God's wrath could be exorcised from it.[60]

Albrecht Ritschl rejects Luther's notion of the hiddenness of the unpreached God on the basis of his own Neo-Kantian approach to theology. Operating from this theological basis, Ritschl determines that Luther's doctrine of the hidden God violates the teaching of God revealed as a God of love in Jesus Christ, on the basis that it constitutes a remnant of medievalism in Luther's theology, and because it depicts a will of God which cannot correspond to anything in the human being. Ritschl's own understanding of God and interpretation of Luther's theology undergird this multi-faceted rejection of Luther's teaching concerning God preached and God not preached. Above all, Ritschl rejects Luther's view of the hiddenness of the unpreached God because its conception of God's wrath and willing the destruction of the sinner conflicts with his own understanding of God revealed purely as love in Jesus Christ.

Other Ritschlians

Although some of the individual figures within the Ritschlian tradition articulate unique nuances of Albrecht Ritschl's interpretation of Luther's teaching concerning God hidden and God revealed, the Ritschlian tradition is united in its rejection of Luther's notion of the unpreached God of

---

59. Dillenberger, *God Hidden and Revealed*, 12. Paulson, "Analogy and Proclamation," 95. *JR* 3:290–91.

60. *JR* 3:625–27. Dillenberger, *God Hidden and Revealed*, 14–15. Paulson, "Analogy and Proclamation," 95–96.

wrath who wills the destruction of the sinner. Other theologians within the Ritschlian tradition may deviate slightly from some of the aspects of Ritschl's rejection of Luther's teaching. Such theologians include Adolf von Harnack (1851–1930) who, in stark contrast to his father, adopted Ritschl's position on Luther's teaching concerning the hiddenness of the unpreached God with the exception that he sees no positive possibility whatsoever for the concept of divine hiddenness outside of revelation, Ernst Troeltsch (1865–1923) who saw all of Luther's theology and not simply this teaching as hopelessly medieval, and Ferdinand Kattenbusch (1851–1935) who adopted Ritschl's critique of Luther's notion of the unpreached God of wrath with the exception that he sees Ritschl's reworking of God's hiddenness as the true meaning given to the teaching by the reformer.[61] Yet as a whole, the Ritschlian tradition in late nineteenth-century was united in its agreement with Ritschl's rejection of Luther's notion of the unpreached God of wrath who wills the destruction of the sinner.

Karl Holl

The one major Ritschlian theologian who stands as an exception to the rule concerning the Ritschlian tradition's rejection of Luther's doctrine of God preached and God not preached is Karl Holl (1866–1926). In contrast to Ritschl and the rest of the Ristschlian tradition, Holl views Luther's notion of the hiddenness of the unpreached God of wrath in a positive light and interprets it as being in harmony with the heart of Luther's theology. This is, perhaps, due to the fact that, although a Ritschlian and although he evidences a high degree of integrating Kantian thought and Luther's theology with regard to his view of justification,[62] Holl's approach to Luther's doctrine of the hidden God is not quite so tainted by Neo-Kantianism and biased towards a Kantian interpretation of Luther's theology as other figures in the Ritschlian vein of theology. Though he certainly had his own unique interpretations of Luther's theology at points, including a certain revisionist understanding of the nature of the believer's righteousness, in general, Holl endeavored to be faithful scholar of Luther's theology.[63]

61. Adolf von Harnack, *History of Dogma*, vol. 8, 203. Dillenberger, *God Hidden and Revealed*, 15–18, 28–29. Troeltsch, *Protestantism and Progress*, 41–43, 95–99. Ozment, 261–62. Kattenbusch, *Deus Absconditus bei Luther*, 181–83, 204–6.

62. Paulson, *Lutheran Theology*, 198.

63. Cf. Lohse, *Martin Luther's Theology*, 4–5, 87–88. Mannermaa, *Christ Present in Faith*, 7. Though Mannermaa counts Holl amongst his German opponents concerning the interpretation of Luther's understanding of justification, Holl's understanding of justification is much closer to that of Mannermaa and of Osiander than that

While Holl agrees with Ritschl in that he negatively views medieval scholastic theology (nominalist and otherwise) as essentially Pelagian and perceives Luther's teaching concerning God revealed as love in Jesus Christ as something new in theology, he is unlike Ritschl in that he does not reject Luther's notion of the hiddenness of the unpreached God of wrath as something inherently medieval and nominalist.[64] Moreover, Holl does not reject Luther's idea of the hidden God on the basis of its violating the teaching concerning God revealed as a God of love in Christ and its constituting an arbitrary existence and activity of God which cannot be judged by any standard outside of God. On the contrary, Holl sees this teaching as working together with Luther's notion of God's love in Christ and as flowing from Luther's understanding of the Apostle Paul. Furthermore, Holl understands Luther's teaching of God preached and God not preached in *De servo arbitrio* as the embodiment of Luther's earlier teaching concerning the proper and alien works of God articulated in the *Lectures on Romans* of 1515–1516.

Holl essentially agrees with Ritschl that Luther is combating medieval scholastic—particularly nominalist—Pelagianism with his use of his notion of the hiddenness of the unpreached God of wrath.[65] What Holl disagrees with Ritschl about is whether or not Luther's doctrine of the hidden God actually consists of a remnant of medieval nominalism in Luther's theology.[66] While Ritschl maintains that Luther's unpreached God of wrath whose will is not held subject to anything outside of God's self is one and the same as the arbitrary *voluntas beneplaciti* of nominalism, Holl argues that Luther's articulation of the seemingly arbitrary will of the unpreached God of wrath is not an embodiment of medieval teaching but an emphasis on the freedom of God. As Holl understands Luther, God's freedom to will as God alone pleases without being subjected to any external rule is rooted in the idea that

---

of Melanchthon and the German Protestant theological tradition. According to Holl, Luther taught a doctrine of justification in which God's righteousness in Christ is not imputed but imparted to the believer and grows into the righteousness that God demands for eschatological justification through the obedience of love. Cf. Holl, *Die Rechtfertigungslehre in Luthers Vorlesung über den Römerbrief,* vol. 1: *Luther,* 124–25. Holl, *What Did Luther Understand by Religion?,* 5, 11–12, 35–37, 42–43, 80–83, 93–95. Holl, *Die Rechtfertigungslehre im Licht der Geschichte des Protestantismus,* 10–15. Eberhard Jüngel describes this approach and its difference from the overall German approach to the doctrine of justification in his own work on justification. Cf. Jüngel, *Justification,* 210.

64. Holl, *What did Luther Understand by Religion?* 15–24, 40–41, 43, 57–58. Dillenberger, *God Hidden and Revealed,* 19.

65. Holl, *What Did Luther Understand by Religion?* 15–24. Dillenberger, *God Hidden and Revealed,* 19.

66. Schwarzwäller, *Sibboleth,* 33.

if God is not free to will as such then God is not free at all nor omnipotent but a "mere spectator" of events.[67] Holl further argues that Luther in no way allows for the unpreached God to become a topic of theological speculation. In fact, Luther forbids such speculation and respects this truth about God's will as part of the mystery of the divine in a manner that is uncharacteristic of the theology of medieval scholasticism.[68] For Holl, Luther's notion of the hiddenness of the unpreached God of wrath is not a remnant of medievalism in a theology otherwise acceptable for the modern age. Instead, this notion is compatible with the whole of Luther's theology.

Holl's understanding of the meaning of Luther's notion of the hiddenness of the unpreached God of wrath and how it works with God's love flows from Holl's broader understanding of the notion of God revealed as love in Christ.[69] This teaching, says Holl, is in fact new and is discontinuous with the scholastic theology of the Middle Ages. Luther forms this teaching as a direct reaction to medieval scholasticism's Pelagian picture of God as someone who has to be satisfied by the meritorious good works of humans for salvation to be given to them, and it is formulated existentially through Luther's encounter with the theology of Apostle Paul that may be observed in Luther's *Lectures on Romans*.[70]

Holl maintains that the teaching of God's love revealed in Christ flowed from the reformer's pen as a result of the young Luther's intense personal struggle with the teachings of scholasticism and the existentially felt demands of the law for absolute conformity. Luther was only free from this struggle as he rediscovered Paul's teaching concerning a righteousness of God that exists and meets the sinner apart from the law (*ex lege*).[71] In experiencing the message of Paul, Luther understood the love of God to be God's *ex lege* righteousness which justifies humans apart from their performance of the works of the law.[72] Luther broke through his struggle only because he

---

67. Holl, *What Did Luther Understand by Religion?* 56–58. Walter, "Karl Holl (1866–1926) and the Recovery of Promise in Luther," 407.

68. Holl, *What Did Luther Understand by Religion?* 56, 58–59.

69. Dillenberger, *God Hidden and Revealed*, 23. Here, Holl agrees with Ritschl that this point forms the center of Luther's theology.

70. Holl, *What Did Luther Understand by Religion?*, 15–24, 40–41, 43.

71. Ibid., 40–43.

72. This is not to say, however, that Holl understands Luther's doctrine of justification in terms of a declared righteousness of God. Uuras Saarnivaara points out that Holl understands Luther's doctrine of justification in terms of God's actually making the sinner righteous before recognizing the sinner as such. Saarnivaara argues that while this may be true of the early Luther expressed in the *Lectures on Romans*, such cannot be said concerning Luther's later doctrine of justification. Saarnivaara states that Holl has made the error of simplifying Luther's statements about justification misunderstanding

experienced this love of God in Christ which comes apart from the law, and in response he truly broke with the theology of the Middle Ages by making Paul's message his own.[73] Holl agrees with Ritschl that God revealed as a God of love in Christ represents the center of Luther's theology, Luther's break with medieval scholastic theology, and Luther's lasting contribution to modern theology. Unlike Ritschl, however, Holl identifies this teaching of Luther's as being based on God's righteousness in Christ existing and coming to the sinner *ex lege*. Although Holl admits along with the rest of the Ritschlian tradition that Luther's concept of the unpreached God constitutes an existence and operation of God *ex lege*, this does not constitute a serious enough problem for Holl to reject Luther's notion of the hiddenness of the unpreached God.[74] This is because Holl understands Luther's idea of justification as being *ex lege* as well. As Holl understands Luther, justification must come *ex lege* in order for the sinner to be freed from the demands of the law and experience God's love. Holl states that this understanding of justification and God's love apart from the law is, indeed, the center of Luther's thought and his contribution to modern theology.[75]

Because he, unlike Ritschl, understands God's justification in Christ as well as God's hiddenness as being *ex lege*, Holl does not view Luther's notion of the hiddenness of the unpreached God of wrath and his teaching concerning God's love as two conflicting and mutually exclusive themes in the reformer's theology but, instead, views these two themes as working together in Luther's theology. Holl understands the relationship between these two themes of Luther's to be such that the work of the unpreached God takes place necessarily prior to the justifying work of God in Christ. Unlike Ritschl who categorically rejects any notion of predestination as at odds with God's love as revealed in Christ, Holl approaches the working together of the wrath of the unpreached God and the love of the preached God in Christ through Luther's understanding of predestination. According to Holl, Luther maintained that predestination can only properly be understood from the perspective of salvation.[76] Holl understands the work of the unpreached God to be synonymous with predestination, and since predestination cannot be understood apart from salvation, the work of the unpreached God cannot be construed as a venue for theological specula-

---

the doctrine of the early Luther as representative of Luther's overall understanding of salvation. Saarnivaara, *Luther Discovers the Gospel*, 13n38. Cf. Althaus, *The Theology of Martin Luther*, 241–42.

73. Holl, *What Did Luther Understand by Religion?*, 43.
74. Dillenberger, *God Hidden and Revealed*, 19–20.
75. Holl, *What Did Luther Understand by Religion?*, 40–43.
76. Schwarzwäller, *Sibboleth*, 32.

tion. Instead, the work of the unpreached God must be understood from the standpoint of salvation.⁷⁷

From this starting point, Holl argues that the hiddenness of the unpreached God's work of wrath functions in Luther's theology as a work necessarily prior to the justifying work of the love of God in Christ. For support for this interpretation of Luther's notion of the unpreached God, Holl appeals to the early Luther's exegesis of the Apostle Paul, particularly as found in the *Lectures on Romans*. Holl maintains that Luther understood that Paul not only taught about God as a God of love but also as a God of wrath, and the reformer took both of these Pauline understandings about God to heart in his own theology.⁷⁸

According to Holl, the work of the unpreached God of wrath found in *De servo arbitrio* is God's alien work (*Deus alienus*) which Luther describes in the *Lectures on Romans*. In these lectures, Luther states that God hides under the mask of his wrath in order perform his alien work of humbling sinners in order to prepare them for God's justifying work in Christ. Such divine hiddenness is not capricious, as it is in nominalism, but is carefully planned by God for the ultimate goal of the justification of sinners in Christ.⁷⁹ God's wrath is, ultimately, a wrath of mercy which humbles sinners, causing them to despair of their own efforts, so that they may receive God's love and forgiveness in salvation.⁸⁰ Hence, the proper work of God is the underlying motivation for the alien work of God; the love of the preached God drives the wrath of the unpreached God. In Holl's estimation, the two works of God, the alien work of the unpreached God's wrath and the proper work of the preached God's love in Christ are thus united in their common *telos* of God's loving work of justification.⁸¹

Karl Holl holds to an overall positive understanding of Luther's teaching of God preached and unpreached, particularly with reference to the wrath of the unpreached God, and in so doing he makes a break with the Ritschlian tradition's interpretation of this concept of Luther's. Holl maintains that Luther's focus on the hiddenness of the unpreached God of wrath is not a lingering locus of medieval scholasticism at odds with the heart of Luther's theology but that it is, indeed, part of the reformer's own original work and congruent with the rest of his theology. Holl identifies the heart

77. Dillenberger, *God Hidden and Revealed*, 20. Holl, *What Did Luther Understand by Religion?* 58–59, 61. Holl, *Die Rechtfertigungslehre in Luthers Vorlesung über den Römerbrief, Band I: Luther*, 125–128.

78. Holl, *What Did Luther Understand by Religion?*, 51–53.

79. Ibid., 54. Dillenberger, *God Hidden and Revealed*, 21.

80. Holl, *What Did Luther Understand by Religion?*, 44, 54–55.

81. Ibid., 54–55. Dillenberger, *God Hidden and Revealed*, 21–22.

of Luther's theology and Luther's lasting contribution to modern theology as God's *ex lege* justification of the sinner which reveals the love of God in Christ. Holl does not reject Luther's notion of the hiddenness of the unpreached God on the basis of its constituting an existence and operation of God *ex lege* precisely because he understands Luther's conception of justification as also occurring *ex lege*, and he identifies this as the very heart of Luther's theology. Moreover, Holl does not view the wrath of the unpreached God and the love of the preached God revealed in Christ as two conflicting themes in Luther's theology. Instead, he understands the wrath of the unpreached God as the necessary precondition for the love of God revealed in Christ through the justification of the sinner which serves as the ultimate motivation even for God's wrath.

In spite of his recognition of the work of the hiddenness of the unpreached God as oriented towards the ultimate end of human salvation and his positive assessment of this teaching of Luther's, Karl Holl's interpretation of Luther's doctrine of the hidden God is one that is incomplete. Holl does not comment on the congruence between the work of the hidden God and the work of God in the law. Although he rightly identifies the hidden work of God as the alien work of God evident through God's work in predestination, he does not relate how Luther describes this alien work as coming from the hidden God to the human through the existential experience of *Anfechtung*. Most significantly, Holl does not distinguish between the hiddenness of the unpreached God outside of revelation and the hiddenness of God in revelation under the sign of God's opposite.

Yet, in contrast to Ritschl, Holl faithfully interprets the intent of the reformer with reference to the hiddenness of the unpreached God of wrath and understands that this concept ultimately is not at odds with Luther's teaching concerning the mercy and love of God revealed in Jesus Christ. In comparison to Ritschl, Holl's interpretation of Luther incorporates more of the reformer's own thoughts and is less biased by the Neo-Kantian epistemology and approach to theology embodied by Ritschl and the majority of his disciples. On the contrary, Holl is able to recognize and understand Luther's doctrine of hiddenness because he rightly identifies God's salvation of the sinner in Christ as the center of Luther's theology. In this way, Holl is unique not only when compared to his fellow Ritschlians but also when compared with other theologians of the late nineteenth century, including the foremost representative of the history of religions school, Rudolf Otto.

The History of Religions School: Rudolf Otto

Rudolf Otto (1869-1937) is regarded as one of the founders of the late nineteenth-century German history of religions school. As a seminal figure in this school of thought, Otto receives and interprets Luther's doctrine of the hidden God through his own views concerning the history of world religions. From this basis and bias, Otto offers a unique interpretation of Luther's notion of the hiddenness of the unpreached God of wrath.[82] Like Holl, Otto does not reject this notion of Luther's out of hand. Otto, however, goes farther than Holl and interprets Luther as portraying the hiddenness of God in God's self and the wrath of the unpreached God as functioning positively in Luther's theology. Building on the foundation of his own philosophy of religion, Otto interprets this notion of Luther's as being identical with his own idea of the human's being confronted with the otherness of God. Far from disparaging the reformer's concept of the hiddenness of the unpreached God of wrath, Otto maintains that God's hiddenness in God's self—God's hiddenness in wrath—actually constitutes the venue for the experience of God's love and grace.

Otto's interpretation and appropriation of Luther's notion of the hiddenness of the unpreached God of wrath is rooted within Otto's philosophy of religion, which is the study of what he terms "the holy" (*das Heilige*) or "the numinous".[83] The numinous is the transcendent and holy God. The experience of the numinous consists of the universal feeling felt by individual humans when encountered by the divine which is categorically other than humans. This feeling comes to the human in stages which Otto identifies as the *mysterium* in which the human initially encounters the numinous for which the human has no descriptive category, the *tremendum* in which the human trembles before the majesty of the divine, and the *fascinans* in which the human is drawn inexorably and intoxicatingly to bliss, to God's grace and love.[84]

This three-stage feeling is deeper and more fearsome than Schleiermacher's mere feeling of the vast immensity of ultimate dependence upon the divine, since in its *tremendum* stage it entails a sense of real dread of the wrath of God.[85] Otto laments that Ritschl—like Schleiermacher before

---

82. Wilson, *Introduction to Modern Theology*, 146.

83. Rudolf Otto, *The Idea of the Holy: An Inquiry into the Non-Rational Factor in the Idea of the Divine and Its Relation to the Rational*, trans. John W. Harvey (Oxford: Oxford University Press, 1958), 5-7. Schwarzwäller, *Sibboleth*, 35.

84. Wilson, *Introduction to Modern Theology*, 147. Otto, *The Idea of the Holy*, 12-40.

85. Wilson, *Introduction to Modern Theology*, 147. Otto, *The Idea of the Holy*, 9-10, 13-15, 18.

him—has neglected the doctrine of divine wrath and the human's interaction with it through the *tremendum*, concentrating only on the love of God. Otto accuses Ritschl and his followers of emasculating religion by removing from it any notion of God's wrath and turning the gospel of Christ into a mere idyll.[86] Morover, Otto is critical of the Ritschlian understanding of the Kingdom of God as a realization of God's love through a new moral order. In contrast to Ritschl's depiction of Christianity, Otto posits that true religion involves not just the experience of divine love but also "shuddering in horror" before the wrath of the transcendent God and that the Kingdom of God is not an ethical ideal but the reality of the numinous breaking into the present age of humanity.[87] Yet, Otto does not relegate the coming Kingdom of God and the experience of the numinous to Christianity alone. Christianity indeed contains the most advanced experience of the divine, but true experience of the numinous can be felt in all religions, since the feeling is universal to all human experience.[88]

In articulating his understanding of the human's experience of the numinous, Otto acknowledges his debt to Luther's *De servo arbitrio* concerning his understanding of the wrath of God. In particular Otto identifies Luther's notion of the hiddenness of the unpreached God as the source of his own understanding of the stage of *tremendum* in the human's experience of the numinous.[89] In his appropriation of Luther's notion of the unpreached God of wrath, Otto voices his disagreement with the Ritschlian tradition's understanding of this concept and advances his own interpretation of this idea of Luther's on three major points.

Firstly, Otto disagrees with Ritschl concerning the origin of Luther's idea of the unpreached God of wrath. Although he acknowledges some similarity between this concept of Luther's and similar teachings in late scholasticism (particularly in the theology of Duns Scotus), Otto estimates that Luther's notion of the unpreached God of wrath was precipitated by the young reformer's own personal experience with the *tremendum* and that it is not simply a remnant of medieval thought in Luther's theology.[90] Secondly, Otto thinks Ritschl is wrong in citing God's revelation of God's

---

86. Ibid, 18, 83.

87. Ibid, 15. Otto, *The Kingdom of God and the Son of Man*, 334–36, 340, 370–74. Wilson, *Introduction to Modern Theology*, 148.

88. Ibid. Dillenberger, *God Hidden and Revealed*, 80. Otto, *The Idea of the Holy*, 38–39.

89. Ibid, 23–24, 99–104. Dillenberger, *God Hidden and Revealed*, 73. Wilson, *Introduction to Modern Theology*, 147.

90. Otto, *The Idea of the Holy*, 96–98. Dillenberger, *God Hidden and Revealed*, 74–75.

self as the venue for the human's knowledge of God and God's love. Instead, Otto views the hiddenness of the unpreached God outside of revelation as the actual venue for the human's experience of God as a God of grace and love, since faith apprehends not the revealed but that which is unseen.[91] Thirdly, Otto actually views the hiddenness of the unpreached God of wrath positively as helpful for the doing of theology, and in so doing he disagrees with Ritschl and the majority of the Ritschlian tradition.[92]

Otto's positive and unique interpretation consists of the opinion that God's hiddenness outside revelation is the means for knowing God as a God of grace and love. According to Otto, Luther teaches that the experience of the unpreached God's wrath is actually the way in which the individual comes to experience God's love. For Luther, says Otto, the unpreached God may be hidden and even unseen and may lie in the realm of the irrational as the arbitrary God of wrath who damns humans through predestination, but this does not mean that the unpreached God is unknown by humans.[93] In fact, the hidden and unpreached God of wrath is the God of love.[94] As one is drawn into the existential knowledge of the unpreached God through the *tremendum* and places one's faith in this divine hiddenness, the unpreached God becomes known as a God of love as the individual passes through the *tremendum* into the *fascinans*.[95]

According to Otto the early Luther's Christ mysticism elucidates how this movement is made possible through a certain cooperation between the divine and the human. The human side to this cooperation takes effect through faith, the inherent and independent human faculty of mystical knowledge. The divine side takes effect through the Holy Spirit who indwells the heart of the individual. While it is not necessary that one holds to Luther's specifically Christian mysticism, since this phenomenon is common to all human religion, the movement into the unpreached God's wrath thereby finding God's love can only happen through this mystical cooperation of the human and the divine and not through any rational knowledge.[96] According to Otto, Luther understands that true knowledge of the unpreached God, which leads to the love of God, takes place in the *tremendum* through the

---

91. Ibid., 73.
92. Otto, *The Idea of the Holy*, 97ff.
93. Ibid., 135. Dillinberger, *God Hidden and Revealed*, 79, 97.
94. Ibid, 97–98. Otto, *The Idea of the Holy*, 100–101.
95. Dillenberger, *God Hidden and Revealed*, 79. Otto, *The Idea of the Holy*, 9–10, 13–15, 18, 102–4, 134–35.
96. In particular, Otto finds that both Buddhism and Hinduism have a better developed mysticism of horror that corresponds to the individual's experience of the *tremendum* than Christianity has.

mystical knowledge of the soul and not through any comprehensions of "the whore reason." For it is only through the irrational and the mysterious that one can come to know God's love through the unpreached God's hiddenness and God's wrath.[97]

Like Holl, Otto does not reject Luther's notion of the hiddenness of the unpreached God of wrath out of hand and, in fact, views it positively. Unlike Holl, however, he does not accurately interpret this notion of Luther's. Instead, Otto imports his own philosophy of religion into Luther's theology in such a way that he interprets the reformer as articulating Otto's own idea of the human's experience of God's love through experiencing God's transcendent wrath. Such an idea is completely foreign to Luther's theology. Although Luther may see the work of the unpreached God preparing the way for the work of the preached God, he does not see these two works as identical. For Luther, the unpreached God is only a God of wrath. Furthermore, Luther, unlike Otto, argues that God's grace, mercy, and love can be experienced only as the preached God is revealed in Jesus Christ and never outside of Christ.

Among the late nineteenth-century theologians who address this concept in Luther's theology, Otto provides a new and unique interpretation of the concept, which flows from his own philosophy of religion. In contrast to the majority of the Ritschlian tradition, Otto views this teaching of Luther's as flowing from his own experience with the numinous rather than as coming from medieval scholasticism. Otto further differs from his predecessors in that, whereas Ritschl and the Ritschlian tradition (including Holl) understood Luther as teaching that God's love could be known only in God's self-revelation in Jesus Christ, Otto holds that Luther teaches that God's love ultimately is to be known through experiencing the hiddenness outside of revelation in God's self, through experiencing the unpreached God of wrath.

The three German theological thinkers of the nineteenth century who address Luther's doctrine of the hidden God present three very different receptions of this doctrine. Of these three, Karl Holl stands out as the theologian who most accurately interprets and best represents Luther's understanding of the hiddenness of the unpreached God of wrath and who best understands the relationship of this concept to Luther's teaching concerning the God of love revealed in Jesus Christ. Holl differs from Ritschl and Otto in that his interaction with Luther's thought on the hidden God is less determined by theological presuppositions. While Ritschl's reception of Luther's

---

97. Otto, *The Idea of the Holy*, 103–4. Dillenberger, *God Hidden and Revealed*, 79–80.

doctrine of the hidden God is formed by his own Neo-Kantian theology and Otto's by his own philosophy of religion, Holl lets Luther speak for himself. Unlike Ritschl and Otto, Holl understands that in *De servo arbitrio* Luther is arguing that the unpreached God of wrath wills the damnation of sinners so that they may be saved by the God of grace, mercy, and love who is revealed only in the preached God who is Jesus Christ.

The Twentieth Century

The conversation in the modern German Protestant theological tradition regarding Luther's doctrine of the hidden God continued into and even broadened within the twentieth and twenty-first centuries. Like the nineteenth-century figures in the German Protestant theological tradition, the twentieth-century thinkers from this tradition who address Luther's doctrine of the hidden God have their own theological ideas and approach Luther in part from their own theological standpoints. Such figures include Walther von Loewenich, Paul Althaus, Werner Elert, Karl Barth, Emil Brunner, Paul Tillich, Gerhard Ebeling, Wolfhart Pannenberg, Jürgen Moltmann, and Eberhard Jüngel and represent the Erlangen, Neo-Orthodox, Marburg, and Trinitarian schools of theological thought.

Erlangen Theology

The first school within the modern German Protestant theological tradition in the twentieth century that addresses Luther's doctrine of the hidden God is comprised of the Erlangen theologians. This group of theologians, which included Walther von Loewenich, Werner Elert, and Paul Althaus, operated around the Friedrich-Alexander Universität Erlangen-Nürnberg, especially during the 1920s, 30s, and 40s, following in the footsteps of the Luther Renaissance inaugurated by Karl Holl.[98] While they may have followed Holl in terms of interest in Luther's theology, they did not follow him in his understanding of Luther's doctrine of the hidden God. Rather, as will be demonstrated below, each of these scholars either misinterpreted or rejected this teaching of Luther's on the basis of their own theological assumptions. It should be noted that these three scholars are treated below not in chronological order but with regard to the various views of Luther's doctrine of the hidden of God that they propound.

---

98. Grass, "Paul Althaus," in *Theologische Realenzyklopädie*, vol. 2, ed. Gerhard Krause and Gerhard Müller, 330.

Walther von Loewenich

The first representative of the Erlangian trajectory in modern German Protestant theology to be dealt with here is Walther von Loewenich (1903–1992), who was the student of both Werner Elert and Paul Althuas, both of whose views on divine hiddenness will be addressed below. Von Loewenich's particular contribution to the pursuit of Luther studies lies in his bringing to light the significance of Luther's *Heidelberg Disputation* of 1518 with its emphasis on the *theologia crucis* (the theology of the cross). In his ground-breaking work *Luthers Theologia Crucis*, von Loewenich describes the theology of the cross as found in the *Heidelberg Disputation* and uses this teaching of Luther's as an interpretive key for the reformer's entire theology. Von Loewenich characterizes all of Luther's theology as *theologia crucis*, seeks to understand other loci in Luther's theology in relation to this overarching teaching, and comments on the historical and theological background of the teaching in late-medieval mysticism. In doing this, von Loewenich reads and interprets Luther's doctrine of the hidden God through his own assumption that the theology of the cross is the controlling feature of Luther's entire theology.[99]

Von Loewenich treats both the hiddenness of God in God's self and the hiddenness of God in revelation as one doctrine of divine hiddenness. Although von Loewenich views Luther's teaching concerning God's hiddenness in God's self favorably, he collapses Luther's two concepts of God's hiddenness into one. On the surface, von Loewenich understands Luther's teaching concerning the distinction between God unpreached and God preached. Von Loewenich approaches this teaching historically, setting it in the context of Luther's argument against Erasmus' libertarian view of the human "free will" in regard to salvation. Luther appeals to this argument, von Loewenich highlights, in response to Erasmus' use of Ezekiel 18:23: "Have I any pleasure in the death of the wicked, says the Lord God, and not rather that he should turn from his way and live?"[100] Luther responds to what he views as Erasmus' misuse of this passage, says von Loewenich, by appealing to the distinction between God revealed in the Word and God hidden in God's self. Von Loewenich points out that this view of God is not merely a fanciful construction of Luther's, but that it is anchored in 2 Thessalonians 2:4 where St. Paul implies that God exists above revelation and not merely within it.[101]

---

99. Rupp, "Forward," in *Luther's Theology of the Cross*, by von Loewenich, 7–8.
100. Von Loewenich, *Luther's Theology of the Cross*, 31.
101. Ibid., 32.

Von Loewenich also recognizes that Luther's articulation of his teaching concerning the distinction between the unpreached and preached God is related to the reformer's distinction between the law and the gospel in *The Bondage of the Will*. As von Loewenich identifies, Luther accuses Erasmus of interpreting Ezekiel 18:23 as law when it is a verse of pure gospel. Luther characterizes this verse as God's enabling promise in the gospel which accomplishes its effect without the aid of "free will." Erasmus has turned this promise which is given by God without conditions into a command which must be fulfilled by the "free will" of the human. Von Loewenich identifies that, for Luther, free will and the gospel do not mix.[102]

Furthermore, von Loewenich understands that Luther's notion of the hiddenness of God in God's self entails a certain sense of unapproachable mystery. Von Loewenich understands that Luther is here arguing for a view of God in which God cannot be held to any human standard or law but in which God is radically free to do as God wills.[103] This God who dwells hidden in divine freedom cannot be grasped by human reason or speculations and Luther, in fact, warns that such speculations will lead only to despair.[104]

Yet, von Loewenich's interpretation of the overall meaning of Luther's doctrine of the hidden God has some drawbacks. Firstly, von Loewenich slightly misconstrues the relationship linking the distinction between God unpreached and God preached with the distinction between the law and the gospel. Though he clearly does not describe the hiddenness of God as being defined exhaustively in terms of the law, Luther does describe the distinction between God unpreached and God preached as parallel to the distinction between God's condemning work in the law and God's saving work in the gospel. This can be seen from the fact that Luther's articulation of the former distinction in *The Bondage of the Will* is contained within his description of the latter distinction.[105] Von Loewenich, however, states that Luther's invocation of the distinction between the law and the gospel is not enough to silence Erasmus' objection through the use of Ezekiel 18:23 and that, because of this, Luther must go into a deeper explanation of why Erasmus' use of this verse does not legitimize his view of "free will."[106] Von Loewenich's interpretation of the hiddenness of the unpreached God as being deeper than the law does not take into account how Luther describes the work of the hidden God and the work of God in the law as consisting of the

---

102. Ibid., 31.
103. Ibid., 43–45.
104. Ibid., 43.
105. *BOW*, 151, 161–65, 169–71, 171–89; WA 18:673, 679–81, 684–86, 686–99.
106. Von Loewenich, *Luther's Theology of the Cross*, 32.

same thing. Nor does it fully take into account how Luther structures his argument against Erasmus by enfolding his articulation of the distinction between God hidden and God revealed within his discourse concerning the distinction between the law and the gospel.

Von Loewenich's main error regarding his understanding of Luther's notion of the hiddenness of God in God's self, however, regards the overall trajectory of Luther's teaching concerning the distinction between God unpreached and God preached. In this distinction, Luther argues that God is both revealed in God's Word and hidden outside of God's revelation in the Word.[107] As von Loewenich identifies, Luther finds this dual existence of God implied by St. Paul in 2 Thessalonians 2:4.[108] Yet, von Loewenich then proceeds to claim that the hiddenness of the unpreached God is not really a hiddenness outside of revelation, but that is actually equivalent to God's hiddenness inside revelation (i.e. the theology of the cross).[109]

Contrary to Luther's clear articulation of the distinction between God as God exists in revelation and God as God is hidden in God's self, von Loewenich collapses God's hiddenness in God's self into God's hiddenness in revelation. He even goes to the extent of warning against turning Luther's distinction between the unpreached and preached God into "a side by side relationship of two [divine] hypostases."[110] In answer to his own question, "What is the relationship of the hidden God to the revealed God," von Loewenich posits that the hidden God is the revealed God and the revealed God is the hidden God.[111] Von Loewenich explains this identification of the hidden and revealed God through the event of God's clothing God's self.[112]

The revealed God, says von Loewenich, is the God who comes to humans clothed in the revelation of God's Word. This is the God clothed in the mercy of the gospel who comes to save and heal sinners, not to condemn them.[113] Yet the hidden God is also the clothed God, according to von Loewenich. The hidden God clothes God's self, in order that sinful humans will not be destroyed by God. The hidden God is the concealed God, who conceals God's self on account of not willing the destruction of sinful humans.[114] The majestic hidden God is not comprehensible to human reason,

---

107. BOW 169–70; WA 18:684–85.
108. BOW, 170; WA 18:685. Von Loewenich, *Luther's Theology of the Cross*, 32.
109. Ibid., 33ff.
110. Ibid., 44.
111. Ibid., 33, 37–38.
112. Ibid., 33ff.
113. Ibid., 33.
114. Ibid., 36.

and therefore the hidden God clothes God's self with revelation in order to be grasped by humans through faith. Through faith alone, the hidden God can be grasped by humans hidden under the veil of revelation.[115]

This view of God's hiddenness is accurate, when one speaks of God's hiddenness within revelation through suffering and the cross, as Luther delineates in his teaching concerning the theology of the cross in the *Heidelberg Disputation*. Luther's teaching concerning God's hiddenness outside of revelation, however, is something altogether different. When Luther speaks of this kind of divine hiddenness in *The Bondage of the Will*, he is not simply restating what he articulates in the *Heidelberg Disputation* concerning God's hiddenness in revelation. Instead, in this treatise of 1525, Luther clearly states that the hiddenness of the unpreached God in God's self is a hiddenness outside of revelation that cannot be grasped by humans at all.[116] Von Loewenich is thus quite mistaken to identify God hidden in God's self with God revealed in the Word by simply appealing to the event of God's clothing God's self with revelation and thus hiding in revelation.

Walther von Loewenich may have contributed greatly to the discipline of Luther scholarship through his focus on the theology of the cross in Luther's thought. He may also comprehend the historical context of Luther's notion of the hiddenness of the unpreached God in God's self and even that this notion entails a great unapproachable majesty and mystery of God. Von Loewenich does not, however, understand the full weight of this notion of Luther's. Von Loewenich fails to note the parallel relationship within *The Bondage of the Will* of the distinction between God's hiddenness in God's self and God's self-disclosure in revelation with the distinction between the work of God in the law and the work of God in the gospel. Moreover, in seeking to delineate Luther's theology of the cross, von Loewenich misconstrues the ultimate trajectory of Luther's notion of the hiddenness of the unpreached God in God's self by mistakenly identifying it with God's hiddenness in revelation. Von Loewenich collapses the hiddenness of God outside of revelation into God's hiddenness in revelation and his positive contribution to the discussion of Luther's doctrine of the hidden God is thus limited.

Werner Elert

Werner Elert's (1885–1954) work, *The Structure of Lutheranism*, constitutes a significant contribution to confessional Lutheran theology in the

---

115. Ibid., 36–37.
116. *BOW* 170–71; WA 18:685–86.

twentieth century. Elert's Luther scholarship and his Lutheran theology are integral to the study of Lutheran theology today. The Erlangen approach to Lutheran theology, which he shared with Paul Althaus, offered a clear alternative both to Ritschlian theology and the dialectical theology of Neo-Orthodoxy, avoiding the rank neo-Kantian intellectualism of Ritschl and his followers while remaining engaged with culture.[117] Due to his significance in the modern German theological tradition and in contemporary Lutheran theology in general, a thorough study of the pedigree of this doctrine would be incomplete without discussion of Elert's reading of Luther on the doctrine of the hidden.

Elert's treatment of Luther's doctrine of the hidden God is similar to that given by von Loewenich in that Elert addresses the two kinds of divine hiddenness in Luther's theology as one homogenous divine hiddenness, identified with Luther's theology of the cross. Furthermore, in agreement with von Loewenich, Elert at least mentions the connection in Luther's thought between the hiddenness of God and the work of God in the law. Unlike von Loewenich, however, Elert also sees the connection in Luther's thought between the hiddenness of God and God's wrath. Nevertheless, Elert does not capture the fullness of Luther's doctrine of the hidden God, collapses Luther's two notions of God's hiddenness into one, and imposes upon Luther's understanding of hiddenness his own view that the human being, and not God, is ultimately responsible for God's wrath.[118]

In his interpretation of Luther's teaching on the hidden God, Elert treats divine hiddenness in the reformer's thought as if it is all of one kind. It is clear from reading Elert that he understands this hiddenness to be the hiddenness of God in revelation. In his work, *The Structure of Lutheranism*, Elert addresses God's hiddenness according to Luther as God's being concealed even in the midst of God's act of self-revelation.[119] Here, Elert plainly has in mind Luther's understanding of God's hiddenness in revelation, which Luther describes in his theology of the cross as God's being hidden under the sign of God's opposite. It is in Jesus Christ as the *Deus incarnatus et crucifixi* that God is simultaneously hidden and revealed and is revealed in a hidden manner, in way that the human does not expect.[120]

Yet, at the same time, Elert does address the hiddenness of God according to Luther as a hiddenness of God in wrath. Such hiddenness Elert identifies as the hiddenness of the revealed God under the law. God is

117. Stayer, *Martin Luther, German Savior*, 80–82.
118. Elert, *The Structure of Lutheranism, Volume One*, 72–73, 211–13.
119. Ibid., 72.
120. Ibid., 72–73.

hidden in wrath and such wrath is revealed to humans in the law.[121] Yet, Elert does not understand this hiddenness ultimately to be any different from the hiddenness of the crucified God in Christ under the sign of God's opposite. In the law, God is hidden as God against humanity, as a God of wrath, as the judge who condemns the sinner on account of his or her sin. Such hiddenness seems to be a contradiction to God revealed in Christ as a God of grace, mercy, and love.[122] This, however, only appears to be a contradiction. Faith, says Elert, is "the settling of differences."[123] According to Elert, God's hiddenness in wrath and in the law is the same hiddenness of God in revelation, under the sign of God's opposite. The difference between these two seemingly different things is only a matter of perspective and not a matter of God's existence or will. For the one who does not have faith in Christ, the hiddenness of God appears as a hiddenness of wrath experienced through the law as "*Urerlebnis*" ("primal experience"). For the believer, however, the hiddenness of God may be seen for what it really is: the alien work of God hidden in revelation.[124]

Furthermore, Elert states that God does not really desire to will wrath in hiddenness against humans but that he is forced to by human sinfulness. Yet, God makes use of this wrath to work for the establishment of the fulfillment of God's real desire which is to save humans.[125] To this end, God wills wrath and damnation against the sinner so that, in Luther's words "The sinner is justified when he is damned; he is alive when he is killed; he ascends to heaven when he sinks down into hell."[126] Thus, for Elert as he understands Luther, God's hiddenness is only a cloak for revelation, and God's alien work of wrath is only a covering for God's proper work of salvation.[127]

Elert's interpretation of Luther's understanding of the hiddenness of God is certainly better than any other interpretation of this doctrine in the modern German theological tradition since Theodosius Harnack, with the possible exception of Karl Holl. Unlike many others in this tradition, Elert understands the connection in Luther's thought between the hiddenness of God and God's work in the law. Moreover, unlike even his student and

---

121. Ibid., 35.
122. Ibid., 35–37, 71.
123. Ibid., 71.
124. Ibid., 71–73, 211–13. Schwarzwäller, *Sibboleth*, 63.
125. Elert, *The Structure of Lutheranism, Volume One*, 35–37, 71.
126. WA 5:164. Quoted in ibid., 59.
127. Elert, *The Structure of Lutheranism, Volume One*, 211–13. Schwarzwäller, *Sibboleth*, 63.

colleague Walter von Loewenich, Elert understands that Luther views the hiddenness of God as a hiddenness of wrath against the sinner.

Nevertheless, Elert's depiction of Luther's teaching concerning the hiddenness of the unpreached God outside of revelation is not completely representative of the reformer's view. While he understands God's hiddenness in terms of God's wrath against sinners and even understands the connection between this hiddenness and God's work in the law and the alien work of God, Elert does not relate this hiddenness to God's work of damnation particularly in reprobation. Though he mentions "predestination" once in connection with the alien work of the hidden God[128] and even points out elsewhere that Luther understands predestination as necessary for the shattering of the sinner's presumption of "free will," Elert does not clarify that Luther sees the alien work of the hidden God as consisting of God's willing of reprobation in order that the "free will" of the sinner be killed in order that the sinner might be saved. Though there is great potential in Elert's thought for this connection to be made, in the end he does not make it. Neither does he grasp the full weight of Luther's understanding of the alien work of God, which takes place through the trials and existential struggle between the hidden God and the human in *Anfechtung*.

Furthermore, there is something in Elert's interpretation of Luther's doctrine that is not present in the reformer's view: the notion that human and not God is the ultimate cause of God's wrath. Doubtlessly, this innovation of Elert's upon Luther's theology colors how he interprets the doctrine of the hidden God. While this notion of Elert's is in completely in harmony with the views of the Concordists as related in Article 9 of the *Formula*, particularly as related in the "Solid Declaration," it is not consistent with Luther's own view as related in *The Bondage of the Will* as well as in his early and later biblical lectures. In these writings, Luther describes God as actually and actively willing wrath and reprobation of the sinner. Though the ultimate goal is indeed that of the sinner's salvation and this is, according to Luther, God's alien work, God is the one doing it.[129]

---

128. Ibid., 71.

129. Cf. Stayer, *Martin Luther, German Savior*, 81–86. Though it would be imprudent to make a firm statement regarding Elert's motivation for not following Luther with regard to the reformer's doctrine of double predestination one might venture that Elert's own concern to distinguish the Lutheran from the Calvinistic doctrine of predestination—as he indeed was motivated by an overriding desire to show the incompatibility of Lutheranism and Calvinism concerning this and other doctrines—prompts him to opt in favor of single predestination over any form of double predestination, as did the Concordists. Certainly, it may be said that if Elert was motivated by such a concern, this further demonstrates his closer proximity to the Concordists than to Luther on this issue, as the Concordists were also concerned with distinguishing the Lutheran

Elert's collapsing of the two kinds of divine hiddenness is also at odds with Luther's teaching. In his understanding of Luther's notion of divine hiddenness, Elert sees Luther as portraying the hidden God as a God of wrath and revealed as a God of love, grace, and mercy simultaneously, in the same form of hiddenness. Elert understands the difference between wrath and hiddenness under God's opposite to be one of mere human perspective. Luther presents these two kinds of hiddenness as two things that God actually does and that God does in different places. While Luther describes the hiddenness of God under the sign of God's opposite as occurring within the revelation of the crucified Christ, he articulates that the hiddenness of God in wrath is a hiddenness of God outside of the revelation of God in Christ.

Though he makes good observations about Luther's doctrine of the hidden God regarding its connection to Luther's understanding of God's work in the law and to Luther's view of the alien work of God, Elert still misses the fullness of Luther's doctrine of the hidden God. In addition to his failure to relate the hiddenness of God in wrath to reprobation and his addition of the human's responsibility for wrath, Elert ultimately collapses these two kinds of hiddenness and in doing so collapses the alien work of God into the proper work and all divine hiddenness into revelation. Elert shares this fallacy of collapsing the two forms of divine hiddenness in Luther's theology with his forerunner at Erlangen, Walter von Loewenich. Yet, this fallacy is not shared by all members of the Erlangen school, as may be seen in the scholarship of Paul Althaus, who does not share Elert's collapsing of the two kinds of divine hiddenness into one, but neither does he share Elert's astuteness regarding Luther's actual view of the doctrine of the hidden God.

Paul Althaus

Paul Althaus (1888–1966) stands as one of the most prolific Luther scholars of the twentieth century as well as a Lutheran theologian in his own right. Althaus' research and work on Luther's theology were extremely influential in the twentieth century. His comprehensive scholarship, particularly *The Theology of Martin Luther*, is only now in the twenty-first century beginning to be surpassed by the work of contemporary German Luther scholars, including Bernhard Lohse and Oswald Bayer.[130] Althaus stands last in the overview of Erlangen theologians here due to the importance attached to his comprehensive scholarship on Luther's theology and to his difference

---

from the Reformed reformational theology.

130. Hillerbrand, "The Legacy of Martin Luther," 236. Nestingen, "Approaching Luther," 250.

with his fellow Erlangians concerning the interpretation of Luther's doctrine of the hidden God.

In the twentieth chapter of *The Theology of Martin Luther*, Althaus openly rejects Luther's teaching concerning the distinction between God hidden in God's self and God revealed in Christ through the Word. Althaus argues that Luther's notion of the hiddenness of the unpreached God in God's self contradicts Luther's teaching concerning God revealed as a God of love in Jesus Christ.[131] In particular, Althaus objects that, in this notion of divine hiddenness, Luther teaches a knowledge of God outside of divine revelation and a divine work in which God damns humans rather than saving them. This rejection of Luther's doctrine of the hidden God, whether or not Althaus admits it, is based upon his own view of the distinction between the law and the gospel, a view which is foreign to Luther's theology.

Althaus' rejection of Luther's teaching concerning the distinction between God hidden in God's self and God revealed in Christ through the Word is mainly a rejection of the two wills or two works of God proposed by Luther. In *The Bondage of the Will*, Luther argues that God wills and effects the human sinner's life and salvation as God is revealed but that God wills and effects the sinner's death and damnation as God exists hidden in God's self.[132] Althaus objects to this double-willing of God propounded by Luther, saying that it abrogates Luther's broader teaching that God can only be known in God's revelation in Jesus Christ through the Word. Here in *The Bondage of the Will*, says Althaus, Luther is teaching that God exists above and beyond the Word and can even be known outside of God's revelation in Christ through the Word.[133] Althaus disagrees with Luther's doctrine of the hiddenness of God outside of revelation, arguing to the contrary that the true hiddenness of God is God's hiddenness in revelation, under the sign of God's opposite.[134] Moreover, Althaus rightly understands Luther's teaching on the God who is hidden outside of revelation to be an articulation of a doctrine of double predestination on the part of the reformer and rejects it entirely in favor of the doctrine of single predestination found in the *Formula of Concord*.[135]

Before critiquing Althaus' assertion that Luther's notion of the hiddenness of the unpreached God in God's self abrogates the rest of the reformer's

---

131. Althaus, *The Theology of Martin Luther*, 278–79.

132. BOW 169–71; WA 18:684–86.

133. Althaus, *The Theology of Martin Luther*, 277. Althaus, *Die Christliche Wahrheit*, 618–19.

134. Althaus, *Grundriss der Dogmatik*, I, 28–29.

135. Althaus, *Die Christliche Wahrheit*, 618–19. Cf. FC,Ep, 517–20, FC,SD, 640–56; BSLK, 790–91.

theology, it should be pointed out that Althaus understands Luther's concept of the hiddenness of the unpreached God to a certain extent. Firstly, Althaus is essentially correct in his description of the two wills of God as delineated by Luther. Secondly, Althaus recognizes that the hiddenness of God in God's self is a different kind of hiddenness than the hiddenness of God in revelation that Luther describes in the *Heidelberg Disputation*.[136]

Althaus states that whereas the hiddenness of God in revelation is a hiddenness of God and God's salvation under the paradox of suffering and death, the hiddenness of God in God's self is a hiddenness of God outside of revelation. While God hidden in revelation is indeed hidden, God also reveals God's self to humans for their salvation in such revelation. The hiddenness of God outside revelation, says Althaus, is a hiddenness of God in which God dwells in the radical freedom to do as God wills, including willing and effecting the death and damnation of sinners.[137]

Despite his correct understandings of Luther's basic idea of God's hiddenness in God's self and of the difference between this kind of divine hiddenness and the hiddenness of God in revelation, Althaus still misunderstands Luther's concept of the hiddenness of the unpreached God in two ways. Firstly, Althaus states that with this concept Luther is advocating a knowledge of God outside of revelation, that God is actually to be found and known as God is hidden in God's self.[138] Secondly, Althaus objects that this concept constitutes an action of God in which God damns rather than saves humans, neglecting the fact that Luther also teaches that God damns sinners through the law.[139] Both of these objections are overruled in light of what Luther actually says in *The Bondage of the Will* regarding the knowledge of God hidden in God's self and the distinction between the work of God in the law and the work of God in the gospel.

In response to Althaus' first objection, Luther does not advocate that God is to be found and known outside revelation, as God is in God's self. In fact, the opposite is true. Luther clearly articulates in *The Bondage of the Will* that God cannot be found and known as God exists in God's self. While believers are to know and be concerned with God as God is revealed in Jesus Christ through the Word, they are to leave alone God as God is hidden in God's self.[140] Luther here teaches precisely the opposite of what Althaus

---

136. Althaus, *Grundriss der Dogmatik*, I, 28–29.

137. Althaus, *Martin Luther's Theology*, 276–77. Althaus, *Die Christliche Wahrheit*, 618–19.

138. Althaus, *Martin Luther's Theology*, 277.

139. Ibid., 278–79.

140. *BOW*, 170; WA 18:684–85.

accuses him of teaching. Humans are not to seek, know, or speculate about God hidden in God's self. Instead it is enough for them to know that such a God exists and that this God wills their death and damnation, to fear this God, and to content themselves with the revealed God in Christ.[141] In objecting to Luther's concept of the hiddenness of God in God's self on the grounds that it posits a knowledge of God outside of revelation, Althaus fails to account for Luther's direct denial of this within the very same passage of *The Bondage of the Will* in which the reformer articulates this concept.

Althaus' second objection to Luther's notion of the hiddenness of God in God's self can also be answered through appealing to the context of Luther's articulation of this notion in *The Bondage of the Will*. Althaus objects that Luther's notion of the hiddenness of God in God's self constitutes a divine action in which God damns rather than saves sinners.[142] While it is true that Luther does posit such an action of God in articulating this concept of divine hiddenness outside of revelation, this does not entail a contradiction of the reformer's overall theology as Althaus purports. Luther posits the same damning action of God in his view of the work of God in the law.

As part of his argument against Erasmus' Pelagian notion that the law is given by God in order for the human being to merit salvation through the use of his or her "free will," Luther argues that the true work of God in the law is not to provide the human with commands to perform for meritorious righteousness but actually to condemn the humans. Command does not imply ability, says Luther. Just because the law places commands on people, this does not mean that people can actually carry out such commands.[143] Instead of providing the human with something to do in the law, God therein condemns and kills the sinner so that he or she may be made alive by God's work in the gospel.[144]

Althaus fails to take this damning work of God in the law propounded by Luther into account when objecting that in his concept of God's hiddenness in God's self the reformer abrogates the rest of his theology by positing an action of God aimed at the damnation rather than the salvation of humans. Althaus does this even though, in *The Bondage of the Will*, Luther articulates his distinction between God hidden in God's self and God revealed within his larger description of the distinction between God's work in the law and God's work in the gospel. Perhaps Althaus neglects this comparison in Luther's thought in *The Bondage of the Will* between the damning will of

---

141. BOW, 170–171; WA 18:684–86.
142. Althaus, *The Theology of Martin Luther*, 278–79.
143. BOW, 171–174; WA 18:686–88.
144. BOW, 161–62, 165–167, 289; WA 18:679, 681–83, 676.

God hidden in God's self and the damning work of God in the law because of his own revisionist view of the law. In his book, *The Divine Command: A New Perspective of Law and Gospel*, Althaus argues that it is not the proper role of the law to accuse and condemn human sinners. Originally, the law functioned as God's creative command with which humans could cooperate in the fulfillment of God's will. After sin, however, the law took on an accidental accusatory nature. The work of the gospel is to restore the command of God to its proper and primary place.[145]

Whether or not Althaus' view of law and gospel colors his misreading of Luther's distinction between God hidden in God's self and God revealed, two things may be said about the matter with some certainty. The first is that Althaus does not share Luther's view of law and gospel. Luther is clear in *The Bondage of the Will* that the law kills and damns and that the gospel saves and gives life. Luther does not share Althaus' high regard for the law as God's primal and positive word to humanity, nor does he view the gospel as a mere interruptive word of God, which allows the law to take its rightful place of primacy again once it has dealt with human sin. The second is that Althaus either completely misses or intentionally neglects the parallelism of the hidden, unpreached God's damning will and the damning work of God in the law. Luther addresses both of these in *The Bondage of the Will*, and his discussion of the former is included within his broader discussion of the latter.

Though he stands as one of the great scholars of Luther's theology, and though he understands the basic concept of Luther's notion of God hidden in God's self, Paul Althaus rejects this concept on false premises. Althaus purports to reject Luther's concept of the hiddenness of God in God's self on the grounds that it violates the reformer's larger theology, namely the teaching that God is revealed as God of love and salvation in Jesus Christ. In this rejection, Althaus objects that in this concept of divine hiddenness Luther teaches a knowledge of God outside of revelation and an unparalleled activity in which God damns rather than saves humans. These objections can be shown to be unfounded when it is seen that, in *The Bondage of the Will*, Luther teaches that God cannot be known as God is hidden outside of revelation and that God works the sinner's damnation through the law in addition to willing it as God is hidden in God's self.

Unlike the other members of the Erlangen school of theology mentioned here, Walter von Loewenich and Werner Elert, Paul Althaus accurately interprets Luther's doctrine of the hidden God to a certain degree but rejects it. Though he excels von Loewenich and Elert in that he actually is

---

145. Althaus, *The Divine Command*, 8, 10, 12–14, 20–21.

able to distinguish the two kinds of divine hiddenness in Luther's theology, unlike them he does not appreciate Luther's view of the hiddenness of God outside of revelation nor does he comprehend its connection with the law or the alien work of God. Althaus' rejection of Luther's understanding of the hiddenness of the unpreached God is closer to the view promulgated by Albrecht Ritschl against the scholarship of Theodosius Harnack than it is to his Erlangen compatriots von Loewenich and Elert. Like Ritschl before him and like his Neo-Orthodox contemporary Karl Barth, Althaus rejects Luther's teaching concerning God's hiddenness outside of revelation because—although he correctly understands this hiddenness to be distinct from God's hiddenness in revelation and to consists of God's being hidden in wrath against the sinner—he does not fully understand that Luther's doctrine of the hidden God includes within it the teaching that the hidden God of wrath cannot and will not be known by humans but that God is known only as revealed in Christ.

Neo-Orthodoxy

Karl Barth, Emil Brunner, and Paul Tillich are categorized here as Neo-Orthodox due to their understanding that God must be spoken of in theology according to how God discloses God's self in revelation. Though these three theologians share this fundamental presupposition, they each have their own distinctive theologies. More importantly for present purposes, they each treat Luther's concept of the hidden God differently. In doing so, each one of these thinkers interacts with Luther on the basis of their own theological ideas.

Karl Barth completely rejects Luther's concept of the hiddenness of God in God's self, concluding that it is antithetical to the idea that God can be known by humans only as God reveals God's self in Jesus Christ. Emil Brunner, on the other hand, partially accepts Luther's concept of God's hiddenness in God's self and utilizes it in his own theology, though he does not accept this concept entirely and rejects Luther's understandings of the bondage of the human will and God's decrees in double predestination. Paul Tillich's treatment of Luther's concept of the hiddenness of God in God's self differs from the treatments offered by Barth and Brunner in that Tillich deals with this concept only by implication. Tillich does not speak specifically about this concept but, instead, mediates it in a specific way in his theology. Whereas Barth and Brunner either openly reject or accept this concept of Luther's, Tillich takes this concept and transforms it into a speculative notion of God's existence as the ground of all being, based on his own existential approach to theology, and utilizes this notion as the foundation for his own doctrine of God.

Karl Barth

The first Neo-Orthodox theologian to be addressed here is the movement's most eminent thinker, the Swiss Reformed theologian Karl Barth (1886–1968), who stands alongside Martin Luther and John Calvin as one of the greatest and most influential Protestant theologians of all time. There are many theological similarities between Barth and Luther including that both men were evangelical reformers of theology, both emphasized the need for a theocentric approach to theology, and they both emphasized the centrality to theology of God's revelation to humanity in Jesus Christ. Barth's theology also embodies Luther's own emphasis on the hiddenness of God in revelation (i.e. the theology of the cross). The theologies of Barth and Luther are not, however, congruent concerning the hiddenness of God outside of revelation.

Whatever other similarities there may be between his theology and the theology of Martin Luther, Karl Barth does not teach a hiddenness of God in God's self as Luther does in *The Bondage of the Will*. In fact, Barth categorically denies that such a divine hiddenness exists. He argues to the contrary in the *Church Dogmatics*:

But in the revelation of God there is no hidden God, no *Deus absconditus*, at the back of his revelation, with whose existence and activity we have also occasionally to reckon beyond his Word and his Spirit, and who also we have to fear and honor behind his revelation. It may often look like this in certain contexts in Luther. But in the witness of Holy Scripture it does not appear like this. [146]

Here, in the first part of the second volume of the *Church Dogmatics*, Barth directly rejects Luther's notion of the God who is hidden outside of God's revelation. There is, says Barth, no such *Deus absconditus*; Luther may think so, but he is wrong. Barth here judges Luther's view as wrong on the basis that it is at odds with the revealed Word of God in Holy Scripture.[147] This same rejection of Luther's view can be found in other places in Barth's theological works as well. Later on in the same volume of the *Church Dogmatics*, Barth states that he would not take issue with Luther's view of the hiddenness of God in God's self if it were merely a confession of the freedom of God, but Barth understands Luther's view as contradicting the truth of

---

146. Barth, *CD* II.1, 210.
147. Ibid., 210–11.

God revealed in Jesus Christ and thus rejects it.[148] Both Barth and Luther seek to express the idea that God is radically free, but for Barth, God freely chooses to reveal God's self totally in Christ and to exist exclusively as a God of love, and that in this way God is, "the one who loves in freedom."[149] For Luther, God's freedom means that God can and does exist above and beyond God's revelation as a God of love in Christ.[150] Both theologians want to uphold God's freedom, but Luther takes this further than does Barth. Concerning God's freedom expressed through being a God of love revealed in Christ, Barth even voices his agreement with Thomas Aquinas over and against Luther that God enters revelation freely of God's own accord, but that once in revelation, we cannot understand God as existing in any way outside of God's freely entered revelation.[151]

Barth's denial of the existence of God hidden outside of God's revelation is based on the central premise of his theology, which is that God freely, uniquely, and totally reveals God's self in Jesus Christ. God does not, according to Barth in *CD* II.2, exist in hiddenness outside of revelation because God exists fully within God's self-determined revelation of God's self to humanity in Christ. This central tenet of Barth's theology finds expression in his descriptions of revelation as the venue of God, of the hiddenness of God in revelation, and of predestination as God's freely willed decision to exist in revelation and not in God's self.[152]

The venue of God, according to Barth, is God's revelation alone. God's existence is to be found completely in revelation, and thus any attempt to find God outside of revelation is doomed to failure and constitutes a grave theological error. Hence, any divine hiddenness must be a hiddenness of God in revelation.[153] John Dillenberger suggests that Barth may theoretically allow for the idea that God exists as Trinity in himself rather than purely in revelation; such a hiddenness can only be said to exist in Barth's theology concerning God's existence before revelation. Yet, Barth does not allow for much speculation about the state of God prior to revelation. Instead, Barth anchors such divine hiddenness in the relationship between the doctrines of the Trinity and revelation. Indeed, this relationship is the starting point for Barth's theology. The doctrine of the Trinity means that, although God in

---

148. Ibid., 541.

149. Ibid., 301. Cf. ibid., 301–21.

150. *BOW*, 170; WA 18:685–86.

151. *CD* II.1, 541.

152. Ibid., 151, 211. Barth, *Church Dogmatics, Volume I: The Doctrine of the Word of God, Part I*, 384, 389. Barth, *Epistle to the Romans*, 331. Busch, *The Great Passion*, 43.

153. *CD* II.1, 210–11. Dillenberger, *God Hidden and Revealed*, 119. Ebeling, *Lutherstudien*, vol. 3, 477.

The Reception of Luther's Doctrine of the Hidden God

God's freedom does not need to relate to humanity, God does freely relate to humanity in revelation as Father, Son, and Holy Spirit. Barth does not think of the existence Trinity distinctly from the revelation of the Trinity. Instead, Barth states that the revelation of God as Trinity actually constitutes God's essence of Trinity. There is not another triune essence of God which resides in God's self outside revelation; God's existence as Trinity resides solely in God's relationship as Trinity. It would be best, says Barth, if the theologian would simply leave alone the question about God's existence of Trinity within God's self and simply deal with the triune God as God has revealed God's self as Trinity.[154]

Barth is suspicious about any existence of God outside of Christ, because he rejects the idea that there can be any knowledge of God outside of the special revelation of God in Jesus Christ. Since he holds that God is known fully and completely in Jesus Christ, Barth rejects any notion of a general or "natural" revelation as a way of knowing and proclaiming God. In the *Church Dogmatics*, Barth argues that any attempt to know God from the natural order can never apprehend an accurate knowledge of God and is doomed instead to establish idolatry. Thus, the theologian must begin the study of God with God's revelation in God's Word rather than with natural revelation.[155] Barth's rejection of the existence of supposed natural revelation is even stronger in response to Emil Brunner's experimentation with the idea of natural revelation. In this response, entitled *Nein!*, Barth identifies the idea of natural revelation as "the great temptation and source of error" upon which the theologian must turn his or her back in deference to God's true revelation in Jesus Christ.[156]

This is not to say that by arguing that God exists and relates to humanity in Jesus Christ alone that Barth completely denies that God exists outside the Church's proclamation of Christ. As Paul Chung highlights in his work, *Karl Barth: God's Word in Action*, later in life, Barth allowed for the idea that God exists outside of the Church's preaching of Christ, even in the natural order.[157] In his *Lecture Fragments* collected by Eberhard Jüngel, and contained in the English volume, *The Christian Life*, Barth acknowledges that

---

154. *CD* I.1, 371–72. Dillenberger, *God Hidden and Revealed*, 138–39. Cf. Karl Barth, *CD* III.2, 65–66. Chung, *Karl Barth*, 351.

155. *CD* II.1, 86–87. Eberhard Busch points out that Barth understood his theological mission in the composition of the *Barmen Declaration* as removing natural revelation as the basis of theology and replacing it with the true revelation of God in God's Word. Busch, *The Great Passion*, 67. *CD* II.1, 175.

156. Barth, *No: A Reply to Emil Brunner*, in *Natural Theology*, 74–75.

157. Chung, *Karl Barth*, 330–31.

God exists in the world outside of and before the Church's witness to God's self-revelation in Christ.

God's name, then, is already holy in the world that he created long before Christianity begins to pray for its hallowing or to be zealous for the honor of God. Is not his name holy in every blade of grass and every snowflake? Apart from us and even in spite of us, it is holy in every breath we draw, in every thought we think, in every effort of man, undertaken and executed well or badly, with praiseworthy of suspicious or plainly wicked intentions, to subdue the earth to himself both in practice and in theory (Gen 1:28).[158]

Here and in *CD* IV.3.1, where he articulates his teaching on "lights," Barth expresses what might be termed by some as a "natural theology": the idea that there may exist truths and lights about the creation of God within God's creation outside of the Truth and the Light reflected in Christian proclamation.[159] Clearly, in this later material, Barth does allow for the possibility that God exists outside of the Church's proclamation of the Word of God revealed in Christ. Yet, this does not mean that Barth allows for the possibility that God exists hidden outside of God's self revelation in Christ. For, as Chung points out, even in his later statements about God's existence in creation outside of the Church's proclamation, Barth never leaves "the sure ground of Christology."[160] The very reason that Barth can and does say that God exists in creation is because that in Jesus Christ, God has reconciled the world to God's self in such a way that "there is no secular sphere abandoned by him."[161]

If, as Chung and the late German Lutheran Barthian scholar Friedrich-Wilhelm Marquardt suggest, these later statements by Barth constitute

---

158. Barth, *The Christian Life*, 121.

159. Chung, *Karl Barth*, 330–33; Barth, *CD* IV:3.1, 117–18, 136–139; Barth, *The Christian Life*, 121–23.

160. Chung, *Karl Barth*, 330.

161. Ibid., 331. *CD* IV.3.1, 119. There might be a real possibility at this juncture of a rapprochement between the theologies of Barth and Luther concerning the ubiquity of Christ (i.e. the *genus majesticum*) in relation to the *communication idiomatum*. Chung's scholarship at this point—though perhaps at odds with the prevailing interpretation in the United States of Barth's theology (e.g., McCormack, *Orthodox and Modern*, 154–56)—is worth exploring. Based on his reading of Barth's Christology expressed in his doctrine of reconciliation, Chung suggests that Barth moves away from Calvin and the Reformed tradition's understanding towards Luther's understanding of the communication of Christ's attributes from the divine to the human natures of Jesus Christ, while at the same time broadening the Lutheran understanding of the Word made flesh to include Christ's assumption of all humanity upon God's self in Jesus Christ. Chung, *Karl Barth*, 345–46, 351–52, 376. Cf. Chung, 344–76. Barth, *CD* IV.2, 60–116.

a kind of natural theology, it is a Christological natural theology.[162] It is a natural theology—or perhaps said better, a theology of creation—that presupposes the unique revelation of God in Jesus Christ that has reconciled the world to God's self. It is, as Chung says, an embracing of the created world that comes through God's reconciliation of the world in Christ.[163] In this Christological context, it is apparent that Barth is not here indicating a shift in his thinking regarding his negative view of Luther's doctrine of the unpreached God hidden outside of Christ but is, on the contrary, speaking still of God as God is revealed in Jesus Christ, even if he is addressing such revelation in more cosmic dimensions that he does in his earlier works.

Aside from the question of whether or not that there can be any true knowledge of God outside of God's revelation in Jesus Christ, Barth certainly does not espouse the idea that God exists outside of God's revelation as a God of wrath precisely because he teaches that God's wrath is part of God's revelation. According to Barth, God's wrath can only ever really be known in God's self-revelation in Jesus Christ.[164] For Barth, the true understanding of God's wrath is interconnected with how the Triune God reveals God's self in the cross of Jesus Christ. In Christ's death, says Barth, God performs God's alien work of damnation. In the death of Christ, God the Father damns God the Son, pouring the full measure of divine wrath out upon the Son who obediently acts as the representative of all humanity. Humanity deserved such wrath on account of its sinfulness, but in the cross the obedient Son experienced the Father's wrath instead. In the event of Calvary, God's wrath is thus revealed in such a way that it can only be known through the love and grace of God revealed in the crucified Christ. For Barth, any knowledge of God, even of God's wrath, must come through God's self-revelation in Jesus Christ. [165]

Even the existence of God in creation posited by Barth in his *Lecture Fragments* is a gracious existence of God revealed in Christ and not a hidden existence of God in wrath outside of Christ. Directly against Luther's idea that such an existence of God in creation is an existence of wrath, Barth argues in his *Lecture Fragments* that that God who exists in creation is the self-revealing God in Christ. Since God hallows God's name in creation,

---

162. Chung, *Karl Barth*, 17. Marquardt, *Theologie und Sozialismus*, 257–64.

163. Chung, *Karl Barth*, 330. Here there is a corollary with Barth's doctrine of creation as expressed in *CD* III.1, where he states: "We believe in Jesus Christ when [we confess that] we believe in God the Father Almighty, Maker of heaven and earth. These words of the first article do not make sense if for all the particularity of their meaning they do not anticipate the confession of the second and also the third articles."

164. *Römerbrief*, 77. Barth, *CD* IV.1,306.

165. Ibid. Barth, *CD* III.3, 307, 355. *CD* 4.2, 400–401. *CD* IV.3, 1, 462–64.

says Barth, we know that God who is in creation is the self-revealing God in Christ, because God is here named, and therefore not hidden or unknown. This leaves out the possibility that God is hidden in creation outside of God's revelation in Christ as a God of wrath.[166]

This does not mean, however, that there is no such thing as divine hiddenness in Barth's theology; it simply means that there is no such thing as divine hiddenness outside of God's self-revelation in Christ. Barth does discuss a certain hiddenness of God in revelation. In agreement with Luther, Barth holds that God comes to humanity hidden in revelation. God, in a sense, veils God's self in God's revelation to humanity in Jesus Christ.[167]

It is precisely in such hiddenness in revelation that Barth locates the wrath of God and the knowledge of God as a God of wrath. Barth consciously locates God's wrath in what Luther refers to as the theology of the cross, where God and God's salvation is revealed under the sign of its opposite. Like Luther, Barth rejects the theology of glory that would place the human in control of his or her own salvation and argues instead that the God who reveals God's self in the hiddenness of the cross of Christ accomplishes this salvation. Such salvation, God's proper work, is revealed hidden under the sign of its opposite, God's alien work of wrath.[168] As Barth states in a series of lectures given in America in the 1960's, God's Yes is "hidden deep beneath this inseparable No" of God's wrath.[169] Yet such divine hiddenness is still a hiddenness within revelation, and Barth vehemently denies that there is any hiddenness of God outside of revelation.[170]

Even Barth's understanding of how God exists in creation outside of the Church's proclamation is framed within the more overarching context of Barth's teaching that God reveals God's self in Jesus Christ alone, as Barth understands any such existence of God only Christologically. Barth may indeed, as Chung suggests, understand God being hidden in creation as Luther does, but Barth's understanding of God's hiddenness in creation is still categorically the existence of God in Christ whose wrath is enveloped by grace.[171] This runs contrary to Luther's understanding of God hidden in

---

166. Barth, *The Christian Life*, 157.

167. *CD* I.1, 320–321. Dillenberger, *God Hidden and Revealed*, 123–25.

168. *CD* I.1, 179. *CD* III.3, 306–7, 353–55. *CD* IV.3, 306–7. Dillenberger, *God Hidden and Revealed*, 120.

169. Barth, *Evangelical Theology*, 154. Dillenberger, *God Hidden and Revealed*, 125.

170. *CD* II.1, 210.

171. Chung, *Karl Barth*, 330–31, 344.

nature as the God who is hidden outside of God's revelation in Jesus Christ as a God of wrath.¹⁷²

Like his view of God's existence, Barth's understanding of God's will in election is irrevocably Christological. Barth's view of the will of God in election corresponds to and flows from his understanding of God's existing only in God's self-revelation in Christ. For Barth, both God's election and God's nature as Trinity are bound up together with God's existence in revelation. As I have stated previously, Barth understands God's existence as Trinity only in terms of God's revelation of God's self as Trinity to humanity.¹⁷³ Such revelation is manifested particularly in the cross of Jesus Christ. In the cross, says Barth, the Father's plan for humanity as the Father's creation was realized. Furthermore, the cross becomes the one message of God that the Holy Spirit communicates and reveals to God's people and, as the content of such revelation, it enables reconciliation between the Triune God and humanity.¹⁷⁴ Similarly, God's will in election is bound up together with God's self-revelation and with God's nature as Trinity. For election is the eternal decision of the Triune God to be in relationship with humanity through God's self-revelation in Jesus Christ.¹⁷⁵

The issue of double predestination in the theology of Karl Barth is a complex one, but ultimately he locates double predestination within the realm of revelation. There are actually two positions within Barth's theology concerning the place of reprobation in the doctrine of predestination. While in the *Church Dogmatics*, Barth teaches this negative side of predestination befalls Christ rather than the individual human, in his earlier *Göttingen Dogmatics* Barth takes the view that reprobation befalls the individual.¹⁷⁶ In the *Church Dogmatics*, Barth addresses reprobation as God's pouring out God's wrath upon Jesus Christ instead of pouring it out upon humanity. Thus reprobation is the action within the Trinity of God's condemning God's self instead of humanity, so that God might be in relationship with humanity.¹⁷⁷ In the *Göttingen Dogmatics*, however, Barth addresses reprobation as the condemnation under which all humans stand, unless they are encountered by God's revelation and thus met with the saving election of God revealed in Jesus Christ.¹⁷⁸

172. *LW* 19:56, 66–67, 75; *WA* 19:208, 226.
173. *CD* I.1, 371–72.
174. *CD* I.1, 389, 409.
175. Barth, *CD* II.2, 5–8.
176. Cf. McDonald, "Barth's 'Other' Election," 134–47.
177. *CD* II.2, 165–67.
178. Barth, *GD*, 457–58.

Barth's understanding of reprobation in the *Göttingen Dogmatics* is perhaps the only possible venue in his theology for a hiddenness of God outside of God's revelation in Christ. Here Barth states that humans are under God's decree of rejection in reprobation unless they receive God's revelation. Yet, even this understanding of reprobation falls under the larger category of God revealed in Jesus Christ. Barth argues that this negative side of predestination cannot be said to exist on its own or in and of itself, but that exists only as the necessary converse of God's gracious will revealed in election through Jesus Christ.[179] Furthermore, Barth here explicitly rejects the idea that reprobation could form a separate hidden and secret will of God which would stand outside God's revealed will in election. Thus God's will in the divine decision of election remains identified solely with God's revelation in Jesus Christ.[180]

This rejection by Barth of two wills of God in predestination and his insistence that wrath exists only within the larger context of love directly parallels his view of the law in relationship to the gospel. Barth rejects the Lutheran "dualism" of law and gospel and argues that the law exists only within the larger context of the gospel, as part of the gospel. Just as God's hiddenness exists only in order to serve God's revelation—and, indeed, is even part of God's revelation—God's "no" in the law exists only to serve God's "yes" in the gospel and God's wrath exists only to serve God's love and salvation. Just like God's condemning reprobation is part of God's broader gracious will in election and God's hiddenness takes place inside God's revelation and is part of the broader event of revelation, God's condemning "no" in the law is subsumed by God's saving "yes" in the gospel and is actually part of this broader "yes."[181] In this way, Barth demonstrates consistency in his disagreement with Luther by rejecting any notion of any will of God outside of God's will in the revelation of God in Jesus Christ, whether it be in reprobation, in the law, or in hiddenness outside of revelation.

In Karl Barth's theology all divine hiddenness takes place within the context of revelation, and within his theology there can exist no hiddenness of God outside of revelation. Barth categorically denies that there is any hiddenness of God outside of God's revelation and teaches instead that God can only be known in Jesus Christ. Barth's teachings on revelation as the venue for the existence of the Triune God, on divine hiddenness and on predestination flow from and complement this foundational tenet of Barth's theology. The picture of God that emerges from Barth's theology is one in

---

179. *GD*, 460–61.
180. *GD*, 462.
181. *CD* II.1, 236. *CD* IV.1, 347.

which the Triune God freely determines to reveal God's self as Trinity in Jesus Christ and the cross.

In contrast to Luther, Barth rejects that there is any venue for God's existence other than God's revelation. Additionally, contrary to Luther's view, Barth locates both God's decree in election and God's wrath within the realm of God's revelation in Jesus Christ and not in any kind of divine hiddenness outside of revelation. Any hiddenness of God in this picture is a hiddenness of God within revelation. Even God's alien work of wrath is located within God's revelation in this picture of God. The will of this God is depicted in the Triune God's freely determined decision to relate to humanity through God's revelation in Christ. Even God's decree of reprobation functions within the picture of God revealed in Christ and does not constitute a will of God outside of God's revelation.

Nevertheless, the rejection of Luther's view of the hiddenness of God outside of revelation is not merely Barth's arbitrary reaction to the reformer's teaching, nor is it an attempt to reign in divine freedom as one might find in the theology of the Ritschlians. Instead, it is based upon the idea that God is fully revealed in Jesus Christ, a foundational tenet of Barth's theology found throughout his works from the early *Römerbrief* to the late *Evangelical Theology*.[182] It is significant to acknowledge this basis for Barth's rejection of Luther's idea, since the idea of God revealed in God's self-revelation in Jesus Christ is a foundational theme in Luther's theology as well. Barth disagrees with Luther concerning whether or not God is actually hidden outside God's revelation in Christ, but Barth does not disagree with Luther concerning how one comes to know God. For Luther, as well as for Barth, the only way to truly know God is in God's revelation in Jesus Christ through God's Word.

Yet, Barth does categorically reject Luther's doctrine of God hidden outside of God's revelation in Christ as a God of wrath. As Barth stands as the most significant theologian of the twentieth century, his rejection of Luther's doctrine of the hidden God must be taken seriously. This rejection reappears, though in a slightly nuanced form, in the thought of Eberhard Jüngel. Furthermore, Oswald Bayer's interpretation and use of Luther's doctrine of the hidden God stands in stark contrast to Barth's rejection of the doctrine.

---

182. *Römerbrief*, 331. *Evangelical Theology*, 11. In the *Evangelical Theology*, Barth implicitly rejects Luther's concept of God hidden in God's self, when he intimates that such a view of God would be counter to the God who is revealed in the gospel of Jesus Christ, saying that such a God would be a God of a *dysangelion* rather than the God of the *evangelion*.

Emil Brunner

Emil Brunner (1889-1966) is like Barth in that he maintains that theology must be formulated on the basis of God's self-revelation to humanity in Jesus Christ.[183] Unlike Barth, however, Brunner does not view Luther's concept of the hiddenness of God in God's self as being mutually exclusive to God's self-revelation in Jesus Christ. While Barth locates God's wrath solely in the realm of God's self-revelation in Jesus Christ, Brunner agrees with Luther that God's wrath is located outside of Jesus Christ in God as God is hidden in God's self.

Brunner understands Luther's distinction between God hidden in God's self and God revealed as the reformer sets it forth in *The Bondage of the Will* and makes use of it when discussing the wrath of God in his own theology. In particular, Brunner understands that Luther's notion of God hidden in God's self entails the wrath of God against sinful humanity and identifies this divine hiddenness with God's work in the law which drives the human to the revealed God in Jesus Christ. Additionally, Brunner understands and appreciates the difference between God's hiddenness outside of God's self and God's hiddenness within revelation. The point where Brunner fails to understand and identify with Luther's teaching concerning the distinction between God hidden in God's self and God revealed is in the area of predestination and "free will."

In the first volume of his *Dogmatics*, entitled *The Christine Doctrine of God*, Brunner interprets and appropriates Luther's understanding of God hidden in God's self as the God of wrath. In agreement with Luther, Brunner describes wrath as the will of God hidden in God's self under which every human stands outside of Christ.[184] Brunner acknowledges here that he is drawing directly on Luther's distinction between God hidden in God's self and God revealed and consciously adopts the reformer's understanding of the hiddenness of God in God's self in order to explain how God relates to humans as a God of wrath outside of Jesus Christ.[185]

The God who is hidden in God's self, says Brunner, is not the God who is "for us." Instead, this God is the God of wrath who dwells outside of revelation in unapproachable majesty.[186] The human cannot truly know this hidden God, since God can only truly be known for who God really is—a God of love—in Jesus Christ alone. God can only truly be known as God

---

183. Brunner, *The Christian Doctrine of God: Dogmatics Vol. I*, 15.
184. *Dogmatics I*, 170. Dillenberger, *God Hidden and Revealed*, 103–4.
185. *Dogmatics I*, 168.
186. Ibid., 170.

is revealed and not as God is hidden outside of revelation, yet the hidden God drives the human to such revelation. The work of the hidden God (i.e. God's alien work) is to drive the sinner to desperation, so that he or she may turn to the revealed God in faith.[187] While Brunner states that this alien work of God hidden outside of revelation takes place through the human's natural knowledge of God, he also maintains that the human's experience of the hidden God should not be called "knowledge" as such. At the most it is a strange and even distorted knowledge of God. Such a natural knowledge can only perceive God as a God of wrath, for God can only truly been known for who God really is in God's self-revelation in Jesus Christ.[188]

Like Luther, Brunner identifies the hidden God's will of wrath with the law. According to Brunner, the law provides to all humans the natural knowledge of God as a God of wrath. Following the logic of St. Paul in his Epistle to the Romans, Brunner argues that all humanity stands under this law and consequently under the wrath of God hidden in God's self.[189] If one does not turn to God in Christ through faith, he or she will remain under the dreadful wrath of God and perish.[190]

In addition to his understanding and appropriating Luther's idea of God hidden in God's self as a God of wrath, Brunner also recognizes the distinction between this concept of God's hiddenness and Luther's notion of God hidden in revelation. Brunner describes God's hiddenness in revelation as God's being veiled (*Deus velatus*) and explains that the veiled God is equivalent to the revealed God and not to God hidden in God's self. The veiled God is the God who comes clothed in the revelation of God's Word. The veiled God is God hidden in the suffering of the cross and not God hidden in God's own unapproachable majesty.[191] Like Luther, Brunner operates with these two distinctive and different notions of divine hiddenness without confusing or collapsing them.

Although Brunner understands, appreciates, and appropriates Luther's distinction between God hidden in God's self and God revealed both in regard to the hidden God as a God of wrath and the difference between God's hiddenness in God's self and God's hiddenness in revelation, he does not understand or appreciate the connection between this distinction and

---

187. *Dogmatics* I, 168–69. Dillenberger, *God Hidden and Revealed*, 105.

188. *Dogmatics* I, 171, 174. One might legitimately ask if the position Brunner takes here concerning the natural human's having no true knowledge of God is a revision of the position he took concerning natural revelation in his work *Nature and Grace*. Cf. Brunner, *Nature and Grace*, in *Natural Theology*.

189. Ibid. Dillenberger, *God Hidden and Revealed*, 104.

190. *Dogmatics* I, 169–70.

191. Ibid., 172. Dillenberger, *God Hidden and Revealed*, 107ff.

Luther's teachings concerning the bound will and double predestination. This rejection of Luther's doctrine of the bondage of the will is evident in how Brunner presents the human who stands under God's wrath as being able to turn to the revealed God in faith or reject God and thereby remain under the hidden God's wrath.[192] Furthermore, Brunner expressly rejects the idea of double predestination as unbiblical and theologically unsound and because of this fails to observe the connection between it and the distinction between God hidden in God's self and God revealed in Luther's theology.[193]

Brunner implies that the will is not bound but free in relation to God, when he portrays the natural human as being able to accept or reject God's self-revelation in Jesus Christ.[194] Moreover, in all of his treatment of the hiddenness of God in God's self, Brunner neglects the fact that the very reason that Luther employs the distinction between God hidden in God's self and God revealed is to silence Erasmus' objection to Luther's doctrine of the bound will of the human.[195] The entire point to Luther's distinction between these two in *The Bondage of the Will* is that the alien work of God hidden in God's self that encounters the humans through the law encounters them precisely in order to kill and damn their well-cherished belief in their own "free wills."[196]

In addition to missing the connection between Luther's doctrine of the hidden God to his understanding of the bound will, Brunner also fails to identify Luther's understanding of the work of the hidden God as the alien work of God which comes through the existential trials and struggle of *Anfechtung*. In this way Brunner misses the connection in Luther's theology between God's negative decree in reprobation and the will of the hidden God effected through the law. In his *Lectures on Romans*, Luther argues that the work of God in reprobation is the alien work of God, whereby God kills and damns sinners in order to make them alive and save them in God's proper work through God's decree in election.[197] Although he correctly identifies the alien and proper works of God hidden in God's self and God revealed in Jesus Christ through the law and the gospel, Brunner overlooks the connection between God's alien and proper works and God's works in double predestination. Instead, Brunner states that Luther had earlier espoused a

---

192. *Dogmatics* I, 169–70.
193. Ibid., 331.
194. Ibid., 169–70
195. BOW, 169; WA 18:684.
196. BOW, 161–62, 165, 169–71; WA 18:679, 681, 684–86.
197. LW 25:371–72, 375, 377; WA: 56:381–82, 385–87.

view of double predestination but changed his mind in 1525. While there is little evidence of this change of mind in Luther, and Brunner argues entirely from the not (i.e. that Luther does not espouse double predestination after 1525 because he does not address it thereafter); Brunner does not even adequately explain the content of Luther's view of double predestination. Instead, Brunner lumps Luther's view of double predestination together with that of Calvin and in so doing fights a straw man of a generic "reformation" doctrine of double predestination. Brunner treats Luther's idea of reprobation as God's will which befalls those who have been destined by God from the beginning to be damned and not to be saved.[198] For Luther, however, reprobation is God's decrees which kills and damns sinners that they may be made alive and saved by God's decree of promise in election.[199] To what end does Brunner fail to adequately address this doctrine of double predestination in Luther's theology? The most likely explanation seems that Brunner does so because he views any concept of double predestination to be unbiblical and theologically unsound. Thus, his treatment of Luther's doctrine of the hidden God ultimately is inadequate because he fails to take into account the fullness of Luther's view of predestination and its connection to the hiddenness of God.

Emil Brunner understands and appreciates Luther's distinction between God preached and God unpreached better than perhaps any theologian before him since Theodosius Harnack.[200] Brunner understands and appropriates Luther's concept of God hidden in God's self as the God of wrath and the difference between this type of divine hiddenness and God's hiddenness in revelation. Nevertheless, Brunner fails to grasp the connection between Luther's concept of God's hiddenness outside of revelation and the reformer's teachings concerning the bondage of the human will and double predestination.

Paul Tillich

In addition to Karl Barth and Emil Brunner, Paul Tillich (1886–1965) is treated in this study as a Neo-Orthodox theologian since his theology also rests on the necessity of divine revelation. Tillich's understanding of the place of revelation in theology differs from that of other Neo-Orthodox thinkers, however. While other Neo-Orthodox thinkers such as Barth and

---

198. *Dogmatics*, I, 321, 324–30, 342–45.

199. *LW* 25:371–72, 375, 377; WA: 56:381–82, 385–87.

200. Cf. T. Harnack,, *Luthers Theologie*, 84–97. *Dogmatics* I, 168. Dillenberger, *God Hidden and Revealed*, 103n11.

Brunner view God's self-revelation as the starting point of theology, Tillich views it as the secondary factor in the formulation of theology. The first factor is reason, which poses certain questions about universal human existence. Revelation then brings the answers to these questions raised by reason.[201] The essential question of human life that is posed by reason is that of being and non-being—the question of human finitude. This question is then answered by God's self-revelation as the ultimate and infinite ground of being.[202] Tillich also differs from the rest of Neo-Orthodoxy in that he does not relegate revelation—even special revelation—to Jesus Christ or the Word. Instead, he proposes that anything can become a venue for God's self-revelation.[203]

Tillich does not necessarily engage directly Luther's teaching concerning the hiddenness of God in God's self or the distinction between the unpreached and preached God, as do Barth and Brunner. Instead, Tillich mediates a transformed view of Luther's teaching concerning God's hiddenness and revelation in his own conception of God's being and revelation. In Tillich's view, the hiddenness of God is expressed as the sheer power of the divine "abyss," and the revelation of God in Christ is expressed in terms of God's work in Christ through the cross.

God, according to Tillich's view, is the ground of all being. God is not an existing entity *per se*; rather God is the ground of existence. This means that everything has its ultimate basis of existence in God, including both good and evil. God in this sense is the great "abyss" of being who encompasses all things, all powers, and all forces within God's self.[204] Although Tillich does not make the direct connection, one can detect a certain similarity here to Luther's concept of the hiddenness of the unpreached God, the God who works all in all, the God who works evil as well as good.[205] There is also, however, a significant difference from Luther's view that must be highlighted. While Luther appeals to the concept of the hiddenness of the unpreached God in order to safeguard the idea that God alone is the one who saves sinners, Tillich actually uses the concept of the God who works all in all as the basis for his understanding of the doctrine of God.[206]

---

201. Tillich, *Systematic Theology I*, 61–65. Grenz and Olson, *20th Century Theology*, 120–21.

202. Tillich, *Systematic Theology I*, 163, 211ff.

203. Ibid., 118, 157. Grenz and Olson, *20th Century Theology*, 123.

204. Tillich, *Systematic Theology I*, 235–37. McKelway, *The Systematic Theology of Paul Tillich*, 123.

205. *BOW*, 169–71; WA 18:684–86.

206. Tillich, *Systematic Theology I*, 237–39.

Tillich both agrees with and departs from Luther concerning the wrath of God. Tillich describes God's wrath in terms of God's disposition towards sinners apart from God's revelation of God in Christ as a God of love.[207] Tillich states, however, that such a picture of God is not a true picture of God, for God essentially is a God of love. The difference between God as a God of wrath and God as a God of love is a matter of human perception, dependent upon whether or not the human has experienced the forgiveness of sins in the revelation of God in Jesus Christ. It is not as if the human being actually stands under some ultimate condemnation of God and is cut off from God because of this condemnation. Instead, the human simply needs to be enlightened as to the true state of affairs concerning God's disposition towards him or her.[208] This is where, for Tillich, God's revelation in Christ comes into the picture. Christ acts as the archetypical new being who comes as a revelation from God to show the human the true state of affairs between God and the human by taking the negative disposition of God into himself—and by so doing also into God's self—in order that the human may see God truly as a God of love.[209]

While this view of God's hiddenness outside of revelation and God's revelation in Jesus Christ bears a certain resemblance to Luther's view, it is only a pale resemblance at best. It is true that Tillich—in a manner similar to Luther—describes God as the one who works all in all both good and evil when he describes God as the ground of all being and as being itself. It is also true that in some sense Tillich, like Luther, identifies God as a God of wrath and God revealed in Christ as God revealed as love. Yet, such a comparison eventually disintegrates, with the emergence of several significant differences between Tillich and Luther.

The first of these differences concerns the way in which each of these theologians approaches the hidden existence of God in God's self. While Luther simply seeks to express in this teaching that God is radically free and that God outside of revelation condemns the human sinner and wills his or her death, Tillich uses God's existence outside of revelation as the basis for his doctrine of God. Unlike Luther, Tillich proceeds to speculate into God's hiddenness outside of revelation in order to establish the beginning of a knowledge of God. Tillich actually draws his definition of God out of such speculation about the hidden God: God is the ground of all being and is, in fact, being itself.

---

207. Tillich, *Systematic Theology II*, 76–77.
208. Ibid., 77–78.
209. Ibid., 78–80, 173–76.

A second difference between Tillich and Luther concerning the hiddenness and revelation of God concerns God's wrath. Luther locates God's wrath outside of the revelation of God in the hiddenness of God in God's self. Tillich seems to posit that God's wrath exists only in human perception. He maintains that God's true disposition towards humans is one of love.[210] Luther, on the other hand, views God's wrath as the genuinely extent will of God outside of God's revelation in Christ. Furthermore, the revealed God in Christ does not merely serve to enlighten mistaken humans. Instead, according to Luther, God actually exists as a God of grace, mercy, and love in the revelation of Jesus Christ through the Word and actually exists as a God of wrath outside of Christ. For Luther, God's wrath and condemnation are real.[211]

Although Tillich's understanding of God as being itself bears a certain resemblance to Luther's understanding of the hiddenness of God in God's self, it is finally only a resemblance. Contrary to Luther's sense of a holy awe concerning the mystery of God hidden in God's self, Tillich builds an entire doctrine of God from such a divine hiddenness. Whereas Luther holds that the God in God's self should not be speculated about, Tillich enters completely into speculation about the hiddenness of the unpreached God. Such disparity between Tillich and Luther on this point of the wrath of God demonstrate the former's divergence from the latter regarding the doctrine of the hidden God.

Though Paul Tillich is unique in that he actually wants to use a speculative interpretation of the hidden God as the starting point for his own doctrine of God, none of these three Neo-Orthodox theologians captures the complete message of Luther's doctrine of the hidden God. Each interacts differently with Luther concerning this theme, but while each of them mirrors something of Luther's teaching, none of them correctly interprets or adopts it fully. Barth correctly identifies Luther's understanding of God's hiddenness outside of revelation as the existence of God in wrath parallel to God's existence in grace through God's self-revelation in Jesus Christ, but he openly rejects Luther's doctrine of the hidden God. Like Althaus, he rejects Luther's notion of God's hiddenness in God's self, even though he shares Luther's understanding that God can only truly be known in Jesus Christ. In fact, as does Althaus, Barth fails to comprehend that Luther is not advocating an actual knowledge of God outside of God's revelation in Christ. Alternately, Brunner accepts Luther's concept of God's hiddenness in God's self in part and uses it in his own theology, but he does not accept Luther's

---

210. Ibid., 76–77.
211. *BOW*, 169–17; WA 18:684–86.

understanding of "free will" and predestination which is inextricably linked with this concept. Tillich appropriates a certain form of this concept, but he then uses a speculative understanding of it as the foundation for his doctrine of God in a way completely foreign to Luther's articulation of this same concept and in a way which Luther actually forbids.

Marburg Theology: Gerhard Ebeling

The Marburg school of theology within the modern German Protestant theological tradition includes such theologians and scholars as Rudolf Bultmann, Ernst Käsemann, Hans Conzelmann, and Willi Marxsen. The important figure from this school for the concerns of the present study is Gerhard Ebeling (1912–2001). A student of Rudolf Bultmann, of Emil Brunner, and of Dietrich Bonhoeffer, Gerhard Ebeling was one of the most important Luther scholars and Lutheran theologians in the second half of the twentieth century.[212] Ebeling approaches his studies of Luther's thought and his own doing of systematic theology from a hermeneutical view of reality, and he understands Luther's view of divine hiddenness in this light. According to Ebeling, reality was begun by and is upheld by word, particularly by God's Word. Moreover, he states that human existence is defined by and in relationship to God, to others, and to the world, through this Word of God. The essence of human existence thus consists of a divine-human *Sprachsituation* (a linguistic situation or a situation of speech).[213] According to Ebeling, this *Sprachsituation*, which defines reality and human existence before God (*coram Deo*) consist of three kinds of speech: *Widersprechen*—God's speech against the human in the law, *Versprechen*—God's speech of promise to the human in the gospel of Jesus Christ, and *Entsprechen*—the speech between the human and God in prayer.[214] This understanding of reality and human existence before God lies in the background of Ebeling's understanding and interpretation of Luther's doctrine of the hidden God.

The accuracy of Ebeling's treatment of Luther's doctrine of the hidden God, driven as it is by Ebeling's hermeneutical understanding of reality and human existence, is somewhat mixed. While Ebeling fails to distinguish between the hiddenness of God in revelation and the hiddenness of God outside of revelation and the connection between the work of the hidden

---

212. Menacher, "Gerhard Ebeling in Retrospective," 166–67.

213. Ebeling, *God and the Word*, 18–23. Ebeling, "Word of God and Hermeneutics," 318–22. Ebeling, *Dogmatik des Christlichen Glaubens*, vol. 1, 189–191. Menacher, "Gerhard Ebeling in Retrospective," 176.

214. Ebeling, *Dogmatik I*, 189–90.

God and the work of God in the law, he does identify the hiddenness of God as incomprehensible and the work of the hidden God as the alien work of God through reprobation (damnation). More importantly, he understands and relates Luther's understanding of the relationship between the hidden God and God revealed in Christ through the Word.

In his volume entitled, *Luther: An Introduction to His Work*, Ebeling addresses the doctrine of the hiddenness of God in Luther's theology, commenting on both Luther's understanding of the hiddenness of God in revelation and the hiddenness of God outside of revelation, but focusing particularly on the latter.[215] The difficulty in approaching Ebeling's interpretation of Luther on the hidden God is that, although he addresses each of these, he does not effectively distinguish between God's hiddenness in revelation and God's hiddenness outside of revelation as two different kinds of hiddenness. Instead, like von Loewenich and Elert, Ebeling addresses the hiddenness of God as if it were of a singular, composite nature in Luther's theology. He relates that the hidden God is the God who is hidden under the sign of God's opposite in the suffering of the cross and more particularly in the crucified Christ. Yet, without distinguishing between the two, he also relates that the hidden God is the God who is hidden beyond revelation as the incomprehensible God who works all things, including wrath and damnation.[216] Such an understanding of divine hiddenness does not quite represent the views of the reformer himself, who certainly is not referring to the same kind of divine hiddenness in the *Heidelberg Disputation* as he is in *The Bondage of the Will*. Yet, it is not as if these two kinds of divine hiddenness in Luther's theology are completely mutually exclusive to one another, as Althaus claims. Instead the hiddenness of God in revelation is part of God's self-revelation, while God's hiddenness outside of revelation is really outside of God's self-revelation.

While he may not clearly distinguish between the two kinds of hiddenness in Luther's theology, Ebeling does depict God's hiddenness as standing in radical paradox to God's self-revelation. Like Luther, Ebeling understands God's self-revelation to be one of grace, mercy, and love given to humans as the promise of God in the gospel of Jesus Christ. In fact, Ebeling identifies God's self-revelation in Christ as "the gospel in person." In Jesus Christ, says Ebeling, God is God's Word of promise to and for humans.[217] Following Luther, Ebeling understands the hiddenness of God in terms of a dialectical

---

215. Ebeling, *Luther*, 226–41.

216. Ibid., 226–28, 240.

217. Ebeling, *Evangelische Evangelienauslegung*, 270–72. Menacher, "Gerhard Ebeling in Retrospect, 165.

and paradoxical relationship with God's revelation in Jesus Christ.[218] Ebeling argues with Luther against the Aristotelian understanding of natural theology propounded by the medieval scholastics. According to this theology, human beings have the capacity, through the faculty of reason, to see God and understand God's will at work in nature as well as the free will to act upon this understanding of God through natural revelation.[219] In agreement with Luther, Ebeling states that though there may be some knowledge of God through nature, such a positive knowledge of God apprehended by reason is impossible and leads inevitably only to speculation and utter despair. Any knowledge of God outside of Christ is a knowledge of the hidden God, says Ebeling, and as such it is neither a true knowledge nor beneficial, because ultimately God will not be known by humans outside of God's self-revelation in the gospel of Jesus Christ.[220] Quoting Luther, Ebeling states that there is no knowledge of God outside of Christ, for to know God outside of Christ is to know God as the devil.[221] In agreement with reformer, Ebeling describes the hidden God as the God who exists hidden, outside of God's revelation in Christ through the Word. This God outside of revelation, says Ebeling, works wrath and determines all things that happen including evil and the work of the devil, in direct paradox to the God of grace and mercy revealed in the promise of God in the gospel of Christ through the Word.[222]

In addition to agreeing with Luther concerning the incomprehensibility of the hidden God, Ebeling represents Luther well when he demonstrates the paradoxical relationship between the hidden and revealed God by describing the work of the hidden God as consisting of God's wrath against and damnation of the sinner. Ebeling identifies the work of the hidden God as God's alien work of damning and killing the sinner, in order that God might then raise to life and save the sinner. In expounding upon this work of the hidden God, Ebeling draws both from *The Bondage of the Will* and from the treatises of the early period of Luther's theological work in order to show how the reformer posits that God first kills the sinner to make the sinner alive, damns the sinner in order to save, and leads the sinner through hell in order to bring the sinner to heaven.[223] Ebeling does not, as such, identify that the alien work of God is enacted by the hidden God in order to obliterate the sinner's false notion of free will, but this much is implied

---

218. Ebeling, *Luther*, 238–40.
219. Ibid., 231–34.
220. Ibid., 229–30. Schwarzwäller, *Sibboleth*, 90.
221. Ebeling, *Luther*, 234–35.
222. Ibid., 240–41.
223. Ibid., 236–37.

by Ebeling's assent to Luther's understanding of the human will as bound rather than free before God[224] and by his description of the alien work of the hidden God as damnation for the sake of salvation.[225]

Ebeling's scholarship regarding Luther's understanding of the work of the hidden God as the alien work of God's condemnation aimed at ultimate salvation constitutes a decisive breakthrough in the modern German Protestant theological tradition's interpretation of Luther's doctrine of the hidden God. Nevertheless, Ebeling could go further in his exploration of Luther's understanding of the work of the hidden God. Though he defines the work of the hidden God as God's alien work and even refers to Luther's early theology to describe it, Ebeling does not identify the work of the hidden God as reprobation within double predestination and does not relate this to the reformer's later understanding of God's alien work through the trials and existential struggle of *Anfechtung*, nor does he relate this work of the hidden God to the work of God in the law, even though he clearly understands and agrees with Luther's teaching that God condemns through the law, in both its natural and written forms, in order to save through the gospel.[226]

Moreover, Ebeling still does not clearly distinguish between the two kinds of divine hiddenness in Luther's theology. Instead, he treats both kinds of hiddenness together as one hiddenness. This can be very confusing for the reader of Ebeling, who will at one juncture speak of hiddenness as God's being revealed in a paradoxical way, and in the next moment speak of hiddenness as that which is outside of revelation and which is seemingly contradictory to revelation itself.[227]

Aside from these drawbacks, however, Ebeling's interpretation of Luther's doctrine of the hidden God stands as perhaps the most accurate from the time of Theodosius Harnack to his own day. Ebeling goes beyond the scholarship of von Loewenich and Elert and the simple rejection of the doctrine by Ritschl, Althaus, and Barth and captures the spirit of the view of Luther himself. Though his depiction of Luther's doctrine of the hidden God is not complete, Ebeling relates the substance of this doctrine: that God is hidden outside of God's revelation of God in Christ through the Word as a God of wrath, that this hiddenness of God is incomprehensible, that it constitutes God's working of all things, that it constitutes God's alien work, and that the ultimate trajectory of this is the sinner's salvation in Christ through

---

224. Cf. Ibid., 208–25.
225. Ibid., 236–37.
226. Ibid., 137.
227. Ibid., 226–27, 240.

the Word. Such an understanding of Luther's doctrine, that God ultimately must be found in Christ the Word and that even God's hiddenness outside of Christ works to this end, may indeed be influenced by Ebeling's own hermeneutical approach to theology. Nevertheless, this view reflects a serious attempt to relate Luther's thoughts on their own terms and may also be seen as an accurate interpretation of Luther's doctrine of the hidden God. In fact, it is likely that Ebeling has not imposed his approach to theology upon Luther but that Luther's doctrine of the hidden God has influenced Ebeling.

Trinitarian Theologians

This section addresses more recent German Protestant thinkers, whose works span the division between the twentieth and twenty-first centuries who directly address and interact with Luther's doctrine of the hidden God. These three contemporary German Protestant theologians are sometimes referred to as "Trinitarian theologians," designating them as practitioners of a certain approach to theology in which the doing of theology itself must consciously be based on the fundamental truth of God's specific definition of God's self as Trinity. These three Trinitarian theologians all treat Luther's concept of God's hiddenness in God's self somewhat differently from one another, but they are united in that none of them accepts or utilizes this concept of Luther as the reformer articulates it. This is due to the fact that each of these theologians approach Luther's doctrine of the hidden God from the basis of their own theological ideas. Jüngel openly rejects Luther's doctrine of the hidden God, operating out of his analogical approach to theology and from the assumption that God's nature is love alone, which ultimately precludes the kind of wrathful God Luther presents in his doctrine of the hidden God. Pannenberg and Moltmann are more subtle. Instead of rejecting Luther's concept of God hidden in God's self, they undermine it by paying lip service to the notion of divine hiddenness while collapsing God's hiddenness in God's self into God's hiddenness in revelation to serve the needs of their own theological projects.

Wolfhart Pannenberg

The first of the Trinitarian theologians whose treatment of Luther's distinction between God hidden in God's self and God revealed I will address in this study is Wolfhart Pannenberg (1928–2014). Pannenberg's approach to the doctrine of God—and indeed his understanding of the whole of theology—is conditioned by two undergirding theological presuppositions. The first of these presuppositions is an eschatological (some might say teleological) approach to the study of God. For Pannenberg, God is working all of reality towards a specific *telos* which will be revealed in the eschaton. Moreover, Pannenberg maintains that God is also moving God's self towards this *telos* in which God will be more fully God's self.[228] The second presupposition is Pannenberg's specifically Trinitarian approach to theology. Inspired by the thought of the Cappadocian Fathers, Pannenberg posits that the three divine persons of the Trinity are defined by their relationships with one another (i.e. *perichoresis*).[229] This particular Trinitarian approach to theology serves as the basis from which Pannenberg addresses every topic in theology, and the hiddenness of God is no exception.

Pannenberg essentially defines the concept of divine hiddenness in the same way that Luther defines the hiddenness of God in God's self, yet Pannenberg collapses God's hiddenness and God's revelation together. For Pannenberg, the entirety of divine hiddenness is eventually (or will be eventually) disclosed through the revelation of the Triune God. Pannenberg approaches this self-disclosure of the hidden God by means of a combination of his eschatological approach to the doctrine of God and his Trinitarian speculative approach to the work of God in the cross of Christ.

In the first volume of his highly influential *Systematic Theology*, Pannenberg describes the hiddenness of God as consisting of God's hiding of God's self from sinners either for salvation or for judgment. Pannenberg states that such hiddenness includes the unsearchability of the divine counsel and the incomprehensibility of the divine essence.[230] While this definition of God's hiddenness is not Luther's verbatim, it is basically equivalent to the reformer's teachings on the hiddenness of God. Mirroring the reformer's description of God's hiddenness in God's self, Pannenberg states that the hiddenness of God includes the hiddenness of both God's counsel and God's essence.[231] Though Luther does not use these exact terms, he does state in *The Bondage of the Will* that God's hiddenness in God's self entails the hiddenness both of God's person and of God's will.[232] Although he does not expressly state that God may be hidden in revelation or in God's self, Pannenberg does state that God's hiddenness may be for salvation or for judgment. One could infer that Pannenberg's idea of God's hiddenness for

---

228. Mattes, *The Role of Justification in Contemporary Theology*, 57–58. Cf. Pannenberg, *Systematic Theology, Volume 1*, 55–56, 185–87, 250.

229. Pannenberg, *Systamtic Theology 1*, 277–79.

230. Ibid., 339–40.

231. Ibid.

232. *BOW*, 169–71; WA 684–86.

salvation might be seen as equivalent to Luther's understanding of God's hiddenness in revelation and Pannenberg's idea of God hidden for judgment as equivalent to Luther's understanding of God's hiddenness in God's self. On the other hand, unlike Luther, Pannenberg speaks of these two venues of divine hiddenness as constituting a single form of God's hiddenness. Rather than distinguishing God's hiddenness in revelation and God's hiddenness in God's self, Pannenberg collapses the latter into the former through his explanation of how God's hiddenness is disclosed through revelation and through the cross event.[233]

Pannenberg's collapsing of God's hiddenness in God's self into God's hiddenness in revelation may be observed in how he explains the hiddenness of God as being revealed. Appealing to John 1:18 ("No one has ever seen God; the only Son who is in the bosom of the Father, he has made him known"), Pannenberg states that God's hiddenness from humanity is revealed through the Incarnation of Jesus Christ. What was hidden about the Triune God, thus has been revealed through the work of the Father in the life of the Son. "This process," says Pannenberg, "will be completed, of course, only in the eschaton."[234] Nevertheless, God's hiddenness has been, is being, and will be disclosed in God's revelation in history through Jesus Christ. Pannenberg even projects this view of God's hiddenness onto Luther, saying that this is what Luther's doctrine of divine hiddenness really means and that the reformer never intended to convey a dialectical view in which God is simultaneously hidden and revealed.[235]

This articulation by Pannenberg of God the Son's complete disclosure of divine hiddenness through progressive revelation evidences two things. The first is, as has been stated, that Pannenberg collapses God's hiddenness in God's self into God's hiddenness in revelation and simply calls it the hiddenness of God. Pannenberg describes such hiddenness in terms of Luther's concept of God's hiddenness in God's self (i.e. that God's person and will are incomprehensible), but he then goes on to say that such hiddenness is disclosed in revelation. The second thing evidenced by this view of divine hiddenness is that Pannenberg either misunderstands or misrepresents Luther's understanding of God's hiddenness in God's self. While it is true that Luther defines the content of such hiddenness in much the same way as Pannenberg, Luther does explicitly teach a dialectical view of God in which

---

233. Pannenberg, *Systematic Theology 1*, 339–40.
234. Ibid., 340.
235. Ibid.

God's hiddenness in God's self and God's self-disclosure in revelation exist parallel to each other.[236]

Another place in which Pannenberg's collapsing of God's hiddenness in God's self into God's hiddenness in revelation may be observed is his explanation of God's disclosure of God's hiddenness through the cross event. Here Pannenberg mirrors Luther's understanding of God hidden in God's self by identifying the hiddenness of God with God's wrath against humans for their rebellious sin against God. Yet here Pannenberg again departs from Luther's understanding of such divine hiddenness by means of a Trinitarian, speculative Good Friday.[237] In his understanding of the cross event, Pannenberg relates that through the cross God the Father judges God the Son instead of humanity. God does this because God cannot have two wills towards humanity. God's true will towards humanity, says Pannenberg, is one of love. Thus, God must be rid of God's will of judgment, and God does this through the cross. The hiddenness of God is thus, through a perichoretic action of the Trinity, completely disclosed through the Father's judgment of the Son on the cross such that both God's judgment and God's hiddenness are completely fulfilled and no longer remain with God.[238]

The contrast between Pannenberg's view of God's hiddenness completely disclosed in the cross event and Luther's understanding of the distinction between the hiddenness of God in God's self and God's self-disclosure in revelation is not difficult to detect. For Luther, God's hiddenness in God's self stands over and against God's self-disclosure of God's self in revelation. Luther points out directly that one must distinguish between these two any time one speaks of God or God's will.[239] It is true that Luther also sees the cross in terms of Christ's taking God's judgment instead of humanity, and this is a prominent theme in Luther's understanding of the atonement as the *Frohliche Wechsel*.[240] Yet, Luther is also clear that God's gracious will of mercy and forgiveness revealed in Christ belongs to the revelation of God

---

236. BOW, 169–70; WA 18:684–86.

237. The term "speculative Good Friday" comes from Hegel and is referenced in Mark Mattes' book *The Role of Justification in Contemporary Theology* wherein Mattes uses the term to refer to Pannenberg's approach to the work of God in the cross from the perspective of intellectual speculation and Hegelian theology. I add the qualifier "Trinitarian" both in order to attempt communicate the full weight of Pannenberg's use of Trinity in all of theology and in order to correlate Pannenberg's understanding of the atonement with his view of progressive revelation. Mattes, *The Role of Justification in Contemporary Theology*, 80n87. Cf. Hegel, *Faith and Knowledge*, 43.

238. Pannenberg, *Systematic Theology, Volume 2*, 391–92.

239. BOW, 169–170; WA 18:684–85.

240. LW 26:276–90; WA 40.1:432–52. Luther, *The Freedom of a Christian*, 62–65.

and not to the hiddenness of God in God's self.[241] It is also true that Luther also sees a certain hiddenness of God being revealed in the cross, but it is the hiddenness of God in revelation not the hiddenness of God in God's self. Pannenberg does not distinguish between these two types of hiddenness, and therein lies his departure from Luther concerning the hiddenness of God.

Wolfhart Pannenberg may follow Luther's explanation of the hiddenness of God to a certain point, but the overall trajectory of his understanding of divine hiddenness diverges sharply from Luther's. This divergence consists of Pannenberg's failure to distinguish between the hiddenness of God in God's self and the hiddenness of God in revelation. In contrast to Luther, Pannenberg collapses God's hiddenness into God's self disclosure in revelation, motivated by the concerns of his own Trinitarian approach to theology. This may be observed particularly in how Pannenberg relates God's hiddenness to his notion of the Triune God's progressive revelation and to his understanding of the work of the Triune God. In this way, Pannenberg removes the concept of divine hiddenness from its context in Luther's theology and tailors to his own theology.

Jürgen Moltmann

Like Pannenberg, the Trinitarian theologian Jürgen Moltmann (1926–) espouses Luther's understanding of the hiddenness of God to a certain extent, but he ultimately collapses the hiddenness of God in God's self into God's self-disclosure in revelation. Moltmann does this by describing the hiddenness of God in terms of God's hiddenness in revelation without any mention of God's hiddenness in God's self. Moltmann's one-sided description of the hiddenness of God flows from and manifests itself in terms of his rejection of traditional theism's understanding of an absolute God. In collapsing the two kinds of divine hiddenness, Moltmann thus utilizes Luther's views regarding God's hiddenness only insomuch as they serve his own theological project. Such selective reading of Luther fails to portray accurately the reformer's understanding of the hiddenness of God.

In his work, *The Crucified God*, Moltmann addresses Luther's concept of the hiddenness of God in revelation (i.e. the theology of the cross) at some length and appropriates and reinterprets this concept for his own theological enterprise.[242] True theology, says Moltmann, begins not with speculations about God and God's nature but with God revealed in Christ through

241. *BOW*, 170–71; WA 18:685–86.
242. Moltmann, *The Crucified God*, 207ff.

the suffering of the cross. Whoever wants to know God, says Moltmann, cannot know God any other way than through the crucified God in Jesus Christ.[243] Here Moltmann is in basic agreement with Luther. As Moltmann identifies, Luther articulates this same view in his *Heidelberg Disputation* of 1518.[244] Although Moltmann does not distinguish, as does Luther, between the hiddenness of God in revelation and the hiddenness of God in God's self, he does at least to an extent accept Luther's understanding of God's hiddenness in revelation.

Yet, Moltmann takes even this form of divine hiddenness and turns it into something contrary to Luther's understanding of it. For Luther, God reveals God's self in Christ in order that humans might be forgiven of their sins and live in communion with God in Christ.[245] Moltmann, on the other hand, uses Luther's understanding of God hidden in revelation as a starting point for his own political-theological praxis. For Moltmann, God's hiddenness in revelation means that God comes hidden not only in the suffering of the cross but in all suffering and that identifying with the suffering and oppressed peoples of the world constitutes identification with God. Moltmann thus develops Luther's theology of the cross, which the reformer uses to speak about God's revelation to humanity, into a theological basis for leftist political activism.[246]

While Moltmann at least to some extent adopts Luther's understanding of God hidden in revelation, he is completely silent about the hiddenness of God in God's self. The only form of divine hiddenness to which Moltmann holds is God's hiddenness in revelation; it might thus be said that Moltmann, much like Pannenberg, collapses God's hiddenness into God's self-disclosure in revelation. This phenomenon may be observed in how Moltmann addresses the claims about God's absolute nature posited by traditional theism. Moltmann is highly critical of how traditional theism views God as immortal, impassive, and omnipotent. Anyone who espouses such a view of God, says Moltmann, does not understand the hiddenness of God in revelation evident in the theology of the cross.[247] Instead of seeing God as immortal, impassive, and omnipotent, Moltmann sees the crucified God

---

243. Ibid., 208–9, 212–13.

244. *LW* 31:40–41; *WA* 1:354–55.

245. Cf. *SC*, The Second Article of the Creed; *BC*, 355.

246. Moltmann, *The Crucified God*, 25. Mattes, *The Role of Justification in Contemporary Theology*, 99.

247. Moltmann, *The Crucified God*, 215–26.

as a vulnerable and suffering God who identifies with and may be found amongst the vulnerable and suffering peoples of this world.[248]

It is clear from Moltmann's critique of traditional theism that he fails to grasp or purposely rejects Luther's distinction between God revealed and God hidden in God hidden in God's self. It is true, says Luther, that God is limited by revelation, but God does not exist only in revelation. God is also radically free above and beyond revelation. The God who is hidden in God's self is does not exist within limits. Instead, God hidden in God's self works all things and holds dominion over all things.[249] For Luther, God may be hidden under the suffering of the cross, but at the same time God also dwells in unapproachable radical freedom as God is hidden in God's self. Luther depicts these two venues of God's existing as being distinct from one another and parallel to one another, but Moltmann collapses the hiddenness of God into God's revelation under the suffering of the cross.

Jürgen Moltmann may agree with Luther's understanding of God's hiddenness in revelation under the suffering of the cross to some extent, but he does not agree with Luther concerning the hiddenness of God in God's self. Moltmann does not even mention such divine hiddenness but, instead, collapses all divine hiddenness into God's revelation in the cross. This is observable in how Moltmann speaks of the theology of the cross as mandating that Christian theology lay aside traditional theism's claims about the absolute nature of God for a picture of the vulnerable and suffering God who identifies and dwells with those of this world who are also vulnerable and suffering. Such a notion of God as vulnerable may be compatible with the picture of God Luther gives in his theology of the cross, but it is hardly compatible with that portrayed by Luther in his articulation of the unpreached God hidden outside of revelation.

Eberhard Jüngel

The last of the three Trinitarian theologians to be discussed here, and the most significant in terms of interaction with Luther's doctrine of the hidden God, is Eberhard Jüngel (1934 -). Like Althaus, Jüngel rejects Luther's teaching concerning God unpreached and God preached on the basis that violates the teaching of God revealed as a God of love in Jesus Christ. Like Karl Barth, Jüngel argues that God is fully revealed as a God of love in Jesus Christ, so that there is no longer any divine hiddenness. Since he interacts with Luther's doctrine of the hidden God (particularly the hiddenness of

---

248. Ibid., 25, 214–16, 229.
249. *BOW*, 169–70; WA 684–85.

God in God's self) from his own analogical approach to theology and since he views God's very nature as that of love itself, Jüngel sees any hiddenness of God as being revealed in the Triune God's revelation of God's self as love in and through the cross of Jesus Christ.

Jüngel rejects Luther's teaching concerning the unpreached and preached God, because he believes it to contradict God's love as revealed in Jesus Christ and the cross. Jüngel here agrees with Barth against Luther that there can be no essential dichotomy in God's nature, nor can there be such in God's revelation. God cannot exist both as love and hidden in wrath. Any *Deus absconditus* must consist of God's hiddenness in the revelation of God's love in Jesus Christ. There cannot be any hiddenness of God as a *Deus absolutus* alongside the revelation of God as a God of love in Jesus Christ.[250]

In his work, *God as the Mystery of the World*, Jüngel takes up the critique of Ludwig Feuerbach against Christian theology. Feuerbach argues, and Jüngel repeats, that all too often theology has preoccupied itself with the study of the *potentia absoluta* of God to the neglect of the love of God. Jüngel takes this accusation of Feuerbach against Christian theology seriously and states that theology, "must be careful not to differentiate God and love ontologically in the sense that God's being is not defined by love."[251] Consciously building on Feuerbach, Jüngel argues that in theology love must be exalted to the status of a substance.[252] This is what is meant by the biblical phrase, "God is love." For Jüngel, this phrase becomes an axiom of the definition of the divine substance. God is love does not mean that all love equals God, but it does mean that the divine substance is defined very narrowly as pure love.[253] If love is not thus exalted to the status of the divine substance and there is instead some divine subject behind love, then the Christian view of God devolves into a picture of a diabolical and demonic monster.[254]

In his essay *The Revelation of the Hiddenness of God*, Jüngel accuses Luther of committing this precise error. Luther, says Jüngel, should be content to speak of God hidden in God's revelation, but he is not. Instead, the reformer blunders into the articulation of a *Deus absconditus et absolutus* who works all things in the universe by virtue of this God's secret will and *opus alienum*.[255] This view of hiddenness of God and its corresponding

---

250. Jüngel, "The Revelation of the Hiddenness of God," in *Theological Essays II*, 137–38. Mattes, *The Role of Justification in Contemporary Theology*, 40.

251. Jüngel, *God as the Mystery of the World*, 316. Paulson, "Analogy and Proclamation," 2. Cf. Feuerbach, *The Essence of Christianity*, 50–54.

252. Jüngel, *God as the Mystery of the World*, 316.

253. Ibid., 316–17.

254. Ibid., 316.

255. *TE II*, 136. Mattes, *The Role of Justification in Contemporary Theology*, 40.

teaching of a hidden divine will contradicts the God of love, whom Luther rightly identifies as the God revealed in Christ through the Word. Such a view of God has no place in Christian theology and only complicates the appropriate understanding of the revealed God, says Jüngel. Theology must leave behind this demonic understanding of God and content itself with the *Deus revelatus* and with the *opus proprium* of the revealed God.[256]

Jüngel recognizes Luther's doctrine of the hidden God better than most twentieth-century theologians. He correctly identifies this teaching as the reformer's notion of the distinction between the law and the gospel applied to the very being of God itself.[257] Jüngel does not completely reject the terminology of God's hiddenness. What he does is subsume the hiddenness of God under the category of the revelation of God, so that the only hiddenness of God there is left in his theology is the hiddenness of God in revelation, described by Luther in his *theologia crucis*.[258]

Jüngel ultimately rejects the idea of the unpreached God's hiddenness outside of revelation, because he holds that God's nature is not divided but consists of pure love. The teaching concerning God's hiddenness in God's self constitutes an understanding of God's wrath that contradicts God's essential being as love. For Jüngel, the ultimate venue for God's self-revelation as a God of love is the cross. The cross constitutes the triune God's self-revelation in history as the interruption of the ages, and in this way the cross as revelation serves a critical function in theology. The cross as the embodiment of God's love is the criteria by which theology must be judged and around which theology must be centered.[259]

From this methodological standpoint, Jüngel rejects the idea that there is a hiddenness of the unpreached God in God's self, though he does retain that there is a certain hidden work of God.[260] In the hidden work of God, God works through wrath to destroy all evil in the world, particularly through the cross of Christ.[261] This *opus Dei alienum et absconditum* is thus not a work contrary to the revealed work of God, nor is it the hidden work of the hidden God. Instead, it is the hidden work of the revealed God of

---

256. TE II, 136–37. Mattes, *The Role of Justification in Contemporary Theology*, 40.

257. Jüngel, *God as the Mystery of the World*, 345.

258. TE II, 130, 143–44.

259. Jüngel, *God as the Mystery of the World*, 302, 310ff. Paulson, "Analogy and Proclamation," 233.

260. TE II, 137.

261. TE II, 130, 137, 139–42.

the cross. Such a work has no existence on its own but is located within the greater work of the God of love revealed in the cross.[262]

Jüngel rejects Luther's teaching concerning the distinction between God's hiddenness in God's self and God's revelation, because Jüngel posits that God's nature is unitary and not divided. God has revealed God's self as a God of love, says Jüngel, and God does not contradict God's self.[263] For Jüngel, God's nature is solely one of love, and he rejects any attempt to have a divine subject behind the divine substance of love as dangerous to theology and ultimately demonic. Jüngel also rejects that there is any will of God's wrath which stands on its own. Instead, he locates God's alien work of wrath within the larger category of God revealed as a God of love in the cross of Christ. Jüngel thus subsumes God's will of wrath under God's will of love revealed in the cross of Jesus Christ and, in so doing, subsumes the hiddenness of the unpreached God in God's self under the hiddenness of the preached God in revelation.

Jüngel may recognize Luther's doctrine of the hidden God for what it really is. Ultimately though, Jüngel has no place for Luther's understanding of divine hiddenness outside of revelation because it does not fit into his own theology. In this theology, not only does God's wrath disappear entirely into the generalized category of love, but the revealed God is also defined completely in terms of an idealized love. In Jüngel's dogmatic scheme, love actually loses its point of reference in the work of God in Jesus Christ over and against God's wrath, and in so doing becomes a general truth against which God's revelation in Christ must be judged, just as von Loewenich warns against.[264] Such a view of God as generalized love stands in direct contrast to Luther's dialectical view of God as a God of wrath outside of God's revelation in Christ and as a God of grace, mercy, and love in God's revelation in Jesus Christ.

Summary

Luther's doctrine of the hidden God was neglected until Theodosius Harnack revived it in the nineteenth century. Immediately after T. Harnack however, beginning with Albrecht Ritschl, the doctrine was generally maligned in the modern German Protestant theological tradition, even though each of the aforementioned figures within this tradition handled Luther's distinction

---

262. *TE* II, 143–44.

263. Jüngel, *God as the Mystery of the World*, 313–17. *TE* II, 141. Reinhuber, *Kampfender Glaube*, 105.

264. Von Loewenich, *Luther's Theology of the Cross*, 38.

between God hidden and God revealed generally and the concept of God's hiddenness in God's self specifically in their own ways.

Ritschl and his followers approach and negatively assess Luther's doctrine of the hidden God from their own Neo-Kantian framework, while Rudolf Otto interprets this doctrine in line with his own philosophy of religion from the History of Religions School. Karl Holl, on the other hand, represents a somewhat rogue figure within the late-nineteenth century in general and the Ritschlian school in particular in that, while he integrates Kantian thought and Luther's theology in his approach to justification, he manages to relate Luther's doctrine of the hidden God somewhat accurately. In the twentieth century, the theologians from the Erlangen, Neo-Orthodox, Marburg, and Trinitarian schools also approach Luther's doctrine of the hidden God on their own theological terms. In the Erlangen school, while von Loewenich interprets this doctrine through his own understanding of the theology of the cross as the center of Luther's theology, Elert and Althaus interpret Luther's view of divine hiddenness from their own respective metheological viewpoints regarding the human as the one responsible for God's wrath and a revisionist view of the dialectic between the law and the gospel. While Ebeling looks seriously at Luther's theology on its own terms, he also approaches Luther's doctrine of the hidden God from his own hermeneutical approach to theology. The Trinitarian theologians also view this doctrine from their own theological standpoints. While Pannenberg selectively interprets and uses some of Luther's teaching concerning divine hiddenness from the basis of his social-Trinitarian and eschatological approach to theology, Moltmann interprets Luther's views on God's hiddenness from and orients this interpretation back towards his critique of the traditional doctrine of the absolute God. Finally, Jüngel, rejects Luther's doctrine of the hidden God on the basis of his own analogical approach to theology and his notion that God's nature is love alone.

Yet, while each of these theologians approaches Luther's doctrine of the hidden God from their own theological standpoints, I will note some trends evident among them. One trend evident amongst these theologians is the tendency to collapse God's hiddenness in God's self into God's hiddenness in revelation. The ways in which Holl, von Loewenich, Elert, Pannenberg, Moltmann, and even Ebeling interact with Luther's teachings on divine hiddenness represent this trend. Another trend is represented by Althaus, Barth, and Jüngel, who completely reject Luther's concept of God hidden outside of revelation on the basis that it contradicts more fundamental theological truths. Still another trend is evident in how Otto, Brunner, and Tillich all adopt Luther's concept of God's hiddenness in God's self but modify the reformer's articulation of this concept in some way to a lesser or greater extent.

Though some of these theologians come closer to Luther's own articulation of the concept of God's hiddenness in God's self than others, none of these theologians express this concept in quite the same way as the reformer himself does. Albrecht Ritschl rejects this theme in Luther's theology on the basis that it contradicts Luther's teaching of God revealed in Christ as a God of love, but in doing this Ritschl fails to comprehend the depth of Luther's doctrine of the hidden God and its relationship to salvation through Luther's understanding of God's alien work. Karl Holl identifies aspects of Luther's doctrine of the hidden God, including God's alien work through double predestination, but he fails to see the parallel in Luther's theology between this work and the work of God in the law. Rudolf Otto understands something of Luther's doctrine of the hidden God, but stands Luther's teaching on its head by using this doctrine for a springboard into a theology that is completely at odds with the subject of Luther's doctrine. Walther von Loewenich comprehends the historical context of Luther's concept of the hidden God and understands that this concept entails the unapproachable mysteriousness of God, but he fails to see the parallel relationship of the distinction between God hidden in God's self and God revealed with the distinction between the law and the gospel and collapses the hiddenness of God outside of revelation into God's existence in revelation. Althaus rejects Luther's concept of God's hiddenness in God's self out of hand, failing to see the connections in Luther's theology between the will of God hidden in God's self and God's work through the law and God's will in reprobation. Barth, like Althaus, rejects Luther's notion of God's hiddenness in God's self, even though he shares Luther's understanding that God can only truly be known in Jesus Christ. Brunner accepts Luther's concept of God's hiddenness in God's self in part and uses it in his own theology, but he does not accept Luther's understanding of "free will" and predestination which is inextricably linked with this concept. Tillich appropriates a certain form of this concept, but he then uses a speculative understanding of it as the foundation for his doctrine of God in a way completely foreign to Luther's articulation of this same concept. Jüngel, like Barth and Althaus, rejects this concept of Luther's, but he is unique in that he does so from the standpoint of God's nature being defined solely in terms of idealized love. Pannenberg and Moltmann pay lip service to a divine hiddenness described by Luther, but they both collapse Luther's concept of God's hiddenness in God's self into the concept God's hiddenness in revelation in order to better fit Luther's descriptions of divine hiddenness into their own theologies.

Of all of these figures, the closest to Luther himself, in terms of correctly interpreting Luther's doctrine of the hidden God, is Gerhard Ebeling. Yet even Ebeling falls short in his description of Luther's teaching on the hiddenness of God. Ebeling understands and relates Luther's understanding of God's hiddenness outside of revelation correctly in so far as he depicts it as consisting of the incomprehensible work of God that accomplishes all things and works wrath, of God's alien work of damnation against the sinner, and as ultimately, though paradoxically, compatible with Luther's understanding of God revealed in Christ. Yet he still appears to collapse both kinds of divine hiddenness into one. Furthermore, he does not relate the connection between the hidden God's alien work and God's work in the law, nor does he identify this divine work with God's will of reprobation in double predestination or understand it in terms of the trials and existential struggle of *Anfechtung*.

In fact, none of these figures of the modern German Protestant theological tradition and, for that matter, none of Luther's theological successors before the nineteenth century seem to understand the significance of *Anfechtung* for Luther's teaching concerning the hidden God. Though biographers and psychologists of Luther have made much of *Anfechtung* with regard to Luther's personal experience with God,[265] Luther scholars and theologians seem to have somewhat overlooked its importance as the work of God that contradicts God's work in salvation. A few of these figures in the modern German Protestant theological tradition—namely, Harnack, Holl, Elert, Brunner, and Ebeling—attempt to varying degrees of success to relate and interpret Luther's doctrine of the hidden God as it features in Luther's own theology, with its center of God's salvation of the sinner in Christ. Others, particularly Otto and Tillich, seek to utilize Luther's doctrine of the hidden God in their own theology, but none of the figures addressed above attempts to integrate this doctrine as it is actually found in Luther's theology into their own theologies.

As will become apparent further on in this work, such is not the case with Oswald Bayer. Though he may share some of the same views of Luther's understanding of the hidden God with other scholars and theologians of the German Protestant tradition, and though he himself stands within the tradition, at this point, he highlights the relationship of the hidden God to *Anfechtung* as something within Luther's teaching on the hidden God missed by the tradition and uses it extensively in his own theology. Moreover, unlike those before him, Bayer actually takes up Luther's doctrine of

---

265. Bainton, *Here I Stand*, 42, 62, 335, 357, 361. Erikson, *Young Man Luther*, 110–15, 237–38, 241–50. Oberman, *Luther: Man between God and the Devil*, 226. Oberman, *The Dawn of the Reformation*, 112, 148. Kittelson, *Luther the Reformer*, 56–57.

the hidden God and integrates it into his approach to doing theology, gives it a prominent place in the content of his theology, and defines it with reference to God's justification of the sinner in Christ, which he sees as the center of Luther's and all Lutheran theology. Otto may function as a precursor to Bayer in this way, but Otto's misinterpretation of Luther's doctrine of the hidden God ensured that he would be unable to understand it properly within its context in Luther's theology. In any event, Bayer by no means duplicates Otto's view.

Of the figures whose interpretation of Luther's doctrine of the hidden God I have addressed here, T. Harnack, Ritschl, Holl, Otto, Elert, Althaus, Barth, Ebeling, and Jüngel's views are the most relevant for comparing with Bayer's understanding and use of this doctrine. I will compare their views with that of Bayer in chapter eight of this work, while in chapters six and seven I will address how Bayer himself interprets and uses Luther's doctrine and how he compares to the reformer himself. Before embarking on these tasks, however, I will first discuss how it is that Bayer approaches theology and what he understands to be the nature of justification.

4

Bayer's Approach to Theology

OSWALD BAYER'S INTERPRETATION AND use of Luther's teaching concerning the hidden God is conditioned by his overall approach to the doing of theology. In particular, Bayer's treatment of hiddenness is formed by and is integrated into his theological method, as well as his views of the mode, subject matter, and data of theology. In order to understand the place of divine hiddenness in Bayer's theology, it is first necessary to explore how it is that Bayer does theology and what he sees as the subject and trajectory of theology.

Throughout his theological works, Bayer shows a great appreciation for and debt to the theology of Martin Luther. From his writings it becomes clear that Bayer understands himself as a specifically Lutheran theologian and as a contemporary interpreter of the sixteenth-century reformer's theological thought. The Lutheran trajectory that Bayer sets for himself as a theologian determines how it is that he approaches the doing of theology.

In the opening pages of his work, *Martin Luther's Theology: A Contemporary Interpretation* (*Martin Luthers Theologie: Eine Vergenwärtigung*), Bayer argues that while Luther never composed a systematic theology like the *Summa Theologiae* of Thomas Aquinas or Philip Melancthon's *Loci Communes*, Luther was a systematic theologian.[1] Bayer is clear, however, that he does not mean that Luther was a systematician in the sense that his theology fits together nicely into a functional whole without contradiction or conflict within it. Instead, he maintains that Luther was a systematic theologian in that his theology has an "internal coherency" presented in a series of central themes that address what the Christian faith means. Such themes include freedom in Christ, the distinction between God's Word in the law and God's

---

1 Bayer, *Martin Luther's Theology*, xv; Bayer, *Martin Luthers Theologie*, VII.

Word in the gospel, and justification by faith alone.[2] These themes, says Bayer, are not merely sixteenth-century concerns that have no bearing on the doing of theology today. Instead, Luther's theology addresses timeless questions that are relevant to all Christians and indeed to all humans in all ages, questions about what it means to be human in relationship to God, questions about sin and salvation, death and life. Because of the persistence of such questions in the midst of human existence and because of the fact that Luther's theology addresses these questions, says Bayer, Luther's theology forces itself upon us.[3]

Yet, Bayer does not merely seek to replicate Luther's theology today. Instead, he has taken Luther's central themes and interpreted them for contemporary times and in so doing takes into account his own contemporary temporal setting and developments in theology and philosophy since Luther's time in order to formulate his own contemporary Lutheran approach to doing theology. Bayer's use of Luther in this approach is illustrated by how he explains the mode of theology, how he formulates his theological method, how he defines the subject of theology, and what he sees as the data given for the doing of theology. In following Luther in these areas of what some might term the prolegomena of theology, Bayer deliberately seeks to realign contemporary evangelical theology, which has been deluded by the "narcissism of modernity," with its reformational heritage.[4]

Theologie als Weisheit: The Mode of Theology as Experiential Wisdom

By using the terminology of "the mode of theology," I am importing a classification into Bayer's description of theology. Bayer does not use the term "mode" in his description of his approach to the doing of theology. Nevertheless, I have used this term here to describe both "what kind of knowledge theology is" and the *Sitz im Leben* of both theology and the theologian formed by such knowledge as Bayer describes them.[5] By describing what Bayer understands as constituting the true mode of theology, I am addressing what exactly Bayer says theology is, what its genre is, and within what

---

2. Bayer, *Martin Luther's Theology*, xvi-xvii; Bayer, *Martin Luthers Theologie*, VIII-IX.

3. Bayer, *Martin Luther's Theology*, xix; Bayer, *Martin Luthers Theologie*, X-XI.

4. Helmer, "The Subject of Theology in the Thought of Oswald Bayer," 21-25. Cf. Mattes, *The Role of Justification in Contemporary Theology*, 145ff. Bayer, "The Modern Narcissus," 304-5; Bayer, "Der Neuzeitliche Narziß," in *Gott als Autor*, 75-77.

5. Bayer, *Martin Luther's Theology*, 29-30ff.; Bayer, *Martin Luthers Theologie*, 27-28.

kind of setting it is done. In other words, by the use of the term "mode," I intend to communicate what Bayer understands to be the true nature of systematic theology.

Before exploring how Bayer understands the nature of systematic theology, however, it is necessary first to discuss what Bayer says theology is not. Bayer constructs his own reformationally oriented theology in opposition to what he identifies as transformations of the true nature of theology present in both Roman Catholic and modernistic Protestant theologies.[6] With regard to the mode of theology, Bayer thus assesses all theological thinking since the time of the ancient Greeks and focuses on these two main ways of doing theology that he subsequently criticizes: the Aristotelian (i.e. the classic Roman Catholic way) and the modern way. Bayer's critiques both the theologians of the Aristotelian way of doing theology, from Aristotle to Pannenberg, and those of the modern way, from Kant to Bultmann, on account of how they portray the mode of theology as metaphysical science over mythology and in how they see all theological work in dualistic terms as consisting of and being divisible between contemplation and action, between theory and praxis.[7]

Over and against these two forms of metaphysical theology, Bayer argues that the true mode of theology lies not in science (*scientia*) but in wisdom (*sapientia*), not in metaphysical speculation, but in the tension between mythology and metaphysics.[8] However, unlike the Greek mythologists, Bayer does not devolve into thinking of theology purely in terms of mythological stories with morals to be retrieved and taken to heart.[9] Bayer also rejects the division of theology between theory and praxis, embodied by the Aristotelian and modern ways of theology. Instead, drawing on Luther's early theological work, Bayer understands the mode of theology as "experiential wisdom" (*sapentia experimentalis*). This does not mean that Bayer understands theology as simply being based on experience itself or on some general, universal human experience of dependence upon God. Bayer is not proposing here a contemporary return to Schleiermacher and clarifies this by consciously distancing himself from Schleiermacher regarding the

---

6. Bayer, *Theology the Lutheran Way*, 28–29, 34, 139; Bayer, *Theologie*, 49–51, 58–59, 453–54.

7. Bayer, *Theology the Lutheran Way*, 6–7, 14, 21, 28–29, 106–9, 114–19; Bayer, *Theologie*, 24–25, 32, 49–51, 418–21, 426–32.

8. Bayer, *Theology the Lutheran Way*, 28, 8–9; Bayer, *Theologie*, 49, 26–27. Bayer, "Entmythologisierung? Christliche Theologie zwischen Metaphysik und Mythologie im Blick auf Rudolf Bultmann," 110.

9. Bayer, *Theology the Lutheran Way*, 8–9; Bayer, *Theologie*, 26–27.

nature of theology as experiential.[10] On the contrary, as I shall explain more fully below in describing Bayer's understanding of the subject and the data of theology, he understands the experiential nature of theology to consist of the specific experience of being encountered and addressed by the living God who kills and makes alive, who accuses and justifies.[11] Bayer states that this mode of theology, this experiential wisdom, encounters the theologian and that, instead of theorizing upon a theology to be acted upon, the theologian suffers this experiential wisdom in what Bayer describes as "the passive life" (*vita passiva*). In the passive life, the false dialectic of theory and praxis is replaced by suffering. Instead of theorizing and acting, the theologian suffers what happens to him or her passively. Instead of being a thinker and an actor, in the understanding of the mode of theology as expressed in the passive life, the theologian is one who undergoes theology.[12]

Bayer does not fabricate this understanding of the mode of theology out of thin air. Though Bayer certainly articulates and nuances his understanding of theology as experiential wisdom as a response and an alternative to the Aristotelian and modern approaches to theology, he also draws on one pre-modern and one modern figure who have had a profound influence upon his theological thinking. In articulating this view of experiential wisdom as the mode of theology over and against metaphysical science, Bayer demonstrates how he has been influenced by both the pre-modern reformer Martin Luther and the modern Enlightenment thinker Johann Georg Hamann.

In *Martin Luther's Theology*, Bayer identifies how Luther defines the "kind of knowledge" that constitutes theology. Bayer relates how Luther addresses this as one of a series of questions posed to by the late scholastic theologian Gabriel Biel.[13] By defining the mode of theology as experiential wisdom, Bayer does not allow the minimzing the mode of theology to a distinction between theory and praxis, between contemplation and experience but, instead, brings experience into the mode of theology itself.[14] Much was written in twentieth-century Luther studies concerning Luther as a student

---

10. Bayer, *Martin Luther's Theology*, 104; Bayer, *Martin Luthers Theologie*, 95. Bayer, *Theology the Lutheran Way* 113; Bayer, *Theologie*, 425.

11 Bayer, *Theology the Lutheran Way*, 112–14; Bayer, *Theologie*, 424–26. Bayer, *Martin Luther's Theology*, 36–39.

12. Bayer, *Theology the Lutheran Way*, 21–23; Bayer, *Theologie*, 45–46. Bayer, *Martin Luther's Theology*, 42–43; Bayer, *Martin Luthers Theologie*, 38–40.

13. Bayer, *Martin Luther's Theology*, 29–30; Bayer, *Martin Luthers Theologie*, 27–28. Bayer, *Theology the Lutheran Way*, 13–14; Bayer, *Theologie*, 31–32. Bayer, *Zugesage Gegenwart*, 41.

14. Bayer, *Theology the Lutheran Way*, 28–29; Bayer, *Theologie*, 49–52.

in the stream of Biel's nominalistic/Ockhamistic theology.¹⁵ Yet Bayer makes an original contribution to this aspect of the contemporary field of Luther studies when he focuses on how Luther answers these questions posed by Biel by employing his understanding of theology as experience in such a way that he suggests a new experiential approach to doing theology.¹⁶ Bayer demonstrates how Luther forms his reformational approach to theology as a response, at to some extent, to three formative questions about the task of theology given by Biel.

Biel outlines these questions in his *Collectorium circa quattuor libros Sententiarum*. As the title of this work suggests, the questions that Biel articulates here are developed from Peter Lombard's *Sentences*. While the first and third of these questions inquire as to the nature of the knowledge entailed by the discipline of theology, the second asks what the subject of theology is.¹⁷ Bayer takes up Luther's response to the second of these questions in his own exploration of what forms the subject matter of theology, but first he shows how Luther answers the first question in his notes on one of Johannes Tauler's sermons (c.1516) by arguing that theology is neither speculative nor practical in nature, rejecting both metaphysical and moralistic approaches to defining the nature of theology, but that it consists of "experiential wisdom."¹⁸

According to Luther, "experience alone makes one a theologian."¹⁹ Bayer relates that Luther understands such experience as being the specific experience of being addressed by the Word of God.²⁰ Since one is addressed by God, this experience of the theologian is one that is characterized by passivity. This is the notion of the *vita passiva*, which Bayer adopts from Luther and utilizes in place of the dialectic between theory and praxis, between the *vita contemplativa* and the *vita activa* of medieval scholasticism.²¹

---

15. Cf. Scheel, *Martin Luther*, Zweiter Band, 80-97, 129-40ff. Oberman, *The Dawn of the Reformation*, 93-103, 113-14. Oberman, *The Harvest of Medieval Theology*, 1-3, 18, 55, 143-44, 232-33, 427. Oberman, *Luther: Man between God and the Devil*, 118-122. Steinmetz, *Luther in Context*, 56-57, 63-67. Lohse, *Martin Luther's Theology*, 20-27, 47-49, 98-99. Saarnivaara, *Luther Discovers the Gospel*, 25-27, 30, 55.

16. Bayer, *Martin Luther's Theology*, 29-30; Bayer, *Martin Luthers Theologie*, 27-28.

17. Bayer, *Martin Luther's Theology*, 29; Bayer, *Martin Luthers Theologie*, 27. Bayer, *Theology the Lutheran Way*, 13-14; Bayer, *Theologie*, 31-32. Cf. Biel, *Collectorium crica quattuor libros Sententiarum*, vol. 1, 8.

18. Bayer, *Martin Luther's Theology*, 29-30; Bayer, *Martin Luthers Theologie*, 27-28. Bayer, *Theology the Lutheran Way*, 23; Bayer, *Theologie*, 44. Cf. WA 9:98.

19. Bayer, *Martin Luther's Theology*, 22; Bayer, *Martin Luthers Theologie*, 20.

20. Bayer, *Martin Luther's Theology*, 22; Bayer, *Martin Luthers Theologie*, 20-21. Luther, *Table Talk*, in LW 54:7; Luther, *Tischreden*, WA TR 1:16.

21. Bayer, *Zugesagte Gegenwart*, 41.

According to Bayer as he draws from Luther's response to Biel's first and third questions by defining for himself the nature of the knowledge in theology—not as science but as wisdom, not as speculation or as action but passivity—the theologian engages in theology not as an acting party, but as one who undergoes the Word of God and meditatively reflects on it, forming such experience into thoughts. In this way, theology is not so much a matter of doing as it is of suffering (*passio*), suffering the Word of God.[22]

Luther is not, however, the only influence on Bayer's view of the mode of theology as experiential wisdom passively suffered by the theologian. In this view, Bayer also evidences how indebted he is to Hamann's critique of the German Enlightenment philosophy of Immanuel Kant. According to Bayer, Kant is responsible for transmitting the false dialectic between theory and praxis to modern philosophy and modern Protestant theology through his attempt to separate the "scientific" side of philosophical knowledge from the aesthetic, the realm of the empirical from that of the purely rational, practical reason from pure reason. In advancing this false dialectic, says Bayer, Kant intentionally made moral activity the ultimate goal of religion, and thus modern Protestant theology, following Kant, made this concern forefront in systematic theology.[23]

Indeed, in both his third critique (*The Critique of Judgment*), *Religion within the Limits of Reason Alone*, and his *Lectures on Philosophical Theology*, Kant sets forth his critique of the Christian religion on the basis of his distinction between these two aspects of philosophy. What religion needs in the Modern Age, says Kant, is to jettison the otherworldly pursuit of knowledge based on pure reason through erudite doctrinal theology or the interpretation of divine revelation and to focus instead moving humans through the moral law to the goal of ethical action.[24]

Over and against his more famous contemporary in Königsberg, Hamann taught that humans are not primarily actors in their own destiny but passive suffers. In contrast to Kant's focus on moral *actio*, Hamann focused on *passio* as the goal of humanity and the trajectory of religion. It is not that

22. Bayer, *Martin Luther's Theology*, 21; Bayer, *Martin Luthers Theologie*, 20. Bayer, *Theology the Lutheran Way*, 21–24, 28–29; Bayer, *Theologie*, 42–46, 49–50.

23. Bayer, *Theology the Lutheran Way*, 107–8, 115–16; Bayer, *Theologie*, 419–20, 427. Cf. Kant, *Critique of Practical Reason*, in *The Critique of Pure Reason, the Critique of Practical Reason, and the Critique of Judgment*, 297–98ff. Kant, *Fundamentals of the Metaphysics of Morals*, in *Basic Writings of Kant*, 146–49.

24. Kant, *Critique of Judgment*, in *The Critique of Pure Reason, the Critique of Practical Reason, and the Critique of Judgment*, 588–596. Kant, *Religion within the Limits of Reason Alone*, 94–98, 156–63. Kant, *Lectures on Philosophical Theology*, trans, 23–25. Wilson, *Introduction to Modern Theology*, 35–36. Cf. Wood, "Rational Theology, Moral Faith, and Religion," in *The Cambridge Companion to Kant*, 394–416.

Hamann saw no place for human action, even moral action, but such action flows from and is part of a larger overall picture of suffering as that which characterizes human existence.[25]

It is important at this juncture to note that by using the term "suffering," (*passio*) Bayer does not intend to communicate that suffering *per se*—undergoing pain, stress, or catastrophic events—makes one a theologian. Instead by "suffering" Bayer clearly means the particular experience of being acted upon by God. Bayer uses the terminology of suffering simply to communicate the nature of passivity in which the human undergoes God's work. Since God is author, the human existence as suffering is one of suffering (or undergoing) the language of God. Thus, for Hamann, the human being is not essentially an actor who reasons and wills his or her own moral destiny but is one who undergoes being addressed by God.[26]

Bayer nuances his understanding of the mode of theology as experiential wisdom functioning between metaphysics and mythology by using Hamann's critique of Kant, adopting and further clarifying Hamann's position against Kant on human existence as suffering (*passio*). For Bayer, Hamann's replacement of Kant's *actio* with his own notion of *passio* is key not only in order to understand human existence, but also to form what the mode of theology as experiential wisdom means. It means living and learning what it means to do theology by suffering the speech of God. Instead of humans existing as active entities, humans exist and theologians operate (or are operated upon!) in the *vita passiva*, the passive life, which becomes the way for the theology to undertake the experience of theology.[27] The foundational motif for the enacting of such a work of God upon passively suffering humans for Bayer, as he interprets Hamann, is the cross of Jesus Christ. Here, says Bayer, is the true identity marker of human destiny, not critical reason and judgment employed under the motivation of the moral law towards ethical action, but the negation of all human reason and all human action in the scandal of the divine-human suffering of the cross.[28]

Bayer juxtaposes Hamann's understanding of suffering through the cross with Martin Luther's theology of the cross as expressed in the

---

25. Bayer, *Zeitgenosse im Widerspruch*, 185; Bayer, *A Contemporary in Dissent*, 162. Hamann, *Letztes Blatt*, 54–55. Bayer and Knudsen, *Kreuz und Kritik*, 103–6, 110–11.

26. Mattes, *The Role of Justification in Contemporary Theology*, 150. Cf. Bayer, "God as Author of My Life History," 437ff; Bayer, *Gott als Autor*, 21–40.

27. Mattes, *The Role of Justification in Contemporary Theology*, 150–51. Bayer, "God as Author of My Life History," 436–440; Bayer, *Gott als Autor*, 21–24. Bayer, *Autorität und Kritik*, 108–9. Bayer, *Theology the Lutheran Way*, 21–23; Bayer, *Theologie*, 42–43.

28. Bayer and Knudsen, *Kreuz und Kritik*, 110–11. Bayer, *Autorität und Kritik*, 32, 110, 117–24.

Heidelberg Disputation of 1518. The theology of the cross, says Bayer, is what theology as true passivity, as true experiential wisdom means. It means the negation of human reasoning and human activity as the means for self-definition and explaining the divine. It means dispensing with the dialectic of theory and praxis and understanding theology instead as passively suffering God's work.[29]

This is not to say that Bayer's understanding of the mode of theology lacks any kind of dialectic. Though he rejects the dialectic between theory and praxis immanent within Aristotelian and modern theology, Bayer does not reject the concept of dialectical thinking altogether. Instead, Bayer seeks to realign evangelical theology with a more reformational—and therefore a more evangelical—dialectic. Drawing once again from Luther, Bayer posits that the true dialectic of systematic theology is one between the monastic and scholastic aspects of theology, between the experience of the Christian Church's corporate worship, confession, and petitioning of the Triune God on the one hand and the role of systematic theology as an academic discipline complete with a methodology and hermeneutics on the other hand.[30]

Both sides of this dialectic are united, however, in that they are both oriented towards the same goal, which makes up the true task of theology: *Gottesdienst* (divine service or worship). Bayer argues that, instead of divorcing theological knowledge and understanding from the experience of the everyday life of the Christian and thus creating a false distinction between theory and praxis in theology, his Lutheran methodology for doing theology anchors academic, systematic theology firmly within the Christian community's public and private life of worship and devotion.[31] The scholastic side of theology thus works in tandem with and even in service to the monastic side so that "academic" systematic theology is done as a catechetical exercise. In this way, even the university faculty of systematic theology exists to serve the monastic theology of the Church and its members, teaching them what it means to confess faith in the Triune God. Once again, Bayer here acknowledges his debt to Luther. Bayer notes that it was to this same end that the reformer composed his *Large Catechism* for the theological training of the preaching ministers of the church and his *Small Catechism* for the theological learning of all Christians. As a result, not only was there a dissemination of the theological program of the Reformation, but there was also a leveling amongst people so that, in the words of Karl

---

29. Bayer, *Gott als Autor*, 256–260. Bayer, *Martin Luther's Theology*, 42–43; Bayer, *Martin Luthers Theologie*, 38–40.

30. Bayer, *Theology the Lutheran Way*, 28–32; Bayer, *Theologie*, 49–55.

31. Bayer, *Theology the Lutheran Way*, 34; Bayer, *Theologie*, 58–59.

Marx, "the monks became laypeople and the laypeople became monks."[32] Thus, in Bayer's thought, the experiential wisdom of systematic theology takes place as a form of worship oriented towards God for the benefit of the whole Church. Such divine service exists as a sacrifice of thanksgiving in response to God's gracious address of divine service of address to the theologian through the Word and Sacraments.[33]

Bayer articulates this view of the mode of theology as experiential wisdom, with its basis in divine service, as a clear alternative to what he sees as the faulty modes of theology prescribed by the Aristotelian and modern approaches to theology. According to Bayer, these approaches to theology portray theology as a metaphysical science expressed through a dialectic of theory and praxis. Bayer rejects the metaphysical-scientific understanding of theology with its dialectic and offers instead his own view that theology is actually an experiential wisdom. Incorporating Luther and Hamann into his account of the mode of theology in order to nuance his understanding of theology as experiential wisdom, Bayer argues that only the experience of being addressed by God makes a theologian and that consequently the theologian experiences theology through the passive life brought about by being addressed by God. In place of the dialectic between theory and praxis, Bayer describes the experiential wisdom of theology as having a scholastic as well as a monastic dimension. Both of these sides of theology are united in that they are both divine service undertaken by the theologian as worship in response to God's prior address to the theologian.

Oratio, Meditatio, Tentatio: Towards a Reformational Theological Method

Bayer's view of the method of theology flows from his view of the mode of theology of experiential wisdom. Following the theme of the way of the theologian as the passive life, Bayer approaches the method of doing theology not only as a rule for how one undertakes the theological task but also as the rule that characterizes the experience of the theologian. As in his view of the mode of theology, Bayer here draws heavily from Luther in his own description of the method of theology, adopting the rule of the theologian set forth by the reformer. Like Luther, Bayer does not relegate this rule of

---

32. Bayer, *Theology the Lutheran Way*, 67–68; Bayer, *Theologie*, 106–8. Cf. Marx, *A Contribution to the Critique of Hegel's 'Philosophy of Right': Introduction*, in *The Critique of Hegel's 'Philosophy of Right'*, 138; Marx, *Zur Kritik der Hegelschen Rechtsphilosophie: Einleitung*, in *Karl Marx-Friedrich Engels Werke, Band 1*, 386.

33. Bayer, *Theology the Lutheran Way*, 90; Bayer, *Theologie*, 400.

theological method to the experience of the "professional" theologian alone but, rather, describes it as something that happens to all Christians in so much as, to some extent, all Christians are theologians. Bayer thus uses the terms "theologian" and "believer" somewhat interchangeably in his description of the method of theology.[34]

Following on the idea that the mode of theology is experiential wisdom, which the theologian suffers through the passive life, Bayer circumvents the metaphysical approaches to theology and proposes a return to a reformational theological method that he receives from Luther's theological writings.[35] This method consists of a three-fold rule that Bayer gleans from Luther's brief exposition of Psalm 119 in his *Preface to the German Writings* of 1539. In this rule, Luther states that the task of the theologian must be guided by *oratio* (prayer), *meditatio* (meditation), and *tentatio* (*Anfechtung*/ agonizing struggle).[36]

Bayer highlights that this rule for doing theology was not relegated only to this single text in the reformer's works but informed all of Luther's theology and, indeed, survived him as a methodological legacy that was practiced in subsequent generations of Lutheranism, including both Lutheran Orthodoxy and Lutheran Pietism. This common Lutheran methodology inherited from the reformer emphasized how theologians were formed through undergoing these three experiences.[37] Bayer argues that this theological method stands as a clear and preferable alternative to the purely metaphysical approaches evident in the scientific theological method of those of the Aristotelian of theology such as Aquinas and Pannenberg and to the demythologizing method of the modern theologians such as Bultmann. Bayer states that, instead of divorcing theological knowledge and understanding from the experience of the everyday life of the Christian and thus creating a false distinction between theory and praxis in theology, his Lutheran methodology for doing theology anchors academic, systematic

---

34. Bayer, *Martin Luther's Theology*, 16–17; Bayer, *Martin Luthers Theologie*, 15–17.

35. Bayer, *Theology the Lutheran Way*, 32–33; Bayer, *Theologie*, 55–57. Bayer, *Martin Luther's Theology*, 31–32; Bayer, *Martin Luthers Theologie*, 29–30.

36. Bayer, *Martin Luther's Theology*, 32; Bayer, *Martin Luthers Theologie*, 29–30. Bayer, "'die größte Lust zu haben / allein an deinem Wort,'" 795. Cf. Luther, *Preface to the German Writings* (1539), *LW* 34:285–87; Luther, *Vorlesung zur Deutsche Schfriten* (1539), WA 50:659–661. Although *tentatio* could be—and indeed has been by Mark Mattes—translated as "temptation," I have followed Thomas Trapp's translation "agonizing struggle," which I believe fits better with Luther's idea of *Anfechtung* that Bayer is seeking to employ here.

37. Bayer, *Theology the Lutheran Way*, 33–34; Bayer, *Theologie*, 55–58.

theology firmly within the Christian community's public and private life of worship and devotion (*Gottesdienst*).[38]

By shaping his thought along the methodological contours of prayer, meditation, and agonizing struggle, Bayer ensures that his experiential understanding of theological method will not be confused with that of other existential theologians such as Schleiermacher. By adopting and advocating the Lutheran rule of theological method, Bayer specifies that his theological method rests not on general human experience but on the particular human experience of being addressed and acted upon by the living God through the Word. For Bayer, prayer and meditation are not general concepts for study or introspective spiritual exercises but the particular experience of the human who is encountered by God in God's objective and external Word of God.[39] Prayer in this sense is the specific prayer of humility that God would enable the theologian to be a theologian, to be addressed by God's Word and thereby to grasp its wisdom.[40] Meditation is not a practice of turning inward in the quest for truth but meditation on the external truth of the Word wherein God addresses the theologian.[41] The agonizing struggle of *Anfechtung* is not simply some form of a generic human angst but the experience of the theologian—and indeed of every Christian—who is addressed by God's Word. This experience, says Bayer, is the experience of the contradiction of God's Word of promise; it is the contradiction apparent in reality against what God says in the Word. It is the touchstone of being addressed by God's Word experienced by everyone who meditates upon that Word.[42]

Although in Bayer's thought prayer and meditation are related to divine hiddenness as well, the last aspect of Bayer's reformational theological method, *Anfechtung*, is the most important for understanding how Bayer interprets Luther's doctrine of the hidden God and uses it in his own theology. For Bayer the theologian's experience of *Anfechtung* is the experience of

---

38. Bayer, *Theology the Lutheran Way*, 34; Bayer, *Theologie*, 58–59. Here there appears an echo of Bonhoeffer's notion of life under the Word, as expressed in Life Together, where Bonhoeffer describes the formative nature of the Word on personal and corporate worship, devotion, prayer, and meditation. Cf. Bonhoeffer, *Life Together* in *Dietrich Bonhoeffer Works*, Vol. 5, 31–32, 51–53, 84–92; Bonhoeffer, *Gemeinsames Leben*, in *Dietrich Bonhoeffer Werke*, Band 5, 18–20, 37–41, 66–76.

39. Bayer, *Theology the Lutheran Way*, 44–49, 52, 55–56; Bayer, *Theologie*, 72–82, 85, 89–91.

40. Bayer, *Martin Luther's Theology*, 32–34; Bayer, *Martin Luthers Theologie*, 30–31. Bayer, *Theology the Lutheran Way*, 47–48; Bayer, *Theologie*, 77–80.

41. Bayer, *Martin Luther's Theology*, 34–35; Bayer, *Martin Luthers Theologie*, 31–32. Bayer, *Theology the Lutheran Way*, 56–59; Bayer, *Theologie*, 90–95.

42. Bayer, *Theology the Lutheran Way*, 63–64; Bayer, *Theologie*, 100–103. Bayer, *Martin Luther's Theology*, 20–21, 35–37; Bayer, *Martin Luthers Theologie*, 19–20, 33–34.

the attack on the believer's faith in God's saving promise in justification in Jesus Christ.[43] Such an experience, says Bayer, is not driven by the believer nor is it driven by another person or external environmental factors. Instead, *Anfechtung* stands as a work done by God.[44] In addressing the subject of divine hiddenness itself, Bayer later defines this experience of agonizing struggle as the experience of the radical contradiction of the promise of God in justification at the hand of the hidden God.[45] This description of *Anfechtung* will be dealt with in chapters six and seven of this work.

Bayer sets forth his method of doing theology as consisting of meditation, prayer, and the agonizing struggle of *Anfechtung*. Bayer adopts this theological method from Luther, and it also flows from Bayer's understanding, via Luther, of the mode of theology as experiential wisdom. In short, this experiential method of theology is the description of what happens when one is made a theologian by the God who encounters humans through the Word. The encounter between God and the human in the Word not only informs Bayer's theological method; as it consists of God's address to the human, it also ensures that this divine action to the human will serve as the basis for Bayer's understanding of the subject for theology.

The Subject Matter of Theology: "Was ist Evangelisch?"

Bayer's view of what constitutes the true subject matter of the theology is essential to his entire theological endeavor and forming the way he approaches theology as a whole as well as individual themes within it such as the doctrine of the hidden God. Bayer rejects the often-assumed notion that the subject of theology is simply "God" and voices his criticism of theologians past and present who define the subject of theology as such, especially Thomas Aquinas and Wolfhart Pannenberg. Instead, Bayer proposes that the true subject of theology is narrower than simply the study of God; it consists of God's justification of human sinners in Jesus Christ.[46] This definition of the subject of theology is not unique to Bayer, and here, continuing

---

43. Bayer, *Theology the Lutheran Way*, 61; Bayer, *Theologie*, 98.

44. Bayer, *Theology the Lutheran Way*, 62–63; Bayer, *Theologie*, 100–101.

45. Bayer, *Martin Luther's Theology*, 39–40, 213; Bayer, *Martin Luthers Theologie*, 36–37, 192. Bayer, *Theology the Lutheran Way*, 102, 104; Bayer, *Theologie*, 413, 415–16.

46. Bayer, *Theology the Lutheran Way*, 98; Bayer, *Theologie*, 408–9. Bayer, *Martin Luther's Theology*, 37–38; Bayer, *Martin Luthers Theologie*, 36–37. Cf. Thomas Aquinas, *Summa Theologiae*, Ia.I, 24–27. Pannenberg, *Theology and Philosophy of Science*, 297–99.

his conscious utilization of Luther's thought for the formation of his own approach to theology, Bayer opens his view of the subject matter of theology by describing the reformer's answer to Biel's second question regarding the doing of theology. Adopting Luther's view of the subject matter of theology, Bayer then utilizes this in his own systematic theology, identifying God's justification of the human sinner as the norm, basis, and boundary of theology. In defining the subject of theology thus, Bayer identifies and rejects what he identifies as the improper reception of the reformational approach to the subject matter of theology as justification within both Roman Catholicism and Protestantism.

Biel's second question answered by Luther inquires as to what constitutes the subject of theology, giving the discipline of theology its unity.[47] Bayer notes that Luther, unlike Aquinas, Pannenberg and others, does not define the subject of theology and what gives theology its unity by addressing theology as "the study of God," or some similar broad category of the knowledge or the experience of divine things. Instead, Luther defines the subject matter and unity of theology very narrowly, and Bayer takes the reformer's lead in doing this. For Luther, as for Bayer, the true subject matter of all theology is the "the sinning human being and the justifying God."[48]

In particular, Bayer adopts this definition from Luther's commentary on the fifty-first Psalm, where Luther states that the true subject matter of all theology is the guilty human sinner and the God who justifies this sinner.[49] In defining the subject of theology as such, Luther –and Bayer following him—brings the human as subject into the subject matter of theology, not in such a way that the divine subject is defined by the human subject but in such a way that the human subject can only be defined by the divine subject.[50] Thus, for Bayer, the subject of theology is no longer simply "God" but the human as accused and justified by God and the God who accuses and

---

47. Bayer, *Martin Luther's Theology*, 37; Bayer, *Martin Luthers Theologie*, 34. Bayer, *Theology the Lutheran Way*, 17; Bayer, *Theologie*, 36

48. Bayer, *Martin Luther's Theology*, 37; Bayer, *Martin Luthers Theologie*, 34. Bayer, *Theology the Lutheran Way*, 17; Bayer, *Theologie*, 36.

49. Luther, *Psalm 51* (1538), LW 12:311; WA 40.2:328. Bayer, *Martin Luther's Theology*, 37–39; Bayer, *Martin Luthers Theologie*, 34–36. Bayer, "Justification as the Basis and Boundary of Theology," 287; Bayer, *Leibliches Wort*, 34.

50. LW 12:311; WA 40.2:328. Bayer here references Bonhoeffer's notion of self-understanding only in relationship to how the self is known by God: "Who am I? Thou knowest me. I am thine, O God." Bonhoeffer, *Dietrich Bonhoeffer Works, Volume 8: Letters and Papers from Prison*, 459–60; Bonhoeffer, *Dietrich Bonhoeffer Werke, Band 8: Widerstand und Ergebung: Briefe und Aufzeichen aus der Haft*, 513–14. Bayer, *Living by Faith*, 25; Bayer, *Aus Glauben Leben*, 35. Bayer, "Justification as the Basis and Boundary of Theology," 287.

justifies the human.[51] For Bayer, this is what it means to do theology in the reformational tradition, this is what it means to do theology as an evangelical Lutheran, that the subject of theology consists both of the accused and justified sinner and the accusing and justifying God.[52]

In his essay entitled, "Was ist evangelisch?" ("What is Evangelical?") Bayer states that the adjectives "evangelical," Lutheran, and "reformational," describe a certain way of doing theology, namely, doing theology around the central subject matter of the God who justifies sinners in Jesus Christ.[53] Here, Bayer traces what it means to do theology this way by going back to the inception of reformational theology in the early thought of Luther. According to Bayer, as he has developed in more detail in *Promissio*, God's justification of the sinner became the definitive center of Luther's theology by the time of his debate with Cardinal Cajetan in Augsburg in 1518.[54] Here, before one of the greatest scholars of his day, Luther was forced to defend the essence of his new theology, which stated that "no one can be justified except by faith" and that "the righteous live not by their disposition [i.e. towards God] but by faith," in the face of the proxy of the Roman pope and curia.[55] Through the process of defending his new evangelical theology, says Bayer, Luther rightly came to understand the center of this theology as God's action of justifying the sinner by faith alone, as Cajetan also recognized by his statement: "This means constructing a new church" ("Dies bedeutet, eine neue Kirche zu bauen").[56]

In "Was ist evangelisch?" Bayer then demonstrates how Luther understood that it would be categorically unchristian of him, as a theologian of the Church, to renounce his belief in God's justification of the sinner, because this belief was the fundamental belief of Christianity and the very center

---

51. Bayer, *Martin Luther's Theology*, 37–39; Bayer, *Martin Luthers Theologie*, 36–37. Bayer, *Theology the Lutheran Way*, 17–18, 97–98; Bayer, *Theologie*, 36–38.

52. Ibid. Bayer, *Martin Luther's Theology*, 53–54; Bayer, *Martin Luthers Theologie*, 49.

53. Bayer, *Zugesagte Gegenwart*, 22–33; Bayer, "What is Evangelical?," 1–15. On the human sinner and the justifying God in Christ as the center of Luther's theology, see Schwarzwäller, *Theologia Crucis*, 46–48; Kolb, *Bound Choice, Election and Wittenberg Theological Method*, 20; Cf. Forde, *The Captivation of the Will*, Chapter 4. Bayer, *Martin Luther's Theology*, 50; Bayer, *Martin Luthers Theologie*, 46.

54. Bayer, "Rückblick," 161. Bayer, *Promissio*, 346. Bayer, "Die reformatorische Wende in Luthers Theologie," 107. Bayer, *Martin Luther's Theology*, 50; Bayer, *Martin Luthers Theologie*, 46.

55. Bayer, "What is Evangelical?" 4–5; Bayer, *Zugesagte Gegenwart*, 25–27. Luther, *Proceedings at Augsburg* (1518), LW 31:270–71; *Acta Augustana*, WA 2:13–14.

56. Bayer, "What is Evangelical?" 5; Bayer, *Zugesagte Gegenwart*, 26–27. Cardinal Cajetan, *Augsburg Treatises* (1518), 55.

of both Christianity and Christian theology. Thus Bayer relates Luther's response to the challenge laid down by Cajetan for him to recant his views: "I will not become a heretic by renouncing what made me a Christian."[57] Bayer then argues that this belief in the God who justifies the sinner by faith constitutes and continues to be the true and only center of evangelical, Lutheran, and reformational theology. This center is not unmovable, however, and it must be tried and tested in every generation, says Bayer. Nevertheless it is the center of reformational theology, and as such should not be jettisoned in favor of an ecumenical endeavor of "unity at any price."[58] The center of theology as the sinning human and the justifying God cannot be sacrificed for the sake of the ecumenical unity or for some deeper common truth, Bayer argues, because as the center of theology, it is not merely one doctrine within a larger theological system but that which is constitutive of the whole of theology. As such, then, God's activity of saving the human sinner is not merely a point in theology but the norm of reformational theology. It is what makes evangelical, Lutheran, and reformational theology evangelical, Lutheran, and reformational.[59]

Bayer does not, however, see the subject of the sinning human and the justifying human as the norm of reformational theology alone. According to Bayer, Luther saw the evangelical faith as the faith, the faith that brings justification by God in Christ as the only true faith. Bayer argues that the fact that Luther understood the rejection of God's justification of the sinner by faith alone as the rejection of Christianity itself, tantamount to heresy and apostasy, demonstrates that he understood faith in God's justifying act and Christian faith to be identical. Seeking to be faithful to Luther he sees it as the only real and true norm of all theology.[60] By presenting the subject of God's justification of human sinners as the subject matter and norm of theology, however, Bayer does not reduce theology to a single doctrine or to a single theological point. Instead, he describes this subject matter as forming the basis, boundary, and sum total of all of theology.

Defining the subject matter of theology as God's justification of the human sinner in Christ, says Bayer, does not amount to a theological reductionism or to a monotony of themes as one might first think. Bayer addresses such a misunderstanding of the reformational notion of the subject matter of theology in his essay entitled "Justification as the Basis and Boundary of

57. Bayer, "What is Evangelical?" 7; Bayer, *Zugesagte Gegenwart*, 28.
58. Bayer, "What is Eavangelical?" 3, 7–8; Bayer, *Zugesagte Gegenwart*, 23, 28.
59. Bayer, "What is Evangelical?" 11–12; Bayer, *Zugesagte Gegenwart*, 32–33.
60. Bayer, "What is Evangelical?" 3, 6–8, 11–12; Bayer, *Zugesagte Gegenwart*, 23, 28–29, 32–33. Bayer, "Die reformatorische Wende in Luthers Theologie," 104.

Theology," wherein he describes in greater detail the meaning of his definition of the subject of theology as God's justification of the sinner.[61] In the beginning of this essay, Bayer acknowledges that Luther's understanding of the subject of theology as God's justification of the sinner has often been perceived as a kind of theological reductionism that is "monotonous, empty, and even obsessive." He relates Erik Peterson's account of Immanuel Swedenborg walking up and down a dark room "without windows or doors" unable to do anything other than repeat to himself: "I am justified by faith alone; I am justified by faith alone; I am justified by faith alone."[62] Bayer vehemently disagrees with such an assessment of Luther's and Lutheran theology. Such an image portrays reformational theology of justification as "a denial of all this-worldly relationships" and as "complete unworldliness."[63] Against this parody of reformational theology as otherworldly, Bayer argues to the contrary that justification bears a definite ontological, existential, and relational significance for all of theology, and indeed for all of life. As I will describe more fully when I outline the content of Bayer's doctrine of justification below, Bayer understands justification as opening up new relationships between God and the human, the human and other humans, the human and fellow creatures, and the creation itself to the human.[64]

Bayer also takes up this theme of justification as the norm of theology in his short work on the subjects of justification and sanctification entitled *Aus Glauben Leben*. In the "Preface to the First German Edition" of this work, Bayer argues that far from being a single doctrine, justification is the sum total of all theology, which should be appreciated in its "breadth and depth."[65] Justification first of all concerns the justifying God's encountering the human in Jesus Christ with the forgiveness of sins and salvation, but, says Bayer in his "Preface to the English Edition" of this work, precisely because of this, justification also leads to and encompasses the theology of creation and eschatology and defines them as God's gracious works done "without any merit or worthiness" on the part of the human, fellow creatures, or creation but upon the basis of God's goodness alone.[66] Justifica-

---

61. Bayer, "Justification as the Basis and Boundary of Theology," 273-92; Bayer, *Leibliches Wort*, 19-34.

62. Bayer, "Justification as the Basis and Boundary of Theology," 273, 288 n. 1; Bayer, *Leibliches Wort*, 19.

63. Bayer, "Justification as the Basis and Boundary of Theology," 273-74; Bayer, *Leibliches Wort*, 19-20.

64. Bayer, "Justification as the Basis and Boundary of Theology," 286-87; Bayer, *Leibliches Wort*, 33-32.

65 Bayer, *Living by Faith*, xi-xii; Bayer, *Aus Glauben Leben*, 9.

66. Bayer, *Living by Faith*, xiii-xvi (not in German editions).

tion, therefore, is not just a doctrine of salvation, nor is it only the "article upon which the Church stands or falls." In addition to these, says Bayer, justification entails all of theology, personal history, world history, and even natural history in as much as it defines who God is in relation to the created order and the eschaton as well as what human beings and fellow creatures are in relation to the gracious, justifying God.[67] For, justification is not one theme of theology amongst others but is constituent of the whole of theology. There is in fact no other theme outside of justification, says Bayer in *Aus Glauben Leben*. Justification embraces all of theology and all of reality.[68] This inclusive description of justification shapes how Bayer addresses problems he sees within both Roman Catholic and Protestant theology.

Bayer identifies two problems with Roman Catholic theology with regard to justification as the subject matter of theology. The first of these problems arises out of the ecumenical dialog surrounding the *Joint Declaration on the Doctrine of Justification* composed and signed by the Lutheran World Federation and the Roman Catholic Church. According to Bayer, the main flaw in the *JDDJ* is that it approaches justification as one doctrine amongst others rather than that which categorizes the whole of theology. In so doing, *JDDJ* fails because it does not actually address the reformational view of justification with all of its breadth and depth.[69]

The second problem with Roman Catholic theology in relation to justification as the subject matter of theology is that God's gracious justification of the sinner in Christ does not form the sole content matter of theology in the traditional (i.e. Thomistic) Catholic approach to theology. In fact, Catholicism, following Aquinas, has taken an Aristotelian approach to theology as "the science (or knowledge) of God."[70] In the Thomistic approach, the subject matter of theology is defined simply as "God." Bayer identifies that this presents all sorts of theological problems because it brings the content of philosophy directly into theology, violating the distinctions between the two disciplines and muddling the true subject matter of theology with other concerns and kinds of knowledge.[71] This confusion of philosophy and theology in Thomistic thought is driven by the desire for

---

67. Ibid, xi–xii; Bayer, *Aus Glauben Leben*, 9–10. Bayer, "Justification as the Basis and Boundary of Theology," 274–75; Bayer, *Leibliches Wort*, 20–21.

68. Bayer, *Living by Faith*, 9; Bayer, *Aus Glauben Leben*, 21.

69. Bayer, *Living by Faith*, xiv, 9; Bayer, *Aus Glauben Leben*, 21. Bayer, "What Is Evangelical?" 2, 11–12; Bayer, *Zugesagte Gegenwart*, 23, 32–33.

70. Bayer, *Theology the Lutheran Way*, 98; Bayer, *Theologie*, 408–9. Bayer, *Martin Luther's Theology*, 37–38; Bayer, *Martin Luthers Theologie*, 34–35. Cf. Thomas Aquinas, *Summa Theologiae*, Ia.I, 24–27.

71. Bayer, "What is Evangelical?" 12; Bayer, *Zugesagte Gegenwart*, 33.

a synthesis of all knowledge through theology, an Aristotelian metaphysic uniting general truth through an all embracing system.[72] Such working towards a harmonious summary of all general truth of reality, says Bayer, is incompatible with the reformational understanding of the subject matter of theology and presents a serious (perhaps insurmountable) obstacle for an ecumenical theology.[73]

Yet, in Bayer's opinion, Roman Catholic theology is not the only tradition that has mistreated the subject of theology. If Thomistic Catholicism has focused on the vague "knowledge of God" and general knowledge of reality to the expense of God's justification of the sinner as the true subject matter of theology, Protestant theology, particularly the modern German Protestant theological tradition, has moved the focus of theological study away from the God and God's justification of the human sinner, to the human self alone. Bayer has labeled this introspective view of modernity, embodied first and foremost by Kant's turn to the subject, as "the modern narcissism."[74] Bayer maintains that the turn of the human inward embodied in German philosophy and theology from Kant onwards has transformed the subject of theology from God's justification of the human to the human itself alone.[75]

Like the young man in the classical Greek myth, says Bayer, the human being through modern German philosophy and theology is subjectively obsessed with itself alone. While it is true, admits Bayer, that narcissism is not relegated to the era of modernity and has, as the myth relates, been present in humanity since ancient times, never before has narcissism so categorized the philosophy and *Zeitgeist* of an era quite like it has in modernity. For, in modernity, the human self loves and has become obsessed with its own reflected image, as was the youth looking into the water. In modernity, the entirety of the human species in a particular epoch has taken the narcissism upon itself so that the human does not look outside itself for an explanation of its existence. Yet, modern philosophy and theology has surpassed narcissism of other eras, in that it has spiritualized and absolutized this self obsession of the human with its own reflection.[76] Not being satisfied with simple self-love at the expense of others, the modern human, through mod-

---

72. Bayer, "What is Evangelical?" 10–11; Bayer, *Zugesagte Gegenwart*, 31–32. Bayer, *Martin Luther's Theology*, 31–32, 37; Bayer, *Martin Luthers Theologie*, 29, 34.

73. Bayer, "What is Evangelical?" 10–11; Bayer, *Zugesagte Gegenwart*, 31–32. Bayer, *Martin Luther's Theology*, 37; Bayer, *Martin Luthers Theologie*, 34.

74. Bayer, "The Modern Narcissus," 301–2; Bayer, "Der neutzeitliche Narziß," in *Gott als Autor*, 73–74.

75. Bayer, *Was ist das: Theologie?*, 24.

76. Bayer, "The Modern Narcissus," 301–2; Bayer, *Gott als Autor*, 74

ern philosophy and theology, has sought to identify and relate to not only itself but also others, the world of nature, the cosmos, world history, and freedom from no other basis than its subject self.[77]

Bayer faults Kant directly for the modern human's turn inward upon itself. In particular, he identifies Kant's turn towards the subject and assertion of the importance of freedom through autonomy realized in ethical action as the tangible cause for the modern narcissism.[78] Kant, says Bayer, begins his theories from no other starting point that the human self and orients them ultimately towards nothing outside the human self. According to Bayer, Kantian thought is not just solipsistic and narcissistic, ultimately, it is atheistic, for Kant admits no truth outside of the consciousness, reason, and will of the individual, autonomous humans self.[79] Even the law, which Bayer sees as God's external means for informing and guiding human ethical thought and action, is secularized and humanized. Stripping the law of its divine origin and existence external to the human, Kant turns the law into the internal "categorical imperative" of the human conscience. Furthermore, says Bayer, since Kant understands human freedom as coming from the human will's enacting of the internal law, freedom itself is inherent to the human as a self-realized act of will.[80] Bayer identifies that by doing this, Kant has set the stage for a definite tradition of narcissism in modern philosophy and theology of self-creation, a tradition in which the human self constitutes itself in its own image.[81]

The result of this modern turn inwards begun by Kant is a series of transformations of the subject of theology from God's justification of the human sinner to the individual, autonomous human's assertion of itself. Though Bayer ultimately places blame on Kant for this curving of the modern self inward upon itself,[82] he negatively asseses other modern philosophers and theologians of the German tradition as participating in and even furthering this realignment of the subject of theology with the self and forming various secularizing, anthropocentric, and ultimately atheistic transformations of the subject of theology.[83] Bayer sees Fichte and

77. Bayer, "The Modern Narcissus," 301–2; Bayer, *Gott als Autor*, 74.

78. Bayer, *Leibliches Wort*, 36. Freedom in Response, 140; Freiheit als Antwort, 166.

79. Bayer, *Freedom in Response*, 140; Bayer, *Freiheit als Antwort*, 166.

80. Bayer, *Freedom in Response*, 140–41; Freiheit als Antwort, 166–167. Bayer, "The Modern Narcissus," 302; Bayer, Bayer, *Gott als Autor*, 74.

81. Bayer, "The Modern Narcissus," 302; Bayer, *Gott als Autor*, 74.

82. Bayer, "The Modern Narcissus," 302; Bayer, *Gott als Autor*, 74. Bayer, *Leibliches Wort*, 36.

83 Bayer, *Was ist das: Theologie?*, 24. Bayer, *Theology the Lutheran Way*, 139ff.; Bayer, *Theologie*, 453ff. Bayer, "Justification as the Basis and Boundary of Theology,"

the early Romantics, such as Novalis, as radicalizing this anthropocentric revolution and building an educational program along these lines, aimed at self-realization.[84] Hegel, says Bayer, rationalizes and spiritualizes Kant's turn inwards by grounding the common human existence, world history, and the spirit (*Geist*) of the universe in relation to the reason of the human self. For Bayer, Hegel thus represents a rationalist, anthropocentric transformation of the subject of theology in which the human self frees itself by its own rationalist spirit.[85] Though Bayer does admit that Hegel tried to react against Kantian subjectivity with his theo-philosophy of *Geist*, he ultimately succeeded only in rationalizing or spiritualizing the subjectivity by connecting the human *Geist* with the universal *Geist* of the cosmos.[86]

Bayer even sees the contemporary and friend of Hamann, Johann Gottfried Herder, as participating in this modern tradition of Narcissism. In his philosophy of "creation working itself out," Herder posits that through the ongoing work of creation, the human becomes a self-creator, as the representative and image of God on earth.[87] This idea of self-creation is heightened by Nietzsche who, as Bayer highlights, is quite open about the fact that he seeks to displace God's work upon the human with the human's own work of self-creation.[88] It is Marx, however, who Bayer sees as the great example of the modern human's self-creation at its height, since Marx depicts the human being as actually creating itself and its meaning through its own work.[89]

Yet, the figure subsequent to Kant in the modern German philosophical and theological tradition to whom Bayer has given the most attention is the great liberal Protestant theologian, Friedrich Schleiermacher. According to Bayer, Schleiermacher theologizes and existentializes the modern human's turn inward.[90] Schleiermacher has accomplished this, says Bayer, by mak-

---

277; Bayer, *Leibliches Wort*, 23.

84. Bayer, "The Modern Narcissus," 302; Bayer, *Gott als Autor*, 74. Bayer, "Justification as the Basis and Boundary of Theology," 277–79; Bayer, *Leibliches Wort*, 23–26.

85. Bayer, "The Modern Narcissus," 302; Bayer, *Gott als Autor*, 74. Bayer, *Theology the Lutheran Way*, 146–147; Bayer, *Theologie*, 460–62.

86. Bayer, "The Modern Narcissus," 303–304; Bayer, *Gott als Autor*, 75–76.

87. Bayer, "Self-Creation? On the Dignity of Human Beings, 275–76; Bayer, "Selbstschöpfung?: Von der Würde des Menschen, in *Zugesagte Gegenwart*, 272–73.

88. Bayer, "Self-Creation?" 275–76; Bayer, *Zugesagte Gegenwart*, 272–73.

89. Bayer, "With Luther in the Present," 3–4; Bayer, "Mit Luther in der Gegenwart: Die diagnostische Kraft reformatorischer Theologie," in *Zugesagte Gegenwart*, 11–12. Bayer, *Theology the Lutheran Way*, 111; Bayer, *Theologie*, 423. Bayer, "Justification as the Basis and Boundary of Theology," 277; Bayer, *Leibliches Wort*, 23.

90. Bayer, *Was ist das: Theologie?*, 24. Bayer, *Theology the Lutheran Way*, 148ff.; Bayer, *Theologie*, 463ff.

ing God's existence fit within the broader category of human consciousness. For Schleiermacher, God is therefore subject to the consciousness of the individual human self through the "feeling of absolute dependence."[91] Accordingly, it should come as little surprise that Bayer has largely rejected the contemporary German Schleiermacher renaissance.[92]

According to Bayer, all of these various facets of the modern narcissism have in common that they begin from the human alone and that in so doing, they have transformed the subject of theology from God's justification of the human sinner into something else. In so doing, says Bayer, they have destroyed the true subject of theology in modern thought and have put the human self in the place of God's work of justification in Christ.[93] The final result of this tradition of transformation is, ironically perhaps, that, instead of finding comfort in being the final creator and interpreter of its own existence, the human self becomes isolated, alienated, and meaningless.[94] By removing the God who justifies from the subject of theology, the modern self condemns itself to an existence of always futilely seeking some sense of self-justification,[95] like Josef K. in Kafka's *Der Prozeß*,[96] descending into "a hell of self-knowledge."[97] As Bayer is an inheritor of this modern German tradition of the autonomous self, it is in opposition to these secular and anthropological transformations of the subject of theology that he articulates his own theology with its theological center of justification.[98]

---

91. Bayer, *Theology the Lutheran Way*, 148-150; Bayer, *Theologie*, 463-465. Bayer, "The Modern Narcissus," 302-3; Bayer, *Gott als Autor*, 74-75. Bayer makes this argument against Schleiermacher along other lines in his essay "Schleiermacher und Luther," which he presented to the International Schleiermacher Congress in Berlin in 1984. Here, Bayer argues that Schleiermacher transformed Luther's "doctrine of the Word" in which the human is addressed by God into a "doctrine of faith" in which God is subject to the subjective of the human self. Oswald Bayer, "Schleiermacher und Luther," 1006-9.

92. Helmer, "The Subject of Theology in the Thought of Oswald Bayer," 21.

93. Bayer, *Theology the Lutheran Way*, 111; Bayer, *Theologie*, 454.

94. Bayer, "With Luther in the Present," 3-4; Bayer, *Zugesagte Gegenwart*, 11-12. Bayer, "The Modern Narcissus," 301-2; Bayer, *Gott als Autor*, 73-74.

95. Bayer, *Living by Faith*, 10; Bayer, *Aus Glauben Leben*, 22. Bayer, *Autorität und Kritik*, 3. Here, Bayer adopts Friedrich Engels' image of the human being standing always before "Richterstuhl der Vernunft" having to give a self-justification for its existence. Cf. Engels, *Anti-Dühring*, in *Marx-Engels Werke, Band 20*, 16.

96. Cf. Kafka, *Der Prozeß*, 45ff.; ET *The Trial*, 39ff.

97. Bayer, "Justification as the Basis and Boundary of Theology," 281; Bayer, *Leibliches Wort*, 23.

98. Bayer, *Theology the Lutheran Way*, 111, 170-71ff.; Bayer, *Theologie*, 454; 486-87ff. Helmer, "The Subject of Theology in the Thought of Oswald Bayer," 21.

Bayer's definition of the subject matter of theology as God's justification of the human sinner stands in contrast to other approaches to theology, which define theology as the study of God. Bayer adopts his view of the subject matter of theology from Luther and argues that it is the essential core and norm of reformational theology as well as of all true theology. Bayer explains that this view of the subject matter of theology is not reductionist but that it presents God's action in Christ as the basis and boundary for theology, the source from which all statements in theology flow from and to which they are oriented. Bayer argues that other approaches to the subject matter of theology have not treated the reformational view correctly. While the Roman Catholic ecumenical endeavor surrounding the *Joint Declaration on the Doctrine of Justification* has not taken the breadth and depth of the reformational view of justification as the subject of theology seriously, the German Protestant tradition in philosophy and theology has transformed the subject matter of theology into a narcissistic obsession of the human being with itself. Bayer offers his contemporary reformational view of the subject matter of theology as an alternative course for doing theology.

The reformational definition of the subject matter of theology as God's justification of the human sinner, which Bayer adopts from Luther, functions as the essential core of Bayer's theology. Defining the subject matter of theology as God's justification of the sinner certainly shapes Bayer's overall approach theology, but it also affects how Bayer approaches particular themes in systematic theology. One of these themes is the doctrine of the hidden God. Since Bayer understands justification as the only true subject matter of theology and as the norm that forms the basis and boundary for everything said in theology, his understanding of the hidden God is ultimately and inextricably linked with justification. In order to understand the exact nature of this connection, however, it will be necessary to explain first how Bayer describes justification as taking place. This I will do in chapter five, where I will describe Bayer's teaching on the nature of justification in some depth, but at the present, I will turn to address how Bayer defines the data of theology.

Gott als Poet: Hermeneutics and the Divinely Given Data of Theology

Bayer's definition of the subject matter of theology inevitably carries with it a certain approach to identifying and understanding the nature and function of the data of theology. Just as Bayer restricts the subject matter of theology to the sinning human and the justifying God, he relegates what constitutes the data given for the doing of theology to God's words of condemnation and justification in the law and the gospel and to God's hiddenness. For Bayer, the data of theology as such are not things extent in the empirical world for humans to discover and interpret through use of their rational faculties. Instead, argues Bayer, showing once again how Hamann has influenced his theological thought, the data of theology are God's external words, which come to the human from outside the human and interpret and effect the destiny of the human. Following Luther, Bayer states that God encounters the human sinner particularly through the means of the effective words of God's command in the law and God's promise in the gospel. These two words of God's to humans must not, says Bayer, be collapsed but distinguished. Nevertheless, it is clear that Bayer also understands the gospel as the more ultimate of these two words. Furthermore, Bayer also identifies a third data for theology, a third way in which God encounters humans: hiddenness. By including hiddenness within the data of theology, alongside law and gospel, Bayer brings Luther's doctrine of the hidden God into the very method of theology itself. Though this move by Bayer will have to be discussed at more length in chapter six, I will introduce it here in the context of how Bayer delineates the data given to theologian for the doing of theology.

Since the subject of theology is not "God" generally but specifically God's accusation and justification of the human sinner, the parameters of what constitutes the data of theology are also very specifically defined by Bayer. The data of theology, says Bayer, are precisely the words that God uses to condemn and to justify the sinful human, namely, the law and the gospel.[99] God encounters the human sinner particularly through the means of these effective words of command and promise. There is no other way of human encounter with the divine and no other way of human knowledge of the divine. Bayer argues that there is no general knowledge of God accessible through human reason or, as Schleiermacher taught, through a universal human experience of God in the natural order—at least not a positive and quantifiable one. To the contrary, Bayer maintains that true knowledge of God—particularly of God's condemnation and justification of the sinner—comes only through God's revelatory address to the human, address in law and gospel. The theologian's knowledge of the subject matter of theology must, therefore, be a knowledge taken precisely from these divinely given data, wherein God comes to the human as the condemning

---

99. Bayer, *Theology the Lutheran Way*, 17; Bayer, *Theologie*, 36–37.

judge in the command of the law and as justifying Savior in the promise of the gospel.[100]

Bayer operates under the idea that the kind of knowledge entailed in the doing of theology (i.e. the mode of theology) is experiential wisdom. For Bayer, adopting the idea from Luther that the subject and norm of theology is not a general knowledge of God but the specific subject matter of the human sinner and the justifying God, the experience that makes a theologian is not experience in general, nor is it the experience of a feeling of dependence as it is for Schleiermacher. Instead, drawing from both Luther and Hamann, Bayer understands such experience as the particular experience of being addressed by the living God.

As has already been noted, Bayer uses Hamann's understanding of human existence as *passio*, in contrast to Kant's view of human existence as *actio*, in his definition of the mode of theology. This use of Hamann's critique of Kant extends also to Bayer's definition of the data of theology. Bayer's specific use of Hamann in his articulation of the data of theology may be seen in his adoption of Hamann's view of *Gott als Autor* (God as author) or *Gott als Poet* (God as poet). Bayer has commented extensively on how Hamann formulated his understanding of God as author and poet as a response and alternative epistemology to the transcendental epistemology of Kant.

In the first of his three critiques, *The Critique of Pure Reason*, Kant states that there are certain *a priori* "pure concepts of understanding" or "categories" of the mind, which are immanent within the human subject and through use of which the human subject processes the *a posteriori* data of the sensory world.[101] In his work on Hamann, *Zeitgenosse im Widerspruch*, Bayer argues that Kant, in a way that is atypical for the great Königsberg professor when dealing with most subjects, uncritically presumes that reason is presently extant and that it is timeless and eternal. Kant does not account for or even investigate the question about the origin of human reason.[102] Instead, he assumes that reason is a given, leaving unanswered what Bayer esteems to be a basic philosophical question with regard to epistemology: "How is the ability of thought itself possible?"[103] Bayer states that Kant, by assuming the existence and functionality of reason without qualification,

---

100. Bayer, *Theology the Lutheran Way*, 17, 101–4; Bayer, *Theologie*, 412–15.

101. Kant, *Critique of Pure Reason*, 111ff. Mattes, *The Role of Justification in Contemporary Theology*, 150.

102. Bayer, *Zeitgenosse im Widerspruch*, 187; Bayer, *A Contemporary in Dissent*, 164–65.

103. ". . . wie ist das Vermögen zu denken selbst möglich." Bayer, *Zeitgenosse im Widerspruch*, 187; Bayer, *A Contemporary in Dissent*, 164–65.

grounds human existence and meaning in nothing outside the autonomous human self. Bayer calculates that this error did not end with Kant but that the latter bequeathed this fallacy to the entire German philosophical and theological tradition, which embodies the Kantian turn toward the subject as a modern Narcissism.[104]

While he shows how Kant leaves unanswered the question begged by his entire philosophical project: "How is thought possible?,"[105] Bayer demonstrates that Hamann does not make the same error as his fellow Königsberger. In response to this question raised but ultimately ignored by Kant's philosophy, Hamann brings to the fore the discussion of language. The phenomenon of language, says Hamann, precedes that of thought or reason.[106] Though Hamann does address language empirically in terms of human development, he argues first and foremost from the standpoint of Christian theology. For Hamann, language is not just the phenomenon of humans putting together sounds and syllables. Before that, language is a phenomenon of the divine; it is God's own Word, whereby God created and sustains the world. God created the universe through language, says Hamann, and the world of nature itself and human reason are built upon and dependent upon the language of God. Without language, says Hamann, there is no reason, no world, no reality![107]

In this light, God is seen by Hamann as an author or poet (*Gott als Autor*), who speaks reality into existence and upholds reality by God's Word.[108] Far from seeing religion only in terms of moral obligation and action, Hamann understands theology as the fundamental backdrop for all philosophical understanding of reality. Whereas Kant relegates God to moralism and interprets religion and humanity only ethically, Hamann approaches God, religion, humanity, and all of reality from the standpoint of a linguistic aestheticism. In this aesthetic depiction of reality, human beings are God's creatures whose lives are shaped and interpreted by God's Word.[109] More-

---

104. Mattes, *The Role of Justification in Contemporary Theology*, 155. Bayer, "The Modern Narcissus," 302-3; Bayer, *Gott als Autor*, 73-74.

105. Bayer, *Zeitgenosse im Widerspruch*, 187; Bayer, *A Contemporary in Dissent*, 164-65.

106. Bayer, *Zeitgenosse im Widerspruch*, 187; Bayer, *A Contemporary in Dissent*, 164-65. Hamann, *Sämtliche Werke* 3:231, 240. Beutel, *Aufklärung in Deutschland*, 327.

107. Bayer, *Vernunft ist Sprache*, 4. Bayer, *Zeitgenosse im Widerspruch*, 219-21. Hamann, *Briefwechsel* 5:95.

108. Bayer, *Zeitgenosse im Widerspruch*, 75-83; Bayer, *A Contemporary in Dissent*, 54-62. Bayer, "God as Author of My Life History," 444-46; Bayer, *Gott als Autor*, 30-33. Hamann, *Aesthetica in nuce* (1762), in *Sämtliche Werke*, 2:140, 206. Beutel, *Aufklärung in Deutschland*, 327.

109. Bayer, *Autorität und Kritik*, 5-6.

over, Hamann sees nature (i.e. God's creation) itself as the medium for God's creative and sustaining Word. If God is an author and poet for Hamann, the world and the universe are God's text, the record of God's life-giving speech. In this understanding of reality, the empirical world of nature is not raw data to be processed, analyzed, and judged by the faculty of human reason but that through which God brings about human reason and existence. The human no longer interprets nature but, rather, through nature (i.e. creation) God interprets the human, who passively undergoes the experience of such interpretive address as a sufferer.[110]

The influence of Hamann's understanding of suffering and *passio* may be observed in how Bayer, in discussing the data of theology in law and gospel, deals with the subject of hermeneutics and the interpretation of Scripture. Bayer here quotes Hamann approvingly, adopting the latter's notion that the theologian does not primarily interpret Holy Scripture but, rather, God through Holy Scripture interprets the theologian. In this way, says Bayer again countering Kant, the human subject is interpreted by something external, which he or she experiences, instead of being the subjective interpreter of outward experiences.[111] At this point, Bayer reflects both Hamann's metacritique of Kant's assumption of the preeminence of human powers of reasoning and Hamann's insistence instead on the preeminence of speech—particularly divine speech—as that which determines human destiny. The speech, the address of the author-God comes first, says Bayer in agreement with Hamann, for without God's Word, there is no reason and no reality: "*ohne Wort, kein Welt.*"[112]

Bayer expands Hamann's philosophical teaching of God as author and the human as addressed by God into a linguistic approach to the data of systematic theology that is thoroughly Lutheran in terms of understanding the Word of God to humans as law and gospel. In the law, says Bayer, God speaks to the human and against the human on account of human sin. As such God's address against the human in the law is at the same time both accusation and judgment, conviction and sentence. God's Word in the law thus constitutes direct divine address: "Adam, Eve, where are you?" "You are the man."[113] To be sure, Bayer also understands the law as functioning in a civil or "political" sense as well, to restrain evil and order creation,[114]

---

110. Bayer, *Schöpfung als Anrede*, 13–18. Hamann, *Sämtliche Werke* 2:195–217.

111. Bayer, *Martin Luther's Theology*, 71; Bayer, *Martin Luthers Theologie*, 64–65.

112. Bayer, *Zeitgenosse im Wiederspruch*, 187–92; Bayer, *A Contemporary in Dissent*, 165–70. Bayer, *Schöpfung als Anrede*, 44–45. Bayer, *Martin Luther's Theology*, 95–97; Bayer, *Martin Luthers Theologie*, 87–89.

113. Bayer, *Martin Luther's Theology*, 61; Bayer, *Martin Luthers Theologie*, 55.

114. Bayer, *Theology the Lutheran Way*, 106; Bayer, *Theologie*, 417.

functioning particularly in the realm of ethics through the "three estates of creation."[115] Yet, he understands the primary sense of the law to be its work of accusation and condemnation through God's speech against the human sinner, thereby effecting judgment.[116]

Yet, if the direct address of God in the law effects judgment, according to Bayer, much more does God's Word in the gospel effect salvation. Here Bayer uses Hamann's notion of the author-God's effecting of the human's destiny through divine speech as a tool to aid in constructing a contemporary interpretation of Luther's teaching of justification by faith alone through the promise of God in Jesus Christ. In the gospel, God addresses the human not in accusation and judgment but with a promise. This promise is an effectual address of God that does what it says, justifying the human sinner before God and opening a new relationship between God and the human wherein address becomes dialogue between God and the human, a relationship of communion.[117] In this way, the one and only place where the human and God can coexist peacefully is within the realm of this Word of the author-God, within the space that is opened up by the promise of the gospel in Jesus Christ.[118]

One must be careful, says Bayer to maintain this distinction between the law and the gospel. The law and the gospel are two different and even contradictory words of God, says Bayer. While in the law God demands and condemns, in the gospel God promises, saves, and gives life.[119] Drawing once again from Luther's theological works in the formulation of his own theology, Bayer relates how, according to Luther, the mark of a real theologian is one who knows how to handle properly the data of theology, that is, one who knows how to distinguish between the word of God in the law and the word of God in the gospel.[120] Bayer further appeals to Luther's treatise of 1520, *The Freedom of a Christian*, in emphasizing the importance of both the law and the gospel and the distinguishing between these two in the work of theology.[121] Following Luther, Bayer maintains that the two words that make up the data of theology bring with them their own inherent contradiction: the same God who accuses in the law absolves in the

115. Bayer, *Freedom in Response*, 63–64, 105–8; Bayer, *Freiheit als Antwort*, 45–46, 132–36.
116. Bayer, *Martin Luther's Theology*, 61; Bayer, *Martin Luthers Theologie*, 55. Bayer, *Theology the Lutheran Way*, 102; Bayer, *Theologie*, 413.
117. Mattes, *The Role of Justification in Contemporary Theology*, 150.
118. Bayer, *Martin Luther's Theology*, 39; Bayer, *Martin Luthers Theologie*, 36.
119. Bayer, *Martin Luther's Theology*, 61; Bayer, *Martin Luthers Theologie*, 55–56.
120. Bayer, "Gesetz und Evangelium," 155.
121. Bayer, *Martin Luther's Theology*, 59–60; Bayer, *Martin Luthers Theologie*, 54–55.

gospel. The God who speaks in the data of theology speaks contradictorily, speaking *against* the sinful human on the one hand and speaking *for* the same sinful human on the other hand. Such data for theology, such divinely spoken words, necessitate that theology address this contradictory situation of the human addressed by God.[122]

In his *Twenty-Four Theses on the Renewal of Lutheranism by Concentrating on the Gospel of Justification*, Bayer summarizes his understanding of the proper relationship between the two Words of God in the law and the gospel. The law and the gospel must be distinguished as two divine Words—one condemns and one gives life—but this distinction, says Bayer, exists ultimately in order to serve the gospel.[123] By this, Bayer does not mean that the gospel forms an overarching Word as one might find in the thought of theologians such as Barth. On the contrary, Bayer asserts over and against Barth's "monistic doctrine of the Word of God," that the distinction between God's Word in the law and God's Word in the gospel must be maintained in order for the gospel to come forth clearly as the gospel, as God's radical, pure, free, unmerited, unconditional gift without any law or hint of command in it whatsoever.[124]

In this context of distinction, Bayer's categorization of the gospel as the Word of God that is ultimately served by the distinction cannot be understood as a proposal for the unity of law and gospel underneath a more overarching gracious Word of God. Rather, Bayer describes the gospel not as a greater unity of the Word of God but as the more ultimate Word of God, seeing the gospel as bearing a certain eschatological quality not borne by the law. The Word of God in the gospel, says Bayer, is the final and decisive Word of God concerning the identity and destiny of the human.[125] The Word of God in the gospel is the only Word of God that can make this statement of eschatological finality; the law cannot and a third general divine Word of amalgamated law and gospel that purports to show the character of God certainly cannot.[126] The Word of God in the gospel is opposed to the Word

---

122. Bayer, *Martin Luther's Theology*, 60–62; Bayer, *Martin Luthers Theologie*, 54–56.

123. Bayer, "Twenty-Four Theses," 73; Bayer, *Zugesagte Gegenwart*, 34.

124. Bayer, *Theology the Lutheran Way*, 125; Bayer, *Theologie*, 438. Bayer, "Twenty-Four Theses," 74; Bayer, *Zugesagte Gegenwart*, 35. In his work *Createdness and Ethics*, Hans Schaeffer has noted how Bayer relates in his "Selbstdarstellung," that although he began his theological career heavily under the influence of Barth's theology of the Word. As he became more acquainted with Luther's thought, however, he adopted positions contrary to Barth, including the bodily means of the Word (i.e. *Leibliches Wort*) and the idea that the Word creates its own space to be heard." Schaeffer, *Createdness and Ethics*, 103. "Selbstdarstellung," 303ff. *CD* II.1, 236. *CD* IV.1, 347.

125. Bayer, *Martin Luther's Theology*, 61; Bayer, *Martin Luthers Theologie*, 56.

126. Bayer, *Martin Luther's Theology*, 61; Bayer, *Martin Luthers Theologie*, 56.

of God in the law and actually brings about the human's liberation from the very law through which God speaks against the human. The gospel is the end of the law in so much as God's speaking for the human in the gospel puts an end to God's speaking against the human in the law.[127]

Furthermore, the gospel is more ultimate than the law for Bayer, not only because it is eschatologically ultimate but also because it is primary. Bayer argues that the gospel, and not the law, is the primal and primordial Word of God. Although Bayer does see a certain limited role of the law in ordering creation (i.e. the "political" sense of the law),[128] he is insistent that it was through the promise of the gospel, and not through the law, that God created the universe.[129] God created the universe out of nothing, and there was nothing that the universe or its human inhabitants did in order to be created. When addressing the question of what is the proper sequence of the law and the gospel in theology, Bayer argues that one must understand, as does Luther, that in a certain sense the Word of God in the gospel precedes the Word of God in the law. While the law was added because of sin (Galatians 3:19), the gospel was present in the beginning as the Word through which God gave God's good gifts of creation to humanity.[130] Thus, the Word of God through which God created human beings is one of unconditional gift, and as such it is pure gospel.[131]

For Bayer, the gospel is the primal and ultimate Word of God. This is because God used the gospel, and not the law, to speak the world into existence and to sustain it, and because God's speech for the human in the gospel brings the human liberation from God's speaking against the human in the law. Finally, it is the gospel, and not the law that discloses God's true and ultimate will towards the human, for in the gospel, as in nowhere else, God speaks to the human for the human in such a way that the gospel is the only place in which God and the human sinner can coexist peacefully.

127. Bayer, "Justification as the Basis and Boundary of Theology," 280–84; Bayer, *Leibliches Wort*, 26–30. Bayer, *Martin Luther's Theology*, 61; Bayer, *Martin Luthers Theologie*, 56.

128. Bayer, *Theology the Lutheran Way*, 106; Bayer, *Theologie*, 417. Bayer, *Freedom in Response*, 63–64, 105–8; Bayer, *Freiheit als Antwort*, 45–46, 132–36.

129. Bayer, "The Doctrine of Justification and Ontology," 45–48; Bayer, "Rechtfertigungslehre und Ontologie," in *Zugesagte Gegenwart*, 197–200.

130. Bayer, "The Doctrine of Justification and Ontology," 45–48; Bayer, *Zugesagte Gegenwart*, 197–200. Bayer, *Martin Luther's Theology*, 62–63; Bayer, *Martin Luthers Theologie*, 56–57. Concerning God's work of creation as pure gift: Cf. Bayer, "I believe that God Has Created Me and All that Exists, 151–56; Bayer, "Ich glaube, daß mich Gott geschaffen hat samt allen Kreaturen," in *Schöpfung als Anrede*, 103–7.

131. Bayer, "The Doctrine of Justification and Ontology," 45–48; Bayer, *Zugesagte Gegenwart*, 197–200.

Thus, it is this Word that Bayer understands to be the ultimate source and datum of theology: the Word of God's promise of forgiveness for the sinner, in which the sinning human and the justifying God stand together.[132]

Yet, Bayer also identifies a third data of theology, apart from the law and the gospel: the hiddenness of God. According to Bayer, God's hiddenness is a datum of theology wherein God encounters the human, yet it is not as if God speaks something to the human sinner in this datum of theology. On the contrary, God is unintelligible and even silent towards the human in this encounter.[133] Furthermore, God's hiddenness is categorically different from the law and the gospel. While God displays God's wrath in hiddenness as God also speaks judgment through the law, the wrath of God towards the human sinner in hiddenness is different from God's wrath in the law. God's wrath is understandable in the law, says Bayer, but God's wrath is radically incomprehensible in hiddenness.[134] In hiddenness, the human experiences God as sheer terror or primal dread through "catastrophes of nature, unrectifiable injustice, innocent suffering, starvation, murder, war, incurable illness, and the tragic death of the young" and through the spiritual attack of God against the justified human in the agonizing struggle of *tentatio*.[135]

Bayer thus brings Luther's doctrine of the hiddenness of God outside of revelation into his very approach to theology itself. Bayer identifies the human experience of God's hiddenness as one of the data of theology alongside and distinct from the law and the gospel. In Bayer's thinking hiddenness is not subsumed within the law-gospel distinction but in some way operates outside of it. The exact way this aspect of Bayer's approach to theology works itself and what fruit it bears in his theology will be addressed more fully in chapters six and seven. For the present, however, it must be noted that Bayer is pioneering new territory in contemporary theology, or, at the very least, he is embarking upon a seldom-trodden path by taking Luther's doctrine of the hiddenness of God up into his approach to how theology should be done.

Contrary to any Kantian notion of the data of theology as phenomena to be interpreted by human reason, Bayer describes the data of theology as God's address to the human, which interprets the human. In this respect, Bayer draws heavily from Hamann. Yet, Bayer also demonstrates the influence of Luther upon his theology through his argument for the distinction

---

132. Bayer, *Martin Luther's Theology*, 39–41; Bayer, *Martin Luthers Theologie*, 36–38.

133. Bayer, *Martin Luther's Theology*, 198; Bayer, *Martin Luthers Theologie*, 178–79.

134. Bayer, *Martin Luther's Theology*, 196–199; Bayer, *Martin Luthers Theologie*, 177–79.

135. Bayer, *Martin Luther's Theology*, 198; Bayer, *Martin Luthers Theologie*, 178–79. Bayer, *Theology the Lutheran Way*, 104; Bayer, *Theologie*, 415–16.

between the law and the gospel. While Bayer understands the law as God's speech against the human and the Gospel as God's speech for the human, he sees the gospel as the more final Word of God in that it brings liberation from God's accusation in the law and in that it is both the primal and the eschatologically ultimate Word of God. In addition to these two Words of God, Bayer identifies the hiddenness of God as a third data of theology. Through this datum God enacts God's incomprehensible wrath against the human, which goes beyond the understandable wrath of the law and radically contradicts the gospel.

Summary

In order to understand the place of divine hiddenness in Bayer's theology, one must first have some knowledge of how it is that Bayer does theology. Bayer's approach to theology brings the doctrine of justification directly to the center of the theological enterprise. This approach is characterized by Bayer's particular understandings of the mode, method, subject matter, and data of theology. For Bayer, the mode of theology is not metaphysical science but experiential wisdom, in which the theologian truly experiences the work of God. The method of theology that flows from this mode is also experiential and knows no artificial distinction between theory and praxis. It encompasses prayer, meditation, and the agonizing struggle through which a theologian is made. The subject matter of theology, according to Bayer, is not simply "God" but God's accusation and justification of the sinful human. Narrowly defining the subject of theology does not constitute a minimalist approach to grand scope of theology, but it does determine that all of the aspects of theology will relate to this central point of God's justifying work. Such subject matter, says Bayer, is known from the data that God gives the human God's self: the law, the gospel, and God's hiddenness. These are the places in which the human knows God, as God here encounters and addresses the human. While the human is encountered by God and knows God as a condemning judge and complete terror in the law and God's hiddenness, the human can only ever ultimately know God in the promise of the gospel, where God encounters him or her as justifying Savior in Jesus Christ. In following these understandings of the mode, method, subject matter, and data of theology, Bayer lays the groundwork for a theology of justification. That is, he begins constructing a theology conditioned by and centered on justification, but also one that is ultimately concerned with justification, flowing from the divinely given data of theology that encounters the theologian in the promise of the gospel of Jesus Christ.

Bayer's shaping of his theology along the contours of justification ensures that God's hiddenness will be defined ultimately in terms of its relationship to God's justification of the sinner. Before describing the nature of this relationship, however, it is imperative first to describe the nature of justification itself, as described by Bayer. While one can see from the overall thrust of Bayer's approach to theology that hiddenness will be defined in relation to justification (as the norm of theology), one must first comprehend Bayer's actual teaching of justification, in order to understand his definition and description of God's hiddenness.

5

Bayer's Theology of Justification by the Promise

WHILE EVERY ASPECT OF Bayer's theology is determined at least in part by the central role assigned to God's justification of the human sinner, his specific understanding of the nature of justification gives a particular shape to his theology as a whole and to its component parts, including his understanding of the hiddenness of God. Bayer describes hiddenness as the radical contradiction of the gospel, that is, of God's justification of the sinner. To understand what this means in its fullness and what further effects it has on divine hiddenness in theology, it is imperative to understand that, for Bayer, justification entails God's speaking the Word of the gospel, which effects a new state of being for the human.

The Lutheran Doctrine of Justification

In defining the heart of theology in terms of God's justification of the sinner, Bayer stands in the trajectory of the Lutheran tradition flowing from the thought of the reformers and continuing through Lutheran orthodoxy into today. Bayer further echoes the teaching of the reformers that justification is a declaration of righteousness proclaimed by God for the believer on account of the righteousness of Jesus Christ. In the Lutheran understanding of this doctrine, God declares the sinner righteous by virtue of Christ's righteousness, which is given to the sinner by faith in Jesus Christ, a faith that is itself the gift of God.[1] This is the classic understanding of justification that

---

1. Cf. *Ap*, 5, in *BC* 126–27, 136–39; *BSLK*, 151–53, 166–67. *FC,Ep*, 3, in *BC* 495–96, *FC,SD*, 3, in *BC* 563–64.

both Luther and Melanchthon taught. In this understanding of justification, God declares the human being righteous for Christ's sake in God's sight through God's performative Word of the gospel, which comes to the human through the preaching office.[2]

Yet this reformational doctrine of justification so central to the Lutheran understanding of the Christian faith has not gone unchallenged and uninterpreted. There has, in fact, been a plurality of interpretations of Luther's and the Lutheran understanding of justification, including the important deviation of "essentialism" in the history of the modern German theological tradition. Albrecht Ritschl interpreted Luther's understanding of justification in terms of God's redemption of humanity in Jesus Christ in order to re-orient the human morally towards his or her neighbor in love through vocation in preparation for the coming ethical kingdom of God.[3] Karl Holl, on the other hand, interpreted the reformer's teaching on justification in the light of medieval mysticism to form a view of justification in which the human becomes essentially righteous through imparted faith and love. In Holl's estimation, such justification makes the human essentially righteous and works itself out through obedience demonstrated in ethical actions done in love by the human.[4] A slightly variant essentialist understanding of justification was present in Luther's own day in the theology of Andreas Osiander, who was opposed by both Luther and Melanchthon during Luther's lifetime and then later by Melanchthon and Calvin. Osiander taught that it was not sufficient for the sinner to be declared righteous before God for Christ's sake, as Luther and Melanchthon taught, but that the sinner had to become essentially righteous through God's infused grace and love.[5] Luther and Melanchthon rightly understood Osiander's divergent view on justification as an attack on the theological heart of the Reformation and as an interpolation of the power of the human being to participate in God's grace into the doctrine of justification *sola fide*, *sola gratia*, and *solus Christus* and thus condemned Osiander's teaching as heterodox.[6]

---

2. Luther, *Freedom of a Christian*, 59–61; WA 7:53–54. *LW* 36:37–39; WA 7:513–16. Luther, *Lectures on Galatians* (1535), *LW* 226–36; WA 40.1:358–73. *Loci* (1521), 171–72. CA 4–5, in *BC*, 38–41; *BSLK* 62–63. Ap, 4, in *BC*, 120–21ff.; *BSLK*, 142–43ff.

3. Ritschl, *The Christian Doctrine of Justification and Reconciliation*, 194–96, 394–96. Wilson, *Introduction to Modern Theology*, 128–29.

4. Holl, *Gesammelte Aufsätze zur Kirchengeschichte, Band I*, 124–25. Holl, *What Did Luther Understand by Religion?* 5, 11–12, 35–37, 42–43, 80–83, 93–95. Holl, *Die Rechtfertigungslehre im Licht der Geschichte des Protestantismus*, 10–15.

5. Wengert, *A Formula for Parish Practice*, 48–50.

6. Ibid. Paulson, *Lutheran Theology*, 147.

Various versions of the essentialist view have become very popular in New Testament studies, systematic theology, and ecumenical endeavors in wider Christian circles in recent decades. The prevalence of the "New Perspective of Paul,"[7] the moral theology of New Testament theologians such as Richard Hays,[8] the Lutheran-Catholic dialogue culminating in the *Joint Declaration on the Doctrine of Justification*,[9] and ecumenical systematic work such as that undertaken by Catholic-leaning Protestant theologians such as Michael Gorman,[10] and perhaps most significantly the "New Finnish" school's interpretation of Luther's understanding of justification[11] all reflect a desire to abandon what they fear is a "legal fiction" in the reformational understanding of justification in favor of a "participatory" form of justification in which the believer becomes righteous and "divinized" through a combination of infused grace and obedience to God.[12]

The New Finns, Gorman, and other theologians of the of the ontological, essentialist view of justification, including Wolfhart Pannenberg amongst others,[13] see justification by faith as primarily ontological in nature over and against justification as a declaration of the sinner's righteousness made by God for Christ's sake. According to this way of thinking, God does not simply declare the sinner righteous in God's sight. Instead, the sinner

---

7. Cf. Heen, "A Lutheran Response to the New Perspective on Paul," in *LQ* 24 (2010): 263–91. Sanders, *Paul and Palestinian Judaism*, 100, 438–42, 487–97. Dunn, *The Theology of Paul the Apostle*, 335–38.

8. Cf. Hays, *The Faith of Jesus Christ*, 30, 119–24. Hays, *A Moral Vision of the New Testament*, 29–32.

9. Cf. Gottfried Martens, "Inconsequential Signatures?" The *Joint Declaration on the Doctrine of Justification*, esp. the "Official Common Statement," 41–43.

10. Gorman, *Inhabiting the Cruciform God*, 41–44.

11. Having grown out of the ecumenical dialogue held in the nineteen-seventies between the Evangelical Lutheran Church of Finland and the Orthodox churches of both Finland and the Soviet Union this school has its roots and its most classic expression in the work of the Helsinki theologian Tuomo Mannermaa, *Christ Present in Faith*. According to Mannermaa, faith does not justify before God on the strength of a forensic declaration made by God that a sinner is righteous who has not really become righteous. Instead, the faith that justifies a sinner is one that entails a real, ontic bond between the sinner and Christ so that the human actually becomes righteous by his or her participating in Christ and Christ's indwelling of him or her. Cf. Mannermaa, *Christ Present in Faith*; Braaten and Jenson, eds., *Union with Christ*.

12. Gorman employs the terminology of "legal fiction" as a label of what he describes as God's lying about the righteousness of the supposedly justified sinner when he castigates the reformational understanding of the sinner's declared righteousness before God. Gorman, *Inhabiting the Cruciform God*, 82; see also 1–2, 41–44, 60–63, 67.

13. Pannenberg, *Systematic Theology, Vol. 3*, 214, 218–19. Pannenberg, *Anthropology in Theological Perspective*, 71, 85. Mattes, *The Role of Justification in Contemporary Theology*, 63–64, 68.

becomes righteous before God by a process of God's indwelling the sinner and the sinner's participation in God.[14]

In this context of the refutation and reinterpretation of the Lutheran doctrine of justification in modern theology, Bayer's view of justification appears as a unique interpretation of this doctrine that does not reject the declarative nature of justification but also addresses a new ontology brought about by justifying faith. Bayer avoids both the "legal fiction" rejected by the essentialist view as well as the essentialist claim that justification is first and foremost ontological and not forensic. While the essentialists pit declaration against ontology with regard to the justification of the sinner, Bayer sees God's declaration of justification as actually effecting the righteousness that it proclaims and what might be termed a new ontology precisely because it is declarative in nature. According to Bayer, God's work of justification effects a new state of affairs not only in the personal realm of the individual human being's relationship with God and other humans, but also in cosmic dimensions, as creation itself is opened to renewal through God's justifying promise.

In defining justification in this way, Bayer both continues in the confessional tradition of interpreting Luther and develops his own interpretation of the reformer's teaching on justification through his own original research on Luther's understanding of God's active Word of promise. From this research and interpretation of Luther, Bayer formulates an understanding of justification in which the sinner is made righteous by God's active Word. This sinner is declared to be righteous, but this declaration is no legal fiction. Instead, it is an active Word that "does what it says."[15] In order to explain how this active, performative Word of God in the promise functions, Bayer employs the British philosopher of language J. L. Austin's theory of speech act to interpret Luther's understanding of the justifying promise of God. In defining what it is that this active Word of God actually does, Bayer states that God's performative promise makes the sinner righteous and forgives the sinner, liberating him or her from the bondage of sin and the accusing law. Furthermore, according to Bayer, the justifying work of God's promise in the gospel of Christ opens up a new relationship between God and the justified sinner, which was not before in existence. Yet, Bayer does not relegate the effects of God's justifying promise in Christ to the individual and his or her relationship with God. Instead, Bayer states that the promise opens a new relationship between the justified sinner and other humans beings, as well as to all creation. In articulating this, Bayer

---

14. Mannermaa, *Christ Present in Faith*, 9.
15. Bayer, "Selbstdarstellung," 303.

thus consciously moves from personal justification to creation, arguing for a relationship of mutual togetherness between God's work in justification and God's work in creation. The same promise spoken by God in justification opens creation itself, so that God speaks this promise to human—and to creation—through creation. Creation understood thus through justification forms the backdrop of Bayer's discussion of the hidden God. Moreover Bayer's very definition of the hidden God and the hidden God's work is largely defined by Bayer's overall discourse on justification by God's active Word of promise, making Bayer's definition of justification crucial for understanding his view of the hiddenness of God.

Bayer's Study of Luther's Theology and God's Active Word of Promise

Bayer's view of justification by the divine speech act of the promise is built upon his study of the place of this promise in the early theology of Luther. This study is in part built upon the exploration of Luther's understanding of the active Word of God made by two other contemporary German Lutheran theologians. Ernst Bizer, Bayer's own teacher, as well as Gerhard Ebeling have contributed significantly to the study of the active Word of God, especially as it features in Luther's theology. In the foreword to *Promissio* and in his "Selbstdarstellung," Bayer acknowledges his debt to these two theologians in his groundbreaking research with regard to Luther's view of the promise.[16] Bizer's contribution to the background of Bayer's study lies in his observations concerning the important place of the preached and heard Word of God as a means of grace and its connection with "the righteousness of faith" in Luther's early theology. Furthermore, Bizer demonstrates the importance of this aspect of Luther's evangelical breakthrough evidencing itself so clearly in the reformer's early career through his confrontation with Cajetan.[17] Bayer notes that, although he was first exposed to the idea of God's active Word via the theology of Barth, it was Bizer who shaped his studies of the saving action of the Word of God preached. In Bayer's words, Bizer helped him come to the recognition that "Ein solches Wort tut, was es sagt; es gibt Freiheit" ("Such a word does what it says; it gives freedom").[18]

Ebeling describes the featuring of this active Word of God in Luther's early theology from the *Lectures on the Psalms* (1513–1515) through the budding reformer's debate with Cajetan (1518) and up to the composition

---

16. Bayer, *Promissio*, "Vorwort." Bayer, "Selbstdarstellung," 302–3.
17. Bizer, *Fides ex audito*, 170–73.
18. Bayer, "Selbstdarstellung," 303.

of *The Babylonian Captivity of the Church* (1520). Ebeling focuses primarily on the active Word of God in Luther's theology as it relates to hermeneutics, and adopts Luther's view that that the Word of God accomplishes what it says into his own hermeneutical theology.[19] Yet, neither Bizer nor Ebeling undertakes the exhaustive study of the featuring of the performative Word of God's promise and its connection to justification in Luther's theology as Bayer does, nor do they construct a contemporary systematic theology of justification through this promise as Bayer does.

Building on the work of Bizer and Ebeling early in his career, in *Promissio*, his dissertation and habilitation, Bayer began an extensive study of God's active Word of promise and justification in Luther's early theology. In *Promissio*, and other works in which he addresses Luther's understanding of the promise of God in the gospel, Bayer argues that this theme is the central theme in Luther's theology and what constitutes the turning point in Luther's thought from medieval Augustinianism to reformational, evangelical faith. Quoting from Luther's *Preface to the Latin Writings* of 1545, Bayer states that it was this notion of God's promise as a performative Word that does what it says—namely freeing the sinner from the law and forgiving the sinner's sin, and giving righteousness before God—that opened the gates of paradise to Luther, freeing him from the terror of God's wrath and giving him the assurance of faith in God in Jesus Christ.[20]

In defining Luther's reformational turning point (*die reformatorsiche Wende*) as the young reformer's discovery of the *promissio* of God, Bayer rejects several commonly postulated suggestions for what constitutes this turning point. These suggestions include the reformer's discovery of "the righteousness of God" in St. Paul's theology, the distinction between the law and the gospel, and the theology of the cross. It is not as if Bayer rejects these ideas as being present in and even central to Luther's theology. On the contrary, Bayer recognizes them and employs them in his own theology as well. Yet, Bayer interprets and utilizes them only in the light of the *promissio*—especially as it appears in the *Babylonian Captivity*—as the more essential and central reformational point in Luther's theology and as that which may be identified as the reformational turning point in Luther's theology. Bayer respects these suggestions, gives them their due, and actually recognizes the themes of God's righteousness, the distinction between the law and the gospel, and the theology of the cross as important; however, he believes

19. Ebeling, *Luther*, 71–73. Ebeling, *Lutherstudien*, Band I, 34, 257, 267–78, 294–95, 298–99.

20. Bayer, *Promissio*, 11–14, 163. Bayer, *Martin Luther's Theology*, 46–47; Bayer, *Martin Luthers Theologie*, 44–46. Bayer, "Die reformatorische Wende in Luthers Theologie," 98–101ff.

that he, with help from Bizer, has identified the actual reformational turning point in Luther's life and theology in the *promissio*.[21] Whether or not Bayer is correct in this understanding of the reformational turning point in Luther is not my focus in this work. Yet, I must note here how Bayer sees the *promissio* as such, and I will return to this later, observing how Bayer's focus on this theme as the turning point may preclude observing some important material in Luther's earlier writings, which themselves have bearing on the discussion of the teaching of the hidden God in Luther's theology.

Although he does observe and describe the first beginnings of and movement towards this theme in the earliest works of Luther's theology, including the *Lectures on the Psalms*,[22] the *Sermon on the Prologue of John* (1514),[23] the *Lectures on Romans*,[24] and the *Lectures on Hebrews*,[25] Bayer states that the real commencement of this evangelical and reformational turning in Luther's theology occurs in the years 1518-1520. The real *initia Lutheri* and *initia reformationis*, says Bayer may be found in the intellectual and dialogical struggle between Luther and Cajetan at Augsburg in October, 1518, where Luther put his finger on the *promissio* of God in Christ as that which brings faith into being and that which forms the essence of his new teaching.[26] As I noted already in the last chapter, Bayer argues that, when he defended his position before Cajetan at Augsburg, Luther understood the *promissio* not only as the center of his new theology but also as the center to all true theology and the very essence of Christian faith itself, the very thing by which God justifies the ungodly. Wherefore, says Bayer, Luther responds to the call to recantation given by the papal nuncio, "I will not become a heretic by renouncing that which made me a Christian. I would rather die, be burnt, excommunicated or accursed."[27]

Bayer argues that what Luther lifts up in his debate with Cajetan as the center of his refomational theology, the reformer describes more extensively in *The Babylonian Captivity of the Church*. It is here, in this writing of 1520,

---

21. Bayer, *Martin Luther's Theology*, 45-50; *Martin Luthers Theologie*, 41-46. Cf. Luther, *The Babylonian Captivity of the Church* (1520), in *LW* 36:36-49, 66-67; *WA* 6:513-21, 533-34.

22. Bayer, *Promissio*, 17-31.

23. Ibid.

24. Ibid., 32-144.

25. Ibid., 203-25.

26. Bayer, "Rückblick," 161. *Promissio*, 346. Oswald Bayer, "Die reformatorische Wende in *Luthers Theologie*," 107. Bayer, *Martin Luther's Theology*, 50; Bayer, *Martin Luthers Theologie*, 46.

27. Bayer, "What is Evangelical?" 5; Bayer, *Zugesagte Gegenwart*, 26. *LW* 31:270-71; *WA* 2:13-14.

says Bayer, in contrast to the early biblical lectures or the *Heidelberg Disputation*, that one finds the true early manifesto of Luther's theology.[28] Bayer highlights how Luther articulates his view of the *promissio* through his arguments against the seven-fold sacramental system of the Roman Catholic church. Whereas the Roman church had taught that the Sacraments provide grace to their recipients by the virtue of the work performed in the Sacraments themselves (*ex opere operato*), Luther focuses on the words of institution said with the Sacraments. Moreover, as Bayer points out, Luther teaches that the words of institution and not the acts of the Sacraments themselves are what really perform grace. Bayer focuses in on this idea of Luther's that the words of institution actively forgive sins.[29] Luther, says Bayer, understands that God's Word of promise accomplishes what it says, it is not merely a descriptive word but also an effectual, performative word, through a specific word or words of God to the sinner, which effect the sinner's justification.[30] For Luther, says Bayer, God's justifying Word of promise in the specific gospel proclamations given to sinners through preaching and the Sacraments does not merely describe something that has already taken place or will take place, rather, like the words of institution actually make the forgiveness happen that is proclaimed in the Sacraments, the Word of God's promise in Christ actually creates something not before in existence; it does not just describe a state of affairs but actually constitutes it.[31] This, says Bayer, is the very center of Luther's theology and the thing that truly makes reformational theology reformational. Moreover, Bayer uses this understanding of the effectual Word of God's promise as the center for his own contemporary Lutheran theology.

Bayer's Theology of Justification by the Promise

The Promise as Divine Speech Act

Bayer compares Luther's understanding of the effectual promise of God in Christ to the British linguistic philosopher J. L. Austin's theory of speech act and uses Austin's theory as a contemporary hermeneutical matrix for

28. Bayer, *Martin Luther's Theology*, 46; *Martin Luthers Theologie*, 42.

29. Bayer, "Die reformatorische Wende in Luthers Theologie," 110. Bayer, *Promissio*, 186.

30. Bayer, *Martin Luther's Theology*, 50; *Martin Luthers Theologie*, 46. Bayer, *Theology the Lutheran Way*, 128–29; Bayer, *Theologie*, 443–444.

31. Bayer, *Martin Luther's Theology*, 50; Bayer, *Martin Luthers Theologie*, 46. Bayer, *Theology the Lutheran Way*, 128–29; Bayer, *Theologie*, 443–44. Bayer, *Living by Faith*, 42–43; Bayer, *Aus Glauben Leben*, 50–51.

building his own contemporary Lutheran theology of justification by the promise. In his seminal essay, *How to Do Things with Words*, Austin describes what he calls a "performative utterance" as a given phrase which actually accomplishes what it says, as opposed to a strictly descriptive phrase.[32] As examples of this linguistic phenomenon, Austin offers the utterance of a groom at his wedding, the christening of the ocean liner *Queen Elizabeth*, a bequeathed inheritance in a will, and even a wager concerning the next day's weather.[33] Austin further distinguishes between locutionary, illocutionary, and perlocutionary acts of a given utterance. A locutionary act simply refers to the straightforward grammatical meaning of the utterance. The term illocutionary act, on the other hand, regards what is actually being accomplished by the utterance. The perlocutionary act is the act after the utterance and regards psychological effects.[34] Of these three kinds of speech acts articulated by Austin, the illocutionary act is the most important for the purposes of the present study concerning speech acts in of Bayer's understanding of justification. Bayer capitalizes on the particular example of a promise in Austin's development of his basic theory of speech acts, particularly with regard to the illocutionary speech act. Bayer relates how Austin sees a promise constituting a particular kind of illocutionary speech act through which the one promising establishes a previously nonexistent relationship with the one to whom he or she is speaking the promise.[35]

Bayer equates Austin's understanding of a promise as a performative, illocutionary speech act with Luther's understanding of God's promise in the gospel of Christ given through preaching and the Sacraments. Describing Luther's notion of the promise through Austin's concept of speech act, Bayer notes that God's proclaimed promise does not merely describe the way things are but, as an effective and performative speech act, which establishes the way things are.[36] This, says Bayer, is what takes place through the effectual word (*Verbum efficax*) of absolution, which comes to the sinner through the Sacraments of Holy Baptism and Holy Communion, and especially through the absolution that comes through the preacher after confession: "I absolve you! ("*Ego te absolvo!*")[37] Thus, while Bayer fully ac-

32. Austin, *How to Do Things with Words*, 4–7.

33. Ibid., 5.

34. Ibid., 94–102.

35. Bayer, *Theology the Lutheran Way*, 127–28; Bayer, *Theologie*, 441–42. Bayer, *Martin Luther's Theology*, 50–51; Bayer, *Martin Luthers Theologie*, 46–47. Bayer, "Preaching the Word," 255; Bayer, "Das Wort predigen," in *Zugesagte Gegenwart*, 392–93.

36. Bayer, *Was ist das:Theologie?* 25, 28. Bayer, *Martin Luther's Theology*, 51; Bayer, *Martin Luthers Theologie*, 47–48.

37. Bayer, *Martin Luther's Theology*, 52–53; Bayer, *Martin Luthers Theologie*, 47–48.

cepts Austin's notion of promise as an example of an illocutionary speech act, he develops Austin's concept of promise theologically as well. Bayer is not so much concerned with the idea of a promise in general but with the specific revelatory promise of God's salvation in Jesus Christ that encounters and justifies human beings through revelation in Word and Sacrament.[38] Bayer utilizes Austin's theory of speech act as a hermeneutical tool to interpret Luther's theology of *promissio* in doing systematic theology in today's academic, university context. While some certainly may object to the legitimacy of contemporizing Luther in this way,[39] Bayer still seeks to be profoundly true to Luther while constructing a contemporary theology centered on Luther's dynamic understanding of the sinner's justification by God's active Word of promise. Through his contemporary understanding of the effectual, divine promise as performative speech act, Bayer establishes a theology of justification in which God, through the promise of the gospel, declares the sinner righteous for Christ's sake and thus actually makes the sinner righteous, establishing a new relationship with the sinner, liberating and granting confidence in faith to the sinner, and opening the whole world to the justified sinner as a new creation.

God's Work Effected through the Speech Act of the Promise

In Bayer's estimation, justification is the work of God's performative speech act in the promise of the gospel of Jesus Christ, a promise that Bayer describes as effectual in nature. The promise of God is effectual, because it does what it says: it forgives sin and makes the sinner righteous in God's sight.[40] Though Bayer uses Austin's theory of speech act to describe this

---

38. Bayer, *Living by Faith*, 44; Bayer, *Aus Glauben Leben*, 52. Bayer, *Was ist das:Theologie?*, 28.

39. One such detractor is Paul Hinlicky, who rejects Bayer's theological work from the standpoint that any contemporary interpretation of Luther is in itself wrong. Hinlicky argues that it is not possible to interpret and use Luther in today's world, because the interpreter will "modernize" Luther in the interpretation process. This is certainly what Hinlicky thinks Bayer has done. Hinlicky, *Luther and the Beloved Community*, 5–6. Hinlicky contends that Bayer has "lifted Luther out of the stream of Pauline-Augustinian tradition to which he belonged to offer a reconstructed Luther theology *Sonderweg*, when we today should rather find ourselves within the same, broader stream of theological tradition." Hinlicky, *Luther and the Beloved Community*, 6. While it is true that completely objective study of Luther's theology is impossible, one need not assume Hinlicky's selective depiction of the stream of "the Pauline-Augustinian tradition" in the way Hinlicky does. Hinlicky's objections to Bayer on the hidden God will be dealt with more fully in chapter nine.

40. Bayer, *Martin Luther's Theology*, 52; Bayer, *Martin Luthers Theologie*, 48.

event, he does not hinge the effectualness of the promise on this theory. Instead, Bayer states that the promise of God that justifies the sinner is effectual precisely because it is God's promise alone.[41] Although Bayer does not deny that this promise comes through external means to the human and, indeed, states that it always comes through another human's proclamation and administration of the promise in the external and bodily Word and Sacrament (*das leibliches Wort*),[42] he asserts that it is truly and completely God's Word of promise which is given and not human words.[43] God's promise is God's Word alone; it is not mixed with human words, and it cannot be verified by humans because it is self-verifying in humans. It does this by working its work in humans, but it is God's Word in these words that are effectual.[44] Humans do not contribute to God's declaration of justification either in words or deeds. In the act of justification, the human is not an actor but a passive receptor of God's promise, for justification is God's free gift to human sinners who can only receive and suffer this gift passively.[45] The human is not even a conversation partner in justification. Though the human becomes a conversation partner with God after and on the basis of justification, the speech act of justification is purely God's Word.[46] Echoing Luther's explanation to the third article of the Apostle's Creed, Bayer states that until such time as one is justified by God's speech act, one cannot come to or believe in God. It is into this context of human passivity before God, says Bayer, that God's performative speech act in the bodily Word of Holy Baptism, wherein one is "called through the gospel," is proclaimed and effected. For the efficacy of the promise is not based upon one's "reason or efforts" but solely upon the power of the promise of the gospel as *God's Word*.[47] If the promise that justifies were not God's Word alone, says Bayer, it would not do what it does to the human sinner; it would not create a new relationship between the sinner and God, liberate the sinner, and bring the sinner the confidence of faith.[48]

---

41. Bayer, *Living by Faith*, 52; Bayer, *Aus Glauben Leben*, 60. Helmer, "The Subject of Theology in the Thought of Oswald Bayer," 21–52.

42. Cf. Bayer, *Promissio*, 280–83.

43. Bayer, *Theology the Lutheran Way*, 129–30; Bayer, *Theologie*, 443–44. *Living by Faith*, 44; Bayer, *Aus Glauben Leben*, 52.

44. Bayer, *Martin Luther's Theology*, 55; Bayer, *Martin Luthers Theologie*, 50.

45. Bayer, *Living by Faith*, 19–20; Bayer, *Aus Glauben Leben*, 29–30. Bayer, *Martin Luther's Theology*, 43; Bayer, *Martin Luthers Theologie*, 50–51.

46. Bayer, *Theology the Lutheran Way*, 114; Bayer, *Theologie*, 426.

47. Bayer, *Martin Luther's Theology*, 240–41; Bayer, *Martin Luthers Theologie*, 217–18.

48. Bayer, *Martin Luther's Theology*, 55; Bayer, *Martin Luthers Theologie*, 50.

The effectualness of God's justifying Word of promise is demonstrated in how the promise establishes the relationship of faith between the sinner and God immediately. For Bayer, the validity and power of the promise are not fully reliant on some future event or even on something in the past but are really and fully present in the present, when the promise is given through the external, bodily Word and Sacrament. When the pastor declares God's promise in the words of the absolution "I absolve you," he or she is not making a statement about a forgiveness that is already in the present and being affirmed by the pastor. Instead the pastor is actually handing out God's promise of salvation which actively delivers God's forgiveness to the human in the present. God's promise in the Gospel is thus not a declarative statement but a performative and effectual speech act, an illocutionary speech act. It is not a statement about a righteousness that already exists, nor is it a statement of untruth about a righteousness that does not exist. Instead, it is a performative declaration that actually creates and bestows a righteousness that was not before present.[49]

Bayer argues that the promise of God's salvation in the Gospel of Christ is not a declarative statement of proposition or a prescription but an effectual, performative speech act.[50] Following and developing Austin's concept of performative utterances, Bayer argues that performative utterances are of such a nature that they create their own context and a relationship between the one making the promise and the one to whom the promise is made which did not exist before the promise was given.[51] The effectual promise of God in the Gospel of Jesus Christ thus creates its own context by forming a relationship with the human receptor of the promise that did not exist before the promise was given to him or her. This relationship is the relationship of faith, the relationship that God establishes with the human who was not in this relationship with God before the promise of salvation in Jesus Christ was given to him or her in Word and Sacrament.[52]

This new relationship of faith constitutes the only place in life where God and the human sinner can coexist peacefully. Here in the promise, and nowhere else, God speaks for rather than against the sinner. Bayer contrasts such divine speech for the sinner with God's speaking against the sinner in

---

49. Bayer, *Theology the Lutheran Way*, 130-131; Bayer, *Theologie*, 444-45.Bayer, *Martin Luther's Theology*, 50-53; 46-48. Cf. Bayer, *Promissio*, 280-83. It should be noted, however, that Bayer points out that not only pastors, but all Christians are entrusted with this function of the office of the keys—delivering the promise.

50. Bayer, *Theology the Lutheran Way*, 132; Bayer, *Theologie*, 445-446. Bayer, *Was ist das:Theologie?* 28.

51. Bayer, *Theology the Lutheran Way*, 127-28; Bayer, *Theologie*, 441-42.

52. Bayer, *Theology the Lutheran Way*, 130; Bayer, *Theologie*, 444.

the law and the condemnation that the sinner feels in the experience of the hidden God. The sinner cannot stand before the righteous God of the law, nor can the human survive the existence under the hidden God, where God exists and relates towards the sinner as a God of wrath and sheer terror. God's Word of promise in the gospel of Jesus Christ, which creates a new relationship between God and the sinner, forms the refuge for the sinner from the God of wrath revealed in the law and experienced in the existence under the hidden God.[53] Like the situation of Jacob's wrestling with God on the banks of the Jabbok, the relationship between the sinner and God can only be one of hostility, until God and the sinner grasp one another in the promise.[54] Whereas prior to the sinner's being addressed by God in the promise, God spoke only *against* the sinner, now God speaks distinctly *for* the sinner. Whereas before being addressed by God in the promise, the sinner experienced God only as the hidden one who works wrath, now the sinner experiences God as his or her "rock and castle" from such hiddenness and wrath.[55]

Bayer states that the effectual promise of God's salvation in the Gospel of Jesus Christ liberates the human. Bayer identifies the proclamation of God's forgiveness in Christ given in both absolution and the Sacrament of the Altar as the venue for this liberation. Here through the words "Your sins are forgiven" and "Given and shed for you for the forgiveness of your sins," human sinners are actually forgiven and made free people before God. Precisely here in these words, in the giving of God's promise, God encounters sinners and makes them righteous before God's self.[56] Citing the example of Martin Luther's experience with the promise, Bayer states that the promise of God is truly liberating because it draws humans outside of themselves, outside of their own failed attempts at righteousness and outside of the despair that follows such attempts, and because the promise gives to them a righteousness that is not their own but which they receive as a gift.[57]

Bayer also states that this divine, liberating speech act of the promise of God's salvation in the Gospel of Christ brings confidence to the human being. The confidence brought to the human by the promise of God is not, however, an anthropological confidence in the sense understood by the practitioners of modern philosophy. That is, it is not the recapitulation of

---

53. Bayer, *Martin Luther's Theology*, 39–40; Bayer, *Martin Luthers Theology*, 36–37.

54. Bayer, *Martin Luther's Theology*, 39–40, 202–4; Bayer, *Martin Luthers Theologie*, 36–37, 182–84.

55. Bayer, "Twenty-Four Theses," 74; Bayer, *Zugesagte Gegenwart*, 35, thesis 9. Cf. Luther, "Nun freut euch, lieben Christen G'mein," *EG*, 341; *ELW*, 594; *LSB*, 556.

56. Bayer, *Theology the Lutheran Way*, 129–30; Bayer, *Theologie*, 443–44.

57. Bayer, *Martin Luther's Theology*, 54–55; Bayer, *Martin Luthers Theologie*, 50.

the human's own self-understood identity or the verification of the human's dearly held Narcissism.[58] Instead it is a confidence of certainty that the human is known and loved by the God who is outside of himself or herself. It is such a confidence because it establishes communication between God and the human being. This communication is brought by the new relationship established by God through the promise; for in the promise God addresses humans, speaking to them, creating a relationship with them where there was no relationship before. The confidence brought by the promise of God is a confidence in God, a confidence that the human can have because he or she has a relationship with God.[59] In this relationship of communication, God does not merely speak to and with the human; God speaks God's self to the human. God promises God's very self to the human. God promises here to be a certain kind of God: God for us. Through the proclaimed gospel in Word and Sacrament, God binds God's self to the promise, to honor it, to be a merciful God of forgiveness to the human, to be God for the human and to speak on the human's behalf. It is, above all, this pledge of God's self that gives confidence to the newly justified human.[60]

In addition to effecting the sinner's righteousness before God, bringing the sinner into a new relationship with God, and liberating and giving confidence to the sinner, Bayer articulates that God's speech act of promise in justification opens the whole world anew to the newly justified sinner as a new creation. This feature of the work of God's justifying promise leads to a definite turn towards creation in Bayer's theology, yet in this turning, justification is not abandoned. On the contrary, for Bayer, justification and creation belong together as two interrelated works of God. Creation is really only accessible through justification, and justification has new creation as its ultimate trajectory.[61]

Creation in Bayer's Theology of Justification

Bayer moves in his theology from his definition of justification as the new state of affairs brought about by God's divine speech act of the promise in the gospel of Jesus Christ to the doctrine of creation. This is no arbitrary movement, for Bayer understands justification and creation as being intrinsically

---

58. Bayer, *Theology the Lutheran Way*, 133; Bayer, *Theologie*, 447–48.

59. Bayer, *Martin Luther's Theology*, 9–10, 53; Bayer, *Martin Luthers Theologie*, 8–9, 48. Bayer, "Rupture of Times, 43–44; Bayer, *Gott als Autor*, 156–58.

60. Bayer, "Preaching the Word," 259–60; Bayer, *Zugesagte Gegenwart*, 397.

61. Bayer, "The Doctrine of Justification and Ontology," 44; Bayer, *Zugesagte Gegenwart*, 196.

linked with one another. Bayer describes this relationship as one in which justification and creation are indistinguishable from one another, since they both are constituted by God's gracious and active Word; as one in which the creature is brought into a new relationship with creation; in which creation is itself opened through the promise given in justification; in which God's effectual promise in justification is actually mediated through creation; and in which the reality of the promise is fully present in the present despite the fact that evil persists in the rupture of the ages between the advent of the promise in Christ and the eschatological fullness of the promised renewal of creation. A proper appreciation of this relationship is necessary for understanding how the theme of God's hiddenness functions in Bayer's theology of justification, because the relationship between justification and creation forms the context in which Bayer sees the hidden God at work.

The Relationship between Justification and Creation

Bayer argues that justification and creation belong together because both are the work of God's gracious and active Word of promise. As in justification, in creation God addresses the created order, including humanity. As in justification, the creational address of God is, first and foremost, a unilateral divine speech act, a performative declaration. As in justification, in creation, humanity is not a conversational partner with God in this initial and basic speech act. Rather, humanity—indeed all of the created order—is the passive object of the creative work of God's active Word, and as such this divine work is truly *ex nihilo* and, consequently, *sola gratia*.[62] Thus, as in justification, the speech act of God's promise can be understood only as a gift of God, which creatures in no way participate in generating, and which they in no way merit. Instead, they live in the *vita passiva* formed as the human context for receiving the life-giving, creative Word of God.[63] Furthermore, like the work of God's Word of promise in justification, the work of God's speech act in creation engenders a new relationship between God and God's creatures that did not exist previously. As in the relationship established by God with the sinner in justification, this creational relationship is one that only God calls into being, that can exist only in the Word of God's promise

---

62. Bayer, *Martin Luther's Theology*, 95–97, 101, 103, 107–8; Bayer, *Martin Luthers Theologie*, 87–89, 93, 94–95, 97–98. Bayer, "The Doctrine of Justification and Ontology," 45–47; Bayer, *Zugesagte Gegenwart*, 197–200.

63. Bayer, *Martin Luther's Theology*, 97–98; Bayer, *Martin Luthers Theologie*, 89–90.

and that exists as a relationship of trust, in which God's creatures are given the comfort of faith in their Creator.[64]

Since, according to Bayer, God created the universe and established a discursive relationship with humanity though the promise, creation and this relationship are founded upon God's grace and not upon the law. Drawing once again from Hamann, Bayer reflects that the first word of God to humanity recorded in Scripture is, "You may eat," while the last is "Come for all is ready." In this response, creation appears as the work of God constituted by a categorical gift, by a word of promise without conditions.[65] This context of gift created by God's justifying promise is so great, says Bayer, that it should be understood as defining the meaning of ontology itself, so that creation and all that exists is, in its essence, categorical gift.[66]

In his view of creation as established by God's word of promise, Bayer even goes so far as to identify a particular kind of proto-evangelion. Describing the connection between the justifying promise of God and creation as God's good work, Bayer states that there is a primeval promise, which is valid for all people.[67] Contrary to what one might think though, Bayer does not here advocate a kind of natural theology in which one may be saved outside of Jesus Christ or in which creation functions as "a forecourt of the heathen."[68] God, says Bayer, reveals God's self through the promise as a gracious and giving God in creation, as the Triune God and not as some generic deity to whom one can come to a knowledge of through reason and speculation. But, instead of responding to this "natural" revelation of the promising, Triune God in faith and worship, in their bondage under sin, humans have responded to God's gracious revelation in creation by inventing all kinds of idolatry, exchanging the offspring of their own reason and

---

64. Bayer, *Martin Luther's Theology*, 100–103, 111–12; Bayer, *Martin Luthers Theologie*, 93–94, 101–102. Bayer, "The Doctrine of Justification and Ontology," 47–49;Bayer, *Zugesagte Gegenwart*, 200–201.

65. Bayer, "Schöpfung als Anrede und Anspruch," 141. Bayer, "Schöpfung und Verantwortung," 202. Bayer, *Freedom in Response*, 13; Bayer, *Freiheit als Antwort*, 13–14. Saarinen, "The Language of Gift in Theology," 269. Saarinen differs with Bayer in terms of how he understands creation as gift, as well as in many other ways in his theology, but he recognizes how creation functions as gift in Bayer's theology and the contribution that this has made to contemporary systematic theology.

66. Bayer, "The Doctrine of Justification and Ontology," 45; *Zugesagte Gegenwart*, 197. Cf. Bayer, "I believe that God has Created Me with All that Exists," 142–56; Bayer, *Schöpfung als Anrede*, 89–103.

67. Bayer, *Martin Luther's Theology*, 127; Bayer, *Martin Luthers Theologie*, 116–17.

68. "... kein Vorhof der Heiden." Bayer, *Martin Luther's Theology*, 99; Bayer, *Martin Luthers Theologie*, 90.

imaginations for the gracious, Triune God.[69] Yet, says Bayer, the primeval promise is still present and is alluded to in the first words of the Decalogue, where God affirms God's promissory commitment to be God a gracious and giving God. The way in which God is faithful to this promise, however, takes its form only in Jesus Christ.[70]

Flowing from this understanding of the relationship between the work of God's Word in justification and the work of God's Word in creation, Bayer states that the only way to understand creation is through justification. Bayer holds that the only way to an understanding of the first article of the apostle's creed is by belief in the second article, for even the first article is an article of faith and not merely the domain of some revelation of natural law available to all people. Creation, thus, is not the residence of the righteous pagan or the threshold of belief; rather, it is within the realm of relationship of faith in the Triune God that comes only through God's justifying promise.[71] This view of appropriating and knowing creation and creation's God only through justification, says Bayer, takes into consideration both that the promise is the only way in which God deals with God's creatures both in justification and in creation—indeed, ultimately as the only way in which God deals with God's creatures at all—and the fact that the original relationship of faith in the Word engendered by God is now broken by sin and needs God's promise to be spoken again, in justification, for that relationship to be reestablished.[72]

Justification and the Opening of Creation

God's performative Word of promise in justification not only reestablishes the relationship between God and the human, says Bayer, but also reestablishes the human in the human's proper relationships with other humans and with other creatures.[73] This reflects how Bayer understands justification as not simply one point of doctrine in a broader theology and not even simply the subject of all theology but as the very entrance into life itself.

---

69. Bayer, *Martin Luther's Theology*, 127–30, 134–36; Bayer, *Martin Luthers Theologie*, 116–19, 123–24.

70. Bayer, *Martin Luther's Theology*, 127–28; Bayer, *Martin Luthers Theologie*, 116–18.

71. Bayer, "The Doctrine of Justification and Ontology," 45–46; Bayer, *Zugesagte Gegenwart*, 197–98.

72. Bayer, "The Doctrine of Justification and Ontology," 48–49; Bayer, *Zugesagte Gegenwart*, 201.

73. Bayer, "Justification as the Basis and Boundary of Theology," 286; Bayer, *Leibliches Wort*, 33.

In agreement with Luther, Bayer argues that prior to God's justification through the speech act of the divine promise in the gospel of Jesus Christ, the human sinner is curved in upon himself or herself (*incurvatio in se ipsum*) in such a way that he or she is closed not only to a communicative relationship with God but also to communicative relationships with other humans, other creatures, in total, the cosmos itself.[74] Drawing from a sermon given by Luther on September 8, 1538, Bayer states that in this context of the brokenness of creation and its effects on the relationships of creation, God's performative Word of promise comes as the words of Jesus to the deaf man, recorded in the seventh chapter of the Gospel of Mark: "*Ephatha!*" ("Be opened!").[75]

This opening up of the human to the creation and its relationships then opens all of creation to the justified human as well.[76] All of life thus becomes a new creation to the human recipient of God's speech act of promise. The believer is set free from himself or herself and opened to what Bayer describes as a new worldliness in the very word of promise, "Be opened," in which the old creation is becoming the new creation.[77] Such "worldliness" is not, Bayer emphasizes, "an addiction to the world" that amounts to the affirmation of sin and the denial of the gospel of Christ.[78] It is, rather, an affirmation of the world as God originally created it; it is a return to creation as it was created. It is "worldly piety" that rejects Gnosticism and affirms God's descriptive address of "good" to all of creation before the brokenness brought about by sin. This worldly piety affirms creation and its blessings as God's good gifts and recognizes the inherent goodness of the self, other humans, other creatures, and the environment because they are fellow-recipients of God's address of promise. In this worldly piety, the justified human turns away from introspection outward to the neighbors whom God has given him or her, who need his or her help.[79] Above all, this worldly piety is the embodiment and living-out of the relationships—between God and the

---

74. Bayer, *Martin Luther's Theology*, 110-11; Bayer, *Martin Luthers Theologie*, 100-101. Here Bayer draws from Luther's sermon on Mark 7:31-37, the Gospel text for the Twelfth Sunday after Trinity, preached on September 8, 1538. *LW* 37:68ff.; WA 23:150ff. Bayer, *Martin Luther's Theology*, 106-16; Bayer, *Martin Luthers Theologie*, 97-106.

75. "Tu dich auf!" Mark 7:34. Bayer, *Martin Luther's Theology*, 106-8; Bayer, *Martin Luthers Theologie*, 97-99. Bayer, *Schöpfung als Anrede*, 62.

76. Helmer, "The Subject of Theology in the Thought of Oswald Bayer," 286.

77. Bayer, "Twenty-Four Theses," 74-75; Bayer, *Zugesagte Gegenwart*, 35-36, theses 14-24. Bayer, *Schöpfung als Anrede*, 76.

78. Bayer, "Twenty-Four Theses," 74-75; Bayer, *Zugesagte Gegenwart*, 35-36, thesis 16.

79. Bayer, *Living by Faith*, 39; Bayer, *Aus Glauben Leben*, 47. Bayer, *Martin Luther's Theology*, 108-114; Bayer, *Martin Luthers Theologie*, 99-104.

human, the human and other humans, the human and other creatures, and the human and the cosmos—established by God's address of promise in creation and reestablished by God's address of promise in justification.[80] Such relationships are formed in the "three estates" of creation, which first and foremost are not functions of God's law to curb sin but establishments given by God to humanity through the creational promise of God: the Church, the family, and the state. Though broken by sin, for those moved by the promise into creation, they function as the realms of the new worldliness brought by justification.[81]

While it is true, says Bayer, that the world is still under the curse of brokenness wrought on the old creation, the reality of the new creation has broken into the old in the promise of the gospel in Jesus Christ and is, in the present through the promise, renewing and remaking the old creation into the new.[82] This work of the promise of renewing creation is perceptible to the believer in the promissory Sacraments of Holy Baptism and Holy Communion, in which created elements are sanctified by the justifying promise of God and are thus used as promissory means of grace.[83] Though the renewed creation will dawn more fully in the eschaton, it will dawn not as a result of the movement of the world into the future but as a return to the original creation before the brokenness of sin. Though the world is not now enjoying the complete fullness of this reality, the justified humans has truly been brought into this reality through God's address to him or her in the performative Word of God's promise spoken and made reality in the present.[84]

Leibliches Wort and Schöpfung als Anrede

Another dimension of Bayer's understanding of the relationship between justification and creation concerns how the promise of God in justification comes to the sinner. In keeping with Luther's theology, Bayer identifies the Word and Sacraments as the means through which God's saving promise in Christ comes to sinful humans.[85] Yet, the way in which Bayer approaches the

---

80. Bayer, *Martin Luther's Theology*, 108–14.; Bayer, *Martin Luthers Theologie*, 99–104.
81. Bayer, *Martin Luther's Theology*, 122–23; Bayer, *Martin Luthers Theologie*, 112–13.
82. Bayer, *Martin Luther's Theology*, 116–19; Bayer, *Martin Luthers Theologie*, 106–9.
83. Bayer, *Martin Luther's Theology*, 117; Bayer, *Martin Luthers Theologie*, 107.
84. Bayer, *Martin Luther's Theology*, 116–19; Bayer, *Martin Luthers Theologie*, 106–9.
85. Bayer, *Martin Luther's Theology*, 249–50; Bayer, *Martin Luthers Theologie*.

means of grace forms part of his understanding of the connection between justification and creation and once again shows the influence of Hamann upon his theology. In describing these means of grace, Bayer articulates two important positions that reflect how he understands the connection between justification and creation.[86] The first of these positions is that the Word of God's promise is a bodily Word (*Leibliches Wort*)[87], which comes through created, sacramental means. The second is that creation itself is not only a means for God's address but is itself God's address (*Schöpfung als Anrede*).[88]

In both of these positions, Bayer demonstrates a great reliance upon Hamann as he explains the way in which the divine address of God's justifying promise reaches the human sinner. Against Kant and every one of his followers in modern theology, particularly Karl Barth, Bayer argues that the Word of God does not come to the human subjectively as a merely rational or "purely spiritual Word."[89] Instead, says Bayer, God's address comes to the human always through creational means, always as *Leibliches Wort*. Bayer's Lutheranism here evidences itself when he articulates that the particular means through which God's address comes are the words of the physical preacher in the sermon and in the absolution, the waters of Holy Baptism, and the bread and wine of Holy Communion, which convey the body and blood of Jesus Christ with the promise of the forgiveness of sins, life and salvation.[90] In these means, says Bayer, Jesus Christ comes bodily and embodies the truth and power of God's justifying promise in the words attached to these sacramental elements: "I declare you forgiven of all your sins." "I baptize you in the name of the Father, and of the Son, and of the Holy Spirit." "Take and eat; this is my body for you. Take and drink; this cup is the new covenant made in my blood, shed for the forgiveness of your sins." In these words, says Bayer, Jesus Christ, himself, comes as *the* embodied Word of promise, as the God who exists for sinners, promising himself to sinners, saying, "You belong to me; stay in my hand." "I am *for you*."[91]

---

86. Wyller, *Glaube und Autonome Welt*, 111.

87. Bayer, *Martin Luther's Theology*, 89; Bayer, *Martin Luthers Theologie*, 81. Bayer, "Leibliches Wort," 83. Cf. CA, 5, in BC, 40–41; BSLK, 63.

88. Bayer, *Schöpfung als Anrede*, 13–14.

89. Bayer, *Schöpfung als Anrede*, 3ff. Bayer, *Theologie*, 377–78. Bayer, *Barmen zwischen Barth und Luther*, 29–31.

90. Bayer, *Martin Luther's Theology*, 249–56, 222–23; Bayer, *Martin Luthers Theologie*, 225–29, 200–221.

91. Bayer, *Aus Glauben Leben*, 58. Translation is my own. Cf. Bayer, *Living by Faith*, 51.

Though such a sacramental understanding of God's justifying address of promise to humans is certainly Lutheran and has its roots in the reformer's theology,[92] it is also shaped by Hamann's idea of creation as divine speech. God's address, says Bayer following Hamann, comes to the creature only through the creature.[93] Creation as God's good work and address thus serves as the sacramental vehicle for God's condemnation in the law and for God's justifying speech in the promise. In agreement with Hamann, Bayer emphasizes that all of creation and any creature has the potential to serve as such a vehicle for speech.[94] Bayer does not follow Hamann in saying that all of creation and every creature actually serves as such all the time. Nor does he use Hamann to construct a contemporary version of the romantic *Sturm und Drang* panentheism that is evident in the writings of Herder, Goethe, Schiller, and to some extent even in works of Hamann himself. Bayer uses Hamann's notion of creation as address to explain how it is possible for the created to serve as a medium for the address of the Creator, but the ultimate trajectory of this in Bayer's thought is the classic Lutheran understandings of the incarnation of God in Jesus Christ, of the Word of God as sacramental in nature, and as coming through specific Sacraments. In Jesus Christ, says Bayer, the almighty God puts on human flesh and comes to the human creature as the human creature.[95] In the created means of the Sacraments, of the bodily Word, the almighty God in Christ comes clothed in the created, bodily means of human speech, water, bread, and wine. In this sacramental coming of the author-God, God's address and the created, bodily means that bear it are so intertwined that the Word becomes sacramental and the Sacraments become themselves divine address.[96]

Yet, while he does not affirm romantic panentheism, at the same time, Bayer does state that the creation itself is God's divine speech act, and that God's address to humans is not relegated to "the realm of Sacrament and preaching" but that it also takes place in creation.[97] He echoes Hamann's aesthetic notion that the created world functions as a text recording God's address, that creation is a Bible of sorts.[98] Like Hamann, Bayer regards God as

---

92. Cf. *LW* 36:44–46; *WA* 6:518–20.

93. Bayer, *Schöpfung als Anrede*, 18. Mattes, *The Role of Justification in Contemporary Theology*, 153.

94. Bayer, *Schöpfung als Anrede*, 18–19. Mattes, *The Role of Justification in Contemporary Theology*, 153.

95. Bayer, *Schöpfung als Anrede*, 18–19. Mattes, *The Role of Justification in Contemporary Theology*, 153.

96. Bayer, *Leibliches Wort*, 59.

97. Bayer, *Martin Luther's Theology*, 102; Bayer, *Martin Luthers Theologie*, 93.

98. Baeyr, *Schöpfung als Anrede*, 13. Bayer, *Martin Luther's Theology*, 104; Bayer,

a divine poet and author who has spoken the world into existence, continues to uphold the world by God's speech, and speaks to human creatures through the creation.[99] He also adopts Hamann's idea that creation is God's address itself, that creation is God's "speech to the creature through the creature."[100] Bayer is not, however, advocating that one can be justified through some kind of natural revelation, apart from the Word of God in the Scriptures, preaching, and the Sacraments. For the specific Word of God's promise in these places are the key to opening up nature.[101] As I highlighted above, Bayer understands that though God's speech to humans is indeed present in creation, sinful humans are unable to recognize this, and where they encounter it, they faithlessly and idolatrously misuse it. The world may be God's text and the creation may contain or even be God's speech, but, says Bayer, without the specific sacramental Word of God's promise, this speech goes unheard, for the relationship between the speaking God and the addressed human and the relationship between creation and the human are broken.[102]

In fact, it is the very Word of God in the promise, "Be opened," says Bayer, that serves as the key to open creation. It is the word of Jesus Christ, the Word of God, through the preached, sacramental gospel that opens creation anew as God's speech to the human.[103] For, ultimately, Jesus Christ is God's address in creation, says Bayer. Through his incarnation as a human being and through the created means of the proclaimed *Leibliches Wort* in the preaching and the Sacraments, Jesus Christ himself is preached to sinners and actually is God's Word of justifying promise.[104] In this way, Bayer's Lutheran sacramentology of *Leibliches Wort* and his Hamannian notion of *Schöpfung als Anrede* come together in his understanding of the way in

---

Martin Luthers Theologie, 95.

99. Bayer, *Zeitgenosse im Widerspruch*, 75–83; Bayer, *A Contemporary in Dissent*, 165–70. Bayer, *Gott als Autor*, 30–33. Bayer, "God as Author of My Life History," 437, 444–46. Johann Georg Hamann, *Aesthetica in nuce* (1762), in *Sämtliche Werke*, 2:140, 206.

100. Bayer, *Schöpfung als Anrede*, 14–15. Bayer, *Zeitgenosse im Widerspruch*, 95; Bayer, *A Contemporary in Dissent*, 74. Hamann, *Sämtliche Werke* 2:198. Bayer's student, Johannes Schwanke, has also adopted the perspective of Hamann that God is the author of creation and that creation is God's address "to the creature through the creature" and further investigated Luther's doctrine of creation, particularly in the *Lectures on Genesis*, from this standpoint. Schwanke, "Luther on Creation," 5–6. Cf. Schwanke, *Creatio ex nihilo*.

101. Bayer, *Zeitgenosse im Widerspruch*, 91; Bayer, *A Contemporary in Dissent*, 70. Bayer, *Schöpfung als Anrede*, 10–11.

102. Bayer, *Schöpfung also Anrede*, 19–20.

103. Bayer, *Martin Luther's Theology*, 107–8; Bayer, *Martin Luthers Theologie*, 97–98.

104. Bayer, *Schöpfung als Anrede*, 16–17.

which God's justifying promise in Christ comes to human sinners, forgiving their sins, creating a new relationship between God and them, and opening creation anew to them. According to Bayer, this promise comes as divine address from the Creator to the creature, through the creature, namely through Jesus Christ as the bodily Word.[105]

The Rupture of the Ages: The Brokenness of Creation and the Reality of the Promise

Although creation is opened anew to the believer and the believer to creation through the proclaimed, bodily Word of God's promise in Jesus Christ, still not all is perfect in creation; creation has not returned to paradise. Instead, says Bayer, while the promise is really valid in the present time, both humanity and creation itself still bear the marks of sin. These marks are particularly visible in the inability of humans to understand the speech of God in creation, their failure to recognize creation as God's good work and as God's address to the creature, and the substitution of dumb idols for the speaking God.[106] Furthermore, the promise of life and salvation hardly seems apparent in the present state of creation as humans see it. Instead, evil and death are rampant in creation.[107] As Marx identifies, nature itself, through natural evil and the powers of death wielded by nature, appears to be in revolt, in a revolution, against humanity and against human justice.[108] Such revolt, says Bayer, is indicative of the brokenness of creation under the power of sin, but the solution is not the harnessing and humanizing of nature advocated by Marx.[109] Whether the efforts to subjugate the revolting nature take on a socialist or a capitalist form, they are ultimately doomed to fail and are completely useless; creation still revolts.[110] In stark contrast to the failure of human ideology, the Word of God promises and effects the "better world" of which capitalism knows nothing and of which Marxism can only dream.[111]

---

105. Ibid. Wyller, *Glaube und Autonome Welt*, 112.

106. Bayer, *Martin Luther's Theology*, 110–11; Bayer, *Martin Luthers Theologie*, 100–101.

107. Bayer, *Martin Luther's Theology*, 112; Bayer, *Martin Luthers Theologie*, 102.

108. Bayer, *Schöpfung als Anrede*, 47. Cf. Marx, "Ökonomisch-philosophische Manuskripte," in *Marx–Engels Gesamtausgabe*, vol. 2, 292.

109. Ibid.

110. Bayer, *Schöpfung als Anrede*, 47–48.

111. Ibid. Cf. Bayer, "Für eine bessere Weltlichkeit," 238–260; Bayer, *Leibliches Wort*, 265–86.

According to Bayer, the only solution to the brokenness of creation comes from God as a Word of God, the Word "Be opened!" in which the eschatological reality of salvation and the renewal of all creation is present in the present. While creation awaits its renewal under the curse of death, the promise of such renewal, which itself effects the renewal, exists in the present. Thus, only the believer knows the real creation, the way God intends it, the way it should be, by faith in God's promise.[112] God has promised: "See, I am making all things new," but the evidence of God's work of re-creation and its first fruits in the resurrection of Christ are apparent only to faith in God's promise.[113] What the believer and creation experience in the meantime between the coming of the promise and its final fulfillment in the eschaton is what Bayer identifies as the "rupture of the ages" ("*Zeitenbruch*"). This rupture consist of the cleavage between the "old aeon" of humanity and creation under sin and death, on the one hand, and the "new aeon" of a re-created humanity and renewed creation on the other.[114] Existing in the midst of this rupture, believers know the new creation of God only through faith in God's Word of promise. Living in the present under the promise, however, believers and creation itself are not silent in the face of the brokenness of the world. Instead, they sigh together for God's promised renewal and final eschatological redemption of all things.[115] There is real power in such sighing says Bayer. For believers, this sighing takes on the form of the lament, "Marantha!," which expresses the desire for God to make good on God's promise of the eschatological renewal of all things.[116] Through such lament, believers enter into a verbal exchange (*Wortwechsel*) with the God of the promise, who has promised to hear and answer the prayers of God's people.[117] In Jesus Christ, God even participates in such sighing, in solidarity with the believer and the broken creation, who together await the promised renewal of all things. Moreover, it is in Jesus Christ that God answers such sighing. For it is in Christ that the creator God comes to the creation as a creature and speaks the effectual Word of promise to creation,

---

112. Bayer, *Martin Luther's Theologe*, 111–12; Bayer, *Martin Luthers Theologie*, 101–2.

113. Oswald Bayer, "Toward a Theology of Lament," 213; Bayer, "Theologie der Klage," in *Zugesagte Gegenwart*, 64.

114. Bayer, *Martin Luther's Theology*, 1–2; Bayer, *Martin Luthers Theologie*, 1–2. Bayer, "Rupture of the Ages," 35–37; Byaer, *Gott als Autor*, 149–50.

115. Bayer, *Martin Luther's Theology*, 112; Bayer, *Martin Luthers Theologie*, 103.

116. Bayer, *Martin Luther's Theology*, 112–13;Bayer, *Martin Luthers Theologie*, 103. Bayer, "Erhörte Klage," 263–65; Bayer, *Leibliches Wort*, 338–341. Bayer, "Toward a Theology of Lament," 212–13; Bayer, *Zugesagte Gegenwart*, 63–64.

117. Bayer, *Martin Luther's Theology*, 112–14; Bayer, *Martin Luthers Theologie*, 103–4. Bayer, "Erhörte Klage," 263–65; Bayer, *Leibliches Wort*, 338–41.

"Be opened!"[118] It is in this Word that God gives believers the comfort and the courage to face life, and it is in this Word that God will remake and is remaking the old creation into the new,[119] so that just as the mouth of the mute man spoken of in Mark 7 was opened by the Lord, the Word of God made flesh in Jesus Christ is opening both the believer and the whole of creation anew to live in righteousness before God through the justifying promise of God in the gospel Jesus Christ.[120]

For Bayer, while creation is fallen and still longs for its ultimate redemption, justification and creation belong together in the present. Bayer argues that creation cannot be understood apart from justification, and justification cannot be understood apart from creation.[121] One cannot understand creation without first being justified by God's promise.[122] Yet, once one has been justified by God's promise, all of creation opens up to the human who is himself or herself opened not only to a new relationship with God but also to renewed relationships with all of creation.[123] God's word of justification, says Bayer, comes through creational means,[124] and through the justifying Word of God, "Be opened!," creation itself becomes known and heard as God's speech "to the creature through the creature."[125] Though humans indeed live in the "rupture of the ages," between the complete fulfillment of the promise seen in the renewal of all creation in the eschatological future and the contradiction of this promise evident in the brokenness of the present, the reality of this fulfillment is present already through the promise, which is itself the means by which God will open and is opening the renewal of creation.[126]

---

118. Bayer, *Martin Luther's Theology*, 113; Bayer, *Martin Luthers Theologie*, 103–4.

119. Bayer, *Martin Luther's Theology*, 9–10; Bayer, *Martin Luthers Theologie*, 8–9. Bayer, "Rupture of the Ages," 43–45; Bayer, *Gott als Autor*, 156–58.

120. Bayer, *Martin Luther's Theology*, 113–14; Bayer, *Martin Luthers Theologie*, 103–4.

121. Bayer, "Justification and Ontology," 46; Bayer, *Zugesagte Gegenwart*, 197.

122. Bayer, "Justification and Ontology," 46; Bayer, *Zugesagte Gegenwart*, 197–98.

123. Helmer, "The Subject of Theology in the Thought of Oswald Bayer," 286. Bayer, *Martin Luther's Theology*, 108–14; Bayer, *Martin Luthers Theologie*, 98–104.

124. Bayer, *Martin Luther's Theology*, 89; Bayer, *Martin Luthers Theologie*, 81.

125. Bayer, *Martin Luther's Theology*, 107–8; Bayer, *Martin Luthers Theologie*, 97–98.

126. Bayer, *Martin Luther's Theology*, 9–10; Bayer, *Martin Luthers Theologie*, 8–9. Bayer, "Rupture of the Ages," 43–45; Bayer, *Gott als Autor*, 156–58.

Summary

Bayer's understanding of justification embodies the idea that God declares the human sinner righteous through the divine speech act of the promise of the gospel of Jesus Christ, delivered to the human through the preaching of the Word and Sacraments. In relating this understanding, Bayer draws on Austin's theory of speech act, but ultimately Bayer anchors this understanding in the fact that it is God whose Word declares the human sinner righteous. By means of declaring the human righteous, God brings the sinner into a new relationship with God, forgives, liberates and grants confidence in faith to the sinner, opens the whole world to the justified sinner as a new creation, and, indeed, through created means, opens the justified sinner anew to the created world.

In setting forth his view of justification, Bayer draws from Austin, Luther, and Hamann to forge a theology of justification in which the sinner is justified by God's performative speech act of promise, which does what it says: forgives sins, justifies the sinner in God's sight, and opens up a new creation. This active and effectual Word of God's promise in the gospel of Jesus Christ comes to the human creature through the creation and the creature as bodily Word in the incarnate Christ through preaching and the Sacraments. This theology of justification gives shape to all of Bayer's thought. Consequently, Bayer approaches theological themes such as the Church, the nature of humanity, eschatology, and Christian ethics all through the central theological motif of the performative promise of God in the gospel, which justifies the sinner and opens life in the realm of creation.

Of particular interest here is that Bayer approaches the theme of the hiddenness of God through this view of justification. As I stated at the closing of chapter four, the nature and place of divine hiddenness in Bayer's theology is defined and described in part by how Bayer approaches the doing of theology and by the central role played by justification in Bayer's theology. The specifics of this definition are played out against the backdrop of how Bayer describes justification taking place through God's speech act of promise and what it accomplishes, namely the gracious forgiveness of sins, the giving of confidence to the believing sinner, and the opening of a new creation. In large part, Bayer describes the nature of God's work in hiddenness as the opposite of God's justifying work in the promise of the gospel and as the contradiction of the forgiveness, confidence, and opening of the new creation effected by God's performative speech act of the promise in justification. Before addressing in detail how Bayer defines and describes God's hiddenness according to his understanding of justification, however, it is necessary first to examine how Bayer's view of Luther's doctrine of the hidden God and his adopting and utilizing of it in his own theology is shaped by his approach to theology.

6

The Hidden God in Bayer's Approach to Theology

I HAVE STRIVEN TO illustrate thus far how Bayer undertakes the task of systematic theology from a decidedly Lutheran perspective. Bayer utilizes Luther's theological teachings in defining the mode, method, data, and subject matter of theology. Bayer takes to heart the reformer's admonition that God's justification of the sinner by faith in Jesus Christ is the true subject matter of theology, and correspondingly identifies justification as the subject that defines the true center, basis, and boundary of all Christian theology. Furthermore, by use of his understanding of God's promise as effectual divine speech act, Bayer offers a contemporary interpretation of Luther's doctrine of justification by faith through the gospel of Jesus Christ that takes seriously the reformer's understanding of that promise as an active and effectual Word of God. Bayer's use and interpretation of Luther is not, however, relegated exclusively to his approach to theology and view of justification. From the core teaching of justification, Bayer also embarks on contemporary explorations of Luther's teaching regarding the Church, ethics, the family, civil government, and eschatology, amongst other subjects, interprets them and adopts them into his own contemporary Lutheran theology. Bayer also employs Luther's doctrine of the hiddenness of God in his own theology, articulating and nuancing it in the context of his contemporary Lutheran theology with its experiential approach to theology and its center of justification through God's promise.

Bayer as an Interpreter of Luther on the Hidden God

Unlike many figures before him in the German theological tradition, Bayer recognizes most of the main features of Luther's doctrine of the hidden God, embraces this teaching of the reformer, and utilizes it in his own Lutheran theology. This does not mean, however, that there are not incongruities between Bayer's understanding of divine hiddenness and the theme as it appears in Luther's theology. Bayer does, in fact, develop the theme of God's hiddenness along the contours of his own theology, which, although certainly informed by Luther, entails its own distinctiveness as well. Moreover, there are some aspects of Luther's doctrine of the hidden God that Bayer neglects, leaves underdeveloped or contradicts. My assessment of congruities and incongruities of Bayer's teaching about divine hiddenness with Luther's own teaching on the subject will, however, be left for chapter eight of this work. Before undertaking this comparison between Bayer and Luther, it is first necessary that Bayer's adoption of Luther's doctrine of the hidden God and his use it in his theology be discussed.

Bayer's Adoption of Luther's Doctrine of the Hidden God

The fact that Bayer adopts Luther's teaching concerning the hiddenness of God sets him apart in the modern German Protestant theological tradition, both as a Luther scholar and as a systematic theologian. In his study of Luther's theology, Bayer identifies Luther's distinction between the hidden God and revealed God as an important matrix for understanding Luther's theology and the doctrine of God hidden outside of revelation as one of the reformer's key teachings.[1] Furthermore, Bayer correctly identifies Luther's doctrine of the hidden God as teaching that, outside of God's revelation in Christ, God exists in incomprehensible hiddenness and that this hidden God actively wills wrath against the sinner, works death, and "all things."[2]

---

1. Bayer, *Martin Luther's Theology*, 11; Bayer, *Martin Luthers Theologie*, 10. Bayer, "Rupture of Times," 46; Bayer, *Gott als Autor*, 159.

2. Bayer, *Martin Luther's Theology*, 202; Bayer, *Martin Luthers Theologie*, 182. Bayer, *Theology the Lutheran Way*, 104; Bayer, *Theologie*, 416. Bayer, *Living by Faith*, 71; Bayer, *Aus Glauben Leben*, 77. Bayer, "Die ganze Theologie Luthers," 265. Bayer, "Der

Bayer also captures the heart of Luther's teaching about the hidden God by relating that Luther states that the hidden God and the hidden God's will and work are ultimately areas of God's existence and ways that are forbidden to the believer but that the revealed God exists for the believer as the God who is known as a God of grace, mercy, and love in the gospel of Jesus Christ.[3]

Though he recognizes that Luther's teaching regarding the hidden God of wrath has not been popular in Protestant theology since the time of the Reformation, Bayer teaches it nonetheless, seeking to confess "the whole of Luther's theology" (*"die ganze Theologie Luthers"*).[4] Such a view of God as a God of wrath, says Bayer, is not accidental to God's nature, nor is it a point to be minimized or explained away within some greater, overarching theme such as love itself as a "timeless principle" describing the essence of who God is.[5] Instead of discounting Luther's idea of the hidden God as the God of wrath who wills the death and damnation of sinners and who wills all things, Bayer takes the reformer's teaching in God's hiddenness outside of revelation seriously, saying that in hiddenness, God comes to the human sinner as an enemy.[6] One should not try to explain away or systematize the tension and contradiction in God that the teaching of hiddenness presents. Instead, one must recognize this tension and contradiction in theology, and within God's very self, for what it truly is.[7] Ultimately, says Bayer, while one cannot avoid or mitigate the hidden God, one can, and must, flee for refuge to the revealed God from the hidden God, to "God against God." One must confess the God of the promise of the gospel revealed in Christ over and

Glanz der Gnade," 81. *BOW*, 170; *WA* 18:685.

3. Bayer, *Martin Luther's Theology*, 11–12; Bayer, *Martin Luthers Theologie*, 10–11. Bayer, "Rupture of the Times," 46–47; Bayer, *Gott als Autor*, 159–60. Bayer, *Theology the Lutheran Way*, 18–19; Bayer, *Theologie*, 39.

4. Bayer, "Die ganze Luthers Theologie," 265. Bayer, *Martin Luther's Theology*, 208; Bayer, *Martin Luthers Theologie*, 188.

5. Bayer, "Hermeneutical Theology," 140; Bayer, "Hermeneutische Theologie," in *Zugesagte Gegenwart*, 349.

6. Bayer, *Theology the Lutheran Way*, 18–19, 114; Bayer, *Theologie*, 39, 425–26. Bayer, "Die ganze Theologie Luthers," 265. Bayer, "Poetological Doctrine of the Trinity," 52; Bayer, "Poetologische Trinitätslehre," 76–77; Bayer, "Poietologische Trinitätslehre," in *Gott als Autor*, 145. Bayer, "Gegen Gott für den Menschen : zu Feuerbachs Lutherrezeption," 59; Bayer, "Gegen Gott für den Menschen," in *Leibliches Wort*, 229.

7. Bayer, "Hermeneutical Theology," 140; Bayer, *Zugesagte Gegenwart*, 349. Helmer, "The Subject of Theology in the Thought of Oswald Bayer," 35. Bayer, "Poetological Doctrine of the Trinity," 52; Bayer, "Poetologische Trinitätslehre," 76–77; Bayer, *Gott als Autor*, 145. Bayer, "Poetological Theology" 164–165; Bayer, "Einführung Poietologische Theologie," in *Gott als Autor*, 14–15. Bayer, "What Is Evangelical?" 10–11; Bayer, *Zugesagte Gegenwart*, 31.

against the hidden God of wrath.[8] In this way, Bayer correctly summarizes and adopts Luther's essential definition of the hidden God, as the reformer states it in *The Bondage of the Will*.[9]

Schreckliche Verborgenheit: The Hidden God and the Mode of Theology

Bayer's discussion of the hidden God follows the contours of his definitions of the mode of theology as experiential wisdom, the method of theology as embodied in the three-fold rule he adopts from Luther, the data of theology as God's address to humans, and the definition of the core subject matter of theology as God's justification of the sinner by faith in Christ. As I illustrated in chapter four, Bayer describes both the mode and method of theology as being inherently experiential in nature, eschewing the distinction between theory and praxis, bringing experience directly into the doing of theology itself. Building on this experiential foundation, Bayer grounds the doing of theology in the theologian's experiences of *oratio*, *meditatio*, and *tentatio*. Bayer even goes to the extent of saying, with Luther, "Only experience makes a theologian."[10] But, exactly what kind of experience does Bayer mean when he says that the mode of theology is experiential wisdom; what kind of experience makes a theologian?

It is precisely at this point that the notion of the hidden God enters into Bayer's approach to theology. Some might object to Bayer's use of experience in his approach to theology, claiming that it is too near the existentialist approaches of classic liberal theologians like Friedrich Schleiermacher, and Bayer anticipates such objections. He answers them by saying that his use of experience—indeed the reformational use of experience—in theology is not the same as a purely existential approach because it does not make use of experience in general, or even a universal feeling of dependence through meditation on the divine in the cosmic order as Schleiermacher advocates; rather Bayer addresses the particular experience of being encountered by the living God.[11]

---

8. Bayer, "What is Evangelical?" 10–11; Bayer, *Zugesagte Gegenwart*, 31. Bayer, "The Modern Narcissus," 311–12; Bayer, *Gott als Autor*, 84. Bayer, *Theology the Lutheran Way*, 207. Bayer, *Martin Luther's Theology*, 21, 213.

9. *BOW* 169–171; WA 18:684–86.

10. Bayer, *Martin Luther's Theology*, 21–22; Bayer, *Martin Luthers Theologie*, 20–21.

11. Bayer, *Theology the Lutheran Way*, 112–14, 174–75; Bayer, *Theologie*, 424–26, 490–91. Cf. Schleiermacher, *The Christian Faith*, vol. 1, 131–48.

Bayer states that this particular experience of God's addressing the human takes place primarily in the Word, the only place where God and the human being can peacefully coexist.¹² Correspondingly, the experience that makes a theologian, says Bayer, is not simply a generic universal experience, but the experience of being addressed by the Word through Holy Scripture, an experienced worked out in *oratio*, *meditatio*, and *tentatio*.¹³ But the Word is not the only place where the human is encountered and addressed by the living God; God also encounters and addresses the human outside of the Word, through God's hiddenness.¹⁴

In contrast to the encounter with God in God's Word of promise in the gospel of Christ, in the encounter with the hidden God the human cannot coexist peacefully with God. Instead, the human experiences God as the enemy, the God of wrath who wills and works the destruction of sinners.¹⁵ Bayer states that such an experience of God is indeed universal, but, contrary to Schleiermacher's understanding of experience and its role in theology, it is far from being any benevolent feeling of ultimate dependence that can serve as the starting point for theology. On the contrary, the universal experience of God's hiddenness, of being encountered by God outside of the Word, is one of absolute terror and fear of the divine; it is the experience of God as the primal dread.¹⁶

Here, in hiddenness, God actually fights against the human sinner as an enemy, as one who seeks to destroy the human, as the one who will be the sinner's undoing. In this experience of the divine, the human cannot grasp God. In this experience of God, God is incomprehensible, other than that God fights against the sinner, seeking the sinner's destruction. Like Jacob who wrestled with God at the Jabbok, the human sinner cannot understand the hidden God but experiences God this as if he or she is the object of God's anger.¹⁷ In this experience of God outside the Word, God is indistinguishable from the devil, so great is the hostility of God towards the human sinner.¹⁸ Here the human experiences God not only outside the promise but even contrary to the promise. Here God is experienced not as the one who

---

12. Bayer, *Martin Luther's Theology*, 39; Bayer, *Martin Luthers Theologie*, 35.

13. Bayer, *Martin Luther's Theology*, 22, 36–37; Bayer, *Martin Luthers Theologie*, 20–21, 33–34. Bayer, *Theology the Lutheran Way*, 112–14; Bayer, *Theologie*, 424–26.

14. Bayer, *Martin Luther's Theology*, 11; Bayer, *Martin Luthers Theologie*, 10. Bayer, "Rupture of the Times," 46; Bayer, *Gott als Autor*, 158–59.

15. Bayer, *Martin Luther's Theology*, 39; Bayer, *Martin Luthers Theologie*, 35

16. Bayer, *Martin Luther's Theology*, 39–41; Bayer, *Martin Luthers Theologie*, 35–37.

17. Bayer, *Theology the Lutheran Way*, 18–19, 99; Bayer, *Theologie* 38–40, 409–10.

18. Ibid. Bayer, *Martin Luther's Theology*, 204–5; Bayer, *Martin Luthers Theologie*, 184–185.Bayer, "Die ganze Theologie Luthers," 267.

saves based on a gracious will but as the God of wrath who is out to destroy the human sinner.[19]

This hiddenness, says Bayer, though it constitutes a specific experience of God's wrath, encompasses all of life's experiences. It is the "terrible hiddenness" ("*schreckliche Verborgenheit*") of God, in which God does not appear as the giver of the promise of life alone, but in which God "accomplishes evil as well as good, life as well as death, light as well as darkness, happiness as well as misfortune."[20] According to Bayer, the experience of this hiddenness is not unique to the believer alone but, rather, is the common experience of all human beings and even of creation itself.[21] It is the experience of the evil things that happen in this world, which are seemingly mixed together with the good.[22] It is not only the experience of evil done by humans, though this certainly is part of it, but it is also the natural evils that befall a broken creation, including natural disasters, disease, and the current ecological crisis of the physical environment of the universe.[23] This experience of God's terrible hiddenness becomes tangible in the natural evils of earthquakes, tsunamis, pandemics, and the untimely deaths of children, as well as in evils manufactured by humans, including the horrific genocide of the shoa and the destructive power of nuclear weapons.[24]

---

19. Bayer, *Theology the Lutheran Way*, 99, 102; Bayer, *Theologie*, 409–10, 413.

20. Bayer, *Martin Luther's Theology*, 202; Bayer, *Martin Luthers Theologie*, 182. Bayer, "Poetological Doctrine of the Trinity," 54; Bayer, "Poetologische Trinitätslehre," 78; Bayer, *Gott als Autor*, 146–47. Bayer, "The Plurality of the One God and the Plurality of the Many Gods," 343–44; Bayer, "Die Vielheit des einen Gottes und die Vielheit der Götter," in *Zugesagte Gegenwart*, 100. Bayer, "Der Glanz der Gnade," 79.

21. Bayer, "The Plurality of the One God," 349; Bayer, *Zugesagte Gegenwart*, 105.

22. Bayer, *Martin Luther's Theology*, 202; Bayer, *Martin Luthers Theologie*, 182.

23. Bayer, *Schöpfung als Anrede*, 161. Bayer, "Der neue Mensch," 126–27; Bayer, "Der neue Mensch ," in *Zugesagte Gegenwart*, 244–45.

24. Bayer, "Der Glanze der Gnade," 80. Bayer, *Gott als Autor*, 272. Bayer's description of universal experience of the hidden God in human evil and a creation in which death and chaos overflow might be summarized in the words of Goethe's poem, "Das Göttliche":

Denn unfühlend
Ist die Natur:
Es leuchtet die Sonne
Über Bös und Gute
Und dem Verbrecher
Glänzen wie dem Besten

der Mond und die Sterne.
Wind und Ströme,
Donner und Hagel
Rauschen ihren Weg

Suffering and the experience of evil, both natural and human, are not unique to the Christian experience but are, in fact, universal in scope. Christians and unbelievers both know experientially in this world "'how everything is not of sugar,' as Döblin says in *Berlin Alexanderplatz*, 'but of sugar and dirt all mixed up.'"[25] Not only Christians realize that not all is right in the world, says Bayer. Many humans do, and some of them seek to explain why this is the case. The universal experience of God's terrifying hiddenness thus serves as part of the mode of theology, any theology, Christian or otherwise. One explanation for this experience, says Bayer, is the "mythology of polytheism." Out the uncertainty of experiencing good

Und ergreifen
Vorüber eilend
Einen um den andern.

Auch so das Glück
Tappt unter die Menge,
Faßt bald des Knaben
Lockige Unschuld,
Bald auch den kahlen
Schuldigen Scheitel.

ET:
For the realm of nature
Is unfeeling:
The sun sheds its light
Over evil and good
And the moon and the stars
Shine on the criminal
As on the best of us.

The wind and the rivers
The hail and the thunder
Storm on their way
And snatch one victim
After another
As they rush past.

So too does blind fortune
Grope through the crowd, now
Seizing a young boy's
Curly-haired innocence
And now the bald pate
Of the old and guilty.

Goethe (c. 1783), in Goethe, *Selected Poetry*, 52–55.

25. Bayer, "Creation as History," 261; Bayer, "Schöpfung als Geschichte," in *Zugesagte Gegenwart*, 229. Döblin, *Berlin Alexanderplatz*, 392.

and bad together, polytheistic paganism has endeavored to answer the question of why. "Is it Vishnu in his goodness and at the same time Kali who destroys?"[26]

Polytheism is not the only non-Christian answer to the experience of hiddenness that Bayer identifies. There is also an intellectual approach. For, the universal experience of divine hiddenness in evil serves not only as part of what makes up the mode of theology, but also as what makes up the mode of theodicy. All the great forms of theodicy in philosophical discourse, including ethical, speculative, and political forms, says Bayer, take their starting point from this common human experience of the hiddenness of God through evil in the world.[27] Yet, all of the answers given by secular theodicy ring hollow in the face of the work of the hidden God. Evil still persists; reason and philosophy cannot do away with that fact.[28] The only resolution to the experience of the terrible hiddenness of God is God's promise in the gospel, and that, says Bayer, is something known to the Christian alone. For, no matter how true and applicative the gospel is for all humans, it is not present in all human experience or in all religion, "not even in traces and analogies." Instead, says Bayer, the gospel is present only in the preaching of the Word, Jesus Christ. While God's hiddenness, which makes up part of the mode of theology, is experienced by all humans, God's message of grace and love in the gospel is not.[29]

This does not mean that dealing with the hiddenness of God is any easier for Christians than it is for humans in general. This experience of the hidden God is no less acute for those who are believers than for those who are not. In fact, according to Bayer, it is even more acute for the believer, because the believer experiences the work of the hidden God, already knowing God in the Word of the promise of the gospel of Jesus Christ. God speaks for the believer and forgives the believer in the gospel, yet the believer still experiences God's wrath in hiddenness through the evil things of the world, and in so doing, experiences it precisely as the opposite of the experience of God in the promise of the gospel.[30] The response of the believer, however, is one that is made from the basis of faith in the promise, and thus the believer's questions about the meaning of suffering and evil in the world are also

---

26. Bayer, "The Plurality of the One God," 349; Bayer, *Zugesagte Gegenwart*, 105.

27. Bayer, *Living by Faith*, 9–18, 21–24; Bayer, *Aus Glauben Leben*, 21–28, 31–34.

28. Bayer, *Living by Faith*, 11–13; Bayer, *Aus Glauben Leben*, 22–25; Bayer, *Martin Luther's Theology*, 198; Bayer, *Martin Luthers Theologie*, 179.

29. Bayer, "The Plurality of the One God," 350; Bayer, *Zugesagte Gegenwart*, 106–7.

30. Bayer, *Theology the Lutheran Way*, 102, 104; Bayer, *Theologie*, 413, 415–16.

more acute than those of the nonbeliever: "Is God keeping his promise?" "My God, My God, why have you forsaken me?"[31]

Yet even some forms of Christian theology, says Bayer, want to dispense with the hiddenness of God. Bayer specifically identifies the contemporary Trinitarian renaissance as a theological movement that seeks to smooth over the contradiction between the experience of the hiddenness of God and the experience of the gracious address of God in the promise of the gospel through the unity in diversity of the Trinity. Instead of doing theology under the mode of tension between God's hiddenness and God's promise, says Bayer, the new Trinitarians, particularly Moltmann, have replaced the true mode of theology as it is really experienced with their own idea of the mode of theology based upon God's existence as Trinity.[32]

This tension, however, cannot be relieved so easily. The experienced reality of the work of the hidden God still exists and still grips all humans, especially Christians, and forms part of the experiential wisdom that makes up the mode of doing theology. For this reason, says Bayer, the theologian must do his or her work under the realization of this tension; he or she must wrestle with the hiddenness of God.[33] This does not mean, though, that the theologian is given a license to speculate about all manner of things that might be ascribed to the hiddenness of God. Divine hiddenness as part of the mode of theology does not mean that the theologians should take up speculating about the hidden God. Instead, it means that hiddenness of God actually grips and forms the theologian. This happens as the experience of the hiddenness of God becomes a very particular and personal experience for the theologian, the experience of *Anfechtung*. It is, at least in part, undergoing the experience of the hidden God that "makes a theologian."[34] It is at this point in Bayer's theology that the teaching of the hidden God moves from his explanation of the experiential mode of theology to the experiential method for doing theology, which he adopts from Luther.

The God Who Wrestles with the Theologian: The Hidden God and the Method of Theology

Bayer's expressed method for doing theology from Luther—consisting of prayer, meditation on Scripture, and the agonizing struggle of *Anfechtung*—is

31. Bayer, *Living by Faith*, 69–70, 10; Bayer, *Aus Glauben Leben*, 76–77, 22.

32. Bayer, "The Plurality of the One God," 353; Bayer, *Zugesagte Gegenwart*, 109.

33. Bayer, "The Plurality of the One God," 352–53; Bayer, *Zugesagte Gegenwart*, 108–9.

34. Bayer, *Martin Luther's Theology*, 36–37; Bayer, *Martin Luthers Theologie*, 33–34.

inherently experiential in nature and flows from the experiential mode of theology as experiential wisdom described by Bayer. According to Bayer, all believers are theologians to some extent, and so this experiential theological method befalls not only "professional" theologians but also all Christians.[35] In discussing how Bayer describes the hidden God in the method of theology, I thus use the terms "believer" and "theologian" somewhat interchangeably as Bayer also does.

Following his use of Luther's doctrine of the hidden God in forming part of the mode of theology, Bayer brings this doctrine into his description of how the theologian operates within the framework of the experiential method of theology as well. While Bayer does to some extent relate this doctrine to prayer and to meditation, he mainly connects this doctrine to his description of the role of *Anfechtung* in the method of doing theology and of forming the theologian.

The Hidden God in Conjunction with Prayer and Meditation

Although the agonizing struggle of *Anfechtung* is the main feature in Bayer's Lutheran theological method that relates to and embodies his articulation of the doctrine of the hidden God, there is also some intersection between the doctrine and the other two features of his theological method, prayer and meditation. What is striking about these two things in conjunction with hiddenness in Bayer's thought is how Bayer shows the disjuncture between hiddenness and prayer and hiddenness and meditation. For Bayer, prayer and meditation in the method of theology belong to the experience of the revealed God, not of the hidden God.

Prayer as it functions in the method of theology, according to Bayer, is primarily the prayer of the theologian to God for the gift of theological discernment. This gift is necessary in order for the theologian to do theology, because the knowledge of God as the justifier of the sinful human can never be arrived at by the use of human reason. Human reason is fallen and fallible, and the study of God's saving work requires a divine gift of knowledge outside of ordinary human reason.[36] Furthermore, Bayer rules out any kind of speculation in prayer through what one might label "contemplative prayer." Such prayer, indeed, would involve confronting the hiddenness of God. Yet, Bayer directly prohibits such prayer,[37] just as he, following Luther,

---

35. Bayer, *Martin Luther's Theology*, 16–17; Bayer, *Martin Luthers Theologie*, 15–17.

36. Bayer, *Martin Luther's Theology*, 33; Bayer, *Martin Luthers Theologie*, 31. Bayer, *Theology the Lutheran Way*, 43–47; Bayer, *Theologie*, 71–78.

37. Bayer, *Theology the Lutheran Way*, 45–47; Bayer, *Theologie*, 74–78.

prohibits any kind of speculation concerning the incomprehensible hiddenness of God.[38] This speculative approach to prayer, says Bayer, is precisely what fallen human reason wants to undertake. It wants to look into the hidden things of God, and it is precisely because of this that the theologian must pray to the revealed God for theological discernment to know what human reason does not seek to know: the saving work of the revealed God.[39]

The definition of prayer in Bayer's theological method certainly pertains to the revealed God known through God's revelation in Christ and not to God hidden outside of revelation. If there were any doubt about this, Bayer dispels them by his direct prohibition against the possibility of prayer to the hidden God. The hiddenness of God, says Bayer, is not a divine attribute or a proper name for God, and, thus, the hidden God "can never be used in the vocative voice."[40] Though prayer does come into Bayer's understanding of the believer's response to the hidden God by way of lament to the revealed God—which I will address in chapter seven—there is no prayer *to* the hidden God, and Bayer is clear that the prayer uttered by the theologian, described in his method of theology is a prayer to the revealed God.

Similarly, Bayer's explanation of the place of meditation in the method of theology pertains to the revealed God and excludes meditation upon the hiddenness of God. Bayer, following Luther, defines meditation in theological method very specifically as meditation upon the external Word of God in Holy Scripture.[41] This Word of God, says Bayer, has a proper name: Jesus Christ. The external Word of God in Scripture is Christ, the merciful revelation of God's salvation in the promise of the gospel who, according to Bayer, is the promise of God's own self.[42] True meditation consists of meditating upon God's gracious Word of promise in the Scriptures as that which "drives Christ home" (*was Christum treibet*).[43] This narrow definition of meditation excludes any kind of spiritualist enthusiasm, speculation, or contemplative flights of fancy all of which, in the words of Luther quoted by Bayer, "play 'blind man's bluff'" ("*Blinde Kuh' spielt*")[44] with the hidden God by anchoring the exercise of meditation in the external Word of God's promise.[45]

38. Bayer, *Martin Luther's Theology*, 198; Bayer, *Martin Luthers Theologie*,
39. Bayer, *Theology the Lutheran Way*, 45–46; Bayer, *Theologie*, 74–77.
40. Bayer, *Martin Luther's Theology*, 206; Bayer, *Martin Luthers Theologie*, 186.
41. Bayer, *Martin Luther's Theology*, 35; Bayer, *Martin Luthers Theologie*, 32.
42. Bayer, *Martin Luther's Theology*, 82; Bayer, *Martin Luthers Theologie*, 74.
43. Bayer, *Martin Luther's Theology*, 82–83; Bayer, *Martin Luthers Theologie*, 74–75.
44. Bayer, *Theology the Lutheran Way*, 45, 56; Bayer, *Theologie*, 75, 91. Cf. *LW* 19:55, *WA* 19:207.
45. Bayer, *Martin Luther's Theology*, 35; Bayer, *Martin Luthers Theologie*, 32. Bayer, *Theology the Lutheran Way*, 51, 53–58; Bayer, *Theologie*, 84, 86–94.

Yet, Bayer states that meditation inevitably leads to a confrontation with the hidden God through the experience of *Anfechtung*. Though meditation itself does not entail experience of the hidden God, *Anfechtung* does, and meditation on God's Word of promise in Scripture inevitably leads to the trial of faith in *Anfechtung*. Those who listen to this Word and take it to heart, says Bayer, will face spiritual attack in the form of temptation and doubt, and in the face of the agonizing struggle the theologian's trust in the Word is tested.[46]

Though *Anfechtung* is the definitive aspect of Bayer's method of theology that relates to the doctrine of the hidden God, Bayer at least alludes in a negative way to the hidden God with regard to prayer and meditation. In both cases, Bayer uses the concept of God's incomprehensible hiddenness outside of revelation to qualify what these two are not. Neither payer nor meditation, says Bayer, entail the contemplation of or speculation concerning the hidden God but are, instead, concerned with the revealed God in Christ. This is not the case, however, when one comes to *Anfechtung* in Bayer's theological method, for the agonizing struggle of *Anfechtung* is the experience of the spiritual attack by the hidden God on faith in the promise of the justifying God in the gospel of Jesus Christ.

The Hidden God and Anfechtung

Bayer describes *Anfechtung* as the venue for the hidden God, within the experiential method of theology.[47] In *Anfechtung*, the believer experiences the hiddenness of God as the attack on belief in God's Word of promise on the gospel of Christ. This attack comes through the terrifying issue of double predestination and the evil experienced in this world, calling into question the validity of faith in God's promise.[48] Yet, Bayer sees God's hidden work in *Anfechtung* as ultimately driving faith to trust God's promise in the midst of the experience of its contradiction.

For the believer, the work of the hidden God is perceptible in the evil that happens in the world and in the adversity that the believer feels in *Anfechtung* (*tentatio*).[49] Knowing that God is almighty, the believer experiences evil as the work of God hidden outside the Word of promise. The believer knows this, and this becomes a problem for the believer, precisely because

---

46. Bayer, *Theology the Lutheran Way*, 53–54; Bayer, *Theologie*, 86–88. Bayer, *Martin Luther's Theology*, 36–37; Bayer, *Martin Luthers Theologie*, 33–34.

47. Bayer, *Martin Luther's Theology*, 20–21; Bayer, *Martin Luthers Theologie*, 19–20.

48. Bayer, *Martin Luther's Theology*, 198–199; Bayer, *Martin Luthers Theologie*, 179.

49. Bayer, *Living by Faith*, 71; Bayer, *Aus Glauben Leben*, 77.

the believer knows God as God through the promise of the gospel of grace in Jesus Christ. In the promise of the gospel, the believer knows that God is omnipotent, because the believer has experienced God's omnipotence in God's work through the life-giving promise.[50] Moreover, the reason that the experience of the hidden God is so acute and a problem for the believer, is because the believer has the standard of God's Word of promise as that by which God and God's works are known. Here, the believer is at a loss for how to understand God in God's hiddenness, because here God is acting contrary to how God has given God's self to the human in the promise of the gospel.[51]

The experience of *Anfechtung* is the believer's experience of undergoing and suffering spiritual attack. For the one who believes in the promise of God in the gospel of Christ, this attack is the hidden God's attack on the belief in that promise, and it comes through trials sent to the believer by God.[52] Here the hiddenness of God raises the question of double-predestination in the believer's mind, "Did God really determine from eternity that some human beings would be damned?"[53] It also raises the issue of "the problem of evil," since it appears in such experience that God is directly responsible for evil.[54]

Following Luther, Bayer does not shy away from the fact that God causes evil as well as good.[55] Anything less than this, says Bayer, would amount to the denial of God's omnipotence, and without God's omnipotence, no one could ever be saved, and God would not be who God is. To deny God's responsibility for evil—good, evil, and all things—would be to deny God's omnipotence, and to deny God's omnipotence would be to deny God's very being God.[56] Bayer does not, however, seek to work out a balancing act between divine omnipotence and human freedom that somehow exonerates God and vindicates human "free will." On the contrary, Bayer submits that God's responsibility for evil is true at the same time that the

---

50. Bayer, "God's Omnipotence," 86–87; Byaer, *Zugesagte Gegenwart*, 112–13.

51. Bayer, *Living by Faith*, 70–71; Bayer, *Aus Glauben Leben*, 77. Bayer, *Theology the Lutheran Way*, 102–4; Bayer, *Theologie*, 413–16. Bayer, *Martin Luther's Theology*, 20–21; Bayer, *Luthers Theologie*, 19–20.

52. Ibid. Byaer, *Theology the Lutheran Way*, 59–62; Byaer, *Theologie*, 96–101.

53. Bayer, *Martin Luther's Theology*, 198–99; Byaer, *Martin Luthers Theologie*, 178–79.

54. Bayer, *Martin Luther's Theology*, 199, 201; Bayer, *Martin Luthers Theologie*, 179, 81.

55. Bayer, *Martin Luther's Theology*, 199–202; Bayer, *Martin Luthers Theologie*, 179–82.

56. Bayer, "God's Omnipotence," 87–89; Bayer, *Zugesagte Gegenwart*, 113–15.

promise of God's grace and goodness in Christ is also true. The effect that this has upon the believer, says Bayer, is that the believer is thrown into a life or death struggle with the God who is both hidden and revealed, who does evil as well as good, who works death as well as life.[57] In the midst of this struggle of *Anfechtung* and its context of utter contradiction, the work of the hidden God contradicts the promise of God that the believer knows and as such the hidden God's doings appear utterly incomprehensible and assault the believer's trust in the God of the promise.[58]

This experience of the hidden God in *Anfechtung*, says Bayer, is more than just some form of intellectual angst or a mental pondering of skepticism.[59] In hiddenness, the incomprehensible God comes as the one who wrestles with the believer, indistinguishable from the devil, challenging the believer's belief in the promise through the believer's experience of God's terrifying hiddenness, radically contradicting the promise of God in the gospel.[60] This experience of God's hiddenness in *Anfechtung* is thus a spiritual attack of "the worst kind" in which God's hiddenness radically contradicts God's promise in the gospel.[61]

Yet Bayer maintains that, in spite of God's contradiction of the promise of the gospel and its attack upon the faith of the believer, God is faithful to God's promise and to the believer to whom God has promised God's self. Part of this faithfulness is that the hidden God uses indirect means to attack the believer, instead of engaging in this assault personally as the same promising God. Adopting Luther's opinion, Bayer states that God does not fight directly against the believer in *Anfechtung* but does so by virtue of God's omnipotence exercised through hiddenness, so that while hidden, God uses foreign instruments to carry out God's hidden work in *Anfechtung*. Bayer identifies the instruments used by the hidden God in this work of omnipotence as the devil and evil in the world, both humanly and naturally caused. Evil people and the devil, who think themselves to be carrying fulfilling the

---

57. Bayer, *Martin Luther's Theology*, 201–202; Bayer, *Martin Luthers Theologie*, 181–82.

58. Bayer, *Martin Luther's Theology*, 198; Bayer, *Martin Luthers Theologie*, 178. Bayer, *Theology the Lutheran Way*, 104; Bayer, *Theologie*, 415–416. Bayer, "God's Omnipotence," 88–90; Bayer, *Zugesagte Gegenwart*, 114–15.

59. Bayer, *Zugesagte Gegenwart*, 71. "Anfechtung ist also mächtiger als der radikalste intellektuelle Zweifel, mächtiger beispielweise als das cartesische Gedankenexperiment einer annihilation mundi, das ja der Auffindung und dem Innewerden eines fundamentum inconcussum dient, oder als die radikale Skepsis David Humes."

60. Bayer, "Rupture of times, 37–38; Bayer, *Gott als Autor*, 150–52 . Bayer, *Martin Luther's Theology*, 201–6, 213; Bayer, *Martin Luthers Theologie*, 181–86, 192. Bayer, "Die ganze Theologie Luthers," 267.

61. Bayer, *Theology the Lutheran Way*, 64; Bayer, *Theologie*, 103.

desires of their own will, are actually carrying out God's will, functioning as tools for the realization of God's will. In this way, no entity escapes the all-encompassing, all-working will of the omnipotent God, who does God's hidden work of *Anfechtung* through these means.[62]

The other side of God's faithfulness through *Anfechtung* consists of the fact that even *Anfechtung* plays something of a positive role in the life of the believer and the theologian, validating faith and leading faith back to the promise of God in Christ. Bayer thus describes *Anfechtung* as "the touchstone" ("*der Prüfstein*") in the believer's experience and in the formation of the theologian.[63] This does not mean, says Bayer, that the experience of God's hiddenness through *Anfechtung* proves that faith is real on the part of the believer in the sense of proving the strength of the believer's genuine motive or effort in believing. Rather, it proves the strength of God's Word for the believer and that the believer has been the recipient of God's Word of promise.[64]

Furthermore, according to Bayer, the "touchstone" of *Anfechtung* actually drives the faith to God's Word of promise in the gospel. Certainty of salvation, says Bayer, and not knowledge is the ultimate goal of theology and of the believer's experience of *Anfechtung*. The work of the hidden God in *Anfechtung* calls into question the validity of God's Word of promise, but at the same time, it drives the believer and the theologian to cling to that Word.[65] *Anfechtung* does this by rendering the believer passive in the face of God's hidden work, stripping away every vestige of self-confidence and self-belief in the believer, so that he or she is bare of any defense before God and has only God's Word of promise to which he or she clings for dear life.[66] In this way, the agonizing struggle of *Anfechtung* brings the believer and theologian who has been meditating on Christ as the Word of God's promise revealed in Scripture back to the same Word, teaching him or her to trust the validity of that promise, to trust God's promise alone for deliverance from all evil and from the *Anfechtung* of the hidden God. This, says Bayer,

---

62. Bayer, "God's Omnipotence," 91–93; Bayer, *Zugesagte Gegenwart*, 117–19. Bayer, *Martin Luther's Theology*, 199–201, 204–5; Bayer, *Martin Luthers Theologie*, 179–81, 184–185. Bayer, "Die ganze Theologie Luthers," 265. Cf. *BOW* 105, 203–5; 216–17; WA 18:636, 709–10, 718.

63. Bayer, *Martin Luther's Theology*, 35–36; Bayer, *Martin Luthers Theologie*, 33. Bayer, *Gott als Autor*, 297. Bayer, *Zugesagte Gegenwart*, 170. Helmer, "The Subject of Theology in the Thought of Oswald Bayer," 30–31.

64. Bayer, *Theology the Lutheran Way*, 63; Bayer, *Theologie*, 101; Bayer, *Martin Luther's Theology*, 36–37, Bayer, *Martin Luthers Theologie*, 33–34.

65. Bayer, *Martin Luther's Theology*, 20–21; Bayer, *Martin Luthers Theologie*, 19–20.

66. Ibid.

is how God makes theologians whose theology and existence are anchored in the true subject of theology, in God's justifying promise in Christ alone.[67]

Anfechtung is the place where the hidden God features in Bayer's approach to the method of theology. Though Bayer mentions the hidden God in relation to prayer and meditation in the experiential method of theology, he describes God's hiddenness as being experienced by the believer particularly through the agonizing struggle of *Anfechtung*. Through this struggle, faith in God's promise is called into question and attacked. Through this assault of the hidden God in *Anfechtung*, the defenses of the believer and theologian are taken away so that he or she has no recourse in the face of the hidden God but to trust in the revealed God's promise in the gospel of Christ alone.

The Hidden God and the Data of Theology

This gospel of the justifying promise of God in Christ is one of the God-given data for the doing of theology identified by Bayer. According to Bayer, the data of theology consist of the ways in which God encounters the human sinner: the law, the gospel, and divine hiddenness.[68] In keeping with his experiential approach to theology, including its experiential mode and method, and drawing from Hamann, Bayer describes the data of theology experientially as God's speech, which the theologian undergoes and by which the theologian is shaped.[69] While God encounters the theologian in the law as the accuser and judge who speaks against and condemns sinners, God in Christ encounters the theologian in the gospel as the advocate who speaks for sinful humans and promises them God's very self as a God of grace and mercy.[70] In this latter encounter, God in Christ comes and addresses sinners through created means (*Leibliches Wort*) speaking as the justifier and creator to the creature through the creature.[71] While Bayer

---

67. Bayer, *Martin Luther's Theology*, 36–37; Bayer, *Martin Luthers Theologie*, 33–34.

68. Bayer, *Theology the Lutheran Way*, 17, 102; Bayer, *Theologie*, 36–37, 413.

69. Bayer, *Theology the Lutheran Way*, 17, 102; Bayer, *Theologie*, 36–37, 413. Bayer, *Schöpfung als* Anrede, 13–18. Hamann, *Sämtliche Werke* 2: 195–217.

70. Bayer, *Theology the Lutheran Way*, 102–3, 130; Bayer, *Theologie*, 413–14, 444.

71. Ibid. Bayer, *Living by Faith*, 51; Bayer, *Aus Glauben Leben*, 58. Bayer, *Schöpfung als Anrede*, 18–19. Though Bayer also understands the law as God's speech to the creature through created means, particularly in its first use through the created means of the three estates, especially that of the civil state, this is only a penultimate speech to the creature through the creature that orders chaos and curbs sin. The primary and even primal speech to the creature through the creature, which comes through the bodily means of speech, water, bread, and wine, is God's speech of the promise in the gospel.

certainly uses Hamann to construct his own view of such divine address to humans through created means, this sacramental understanding of how the Word of the gospel reaches human beings also entails a deeply Lutheran understanding of the means of grace.[72] Furthermore, Bayer's description of the law and the gospel as God's address to human sinners embodies the classic Lutheran understanding of the distinction between the law and the gospel.[73] Yet, Bayer holds that the law and the gospel are not the only data of theology, because they are not the only ways in which humans encounter God.

In addition to the law and the gospel, says Bayer, humans also encounter God in God's "terrible hiddenness."[74] Bayer's description of divine hiddenness as a datum of theology is somewhat complex. Bayer qualifies the definition of the hiddenness of God as a datum of theology by comparing it to the other two data of theology, and in so doing he describes hiddenness almost as a third word of God in addition to the law and the gospel. At the same time, Bayer describes hiddenness and God's word in the law very similarly with some qualification between the two. If hiddenness is a third word to Bayer, it is for him something of a non-verbal word that is experienced by the human more through existence in the world of creation itself rather than the direct speech of God. Throughout the various aspects of his description of hiddenness as a datum of theology, however, Bayer is very clear about one thing: hiddenness is a negative datum for theology. It is the experience of God as a terrifying enemy who works wrath against humans and contradicts the promise of God in the gospel to which the believer clings.

The Hiddenness of God as a Third Word of God

Bayer expresses his description of God's hiddenness as a third word of God in the context of his description of the distinction and difference between God's word in the law and God's word in the gospel, which together make up the contradictory data of theology. In the law, says Bayer, God speaks against the sinner, condemning him or her, but in the gospel, God speaks

---

Cf. Bayer, *Martin Luther's Theology*, 120–126, 140–152; Bayer, *Martin Luthers Theologie*, 110–15, 128–38.

72. Bayer, *Martin Luther's Theology*, 249–56, 222–23; Bayer, *Martin Luthers Theologie*, 225–29, 200–221.

73. Bayer, *Martin Luther's Theology*, 58–62; Bayer, *Martin Luthers Theologie*, 53–56. Bayer, *Theology the Lutheran Way*, 102–3; Bayer, *Theologie*, 413–14.

74. Bayer, *Martin Luther's Theology*, 202; Bayer, *Martin Luthers Theologie*, 182. Bayer, "The Plurality of the One God," 343; Bayer, *Zugesagte Gegenwart*, 100. Bayer, "Der Glanz der Gnade," 79. Bayer, *Theology the Lutheran Way*, 102; Bayer, *Theologie*, 413.

for the sinner, justifying him or her.⁷⁵ In describing the relationship between the law and the gospel as such, Bayer stands firmly within the tradition of confessional Lutheran theology. In the twentieth century this tradition expressed its confession of the distinction between the law and the gospel in response to the Barthian belief in the unity of the gospel and the law as one Word of God, and Bayer's description of the relationship between the law and the gospel reflects an attempt to correct a certain aspect of Barth's theology. Furthermore, Bayer's articulation of the distinction between the law and the gospel reflects a characteristically Lutheran position in that he argues that the law and the gospel are two distinct and contradictory words of God that accomplish two different things, and in this way, Bayer understands himself to be functioning within the Lutheran confessional tradition.⁷⁶ Bayer then brings this distinction into his approach to doing theology as a Lutheran, by defining the data of theology as consisting of the law and the gospel. Yet, Bayer adds a third word of God to these two: the hiddenness of God. Bayer describes hiddenness as a third datum of God, and he defines this datum in terms of its differences with the other two words of God. While Bayer does describe hiddenness in somewhat similar terms to the law, at the same time, he sees it as a word of God distinct from the law.

Bayer's Articulation of the Lutheran Distinction between The Law and the Gospel

Typically, confessional Lutheran theology has recognized that God has two words, not merely one, and has sought to maintain the distinction between these two over and against attempts to unify God's address to humans into one, generic, homogenous word of God.⁷⁷ In the twentieth century, however, Karl Barth's rejection of the Lutheran distinction between the law and the

---

75. Bayer, *Theology the Lutheran Way*, 101–2; Bayer, *Theologie*, 413–14.

76. Bayer identifies his own view of the relationship between the law and the gospel and the respective tasks of these two words as following in the trajectory of the theology of Luther, the *Augsburg Confession*, and the *Formula of Concord*. Bayer, "Gesetz und Evangelium," 155- 161; Bayer, "Gesetz und Evangelium," in *Leibliches Wort*, 35–43.

77. LW 39:182–83; WA 7:653–55. BOW 161–63, 165–67, 289; WA 18:679–80, 682–83, 676. Melanchthon, *Loci* (1521), 111, 121, 151–53, 165–67. Melanchthon, *Selected Writings*, 17. Ap, 4, in *BC*, 121, 137, 150; BSLK, 143–44, 167, 186. Ap, 12, in *BC*, 195; BSLK, 278–79. FC,Ep, 5, in *BC*, 500–501; BSLK, 780–83. FC,SD, 5, in *BC*, 581–86. Lohse, *Martin Luther's Theology*, 267–70. Schlink, *Theology of the Lutheran Confessions*, 67–104. Wengert, *A Formula for Parish Practice*, 77–89. Althaus, *The Theology of Martin Luther*, 251–66. Ebeling, *Luther: An Introduction to His Writings*, 110–24. Iwand, *Glaubensgerechtigkeit*, 49–51. Jüngel, *Justification*, 96–102, 227–29. Forde, *The Preached God*, 50–53. Paulson, *Lutheran Theology*, 11–12, 26–27.

gospel, and his re-formulation of the relationship as a unity of gospel-law has dominated the conversation. In Barth's estimation the law and the gospel are not two distinct words of God but constitute one homogenous Word of God. According to Barth, God is one, and so God's Word is also one. It is a whole and not self-contradictory.[78] In the wake of Barth, many Lutheran theologians have sought to articulate anew the distinction between the law and the gospel and respond to his rejection of the Lutheran distinction. Bayer follows this trend within German Lutheranism and articulates his own view of the distinction with an eye toward rebutting Barth.[79] In both *Theologie* and his "Twenty-Four Theses for the Renewal of Lutheranism," Bayer clearly expresses the classic Lutheran distinction between the condemning word of God in the law and the justifying word of God in the gospel over and against Barth's idea of the unity of the gospel and law in one Word. The law may serve the final word of God in the gospel, but the two remain two distinct and even contradictory words of God.[80]

According to Bayer, the words of God in the law and the gospel constitute two different and differing data of theology. They are, in fact, two distinct and contradictory words wherein God says two different things to the sinner/theologian. In Bayer's thinking, these two words both perform something upon the sinner/theologian and, acting as the data of theology, present two different understandings of God.

Consistent with the theme of speech act in his theology, Bayer describes the law and the gospel as two words in which God says two different things, and which perform two different divine works upon the human. In the law, God effects the human's condemnation; while in the gospel, God effects the human's justification.

In the law, God speaks as the judge who accuses and condemns. God comes in the law accusing the human with questions like, "Where is your

---

78. "We hear the law of God when we hear the gospel. The two dare not be separated. This is what concerns me most about the Lutherans" (Karl Barth, *Freie reformierte Synode zu Barmen-Gemarke*, 30; quoted in Sasse, *Here We Stand*, 163). Cf. Barth, "The Problem of Ethics Today" (1922), in *The Word of God and Theology*, 160. Barth, "Gospel and Law," 71–73, 80–84. *CD* I.2 437–38, 498–99. *CD* II.1, 236. *CD* II.2, 511–13. *CD* IV.1, 347. *CD* IV.2, 534–535. Busch, *The Great Passion*, 158–65. Busch, *The Barmen Theses Then and Now*, 35–37ff. Forde, *The Law-Gospel Debate*, 137–49.

79. Ebeling, "Erwägungen zur Lehre vom Gestz," in *Wort und Glaube*, 255–93; ET Ebeling, "Reflexions on the Doctrine of the Law, in *Word and Faith*, 247–81. Ebeling, "Über die Reformation hinaus?: Zur Luther-Kritik Karl Barths," 85–125. Iwand, *Um den Rechten Glauben*, ed. Karl Gerhard Steck (München: Kaiser, 1959), 87–109. Forde, *The Law-Gospel Debate*, 200–215.

80. Bayer, *Theologie*, 413–14; Bayer, *Theology the Lutheran Way*, 102–3. Bayer, "Twenty-Four Theses," 73–74; Bayer, *Zugesagte Gegenwart*, 34–35.

brother Abel?" and with statements like "You are the one."[81] In this way, God's address in the law comes as a harsh, accusatory tone. God's address here is not limited to accusation, however, and moves into condemnation, "You are condemned to death."[82] In the law, God accomplishes the human sinner's death.[83] Such address from God, says Bayer, penetrates into the human and is recognized by the conscience. Yet, at the same time, God's address in the law is more than the mere echo of some Kantian internal, categorical imperative. It is a distinctly external voice, the very voice of God that effectually accuses and condemns the human sinner.[84]

Although he identifies that the ultimate function of the law is condemnation, this is not to say that Bayer sees no constructive role for the law in theology. Following in the tradition of Luther and the *Formula of Concord*, he also recognizes the "first use of the law," wherein God curbs the effects of sin, orders the chaos of the world, and provides for God's creatures in this life through the law as embodied in the three estates of creation: the family, the Church, and most importantly the state.[85] Yet, this use of the law is not the primary function of this word of God, and it is largely limited to the realm of creation and to the discipline of ethics.[86] According to Bayer, the first use—or civil use—of the law is a penultimate work of God's longsuffering effected through the government of the state to order and sustain the old creation before the full advent of the new in the eschaton.[87] Yet, while Bayer recognizes this function of the law in creation, he still views God's

---

81. Bayer, *Theology the Lutheran Way*, 102; Bayer, *Theologie*, 413. Bayer, *Martin Luther's Theology*, 60–61; Bayer, *Martin Luthers Theologie*, 55. Bayer, *Zugesagte Gegenwart*, 16–17. Gen 4:9; 2 Sam 12:7.

82. Bayer, *Theology the Lutheran Way*, 102; Bayer, *Theologie*, 413. Bayer, *Martin Luther's Theology*, 60–61; Bayer, *Martin Luthers Theologie*, 55.

83. Bayer, "Justification as the Basis and Boundary of Theology," 280; Bayer, *Leibliches Wort*, 26–27.

84. Bayer, *Theology the Lutheran Way*, 102; Bayer, *Theologie*, 413. Bayer, *Martin Luther's Theology*, 60–61; Bayer, *Martin Luthers Theologie*, 55.

85. Luther, *Lectures on the First Epistle to Timothy* (1528), LW 28:233–24; *Vorlesung über den 1. Timothensbrief*, WA 26:14–16. LW 26:308–13; WA 479–87. *Die Zweite Disputation gegen die Antinomer* (1538), WA 39.1:441–42. FC,Ep, 5, in BC, 500–501; BSLK, 780–83. FC,SD, Article 5, 581–86. Helmer, "The Subject of Theology in the Thought of Oswald Bayer," 35. Byaer, *Freiheit als Antwort*, 289; not contained in ET. Cf. Bayer, *Martin Luther's Theology*, 121–52; Bayer, *Martin Luthers Theologie*, 111–38.

86. Helmer, "The Subject of Theology in the Thought of Oswald Bayer," 35. Bayer, *Freiheit als Antwort*, 289; not contained in ET.

87. Helmer, "The Subject of Theology in the Thought of Oswald Bayer," 35. Bayer, *Freiheit als Antwort*, 289; Not contained in ET. Bayer, "The Plurality of the One God," 343–44; Bayer, *Zugesagte Gegenwart*, 100. Cf. Bayer, "Evangelium und Gesetz," 162–63; Bayer, *Leibliches Wort*, 44–45.

voice of accusation and condemnation as the primary work of the address of God in the law.[88]

In opposition to the law, the gospel sounds God's address of salvation, forgiveness, justification, and freedom. While in the law, God speaks against the human sinner, accusing him or her, God speaks for the human sinner in the gospel. The gospel is God's voice *pro me*.[89] While in the law God effects the sinner's condemnation, in the gospel, God effects the sinner's justification and righteousness through the speech act of God's promise in Jesus Christ.[90]

These two words of God's address to the human sinner can never be harmonized but must remain distinct from one another, says Bayer, though he certainly understands there to be a definite eschatological quality to the gospel not possessed by the law. Ultimately, the work of God in the law serves the work of God in the gospel and the tension between the two voices of God will be relieved in the eschaton, as the speech of God in the promise for the human will ultimately triumph over the law. In the meantime, however, the distinction between the two words of God must remain.[91] So distinct are these two voices of God, which function as two different and contradictory data for the doing of theology, that they present two different doctrines of God in theology. On the one hand, the law presents the theologian with a "general doctrine of God." On the other hand, the gospel preaches the Triune God. Bayer adopts this view of the two words of God presenting two different doctrines of God from his interpretation of Luther's "hymn of liberation," "*Nun freut euch, leiben Christen g'mein*."[92] According to Bayer, as he interprets Luther's hymn, the understanding of God as Trinity is contained only within the promise of God in the gospel—wherein the Father, Son, and Holy Spirit speak to one another and to the sinner, accomplishing the sinner's salvation—so that God exists as the Trinity for human beings as a God of mercy and grace. God's existence as Trinity thus cannot be thought

---

88. Bayer, *Martin Luther's Theology*, 61; Bayer, *Martin Luthers Theologie*, 54–55.

89. Ibid.

90. Bayer, *Theology the Lutheran Way*, 102–4; Bayer, *Theologie*, 413–15. Bayer, *Zugesagte Gegenwart*, 18–19.

91. Bayer, *Theology the Lutheran Way*, 102; Bayer, *Theologie*, 413. Bayer, "Twenty-Four Theses," 73–74; Bayer, *Zugesagte Gegenwart*, 34–35. Bayer, *Martin Luther's Theology*, 339; Bayer, *Martin Luthers Theologie*, 309. Gerhard Forde exhibits a similar understanding of the gospel's eschatological ultimacy over the law. Cf. Forde, *The Law-Gospel Debate*, 200–215.

92. Bayer, *Martin Luther's Theology*, 337ff; Bayer, *Martin Luthers Theologie*, 306ff. Helmer, "The Subject of Theology in the Thought of Oswald Bayer," 34–35. *EG*, 341; ET "Dear Christians One and All Rejoice," *ELW*, 594, *LSB*, 556.

of speculatively in terms of God's existence in God's self but only in terms of God's gracious address in the promise of the gospel.[93]

The conversation amongst the persons of the Trinity, says Bayer, "is not some speculative notion of Trinitarian theology." It cannot be, because it is "from the very beginning . . . an event pertaining to the sinner as mercy."[94] For, says Bayer, the Trinity itself is nothing other than the revealed God of the gospel.[95] The general doctrine of God, wherein God is understood only vaguely, is taken from the law in its first and second uses and ultimately presents God as a judge full of wrath against the human sinner.[96] Like the law and the gospel, these two doctrines of God cannot be harmonized on this side of the eschaton but necessarily exist dialectically, in tension with one another in the present. They stand in distinction and even in opposition to one another.[97]

God's Hiddenness as a Third Datum of Theology

Bayer argues that there is a third encounter between God and the human being, a third address of God to the human. This third address is the hiddenness of God, which really is a third kind of encounter with God. Bayer thus defines divine hiddenness as an address to the human by God that radically contradicts the gospel and that goes far beyond the law in conveying the wrath of God. It is clear that Bayer thinks of hiddenness in these terms as a kind of third word of God in addition to the law and the gospel that cannot be amalgamated or harmonized with one of these other words of God. Yet, if Bayer understands hiddenness to be a third word of God, it is something of a non-audible word. For in hiddenness, God is incomprehensible and

---

93. Bayer, *Martin Luther's Theology*, 338–39, 341; Bayer, *Martin Luthers Theologie*, 308, 310–11. Bayer, "Poetological Doctrine of the Trinity," 53; Bayer, "Poetologische Trinitätslehre," 77; Bayer, *Gott als Autor*, 146. Bayer, *Zugesagte Gegenwart*, 175–77.

94. Bayer, "Mercy from the Heart," 29–32; Bayer, "Barmherzigkeit," in *Zugesagte Gegenwart*, 56. Bayer, "The Being of Christ in Faith," 142; Bayer, "Das Sein Jesus Christi im Glauben," in *Gott als Autor*, 120.

95. "Die Dreieinigkeit ist nicht anders als der im Evangelium offenbare Gott." *Zugesagte Gegenwart*, 176.

96. Bayer, *Martin Luther's Theology*, 339; Bayer, *Martin Luthers Theologie*, 308–9. Bayer, "Poetological Doctrine of the Trinity, 52–53; Bayer, "Poetologische Trinitätslehre," 76–77; Bayer, *Gott als Autor*, 145.

97. Bayer, *Martin Luther's Theology*, 339; Bayer, *Martin Luthers Theologie*, 308–9. Bayer, "The Plurality of the One God, 352–53; *Zugesagte Gegenwart*, 108–109. Bayer, "Poetological Doctrine of the Trinity, 52–53; Bayer, "Poetologische Trinitätslehre," 76–77; Bayer, *Gott als Autor*, 145. Bayer, "Poetological Theology," 165; Bayer, *Gott als Autor*, 15.

unintelligible. Hiddenness does, however, constitute one of the data of theology for Bayer, since it entails a real experience of God's interaction with humans apart from the law and apart from the gospel.

According to Bayer, the hiddenness of God constitutes a third kind of divine address, making up one of the datum of theology.[98] Bayer argues that divine hiddenness is a distinct datum of theology alongside the law and the gospel that may not be subsumed under either of these other words of God.[99] In fact, says Bayer, the hiddenness of God goes beyond the simple wrath of God expressed as accusation and condemnation in the law and radically contradicts the word of God's promise in the gospel.[100]

God's Hiddenness and the Law

Bayer rejects the idea that the hiddenness of God is simply another way in which one might talk about the work of God in the law. The terrifying hiddenness of God outside of revelation, says Bayer, is more than just part of the working of the law.[101] While Bayer recognizes that both the law and hiddenness portray God as a God of wrath and actually effect God's wrath upon the human sinner, he distinguishes between the kinds of wrath displayed in the law and in hiddenness. Both the law and hiddenness entail the working of God's wrath, but they differ from one another, says Bayer, insomuch as the law embodies God's "understandable wrath" ("*verständlicher Zorn*") and the hiddenness God's "incomprehensible wrath" ("*unverständlicher Zorn*").[102]

God's wrath in the law is understandable to the extent that it operates in "the sphere of actions that bring about consequences."[103] As an example of God's working of this kind of wrath, Bayer highlights the Deuteronomistic History, wherein it is recorded that God sent the punishment that God threatened upon the people of Israel for rejecting God as God and practicing idolatry.[104] In the law, God confronts the sinner and convicts of

---

98. Bayer, *Theology the Lutheran Way*, 102; Bayer, *Theologie*, 413. Bayer, "The Plurality of the One God," 343; Bayer, *Zugesagte Gegenwart*, 100.

99. Bayer, *Theology the Lutheran Way*, 105; Bayer, *Theologie*, 417.

100. Bayer, *Theology the Lutheran Way*, 102; Bayer, *Theologie*, 413.

101. Bayer, *Theologie*, 413, 415. "... nur als Wirkung des Gestzes." ET Bayer, *Theology the Lutheran Way*, 102, 104. "... more than just the effect of the law."

102. Bayer, *Martin Luther's Theology*, 196–198; Bayer, *Martin Luthers Theologe*, 177–179. Bayer, *Zugesagte Gegenwart*, 114–15.

103. Bayer, *Martin Luther's Theology*, 197; Bayer, *Martin Luthers Theologie*, 178. "schicksalwirkenden Tatsphäre."

104. Bayer, *Martin Luther's Theology*, 196; Bayer, *Martin Luthers Theologie*, 177.

sin in a way that is intelligible for the sinner.[105] God's word of wrath in the law consists of real words, understandable questions and statements of accusation and condemnation.[106]

Such is not the case with God's incomprehensible wrath in hiddenness, says Bayer. Here God, even God's wrath, is not intelligible. In hiddenness, God's wrath is experienced as sheer terror or some kind of primal dread. God's wrath in hiddenness is incomprehensible because, unlike the law, it is not intelligible to the human being.[107] Instead of the clear accusation and condemnation of the law, the wrath of God in hiddenness is non-verbal and is only experienced in terms of terror and the evil things that happen in this life.[108] In this way, hiddenness is beyond the law, says Bayer. It is even beyond the distinction between the law and the gospel as the distinction between God's grace and God's wrath. Though hiddenness embodies wrath like the law, it is not encapsulated by the law because it is a non-verbal, unintelligible wrath.[109]

Yet, in spite of this clear distinction that he makes between hiddenness and the law, Bayer still describes the work of God in the law and the work of God in hiddenness in similar terms and, ultimately, as accomplishing the same or at least a similar task. In addition to identifying both the law and hiddenness as embodying God's wrath—albeit different kinds of wrath—Bayer describes both law and hiddenness as part of the general doctrine of God outside the doctrine of the revealed, triune God of grace and mercy, and, ultimately, he describes both as effecting a similar state in the human sinner. These similarities call into question the absolute legitimacy of Bayer's categorizing the law and the hiddenness of God as two distinct data of theology.

In his discussion of a general doctrine of God versus the doctrine of the Triune God, with special reference to Luther's hymn "*Nun freut euch, leiben Christen g'mein*," Bayer describes the hiddenness of God as belonging to the general doctrine of God as does the law, while the gospel alone belongs the realm of the revealed God of the Trinity.[110] In this way, says Bayer, the law—in both its first and second uses—and hiddenness are both "available" and both readily experienced by those outside of Christianity, by

---

105. Bayer, *Theology the Lutheran Way*, 102; Bayer, *Theologie*, 413.
106. Bayer, *Theology the Lutheran Way*, 87, 102; Bayer, *Theologie*, 396, 413.
107. Bayer, *Martin Luther's Theology*, 198; Bayer, *Martin Luthers Theologie*, 178–79.
108. Ibid. Bayer, *Gott als Autor*, 272.
109. Bayer, *Theology the Lutheran Way*, 64, 87; Bayer, *Theologie*, 103, 396.
110. Bayer, *Martin Luther's Theology*, 336–337; Bayer, *Martin Luthers Theologie*, 306–307. Bayer, *Zugesagte Gegenwart*, 177.

THE HIDDEN GOD IN BAYER'S APPROACH TO THEOLOGY   197

those who have no point of contact with the gospel of Jesus Christ through the means of grace. In fact, says Bayer, the experiences of God through the law and hiddenness are the greatest experiences that non-believers and Christians share.[111]

In describing the law and hiddenness together as part of the general doctrine of God over and against the doctrine of the revealed God of the Trinity, Bayer clearly puts the law and hiddenness together in this regard in order to demonstrate the distinctiveness of the gospel. This may be observed in how Bayer clarifies that, although the law and hiddenness are experiences of God common both to non-believers and to believers, the gospel is experienced only by those who become believers through the promise of God in Jesus Christ, preached and distributed in the means of grace.[112] Moreover, Bayer's putting the law and hiddenness together under the label of the general doctrine of God for the sake of the doctrine of the Triune God revealed in the gospel alone may be seen even more starkly in Bayer's warning against a speculative doctrine of the Trinity.

In describing God's threeness-in-oneness, Bayer insists that the theologian must speak of God's nature as Trinity only with reference to the revelation of God in the gospel.[113] When one understands the doctrine of the Trinity only within the realm of the revealed God of the gospel and does not try to make speculative, metaphysical claims about the nature of God as Trinity within God's self, says Bayer, then the Trinity is seen for what it really is: the gracious existence of "God for us" as a God of mercy, as the three-in-one God whose unity consists in the unity of purpose in God's salvation of the human sinner.[114] In the context of Luther's hymn, the Trinity then becomes the three-fold God who is preached as the salvation of the bound and accused sinner rather than the intellectual plaything of the speculative minds of theologians.[115] The problem with much of contemporary theology—including the so called "Trinitarian renaissance"—is that it interprets God's nature as Trinity in terms of the general doctrine of God through anthropological observations as a basis for all truth or for a particular ordering

---

111. Bayer, "The Plurality of the One God," 349–350; Bayer, Zugesagte Gegenwart, 105–6.

112. Bayer, The Plurality of the One God," 350; Bayer, Zugesagte Gegenwart, 106.

113. Bayer, Martin Luther's Theology, 337–40; Bayer, Martin Luthers Theologie, 306–309. Bayer, "Poetological Theology," 165; Bayer, Gott als Autor, 15. Bayer, Zugesagte Gegenwart, 177.

114. Bayer, Martin Luther's Theology, 337; Bayer, Martin Luthers Theologie, 306.

115. Bayer, Martin Luther's Theology, 222–25; Bayer, Martin Luthers Theologie, 200–203.

of society.[116] The result of such Hegelian "post-Christian natural theology," says Bayer, is the complete loss of the gospel. This is precisely why, says Bayer, the two doctrines of God must be distinguished, so that the gospel is not conflated with the law and the hiddenness of God.[117]

It is clear from Bayer's distinction between the general doctrine of God and the doctrine of the revealed Triune God, that he intentionally places the law and hiddenness together in order to preserve the distinctiveness of the gospel. Here, we observe Bayer describing the law and God's hiddenness as being similar over and against the gospel. The same observation may be made when one looks at comments made by Bayer concerning the actual work of the law and of hiddenness in comparison to the gospel.

In an essay entitled, "Gesetz und Evangelium," Bayer describes the hiddenness of God and the law as having similar effects on the human or accomplishing similar works. Bayer here portrays the law as effecting terror and death within the human sinner, a work that Bayer unequivocally attributes to divine hiddenness in other works.[118] The similarity of this description of the work of the law in his writing, in the context of Bayer's broader description of the work of God's hiddenness, casts some doubt on the clear cut distinction Bayer makes between the law and hiddenness as two different data of theology and upon his assertion that hiddenness is not simply part of the work of the law.

Bayer states that God's hiddenness is a datum of theology unto itself and not merely an expression of God's work in the law. Yet, his description of both the law and hiddenness as embodying and communicating God's wrath (even if he does make the fine distinction between them as understandable wrath and incomprehensible wrath), his putting the law and hiddenness together under the category of the general doctrine of God as opposed to the doctrine of the Triune God as pure gospel, and his description of the work and effects of the law in "Gesetz und Evangelium" in terms strikingly similar to his description elsewhere of the work and effects of hiddenness, all work together to call into question the validity of

---

116. Bayer, "Poetological Theology," 165; Bayer, *Gott als Autor*, 15. Bayer, "Poetological Doctrine of the Trinity," 54–55; Bayer, "Poetologische Trinitätslehre," 78–79; Bayer, *Gott als Autor*, 145–46. Bayer, "The Plurality of the One God," 353. The example of such "Trinitarian" theology given here is Moltmann's *Trinität und Reich Gottes*; ET Moltmann, *The Trinity and the the Kingdom*.

117. Bayer, "Poetological Theology," 165; Bayer, *Gott als Autor*, 15. Bayer, "Poetological Doctrine of the Trinity," 54–55; Bayer, "Poetologische Trinitätslehre," 78–79; Bayer, *Gott als Autor*, 145–46.

118. Bayer, "Gesetz und Evangelium," 158, 161; Bayer, *Leibliches Wort*, 40, 43. Bayer, *Martin Luther's Theology*, 198, 202; Bayer, *Martin Luthers Theologie*, 179, 182. Bayer, *Theology the Lutheran Way*, 104; Bayer, *Theologie*, 416.

his distinguishing between hiddenness and the law as two different data of theology. Such uncertainty about Bayer's claims that God's hiddenness is not simply a working of the law and that hiddenness stands outside of the matrix of the law and the gospel becomes heightened when one reads how Bayer portrays hiddenness as the opposite of the gospel, and I will return to this question about the validity of Bayer's identifying hiddenness as a third word, addressing it more fully when I compare Bayer's understanding of God's hiddenness with Luther's teaching on the hidden God in chapter eight of this work.

God's Hiddenness and the Gospel

According to Bayer, the hiddenness of God as a datum of theology is not only distinct from God's working in the law, but it also stands outside God's word in the gospel as a datum of theology that contradicts the theological datum of the gospel. While God's promise in the gospel effects forgiveness, justification, and freedom, the experience of hiddenness contradicts this saving work of God through the gospel.[119] While in the promise of the gospel, the believer knows God as the one who promises God's very self to the believer in Jesus Christ, God "for you," as the one who says, "You are mine," the experience of God in hiddenness is completely different.[120] Here, the same God who promises life, salvation, and the renewal of all things in the gospel "neither deplores death nor takes it away," "but works, life, death, and all things."[121] Thus, in hiddenness, says Bayer, we experience God contradicting God's speech of promise to the sinner for the sake of the sinner, for here we find God working wrath and death.[122] Here, we find God at work against God.[123]

In this context of God working against God, the hiddenness of God experienced as the opposite of God's promise in the gospel, the speech of God becomes incomprehensible. Whereas in the gospel, God's gracious speech consists of the clear and unilateral promise of God for the human sinner in Jesus Christ, says Bayer, the human experiences God's hiddenness in such a way that the human is unable to hear and understand God through hiddenness and, instead, experiences God's work in hiddenness in terms

---

119. Bayer, *Theology the Lutheran Way*, 102, 104; Bayer, *Theologie*, 413, 415–16.
120. Bayer, *Theology the Lutheran Way*, 104; Bayer, *Theologie*, 415–16.
121. Ibid.
122. Ibid. Bayer, *Martin Luther's Theology*, 198; Bayer, *Martin Luthers Theologie*, 178–79.
123. Bayer, *Theology the Lutheran Way*, 104; Bayer, *Theologie*, 415–16.

terror and dread.¹²⁴ Through the work of God in *Anfechtung*, hiddenness becomes a third experience with God, a third datum of theology, wherein God is not dealing graciously with the human sinner, even with the believing one, but actively and even directly contradicting God's promise in the gospel by attacking faith in the promise as God attacked Jacob on the banks of the Jabbok.¹²⁵ In the agonizing struggle of *Anfechtung*, the believing, justified sinner, who knows God according to God's promise in Christ, is attacked by the hidden God. The hidden God then enters into a battle with the justified sinner, hiding God's self, making God's self incomprehensible to the justified sinner. Like Jacob, the justified sinner does not really know who it is that confronts and wrestles with him or her. The hidden God with whom the justified sinner is confronted is shrouded to such an extent that so that the justified sinner is unsure whether he or she is grappling with God or the devil in the encounter with divine hiddenness.¹²⁶

Bayer is quite clear in distinguishing the terrifying hiddenness of God from the gospel, that this distinction means that a sharp differentiation must be made between the terrifying hiddenness of God outside of revelation, in God's self and the hiddenness of God in revelation (i.e. *theologia crucis*). Just as the terrifying hiddenness of God outside of revelation is the exact opposite and contradiction of God's word of promise in the gospel of Christ, so is the hiddenness of God outside of revelation also the opposite of and must be distinguished from the hiddenness of God under the sign of God's opposite in suffering and the cross. The terrifying hiddenness of God outside of revelation, is completely different from the God who is hidden in the humility of the incarnation and suffering of God in Jesus Christ.¹²⁷

This work of God in hiddenness, which is completely the opposite of and contradictory to God's word of promise, cannot be harmonized with the promising word of God in the gospel of Jesus Christ. Some theologians, says Bayer, think that they can get out of this terrible situation of contradictory paradox by unifying of all of theology into a single systematic word that embraces and harmonizes all tensions.¹²⁸ The modern attempts to do this—particularly evident in the philosophy of Jonas and in process theology in which God merely allows evil or cannot hinder it, in the theology of Karl

---

124. Bayer, *Martin Luther's Theology*, 198; Bayer, *Martin Luthers Theologie*, 179.

125. Bayer, *Zugesagte Gegenwart*, 77. Bayer, *Martin Luther's Theology*, 202; Bayer, *Martin Luthers Theologie*, 182.

126. Bayer, *Martin Luther's Theology*, 201–4; Bayer, *Martin Luthers Theologie*, 181–84.

127. Bayer, *Martin Luther's Theology*, 198; Bayer, *Martin Luthers Theologie*, 178–79. Bayer, *Promissio*, 62–63, 340.

128. Bayer, *Theology the Lutheran Way*, 105; Bayer, *Theologie*, 416–17.

Barth in which God's wrath simply becomes the opposite of God's love,[129] and in the Trinitarian renaissance in which all divine truth is understood as being united in correspondence to the eternal being of the Trinity[130]—evidence a major error of the Enlightenment. Bayer identifies this error as the felt need of the Enlightenment and the modern era to systematize everything so that all tensions disappear into a harmonious whole of truth.[131] But the tension between God's word in the gospel and the experience of God in hiddenness, the tension between God and God, will not go away, no matter how creative philosophical or theological attempts at monism become.[132] Instead, like the remaining tension between the God's word in the law and God's word in the gospel, the tension of contradiction between God's hiddenness and the gospel will only finally be relieved eschatologically.[133]

For Bayer, God's terrifying hiddenness outside of God's revelation in Christ stands as one of three data of theology. Although Bayer embraces the traditional Lutheran understanding of the distinction between God's word in the law and God's word in the gospel, he also adds a third word of God's hiddenness to these other two words of God. According to Bayer, hiddenness is distinct from both the law and the gospel. He describes hiddenness as a third experience of God, which, although it entails God's wrath, goes beyond the "understandable wrath" of God in the law, and "radically contradicts" God's word in the gospel.[134] But what kind of word is this third word of God and what does the experience of it look like, especially if it is the opposite of God's word in the gospel in that it is not clearly heard and presents God as incomprehensible?

The Nature and Experience of Hiddenness as a Datum of Theology

Bayer describes the hiddenness of God as somewhat illusive in nature and in experience, as a third experience of God, which is distinct and differs from the experience of God through God's words of law and gospel. Though Bayer certainly understands the law and the gospel to present two different

129. Bayer, *Martin Luther's Theology*, 206–9; Bayer, *Martin Luthers Theologie*, 186–88.
130. Bayer. *Theology the Lutheran Way*, 105; Bayer. *Theologie*, 416–17.
131. Ibid.
132. Ibid.
133. Bayer, *Martin Luther's Theology*, 212–13; Bayer, *Martin Luthers Theologie*, 191–92.
134. Bayer, *Theology the Lutheran Way*, 102; Bayer, *Theologie*, 413.

and even contradictory experiences of God, in comparison to the experience of God in hiddenness, the other two addresses of God to the human have one commonality: they are heard and understood by the human. This is not the case with hiddenness. On the contrary, as Bayer tells it, the datum of theology called the hiddenness of God, is inaudible and incomprehensible in nature and is experienced accordingly through the evil things that happen in life and through the spiritual assault of *Anfechtung*, which come to the unbeliever and believer alike as divine address through a fallen creation.

The Nature of Hiddenness as a Datum of Theology

In contrast to the other two words of God, which together with divine hiddenness constitute the data of theology, Bayer identifies the hiddenness of God as a datum of theology as a non-audible word. This does not quite mean, however, that Bayer thinks of God's hiddenness as non-verbal. It does mean though that the hidden work of God is unintelligible and that it is more experienced than it is heard.

In defining the hiddenness of God in terms of its function as a datum of theology, Bayer states the hiddenness differs from the other two data of theology in that it is not clearly heard as direct address from God to the human being.[135] In the experience of God's address in hiddenness the human "cannot hear him [i.e. God] any longer, or at least cannot 'understand' him any longer, but can 'hear' only in terror and experience him as oppressive, fearsome, sinister."[136] The address of the hidden God, says Bayer, is not immediately discernable as stating something clearly about God for use in theology. Instead, it comes in the form of evil things that happen in the world through God's omnipotence and an intense, gripping struggle through *Anfechtung*, a personal struggle in which God personally assaults the believer with doubts concerning the validity of the promise. In this sense, the third word of God's hiddenness is more felt than heard.[137]

Yet, Bayer does not actually say that the hiddenness of God constitutes a non-verbal word of God, nor does he equate divine hiddenness with divine silence. Instead, referencing Hamann's notion of God's address to the creature through the creation, Bayer states that in hiddenness, "Where God acts outside of law and gospel, his [God's] voice terrifies me. I experience

---

135. Bayer, *Theology the Lutheran Way*, 87; Bayer, *Theologie*, 396.

136. Bayer, *Martin Luther's Theology*, 198; Bayer, *Martin Luthers Theologie*, 179.

137. Bayer, *Martin Luther's Theology*, 198–204; Bayer, *Martin Luthers Theologie*, 178–84.

him as overwhelming, frightening, and uncanny."[138] It is not so much that the hidden God is not speaking, according to Bayer, but that the human is unable to hear the hidden God understandably.

The astute reader of Bayer will note here in this description of the human's inability to hear and understand the hiddenness of God more than a faint echo of Hamann's linguistic understanding of the fall of humanity. As Bayer relates in *Zeitgenosse im Widerspruch*, Hamann understands the fall through the biblical narrative of the Tower of Babel (Genesis 11:1–9). According to Hamann, the fall of humanity entailed, amongst other things, the inability to hear God's speech through creation. In this context, God's work in Jesus Christ through the cross is God's self-address to humanity in order to open humans anew to God's speech.[139] This understanding of the fall seems to lurk in the background of Bayer's description of the inaudible nature of the hiddenness of God.

Yet there is something deeper in Bayer's explanation of the nature of God's hiddenness as utterly incomprehensible than simply mere unintelligibility. For Bayer also speaks of the incomprehensible nature of God's hiddenness as effecting terror in the human recipient of such hiddenness.[140] Bayer does describe the nature of God's hiddenness as being inaudible and incomprehensible to the human and as more experienced than heard; it does not, however, make God's hiddenness any less real to the human. On the contrary, the reality of this form of theological data is grippingly existential.

The Experience of Hiddenness as a Datum of Theology

Bayer argues that the hiddenness of God as a datum of theology is not heard as such by the human as direct divine address in the same way in which the other two data of theology, the law and the gospel, are but that it is more experienced by the human. Bayer describes this experience as the experience of God in terms of dread, terror, and primal fear.[141] Such an experience

---

138. Bayer, *Theology the Lutheran Way*, 87; Bayer, *Theologie*, 396.

139. Bayer, *Zeitgenosse im Widerspruch*, 180–184; Bayer, *A Contemporary in Dissent*, 157–161. Cf. Bayer and Knutsen, *Kreuz und Kritik*, 95–96. Bayer, *Vernunft ist Sprache*, 2–4.

140. Bayer, *Martin Luther's Theology*, 198; Bayer, *Martin Luthers Theologie*, 178–79.

141. Bayer, *Martin Luther's Theology*, 39–41; Bayer, *Martin Luthers Theologie*, 35–37. Bayer, *Theology the Lutheran Way*, 99; Bayer, *Theologie*, 410.

of terrifying hiddenness presents God and God's work as utterly incomprehensible to the human, even to the believer, says Bayer.[142]

Yet, even though he argues that God and God's work are incomprehensible through hiddenness, Bayer still regards the hiddenness of God as a very real experience, which existentially grips the human's entire being.[143] According to Bayer, the human encounters this experience of God—or perhaps is encountered by it—through the reality of evil, both natural and human, in the world, which the believer experiences as the agonizing struggle of *Anfechtung*.[144] This experience thus takes on the form of things like evolutionary mutations in genetics, earthquakes, tsunamis, pandemics, the untimely deaths of children, global warming, the shoa, arms races, and terrorism.[145]

Bayer develops his understanding of the human's experience of the hidden God in these events along the lines of his adoption of Hamann's understanding of creation as divine address. In the midst of these events, God's address to the creature through the creation becomes not merely indiscernible but utterly frightening. God's hiddenness effects utter terror in the human who experiences God's address through creation in this way.[146]

This experience is not a uniquely Christian one, says Bayer, but affects both the unbeliever and the believer alike.[147] Yet, at the same time, the experience of the hidden God befalls the unbeliever and the believer in somewhat differing ways, producing two different results. For the unbeliever, the experience of God's hiddenness actually seems like God's absence and serves to confirm the unbelief of atheism that God is absent, and the human being is nothing more than an animal.[148] For the believer, however, the hiddenness of God is experienced as *Anfechtung*, the agonizing struggle in which the hidden God assaults faith in God's promise in the gospel of

---

142. Bayer, *Theology the Lutheran Way*, 104; Bayer, *Theologie*, 416. Bayer, *Martin Luther's Theology*, 198; Bayer, *Martin Luthers Theologie*, 178–179.

143. Bayer, "Hermeneutical Theology," 140; Bayer, *Zugesagte Gegenwart*, 349.

144. Bayer, *Theology the Lutheran Way*, 104; Bayer, *Theologie*, 416. Bayer, "Der Glanz der Gnade," 78.

145. Bayer, *Schöpfung als Anrede*, 21–24, 161. Bayer, "Der neue Mensch," 126–27; Bayer, *Zugesagte Gegenwart*, 244–45. Bayer, "Der Glanz der Gnade," 80. Bayer, *Gott als Autor*, 272.

146. Bayer, *Schöpfung als Anrede*, 21, 135. Bayer, *Theology the Lutheran Way*, 87; Bayer, *Theologie*, 396.

147. Bayer, "The Plurality of the One God," 349–50; Bayer, *Zugesagte Gegenwart*, 105–6.

148. Bayer, *Schöpfung als Anrede*, 21.

Jesus Christ in what becomes a life and death struggle for faith in the promise over and against the experience of the hidden God.[149]

In this latter instance, the struggle gets very personal. Like Jacob's confrontation with God at the Jabbok, the hidden God comes in pursuit of the believer and attacks his or her faith in the promise. The experience of the hidden God for the believer thus takes on the nature of a wrestling match in which God is indistinguishable from the devil, in which God is the enemy even of the believer. Here, the hidden God and the believer grapple with each other over the truth of the promise in the face of the reality of evil.[150]

Bayer describes the nature and experience of the hiddenness of God, which forms the third datum of theology, as inaudible and incomprehensible. The nature and experience of the hidden God are such, however, that, though unheard and unintelligible, they still evoke terror in the human recipients of the divine address in hiddenness. The hidden God encounters humans through natural and human evil, through the chaos of creation and the harm that humans do to one another. In this context, the address of God in creation becomes an encounter with the incomprehensible God, which the human experiences as utterly terrifying. This experience of the third form of God's address, says Bayer, is one that is common to all human beings, whether unbelievers or believers. Yet, while unbelievers experience the hidden God through the evil in the world as merely confirmation of their own unbelief, believers experience it as *Anfechtung*, the agonizing struggle precipitated by the assault of the hidden God on faith in the promise of the revealed God in the gospel of Christ.

The Hidden God and the Subject Matter of Theology

The central theme, which runs through all of Bayer's discussion of the hidden God like a scarlet thread, is that the hiddenness of God is the opposite and contradiction of the promise of God in the gospel of Jesus Christ. Such a central theme should not be surprising for the attentive reader of Bayer's works, considering that he understands God's justification of the human sinner to be the sum total of the true subject matter of theology as well as its basis and boundary.[151] Though Bayer certainly discusses other themes in

---

149. Ibid. Bayer, *Martin Luther's Theology*, 36–37, 39–40; Bayer, *Martin Luthers Theologie*, 33–34, 36.

150. Bayer, *Martin Luther' Theology*, 39–40, 201–4; Bayer, *Martin Luthers Theologie*, 36; 181–84. Bayer, *Zugesagte Gegenwart*, 77–78.

151. Bayer, "Justification as the Basis and Boundary of Theology," 287; Bayer, *Leibliches Wort*, 34. Bayer, *Theology the Lutheran Way*, 17, 98; Bayer, *Theologie*, 36–37, 408–9.

theology, he seeks to do so only in so much as they flow from, relate to, and are encompassed by the overall theme of God's justification of the sinner, not as another theme amongst many, but as the one and ultimately the only theme of theology.[152]

It is in this light of justification as the true subject of theology that Bayer defines and describes hiddenness. As I have related throughout this chapter, Bayer defines the hiddenness of God outside of revelation as the activity of God in the world towards the human, which is the opposite and contradiction of God's work of justification for the human.[153] While I have noted this definition throughout this chapter, I will address it more fully in the next, discussing how it is related to and formed by Bayer's overall theology of justification, including the specific sub-themes of justification through the speech act of God's promise and the opening of creation through justification. Moreover, I will relate Bayer's teaching concerning the proper response of the believer when faced by the hiddenness of God through the theology of lament. In this chapter, however, I have confined my discussion of Bayer's understanding of the hidden God as it is found in his approach to theology. This discussion has focused upon how Bayer brings hiddenness into his views of the mode, method, and data of theology.

Summary

With regard to the mode of theology, Bayer argues that the experience that makes a theologian is not only the experience of God through the promise in Christ but also the general experience of God outside of the gracious revelation of God in Christ. This general experience of God, which occurs through creation itself, presents God to the human in terrifying hiddenness (*schreckliche Verborgenheit*). This hiddenness grips the believer through *Anfechtung*, helping to make him or her into a theologian. At least in part, it is the experience of God through the terrifying hiddenness evident in the evil things that happen in the world, through human and non-human means, which constitutes the experience that makes one a theologian.

In describing the hidden God and his method of doing theology, Bayer mentions hiddenness in conjunction with prayer and meditation, but he focuses mainly on the connection between hiddenness and the agonizing

---

Bayer, *Martin Luther's Theology*, 37–38; Bayer, *Martin Luthers Theologie*, 34.

152. Bayer, *Martin Luther's Theology*, 38; Bayer, *Martin Luthers Theologie*, 35. Bayer, *Living by Faith*, xiv, 9; Bayer, *Aus Glauben Leben*, 21.

153. Bayer, *Theology the Lutheran Way*, 95, 102, 104–5; Bayer, *Theologie*, 406, 413, 415–17. Bayer, *Martin Luther's Theology*, 213; Bayer, *Martin Luthers Theologie*, 192.

struggle of *Anfechtung*. In fact, Bayer only discusses the hiddenness of God negatively in the context of prayer and meditation. He argues that both prayer and meditation concern the revealed God in Christ alone and not the hidden God. The hidden God may never be called upon in the vocative, and should not be meditated upon. This is because prayer in the method of theology is specifically the prayer for God to give the gifts of understanding and wisdom when doing theology—since theology can never be undertaken correctly under the guidance of fallen human reason—and because meditation is specifically the meditation upon the word of God's promise in Christ, contained in the Holy Scripture. To be sure, Bayer acknowledges that some have attempted to probe into the existence and workings of the hidden God through prayer and meditation. But such speculative attempts to uncover the nakedness of the hidden God do not constitute true theology, which ultimately is concerned only with the proclaimed God of the promise in the gospel of Jesus Christ who justifies sinners.

In contrast to this absence of the hidden God in prayer and meditation, Bayer claims that the presence of the hidden God in the method of theology is to be identified in the agonizing struggle of *Anfechtung*. In *Anfechtung*, says Bayer, the believer and theologian who has come to know the revealed God in Christ through the promise of justification and who has been occupied with that revealed God in prayer and meditation, is assaulted by the hidden God, who calls into question the validity of the promise. In this way, *Anfechtung* becomes the touchstone of faith in the promise and of being made into a theologian. The theologian is made through this experience of the hidden God and becomes one who clings to the reality of the promise through faith, in spite of the attack of the hidden God through *Anfechtung*.

The work of the hidden God in *Anfechtung* forms one of the three data of theology identified by Bayer. According to Bayer, the hiddenness of God constitutes a unique datum of theology in its own right. Though Bayer stands firmly within the Lutheran confessional tradition regarding the distinction between the word of God in the law and the word of God in the gospel, he argues that God's terrifying hiddenness cannot be subsumed by the law or by the gospel but exists on its own as a third form of God's address to humans. As such, hiddenness, while it is similar to the law in that it entails the wrath of God, differs from the law in that it entails a radical and incomprehensible wrath of God in comparison to the straightforward and understandable wrath of the law, and completely contradicts the gracious and justifying promise of God in the gospel.

Hiddenness as a third form of God's address, as a third word, has a distinct inaudible and incomprehensible nature, according to Bayer. Humans thus cannot intelligibly distinguish anything in the encounter with the hidden God but, instead, experience God through evil as sheer terror or primal dread. Though this experience is common to all humans, for believers it becomes more acute through the life and death struggle of *Anfechtung*, in which God comes as the enemy of the believer, indistinguishable from the devil, as the one who grapples with the believer over the validity of the promise.

It is this very subject matter of theology, the promise of God for the believer in the gospel of Jesus Christ, which the hidden God contradicts through *Anfechtung*. Far from teaching a theological monism or a monotonous view of justification by faith, Bayer exudes a theology that embodies paradox, contradiction, and conflict of the highest order. Bayer understands the existence of the believer and the theologian to consist of a life and death struggle between the hiddenness of God and the promise of God. Yet, it is not as if he sees no resolution to this predicament. As I will address in the following chapter, Bayer ultimately sees the promise itself as the only way of escape from the situation of agonizing struggle at the hands of the hidden God.

7

The Hidden God and Bayer's Doctrine of Justification

BAYER ADOPTS LUTHER'S DOCTRINE of the hiddenness of God and endeavors to utilize it in his own theology. Though he accepts Luther's doctrine, Bayer defines and develops his understanding of God's hiddenness along the contours of his own theology. In the previous chapter, I described how Bayer frames his understanding of divine hiddenness within his own approach to theology, including his views of the mode, method, and data of theology. I also introduced how Bayer expresses his understanding of the hiddenness of God in the context of his view of God's justification of the human sinner as the subject matter of theology. In this chapter, I will focus more closely on this, addressing how Bayer defines and describes the hiddenness of God through his own particular Lutheran doctrine of justification.

According to Bayer, God's justification of the human sinner, which lies at the heart of all true theology, occurs through an effectual divine speech act of promise through the proclamation of the gospel in Word and Sacrament. Through this speech act of promise, the revealed God in Jesus Christ declares, and thereby makes, the human righteous. Through the promise, God forgives the sin of the sinner; begins a new, dialogical relationship with the presently justified sinner; opens him or her anew to creation; and opens creation, beginning the work of reconciling and renewing all of creation. This view of justification permeates all of Bayer's theological writings, and, working with the idea of justification as the center, basis, and boundary of all theological work, he approaches all other aspects of theology from the standpoint of this particular depiction of God's justification of the human sinner. Consequently, Bayer defines and describes his view of the hiddenness of God outside of revelation in this context of justification.

Bayer essentially defines the hiddenness of God as the work of God in which God contradicts God's promise of justification. The human experience of this contrary work is an attack by the hidden God on the believer's faith in the promise called the agonizing struggle of *Anfechtung*. *Anfechtung* reveals that God not only contradicts his own promise, but actually assaults the believer's trust in the very promise which grasps the believer, and so wrestles with him or her over the validity of the promise. Bayer identifies the believer's struggle with the issue of double predestination and the believer's experience of the reality of evil in this world (i.e. theodicy) as the two forms in which the hidden God's contradiction of the promise encounters the believer. Such contradiction of the promise forms an existential tension not only in the life of the believer but also in the way in which he or she experiences and understands God, to the extent that any understanding of complete unity in the being and action of God is impossible in the present. This tension cannot be relieved through any rational theory, and Bayer decries the typical attempts at such theorizing. Nevertheless, he does see a future resolution to the contradiction between the justifying promise of God in the gospel and the experience of the hidden God through *Anfechtung* as well as an appropriate response of the human to this contradiction in the present through lament. For, according to Bayer, the ultimate answer to the experience of the hidden God's contradiction of the justifying promise of God is a return to that promise itself. These themes indicate a particular Lutheran approach to the hiddenness of God that will have to be compared to Luther's own in the following chapter. Yet, regardless of how Bayer compares to Luther on hiddenness, God's hiddenness influences his basic theology of justification, which I will take up in this chapter.

The Experience of the Hidden God as The Contradiction of God's Justifying Promise

Bayer defines the hiddenness of God as God's address that contradicts God's promise in justification. Bayer goes on to depict this contradiction as the assault of the hidden God upon faith in the promise, an assault that takes on very personal dimensions within the struggle of *Anfechtung*, wherein the hidden God attacks and wrestles with the believer as God did with Jacob on the banks of the Jabbok. Bayer describes this attack of the hidden God in *Anfechtung* as befalling the believer particularly through the question of double predestination, which calls into question the promise, and through the dilemma brought upon the believer within the realm of creation in terms of the evil that occurs in the world, which casts doubt upon the promised renewal of creation.

Bayer's Definition of God's Hiddenness As the Contradiction of God's Justifying Promise

Bayer's definition of the hiddenness of God is formed by the central theme of his entire theology: the justification of the human sinner before God through God's active and effectual word of the forgiving and restoring promise of God in the gospel of Jesus Christ. The formation of this definition is a negative one. Bayer understands the hiddenness of God to be the opposite and contradiction of the justifying promise of God. Even so, Bayer continues to play off the theme of justification taking place through God's effectual speech act, for he describes the human experience of the hiddenness of God as the opposite and contradiction of effectual God's word of promise in terms of an unintelligible address. Bayer argues that, ultimately, the human cannot hear and understand God's address in hiddenness or even stand before the hidden God because God and the human can only ever coexist in God's address of promise in justification.

In his discussion of the hidden God, Bayer clearly defines the hiddenness of God as an experience through which God encounters the believer and contradicts God's justifying promise in the gospel.[1] In the promise of justification, God speaks for the human being, says Bayer, graciously pronouncing and effecting the forgiveness of sins, a new relationship between God and the human, and the reconciliation and renewal of all creation. The hiddenness of God, however, completely contradicts this work of God's promise. Whereas, in the promise of justification, God grants life and salvation, in hiddenness, God destroys life and works death.[2] In hiddenness, God encounters the believer as one who breaks God's own word of promise. While, in justification, God has promised to be a certain kind of God, God

---

1. Bayer, *Martin Luther's Theology*, 213; Bayer, *Martin Luthers Theologie*, 192. Bayer, *Theology the Lutheran Way*, 95, 102, 104–5; Bayer, *Theologie*, 406, 413, 415–17.

2. Bayer, *Theology the Lutheran Way*, 95–96, 104; Bayer, *Theologie*, 406, 415–16.

for the believer, in hiddenness God contradicts this.³ So radical is this contradiction, that in the midst of the experience of hiddenness, God becomes the enemy of the believer, pursuing the believer and working against the promise.⁴

In tandem with his theme of God's justifying promise in the gospel and hiddenness as two divergent forms of divine address, Bayer describes the situation of the human's confrontation with the hidden God as one entailing a miscommunication between God and the creature. While in justification the human receives the address spoken by God in a gracious and friendly tone through the promise of the gospel in Jesus Christ, the human cannot distinguish God's voice in hiddenness.⁵ The problem is not that the hidden God is silent and says nothing. The problem is that, the human being can no longer understand the voice of God in God's address of hiddenness to the human.⁶ Outside of the law and the gospel, in the address of hiddenness, says Bayer, the voice of God sounds unfamiliar, "uncanny," "overwhelming," and even "frightening." Over and against the forgiving and comforting voice of God in the promise of justification and even in contrast to the pointed, condemning voice of God's revealed wrath in the law, the voice of the hidden God strikes terror in the heart of the human, even in the heart of the believer who has received the address of God's promise in Christ. When faced with this incomprehensible address of the hidden God, the believer flees from the hidden God in fear.⁷

According to Bayer, this situation of miscommunication, terror, and flight from the hidden God takes place because God's word of the promise of the forgiveness of sin and righteousness in the gospel of Jesus Christ is the only place where God and the human sinner can coexist peacefully. This means, says Bayer, that the human cannot coexist peacefully or even understand such hiddenness, for the hidden God is God as God exists outside the Word.⁸ Once again, this idea is not original to Bayer but is adopted by him from Luther's theology. In his lecture on Psalm 51—the same lecture in which the reformer defines the true subject matter of theology as God's justification of the sinner in Christ—Luther states that the human being can only stand in God's presence through the Word wherein God reveals God's

---

3. Bayer, *Martin Luther's Theology*, 20–21; Bayer, *Martin Luthers Theologie*, 19–20.

4. Bayer, *Martin Luther's Theology*, 39; Bayer, *Martin Luthers Theologie*, 36.

5. Bayer, *Theology the Lutheran Way*, 87; Bayer, *Theologie*, 396.

6. Ibid. Bayer, *Martin Luther's Theology*, 198; Bayer, *Martin Luthers Theologie*, 179.

7. Bayer, *Theology the Lutheran Way*, 87; *Theologie*, 396; Bayer, *Martin Luthers Theologie*, 179.

8. Bayer, *Martin Luther's Theology*, 39, 198; Bayer, *Martin Luthers Theologie*, 35–36, 179. Bayer, *Theology the Lutheran Way*, 105; Bayer, *Theologie*, 416–417.

self. Outside of the Word, God dwells as the absolute God in naked majesty, and if the human stands before God in this way, he or she cannot grasp or fathom God, for God can only be understood and grasped, says Luther, in the Word, wherein God reveals God's self as a gracious God of promise for the human.[9] Bayer, following Luther, states that outside of the promise, the believer faces the reality of God's hiddenness as God's contradiction to the promise and cannot reconcile or unify these two contradictory experiences of God's address.[10]

This definition of the hiddenness of God as the address of God that opposes and contradicts God's gracious address in justification presents the situation of hiddenness as one in which God actively contradicts the forgiveness of sins and new life promised in the gospel. In such hiddenness, says Bayer, God does not take away death but works death against life.[11] In the context of this encounter with the hidden God, God and God's work becomes utterly incomprehensible to the believer; the believer hears and yet cannot hear and understand God.[12] This encounter with the hidden God, who contradicts the promise of God in justification, forms the content of the experience of agonizing struggle in *Anfechtung*.

The Assault of the Hidden God upon the Promise in the Believer's Experience of Anfechtung

As I have already mentioned, Bayer sees the believer's experience of *Anfechtung* as the venue for the encounter between the hidden God and the believer. Bayer states that, in *Anfechtung*, the hidden God attacks faith in the promise, making this experience a life and death trial, which serves as the touchstone (*der Prüfstein*), not for the validity of the individual's faith in God's justifying promise, but for the validity of that word of promise itself.[13] In this experience of agonizing struggle, the contradiction of God's promise in justification becomes tangible as a real, gripping struggle between the hidden God and the believer over the promise and over life itself. Following Luther's lead, Bayer illustrates this confrontation with the hidden God by

---

9. LW 12:312; WA 40.2:330. Bayer, *Martin Luther's Theology*, 39; Bayer, *Martin Luthers Theologie*, 36.

10. Bayer, *Theology the Lutheran Way*, 104; Bayer, *Theologie*, 415–16.

11. Ibid. Bayer, *Martin Luther's Theology*, 198; Bayer, *Martin Luthers Theologie*, 178–79.

12. Bayer, *Martin Luther's Theology*, 198; Bayer, *Martin Luthers Theologie*, 178–79.

13. Bayer, *Gott als Autor*, 297. Bayer, *Theology the Lutheran Way*, 63; Bayer, *Theologie*, 101. Bayer, *Martin Luther's Theology*, 37; Bayer, *Martin Luthers Theologie*, 33–34.

referring to the the biblical narrative of the patriarch Jacob's wrestling with God on the banks of the Jabbok.[14] For Bayer, the hidden God is thus not a matter of abstract thinking or speculation but a reality of radical contradiction to be reckoned with in the life of the believer.

The Contradiction of the Promise in Anfechtung

The central point and the overall subject matter of theology, according to Bayer, is God's justification of the sinner. Bayer understands such justification as taking place through the divine, performative speech act of the promise spoken in the gospel of Jesus Christ. In this promise, which reaches the human through the preaching of the Word and Sacraments, God speaks to the human and for the human, declaring the human righteous, bringing him or her into a new relationship with God, liberating and granting him or her confidence in faith, opening the new creation to him or her, and opening him or her anew to the created world.[15]

Yet, God's encountering the human in divine hiddenness contradicts God's justifying Word in the promise through *Anfechtung*. In this agonizing struggle, the justified sinner who knows God according to God's promise in Christ, is attacked by the hidden God, who puts God's self forward as the enemy of the believer. In *Anfechtung*, the hidden God thus enters into a battle with the justified sinner, hiding God's self, making God's self incomprehensible to the believer who is a justified sinner and contradicting God's own Word of promise to be a gracious forgiving God for the sinner.[16] This battle is not just an intangible or inaudible "spiritual" warfare. Instead, according to Bayer, it takes on the very real dimensions of a hostile exchange of words (*Wortwechsel*) between God and the believer over the validity of God's promise.[17]

---

14. Bayer, *Theology the Lutheran Way*, 18–19; Bayer, *Theologie*, 39. Bayer, *Martin Luther's Theology*, 4, 40, 202–4, 228; Bayer, *Martin Luthers Theologie*, 2, 36–37, 182–84, 206.

15. Bayer, *Martin Luther's Theology*, 9–10, 39–40, 53–55; Bayer, *Martin Luthers Theologie*, 8–9, 36–37, 4–51. Bayer, *Theology the Lutheran Way*, 129–30; Bayer, *Theologie*, 443–44. Bayer, "Rupture of Times," 43–44; Bayer, *Gott als Autor*, 156–57. Bayer, "The Doctrine of Justification and Ontology," 44ff; Bayer, *Zugesagte Gegenwart*, 196ff. Helmer, "The Subject of Theology in the Thought of Oswald Bayer," 286.

16. Bayer, *Theology the Lutheran Way*, 104, 114; Bayer, *Theologie*, 416, 425. Bayer, *Martin Luther's Theology*, 39–40; Bayer, *Martin Luthers Theologie*, 36–37.

17. Bayer, *Martin Luther's Theology*, 39–40, 228; Bayer, *Martin Luthers Theologie*, 36–37, 206.

It is hard to imagine a more desperate situation for the believer in which God contradicts the justification worked by God's promise in Christ than the one which Bayer describes. Here, the hidden God's contradiction of the promise of the revealed God in justification is so stark and even so violent that the hidden God comes after the believer as the enemy of the believer. To further illustrate this point, Bayer brings in Luther's interpretation of the antagonistic encounter between God and Jacob on the banks of the Jabbok, recorded by the Elohist in Genesis 32.

The Wrestling God

Following Luther's interpretation of the narrative in his *Lectures on Genesis*, Bayer employs the story of Jacob's wrestling match with God by the Jabbok ford in order to vividly illustrate the struggle in *Anfechtung* between the hidden God and the believer over the validity of the promise.[18] This, says Bayer, is what the human's encounter with God outside the context of the Word looks like. The promise of justification through faith Christ is the only place where God and the human being can coexist, and outside of this promise, God and the human being are enemies. The enmity between God outside of the promise and the human being is such that God is not merely removed from the human being but actually fights against him or her.[19] For the believer, as for Jacob who was also the recipient of God's promise, this confrontation with the hidden God forms the experience of *Anfechutng*, which in this context, becomes a struggle over the truth of the promise.[20]

The nature of this attack by the hidden God is shrouded in a haze of incomprehensibility. In the midst of his fight on the banks of the Jabbok, says Bayer, Jacob could not discern with whom or with what he was wrestling. Was it a man? Was it an angel? Was it God? Was it the devil?

In the same way, says Bayer, it is impossible in the midst of *Anfechtung* for the believer to know whether he or she is struggling with God or with the devil.[21] Here, in the midst of *Anfechtung*, the believer, like Jacob, experiences God as the enemy who takes away life and attacks faith in the promise of God's salvation.[22] Is it God or the devil who attacks the believer in hid-

---

18. Bayer, *Theology the Lutheran Way*, 18–19; Bayer, *Theologie*, 39. Bayer, *Martin Luther's Theology*, 4, 40, 202–4, 228; Bayer, *Martin Luthers Theologie*, 2, 36–37, 182–84, 206.

19. Bayer, *Martin Luther's Theology*, 39–40; Bayer *Martin Luthers Theologie*, 36–37.

20. Bayer, *Zugesagte Gegenwart*, 77.

21. Bayer, *Martin Luther's Theology*, 40; Bayer, *Martin Luthers Theologie*, 36.

22. Bayer, *Martin Luther's Theology*, 40; Bayer, *Martin Luthers Theologie*, 36–37.

denness? According to Bayer, as he uses the confrontation between God and Jacob to interpret the encounter between the hidden God and the human in *Anfechtung*, both are the case. For, in *Anfechtung*, says Bayer, the hidden God becomes the devil to the believer; the hidden God becomes a demonic force that attacks the believer, seeking to undermine faith in the promise.[23]

While he utilizes Luther at this point to demonstrate that God works evil through the agency of the devil, and so the devil functions as a pawn for God's usage in such a way that God avoids direct responsibility for evil, Bayer does not make a clean distinction between the hidden God and the devil.[24] Ultimately, says Bayer, one can never fully distinguish between the work of the hidden God and the work of the devil; because of the incomprehensibility of the hiddenness of God, it is simply impossible to do so.[25]

The work of the hidden God in *Anfechtung* certainly seems more in concert with the demonic than with the gracious and forgiving God, whom the believer has come to know in the promise, says Bayer. For in *Anfechtung*, the hidden God attacks the believer's faith in the promise.[26] Here again Bayer draws from Luther, quoting the reformer's words, "To seek God apart from Jesus Christ—that is the devil."[27] If God gives the believer a promise and then acts contrary to that promise, then the believer will think that "God is merely playing with humans," and consequently that God "is just as frivolous and unreliable" as the devil.[28]

Bayer does not, however, understand himself or Luther to be a Manichean or a dualist of any kind. In fact, Bayer argues that Luther's approach to the question of God's responsibility for evil, which he himself adopts as well, is the direct denial of dualism. Dualism, in any of its many forms, identifies two distinct and eternal beings as responsible for good and for evil respectively. Luther's argument that the hidden God is responsible for evil, and even ultimately for the demonic, makes dualism impossible. If one follows Luther's thinking on the hidden God and evil, says Bayer, one cannot

---

Bayer, *Zugesagte Gegenwart*, 77.

23. Bayer, "Rupture of Times," 37–38; Bayer, *Gott als Autor*, 150–52. Bayer, *Martin Luther's Theology*, 2–4, 204; Bayer, *Martin Luthers Theologie*, 2–4, 184.

24. Bayer, *Martin Luther's Theology*, 204–5; Bayer, *Martin Luthers Theologie*, 184–85.

25. Bayer, *Martin Luther's Theology*, 280; Bayer, *Martin Luthers Theologie*, 254. Mattes, *The Role of Justification in Contemporary Theology*, 168–69.

26. Bayer, *Martin Luther's Theology*, 204–5; Bayer, *Martin Luther's Theology*, 184–185.

27. Luther, *In XV Psalmos graduum* (1540), Luther, "Psalmus, CXXX," in WA 40.3:337. Bayer, *Martin Luther's Theology*, 205; Bayer *Martin Luthers Theologie*, 185. Bayer, "What is Evangelical?" 10; Bayer, *Zugesagte Gegenwart*, 31.

28. Bayer, *Martin Luther's Theology*, 205; Bayer, *Martin Luther's Theology*, 185.

attribute evil and the demonic to the devil alone, for God is ultimately responsible for them and even for the existence of the devil.[29]

The Forms of the Hidden God's Contradiction of the Promise in Anfechtung

Of course, the believer today is not physically attacked by the wrestling, hidden God in the form of a human being. So then, in what form does Bayer understand the hidden God to encounter the believer? Bayer identifies two unavoidable questions raised by the reality of the hidden God, illustrating the forms taken by the hidden God's contradiction of the promise. The first of these questions is, "Did God really determine from eternity that some human beings would be damned?" The second is, "Does God also work evil?"[30] These two questions present two forms of the hidden God's work of contradicting the justifying promise through *Anfechtung*: the problem of double predestination and the cause of evil in the created order (i.e. theodicy). In the former of these the hidden God contradicts God's promise of the forgiveness of the individual believer's sin. In the latter, the hidden God contradicts the promised reconciliation and renewal of the fallen creation.[31]

The Hidden God and Double Predestination

Although he names it as one of the forms in which the hidden God's attack on faith in the promise comes to the believer, Bayer does not comment on the relationship between the hidden God and the question of double predestination at length. Instead, his description of this form of the hidden God's attack in *Anfechtung* is brief. Nevertheless, Bayer recognizes that there is an important connection between the divine hiddenness and double predestination in Luther's theology and addresses it.

According to Bayer, the question of double predestination is raised by the hidden God and afflicts believers with doubts about their own salvation through the situation of *Anfechtung*.[32] Bayer is careful to point out, how-

---

29. Bayer, *Martin Luther's Theology*, 205-6; Bayer, *Martin Luthers Theologie*, 185-86. Bayer, "God's Omnipotence," 90-92; Bayer, *Zugesagte Gegenwart*, 117-19.

30. Bayer, *Martin Luther's Theology*, 198-99; Bayer, *Martin Luthers Theologie*, 179.

31. Bayer, *Martin Luther's Theology*, 198-99, 209; Bayer, *Martin Luthers Theologie*, 179, 188-189. Byaer, "What is Evangelical?" 4, 10; Byaer, *Zugesagte Gegenwart*, 25, 31-32. Bayer, "The Plurality of the One God," 342-43, 345-46, 353; Bayer, *Zugesagte Gegenwart*, 99-100, 102, 109.

32. Bayer, "What is Evangelical?" 10; Bayer, *Zugesagte Gegenwart*, 31-32. Bayer,

ever, that he does not advocate a speculative view of double predestination whereby theological claims are made about the nature of God and salvation based upon the idea that from eternity God divided humanity between the elect and the reprobate and consequently God's revealed will in salvation would merely reveal his prior secret will established before all time. Bayer recognizes such as view as being representative of John Calvin's teaching of double predestination and the hidden God, but Bayer rejects this attempt to resolve the tension between the hidden God and the revealed God as an answer to the question of double predestination.[33]

The problem with such an idea of double predestination, says Bayer, is the attempt to answer the terrifying question of double predestination by speculating about the will of the hidden God. The correct perspective for addressing predestination is Luther's own, that is, the pastoral care of the individual believer.[34] According to Bayer, this perspective precludes Calvin's speculative solution to the question of predestination simply because it fails to take into account the *Sitz im Leben* of *Anfechtung*, in which the hidden God places the believer.[35] As with *Anfechtung* in general, the hidden God's contradiction of the promise in the specific instance of the question of double predestination can be relieved only by the promise itself and, as I shall address more fully below, only eschatologically.

The Hidden God and Theodicy

Bayer spends more time discussing second of the two situations of the hidden God's attack in creation, usually called theodicy or "the problem of evil."[36] Although all people experience this work of the hidden God to some extent, the situation is more acute for the believer who experiences it as *Anfechtung*, as the hidden God's attack on the promise.[37]

In Bayer's thinking, God's work of justification includes not only God's forgiveness and declaring righteous of the individual believer but also the opening of creation itself and its ultimate reconciliation and restoration. As

Martin Luther's Theology, 198–99; Bayer, *Martin Luthers Theologie*, 179.

33. Bayer, *Martin Luthers Theologie*, 209–10; Bayer, *Martin Luthers Theologie*, 188–89.

34. Ibid.

35. Ibid. Bayer, "The Plurality of the One God," 343; Bayer, *Zugesagte Gegenwart*, 99–100.

36. Bayer, *Martin Luther's Theology*," 198–99; Bayer, *Martin Luthers Theologie*, 179. Bayer, "The Plurality of the One God," 345; Bayer, *Zugesagte Gegenwart*, 102.

37. Bayer, "The Plurality of the One God," 349–50; Bayer, *Zugesagte Gegenwart*, 106.

I discussed in chapter five of this thesis, Bayer understands God's justification of the sinner within ontological and cosmic dimensions, and he demands that justification and creation be addressed together and not divided from one another. Bayer consequently understands God's work of justification to entail God's work of opening a new creation, which is actually a recapitulation of the old to its original created state. The problem with this, of course, is that such transformation is not presently visible to believers who still see the world full of suffering, pain, and evil. It is this reality of the "problem of evil" evident in the world, which is at odds with the trust that God is opening a new creation, that constitutes the second form of *Anfechtung*.[38]

Bayer rejects the attempt to say that God is not responsible for evil by saying God is not omnipotent.[39] Here, Bayer follows Luther into the reformer's strongest statements concerning the bondage of the human will and the all-working power of God.[40] Bayer agrees with Luther that God accomplishes everything that comes to pass, including evil, and that if God did not do so, God would not be God. Bayer echoes Luther's strongest claim: without complete divine omnipotence, there is no divinity.[41] It is not as if Luther heretically fabricated the notion that God is responsible for evil, says Bayer. For God describes God's self in Second Isaiah as "the creator of calamity, of evil, and of darkness" saying, "I am the Lord who does all of these things."[42] There can be no possibility of another entity being ultimately responsible for evil because God alone "is the Lord and there is no other."[43] In theology, says Bayer, there can be no denying that God is responsible for evil. Instead, this reality must be faced as it is experienced.

---

38. Bayer, *Martin Luther's Theology*, 199; Bayer, *Martin Luthers Theologie*, 179. Bayer, "What is Evangelical?" 10; Bayer, *Zugesagte Gegenwart*, 31. It is not as if there is a specific and necessary order to these two forms of the hidden God's contradiction of the promise in *Anfechtung*. While in *Martin Luthers Theologie*, double predestination is listed first and theodicy second, the order is the opposite in *Zugesagte Gegenwart*. Hence, Bayer does not delineate a sequence or progression in regard to these two forms. Instead, he describes them as if they were two sides of the same coin. They are complementary questions both raised by the reality of the hidden God encountered by the believer as contradictions of the promise through *Anfechtung*.

39. Bayer, *Martin Luther's Theology*, 205–8; Bayer, *Martin Luthers Theologie*, 185–87.

40. Cf. *BOW*, 80, 170; WA 615, 685.

41. Bayer, *Martin Luther's Theology*, 201–2, 205–8; Bayer, *Martin Luthers Theologie*, 181–82, 185–87. Bayer, "God's Omnipotence," 91–93; Bayer, *Zugesagte Gegenwart*, 117–19.

42. Bayer, "God's Omnipotence," 91–92; Bayer, *Zugesagte Gegenwart*, 117–18. Isa 45:7.

43. Bayer, "God's Omnipotence," 91–92; Bayer, *Zugesagte Gegenwart*, 117–18. Isa 45:6.

But God's working of evil is not equivalent to or part of God's work of justification through the promise. The two are contradictory to one another. The occurrence of evil in the world really is accomplished by God, says Bayer, but it is the work of the hidden God. As such, it is incomprehensible and contradicts the revealed God's justifying promise and is experienced as such by believers.[44]

What this means, according to Bayer, is that all the human and natural evil experienced by humans, unbelievers and believers alike, comes from the hidden God as the contradiction of the promise of God in justification that is experienced by the believer in *Anfechtung*.[45] It is the experience of all the evil things in life that befall humanity and the creation, which afflict the believer by placing him or her in a context where good and evil are intertwined with one another, with the knowledge constantly in his or her mind that it is God who is responsible for all of this.[46] The believer then becomes keenly aware that hurricanes, tornadoes, earthquakes, tsunamis, famines, wars, pandemics, the untimely deaths of children, the current ecological crisis of the physical environment of the universe, the existence and the threat of the use of thermonuclear weapons, and the shoa and all the horrible things accomplished by Hitler and the Nazis, and every other genocide, ultimately serve as the work of the hidden God.[47] The promise encounters the believer in the midst of these excruciating question of theodicy.[48]

Bayer's view of theodicy as one of the ways in which the hidden God's attack on faith in the promise of justification comes to the believer flows from his overall understanding of justification through the promise. According to Bayer, justification and creation intrinsically belong together as the work of God's word of promise. Both are works of God's word of promise and both are unmerited gifts given by God to the human.[49] As in justification, God's work and gift in creation open up a new relationship between God and the

---

44. Bayer, *Martin Luther's Theology*, 202; Bayer, *Martin Luthers Theologie*, 182.

45. Ibid. Bayer, "The Plurality of the One God," 349; Bayer, *Zugesagte Gegenwart*, 105.

46. Bayer, *Martin Luther's Theology*, 202; Bayer, *Martin Luthers Theologie*, 182. Bayer, "Creation as History," 261; Bayer, *Zugesagte Gegenwart*, 229. Bayer, "God's Omnipotence," 92–93; Bayer, *Zugesagte Gegenwart*, 119.

47. Bayer, *Schöpfung als Anrede*, 161. Bayer, "Der neue Mensch," 126–27; Bayer, *Zugesagte Gegenwart*, 244–245. Bayer, "Der Glanze der Gnade," 80. Bayer, *Gott als Autor*, 272.

48. Bayer, "What Is Evangelical?" 10; Bayer, *Zugesagte Gegenwart*, 31.

49. Bayer, *Martin Luther's Theology*, 95–97, 101, 103, 107–8; Bayer, *Martin Luthers Theologie*, 87–89, 93, 94–95, 97–98. Bayer, "The Doctrine of Justification and Ontology," 45–47; Bayer, *Zugesagte Gegenwart*, 197–200.

created human.⁵⁰ Furthermore creation can only be accessed through justification, and justification leads back to creation as its ultimate trajectory.⁵¹ This is because, for Bayer, justification invariably opens the justified human sinner anew to creation and creation anew to the justified sinner.⁵² Finally, justification and creation belong together in Bayer's theology, because in justification God is actually making the old creation new by returning it to the state of goodness in which God originally created it, redeeming and renewing it through the promise.⁵³

In this context, the hiddenness of God as the contradiction of the promise in justification takes on cosmic dimensions. This means that, for Bayer, *Anfechtung* can never be an isolated individualistic experience. Though it does consist of the individual believer's doubt and wrestling with the hidden God through the question of double predestination, personal *Angst* by no means exhausts Bayer's understanding of *Anfechtung* as the hidden God's work of contradicting the promise of justification. Quite the opposite, when the question of theodicy as a way through which the hidden God assaults belief in the promise is seen from the vantage point of justification as the opening and renewing of creation, the whole of created life becomes the realm for the hidden God's work of contradicting the promise. Bayer sees the hidden God as contradicting the promise of justification and attacking belief in that promise through the horrific disasters in nature and the horrors wrought by human beings, because he holds that part of the promise of justification is that the creation is being opened, renewed, and restored.⁵⁴

In these cosmic dimensions of hiddenness, the creature and all of creation itself becomes a vehicle for the wrath of the hidden God.⁵⁵ Thus, it is not as if Bayer simply sees the evil in nature and the evil committed by humans as raising the question of theodicy, which then serves as a means for an intellectual attack by the hidden God on the faith of the individual

---

50. Bayer, *Martin Luther's Theology*, 100–103, 111–12; Bayer, *Martin Luthers Theologie*, 93–94, 101–2. Bayer, "The Doctrine of Justification and Ontology," 47–49; Bayer, *Zugesagte Gegenwart*, 200–201.

51. Bayer, "The Doctrine of Justification and Ontology," 44; Bayer, *Zugesagte Gegenwart*, 196.

52. Bayer, *Martin Luther's Theology*, 106–8; Bayer, *Martin Luthers Theologie*, 97–99. Bayer, *Schöpfung als Anrede*, 62. Bayer, "The Doctrine of Justification and Ontology," 48–49; Bayer, *Zugesagte Gegenwart*, 201.

53 Bayer, *Martin Luther's Theology*, 9–10; Bayer, *Martin Luthers Theologie*, 8–9. Bayer, "Rupture of the Ages," 43–45; Bayer, *Gott als Autor*, 156–58. Bayer, *Martin Luther's Theology*, 116–19; Bayer, *Martin Luthers Theologie*, 106–9.

54. Bayer, *Martin Luther's Theology*, 101–2, 111–12, 116–19; Bayer, *Martin Luthers Theologie*, 94, 101–2, 106–9. Bayer, *Schöpfung als Anrede*, 43–45.

55. Bayer, *Martin Luther's Theology*, 112; Bayer, *Martin Luthers Theologie*, 102.

believer. Though Bayer by no means discounts the intellectual aspect of the hidden God's attack in *Anfechtung*, he does not limit the scope of the hidden God's assault on faith to the realm of the mental or the psychological. Instead, in a way that turns *Schöpfung als Anrede* on its head and contradicts God's gracious promises through the *Leibliches Wort* of created means, in hiddenness, creation becomes the physical means for the direct wrath of the hidden God. Instead of being a vehicle for the proclamation of the promise, creation and its creatures become the embodiment of God's wrath and of the hidden God's activity of contradicting the promise,[56] so that even the "rustling of a leaf" becomes a venue for the work of the terrifying hiddenness of God that assaults faith in God's justifying promise.[57]

This cosmic situation throws the believer into a very desperate situation.[58] On the one hand, the opening and renewal of creation is promised by God in justification, but, on the other hand, much of what is visible and experienced in the creation contradicts this promise and attacks the believer's trust in the promising God. In the midst of *Anfechtung* the believer is caught between the promise and its utter contradiction.[59]

The picture is frighteningly vivid when God comes to wrestle with the believer. The hidden God does this through the existential question of double predestination and through the reality of evil in the world. The hidden God's assault thus comes against the believer not exactly through a direct attack by God in the form of a hostile stranger as it did to Jacob on the banks of the Jabbok but through the question of whether the believer is elect or damned and the evidence of the contradiction of the promised opening and renewal of creation through the horrific natural and human-caused evil present and active in the created world. Through these means, the hidden God drives the believer into a desperate situation, where he or she is trapped between the justifying promise given by the revealed God and its contradiction in *Anfechtung* through the work of the hidden God.

---

56. Bayer, *Martin Luther's Theology*, 111–12; Bayer, *Martin Luthers Theologie*, 101–2. Bayer, *Schöpfung als Anrede*, 43–45.

57. Bayer, *Martin Luther's Theology*, 102–3; Bayer, *Martin Luthers Theologie*, 94.

58. Bayer, *Martin Luther's Theology*, 113; Bayer, *Martin Luthers Theologie*, 103.

59. Bayer, *Martin Luther's Theology*, 11; Bayer, *Martin Luthers Theologie*, 10. Bayer, "Rupture of Times," 45–46; Bayer, *Gott als Autor*, 158–59. Bayer, *Martin Luther's Theology*, 113; Bayer, *Martin Luthers Theologie*, 103.

The Mounting Tension Formed by the Hidden God's Contradiction of the Promise

As Bayer describes it, through *Anfechtung*, the believer experiences a mounting tension between what he or she has experienced and knows of God through God's justifying promise, on the one hand, and the contradiction of that same promise through what he or she experiences in *Anfechtung*, on the other hand. Through *Anfechtung*, the believer "is driven into narrow straights," which close in about him or her and where he or she is "pressed hard" on all sides.[60] This tension is formed, says Bayer, when the believer undergoes the hidden God's attacking contradiction of the justifying promise of God in the gospel of Jesus Christ through the question of double predestination and especially through the cosmic situation of the problem of evil experience of the hidden God's contradiction. In the midst of this experience of contradiction and mounting tension, the believer is thrown the believer into a very desperate situation.[61] On the one hand, the opening and renewal of creation is promised by God in justification, but, on the other hand, all that is visible and experienced in the creation itself contradicts this promise and attacks the believer's trust in the promising God.[62]

According to Bayer, this desperate situation of mounting tension formed by the attack of the hidden God through *Anfechtung*, traps the believer between two different understandings and experiences of God. In this desperate situation in which the believer finds himself or herself trapped between God and God, God's omnipotence is experienced in two different ways. Moreover, this situation of tension evidences an even greater tension within God's very self as experienced by the believer. These tensions between the two forms of God's omnipotence and between the two understandings of God's very self, says Bayer, are irresolvable for the believer on this side of the eschaton. For Bayer, this is what it means to live in the rupture of the ages, to exist as a believer in the midst of the hidden God's contradiction of the promise of justification. Consequently, argues Bayer, the theologian must maintain these distinctions formed by the agonizing struggle of *Anfechtung* rather than seeking to create some kind of false integration or homogenization of what presently cannot be unified.[63]

---

60. Bayer, *Martin Luther's Theology*, 113; Bayer, *Martin Luthers Theologie*, 103.

61. Ibid.

62. Bayer, *Martin Luther's Theology*, 11; Bayer, *Martin Luthers Theologie*, 10. Bayer, "Rupture of Times," 45–46; Bayer, *Gott als Autor*, 158–59.

63. Bayer, "The Plurality of the One God," 343, 352–53; Bayer, *Zugesagte Gegenwart*, 99–100, 108–9.

Two Understandings of God's Omnipotence

The believer who undergoes *Anfechtung*, says Bayer, is presented with two kinds of divine omnipotence.[64] On the one hand, the believer experiences the omnipotence of God's Word, wherein God's all-working power is revealed benevolently in God's salvation of the passive human sinner.[65] On the other hand, there is also an omnipotence of God outside of God's Word. This omnipotence consists of God's working of all things, corresponds to God's terrifying hiddenness, and operates against the believer.[66] Since God is experienced by the believer in divergent ways God's omnipotence cannot be defined or described uniformly but must be addressed according to the two experiences.[67]

The first of the two kinds of divine omnipotence delineated by Bayer is the omnipotence of God in God's Word. The believer encounters this form of God's omnipotence through the gracious revelation of God in the gospel of Jesus Christ. According to Bayer, this kind of divine foreknowledge is linked intrinsically to the assurance of salvation given to the believer through the promise.[68]

Here, Bayer again follows Luther. Concerning the omnipotence of God in God's Word, Bayer echoes the belief expressed by the reformer in *The Bondage of the Will* that the only way by which the believer can be sure and certain of the promise of God in salvation is because there is nothing that is outside the working of God's omnipotence.[69] The omnipotence of God in God's Word, says Bayer, consists of God's specific working of the human being's salvation. If God does not possess the actual power to effect God's will of salvation, then there is little point to believing in God's promise and no assurance of faith, for faith and assurance in the promise rest on God's faithfulness and power to carry out what God promises.[70] Furthermore, says Bayer, yet again echoing Luther, God effects all that comes to pass by virtue of God's immutable foreknowledge, and that if God were not able to effect God's will, God would no longer be God.[71] If God did not effect everything

---

64. Bayer, "The Plurality of the One God," 346; Bayer, *Zugesagte Gegenwart*, 102.

65. Bayer, "God's Omnipotence," 87; Bayer, *Zugesagte Gegenwart*, 113.

66. Ibid.

67. Bayer, "The Plurality of the One God," 345–46; Bayer, *Zugesagte Gegenwart*, 101–2.

68. Bayer, "God's Omnipotence," 86; Bayer, *Zugesagte Gegenwart*, 112.

69. Bayer, "God's Omnipotence," 86–87; Bayer, *Zugesagte Gegenwart*, 112–13. Cf. *BOW*, 83–84; WA 18:618–19. Forde, *Captivation of the Will*, 38–40.

70. Bayer, "God's Omnipotence," 86–87; Bayer, *Zugesagte Gegenwart*, 112–13.

71. Bayer, "God's Omnipotence," 87–88; Bayer, *Zugesagte Gegenwart*, 113–14.

that comes to pass, then there would be some entity more powerful than God, whether another god or the human's supposed "free will." There is no such entity, for God alone is God and there is no other outside or alongside of God.[72]

Yet, God's omnipotence in working all things is not oriented towards the same end as the omnipotence of God in God's Word nor is it even understandable. While God's omnipotence in God's Word is oriented towards the specific end of God's salvation of the human sinner, God's general omnipotence outside of God's Word, works all things, including life and death, good and evil. It is this omnipotence that characterizes the work of the hidden God.[73] As the work of the hidden God, the omnipotence of God outside of God's Word is utterly incomprehensible. This general omnipotence thus stands in contrast to the omnipotence of God in God's Word, wherein the believer not only comprehends God's omnipotence but actually receives confidence and assurance of salvation through God's promise thereby. In contrast to the omnipotence of God in God's Word that works faith in God's promise, says Bayer, the general omnipotence of the hidden God instills fear in the heart of even the believing human being. Such fear, says Bayer, is completely different than the fear and wonder evoked in the believer by the omnipotence of God revealed in the gospel; it is, instead, a fear of utter terror when faced by the all-working omnipotence of the hidden God.[74] Instead of working assurance in the justifying promise of God, the omnipotence of God outside of God's Word, which effects all things by God's immutable will, actually causes anxiety and doubt in the believer. It causes the believer to doubt the promise.[75]

According to Bayer, this bifurcation in divine omnipotence that flows from the distinction between the revealed God and the hidden God means that the theologian can never speak abstractly and speculatively concerning divine omnipotence as a generic attribute of God. Instead, he or she must plainly distinguish between the two forms of God's omnipotence and focus primarily upon the omnipotence of God in God's Word, since this is the form of omnipotence concerned with God's justifying work in the promise

---

Bayer, *Martin Luther's Theology*, 205–6; Bayer, *Martin Luthers Theologie*, 185–86. Cf. *BOW*, 80; WA 615.

72. Bayer, "God's Omnipotence," 91; Bayer, *Zugesagte Gegenwart*, 117. Bayer, *Martin Luther's Theology*, 205–6; Bayer, *Martin Luthers Theologie*, 185–86.

73. Bayer, "God's Omnipotence," 88–89; Bayer, *Zugesagte Gegenwart*, 114–15.

74. Ibid.

75. Bayer, "God's Omnipotence," 96–97, 99; Bayer, *Zugesagte Gegenwart*, 122–23, 124.

of Jesus Christ. Yet, at the same time, the theologian must not deny the reality of the hidden God's all-working omnipotence.[76]

The two differing forms of God's omniscience thus form part of the tension brought about by the conflict between the reality of the hidden God's work and the reality of the revealed God in Jesus Christ through the promise of the gospel. This tension, says Bayer, cannot be relieved, nor can the two forms of God's omnipotence be unified, except eschatologically. According to Bayer, the tension formed by the activity of the hidden God in the context of the believer's experience God's justifying promise is "irreducible" in the present and must be endured by the believer and not lessened or eased by the theologian.[77] This does not mean, however, that the tension is eternal. Rather, it will be relieved but only eschatologically by God God's self.[78] The only thing for the believer and the theologian to do as long as they are "walking by faith on a pilgrimage that takes time" is to endure the tension between the two forms of God's omnipotence with faith in the eschatological power of God's justifying promise in the gospel of Christ.[79]

Two Doctrines of God

The tension between God's justifying promise and God's contradiction of that promise through hiddenness may be seen even more acutely with reference to God's nature. According to Bayer, the tension between the reality of the hiddenness of God and God's justifying promise is so strong that it appears as a division within God's self. As I have already noted, Bayer sees the distinction between the hidden God and the revealed God to be so significant that it affects the understanding of God's nature as Trinity. According to Bayer, there is a marked distinction between the teaching of the Triune God experienced through the gospel and the doctrine of the "general knowledge of God" experienced through the law and the hidden God's work in the world.[80] Bayer argues that God can be said to exist as Trinity only with regard to God's existence in revelation and in no way in regard to the hidden

---

76. Bayer, "The Plurality of the One God," 345–46; Bayer, *Zugesagte Gegenwart*, 102–3.

77. Bayer, "The Plurality of the One God," 343; Bayer, *Zugesagte Gegenwart*, 99–100. Bayer, *Theology the Lutheran Way*, 105; Bayer, *Theologie*, 416.

78. Bayer, "God's Omnipotence," 99; Bayer, *Zugesagte Gegenwart*, 125. Bayer, *Martin Luther's Theology*, 212–13; Bayer, *Martin Luthers Theologie*, 191–92.

79. Bayer, "God's Omnipotence," 91, 99; Bayer, *Zugesagte Gegenwart*, 117, 125. Bayer, "The Plurality of the One God," 343; Bayer, *Zugesagte Gegenwart*, 100.

80. Bayer, "Poetological Doctrine of the Trinity," 52–53; Bayer, "Poetologische Trinitätslehre," 76–77; Bayer, *Gott als Autor*, "144–45.

God.⁸¹ Thus, in addition to two kinds of divine omnipotence, there are two doctrines of God's nature evident in the tension between the experience of the hidden God and the promise of God's justification given to the believer in the gracious revelation of God in Jesus Christ.

Bayer develops his differentiation between the doctrine of God revealed as Trinity and the general doctrine of God along the lines of his interpretation of Luther's hymn *"Nun freut euch, leiben Christen g'mein,"* which he terms "a poetological doctrine of the Trinity."⁸² According to Bayer, the believer and Christian theologian are brought into the revelation of the Triune God through the justifying and liberating work of God revealed in the promise of the gospel of Jesus Christ.⁸³ Corresponding to this, Bayer maintains that God as Trinity can only be known through the experience of the justifying promise of God in the gospel and not through any speculation concerning the "general knowledge of God." Through the promise of the gospel, says Bayer, the believer comes to know the Triune God as the Father, Son, and Holy Spirit who work together to effect human salvation through the "happy exchange" (*"Der fröhliche Wechsel"*), the action of the Triune God in the incarnation, death, and resurrection of Jesus Christ, whereby God takes upon God's self the sin and death of humanity and gives to humans God's own righteousness and life in Jesus Christ. This action of liberating humanity from sin, death, and God's condemnation in the law, says Bayer, is the true and specific means whereby the believer and theologian is to know and speak of the Triune God, not through some vague generalizing speculation about the nature of God.⁸⁴ To know the Triune God is to know God through the promise of the gospel, for the Triune God is the God of the gospel, and the God of the gospel is the Triune God.⁸⁵ As Bayer puts it,

---

81. Bayer, *Martin Luther's Theology*, 339; Bayer, *Martin Luthers Theologie*, 308-9. Bayer, "Poetological Doctrine of the Trinity," 53; Bayer, "Poetologische Trinitätslehre," 77; Bayer, *Gott als Autor*, 145-46. Bayer, *Zugesagte Gegenwart*, 175-77.

82. Bayer, "Poetological Doctrine of the Trinity," 45-46; 51-52, 54-55; Bayer, "Poetologische Trinitätslehre," 70-71, 75-76, 78-79; Bayer, *Gott als Autor*, 144-145, 147. Bayer, *Martin Luther's Theology*, 224-25, 337ff.; Bayer, *Martin Luthers Theologie*, 202-3, 306ff. Helmer, "The Subject of Theology in the Thought of Oswald Bayer," 34-35. *EG*, 341; *ELW*, 594; *LSB*, 556.

83. Bayer, *Martin Luther's Theology*, 222-23; Bayer, *Martin Luthers Theologie*, 200-201.

84. Bayer, *Martin Luther's Theology*, 222-23, 225-27; Bayer, *Martin Luthers Theologie*, 200-201, 204-5. Bayer, "Poetological Doctrine of the Trinity," 50; Bayer, "Poetologische Trinitätslehre," 74. Cf. Luther, *The Freedom of a Christian*, 60-65; WA 7:53-56.

85. Bayer, "Poetological Doctrine of the Trinity," 52; Bayer, "Poetologische Trinitätslehre," 76; Bayer, *Gott als Autor*, 145. Bayer, "Poetological Theology," 164; Bayer, *Gott als Autor*, 14.

"The doctrine of the Trinity considers nothing other than the gospel, the liberation: the freedom, which Christ has acquired for us and brought to us, and by which, in the Word through the Holy Spirit, he has comforted us and imparted it to us in the present."[86] For Bayer, the doctrine of the Trinity is nothing other than "the sum of the gospel."[87]

Yet, says Bayer, though the doctrine of the Trinity concerns and is revealed through the promise of the gospel alone, many modern theologians and philosophers have sought to interpret the Triune God speculatively according to the general knowledge of God.[88] Bayer argues that this method of discussing God as Trinity constitutes "one of the grandiose errors" of modernity, for to know the Triune God is to know God reveled in the justifying promise of the gospel of Jesus Christ alone.[89] This phenomenon of the existence of this speculative misinterpretation of the doctrine of God's self-revelation as Trinity evident in much of modern theology and philosophy—which Bayer identifies as a post-Christian Hegelian natural theology—illustrates the need for maintaining the difference between the doctrine of the Triune God revealed in the promise of salvation and the general doctrine of God.[90]

According to Bayer, there can be no speculative knowledge of the Trinity, because God as Trinity can only be known through the promise of the gospel. This does not mean, however, that Bayer denies that God is known, or at least experienced apart from God's revelation as Trinity in the promise of the gospel. On the contrary, Bayer insists that the theologian must acknowledge the existence of the general knowledge of God, experienced by the human outside of the Triune God's self-revelation in the gospel so that the doctrine of God as Trinity is not conflated with or collapsed into the general knowledge of God and so that theological discourse does not devolve into speculation.[91] It would be nice, says Bayer, if the theologian could speak only of God's existence in God's gracious self-revelation through the gospel, but this is not the case. Though theologians have attempted to take the easy route by addressing the doctrine of God only in terms of God's

---

86. Bayer, *Gott als Autor*, 14. The translation here is my own. Cf. ET "Poetological Theology," 164. Bayer, *Zugesagte Gegenwart*, 176.

87. Bayer, "Poetological Doctrine of the Trinity," 52; Bayer, "Poetologische Trinitätslehre," 76; Bayer, *Gott als Autor*, 145. Bayer, *Martin Luther's Theology*, 337; Bayer, *Martin Luthers Theologie*, 306.

88. Bayer, "Poetological Theology," 165; Bayer, *Gott als Autor*, 15.

89. Bayer, "Poetological Theology," 164–165; Bayer, *Gott als Autor*, 14–15.

90. Bayer, "The Plurality of the One God," 353; Bayer, *Zugesagt Gegenwart*, 109. Bayer, "Poetological Theology," 165; Bayer, *Gott als Autor*, 15.

91. Bayer, "Poetological Theology," 165; Bayer, *Gott als Autor*, 15.

gracious self-revelation (Bayer lays particular blame here on Barth for doing this and for conflating the Triune God with a general knowledge of God), such theologians do not describe the full reality of the human experience of God.[92] The truth is, says Bayer, that human beings experience God in plurality and diversity, and that such plurality and diversity are irreducible. The best thing that the theologian can do is to recognize the diverse human experience of God both as God reveals God's self as Trinity and of the general knowledge of God.[93]

While God's existence as Trinity is uniquely revealed through the gospel alone and is known and experienced only by the believer, the general knowledge of God, says Bayer, is experienced commonly by all people as the experience of God outside of God's gracious promise in Jesus Christ.[94] Though he also understands this general knowledge of God experienced by all humans to consist also of God's address to the human in the law (in both its first and second uses), Bayer states this general knowledge of God ultimately is the knowledge of the terrifying hiddenness of God experienced through the questions of double predestination and theodicy.[95] The general knowledge of God, which is experienced by all humans and which exists in contradiction to the God of grace and love revealed as Trinity for the human through the promise of the gospel in Jesus Christ, consists of the experience of God as the one who works death, destruction, evil, and "all things."[96] The general knowledge of God is not, however, an opportunity for speculation over and against a clear-cut understanding of God in revelation. Instead, the general knowledge of God, if the theologian lingers on it and seeks to comprehend it through rational reflection and speculation, spells the theologian's undoing. For, the God experienced through the general knowledge of God is no abstract principle but a living and destroying God, who exists in "oppressively incomprehensible hiddenness" and who plagues human

---

92. Bayer, *Martin Luther's Theology*, 208, 335; Bayer, *Martin Luthers Theologie*, 188, 305. Bayer, "The Plurality of the One God," 353; Bayer, *Zugesagte Gegenwart*, 109.

93. Bayer, "The Plurality of the One God," 343, 345–46; Bayer, *Zugesagte Gegenwart*, 99–100, 102.

94. Bayer, "Poetological Theology," 164–165; Bayer, *Gott als Autor*, 15. Bayer, "Poetological Doctrine of the Trinity," 53–54; Bayer, "Poetologische Trinitätslehre," 77–78; Bayer, *Gott als Autor*, 145–46. Bayer, *Martin Luther's Theology*, 224–25; Bayer, *Martin Luthers Theologie*, 202–3.

95. Bayer, "The Plurality of the One God," 343; Bayer, *Zugesagte Gegenwart*, 99–100. Bayer, *Zugesagte Gegenwart*, 177. Bayer, *Martin Luther's Theology*, 339; Bayer, *Martin Luthers Theologie*, 308.

96. Bayer, "The Plurality of the One God," 349–50; Bayer, *Zugesagte Gegenwart*, 105–6. Ibid, 177.

beings, hounding them to death.[97] The God who is experienced in the general knowledge of God outside of God's gracious revelation as Trinity is the hidden God who works evil and death, and who is indistinguishable from the devil.[98]

Such a general knowledge of God stands in obvious and stark contradiction to the knowledge of God that comes by God's self-revelation as Trinity and God for us (*Deus pro nobis*) in the justifying promise of the gospel in Jesus Christ. For Bayer, the general knowledge of God is the hidden knowledge of God and the irreducible contradiction between the revealed knowledge of the Triune God and the general knowledge of God is the same as the contradiction between God's gracious promise in the gospel and the hidden God's wrath experienced through double predestination and the problem of evil.[99] Through his articulation of this distinction between doctrine the revealed Triune God and the general doctrine of God, Bayer portrays the tension formed by the conflict experienced by the believer between the hiddenness of God and God's promise as a tension within the believer's very experience of God's self. This tension, which also includes two forms of God's omnipotence that conflict with each other, is one that cannot be relieved by any rational philosophical or theological speculations or arguments.[100]

Bayer describes the believer who has experienced the justifying promise of God as existing in the present under an irreducible tension between the hiddenness of God and the promise of God in the gospel. This tension is of such a nature that the theologian cannot address the omnipotence or the doctrine of God in a unified manner. According to Bayer, in the midst of this tension, the believer experiences two kinds of God's omnipotence and even two forms of God's nature. In the midst of the tension between the revealed God of the promise of the gospel and the hidden God and, there is both an omnipotence of God in God's Word, experienced as God's accomplishing salvation through the promise of the gospel of Jesus Christ and an omnipotence of God outside of God's Word whereby God accomplishes all things that come to pass, including death and evil. The tension between the revealed and hidden God also gives rise to two differing doctrines of

---

97. Bayer, "Poetological Theology," 165; Bayer, *Gott als Autor*, 15–16. Bayer, *Zugesagte Gegenwart*, 177.

98. Bayer, "Poetological Doctrine of the Trinity," 53–54; Bayer, "Poetologische Trinitätslehre," 77–78; Bayer, *Gott als Autor*, 146.

99. Bayer, "The Plurality of the One God," 343, 345–46; Bayer, *Zugesagte Gegenwart*, 99–100, 102.

100. Bayer, "The Plurality of the One God," 352–53; Bayer, *Zugesagte Gegenwart*, 108–9.

God. On the one hand, Bayer affirms that God reveals God's self as Triune through the gospel alone and that God as Trinity exists as God for humans and constitutes the uniquely Christian doctrine of God as a God of grace, mercy, and love. On the other hand, Bayer also maintains that God is active in the world outside of the gospel, and that this activity, including God's working of evil, forms a general doctrine of God that is real and experienced in the present life by both believers and non-believers. This tension, according to Bayer, is undeniable and irreducible. It is one that existentially grips the believer through the questions of double predestination and theodicy through *Anfechtung* and will not simply go away of its own accord. The hidden God continues to vex the believer, badgering, and assaulting him or her through *Anfechtung* in which God is indistinguishable from the devil.[101]

The Resolution of the Hidden God's Contradiction of the Promise

If, as I have laid out, Bayer argues that the hidden God's contradiction of the promise forms an existential tension in the believer, how then is this tension to be resolved? Or can it be resolved? Are believers to be left forever in the tension of contradiction and the rupture of the ages? Do they go to their graves without any hope of resolution? In response to such existential questions, Bayer first describes and dismisses what he understands to be inadequate solutions to the problem of the tension formed by the hidden God's contradiction of the revealed God's justifying promise in the gospel of Jesus Christ. Bayer maintains that the historical solutions offered to this problem by philosophers and theologians are ultimately insufficient to relieve the tension that the believer experiences at the hand of the hidden God, because they are rationalistic or existential humanly manufactured answers to a problem that only God will relieve. According to Bayer, the only true resolution to this tension is an eschatological one, in which God will relieve the tension forever. In the meantime, however, although the believer has a real and sure hope of salvation through the promise, the reality of experience belies this hope. This situation evokes a response from the believer in which the believer cries out to God in lament through the promise. This response of lament is the only proper response to tension formed by the hidden God's contradiction of the promise, and it is the only response that actually brings peace and hope to the believer.

---

101. Bayer, "God's Omnipotence," 91; Bayer, *Zugesagte Gegenwart*, 117.

The False Solutions to the Hidden God's Contradiction of the Promise

Before discussing Bayer's solution to the tension formed by the hidden God's contradiction of the promise, however, it is necessary first to address what false solutions he rejects. These solutions include dualism in its various forms, monism (particularly Hegelian monism in both its philosophical version and its theological version in the contemporary Trinitarian renaissance), the notion of a "suffering God" evident in various forms of contemporary theology, moralism, the Barthian concept that God's wrath is merely a complementary form of God's love, and the traditional Calvinistic doctrine of double predestination. Bayer rejects all of these answers to the problem of the tension because they rationalize it away in a manner that is contrary to God's existence and activity as understood from Scripture and as experienced by the believer. They simplify the complex, living God into an understandable and acceptable syllogism. Furthermore, they do not solve the pastoral care problem brought about by the hidden God's activity and therefore do not actually bring comfort and relief to the believer afflicted by *Anfechtung*.[102]

Dualism

Bayer identifies theological dualism as the first false solution to the problem of the tension experienced by the believer. It is important for Bayer to dispense with this false solution, as one might think that his own approach to the hiddenness of God and his description of the tension formed by the hidden God's work constitutes a kind of dualism. For the astute reader of Bayer's works—especially in the light of his claims regarding the two forms of divine omnipotence and the two doctrines of God—the question naturally arises at this point of whether or not his view of the tension between God's terrifying hiddenness and God's justifying promise in the gospel amounts to an espousal of some form of dualism. Bayer explicitly rejects dualism as an explanation for the problem of evil. In relating and interpreting Luther's understanding of the hiddenness of God outside of revelation, Bayer argues that Luther always considered dualism to be heretical and affirmed the goodness and unity of God, even in the midst of his discussion about the hidden God's causing of evil.[103] Bayer puts forth his interpretation

---

102. Bayer, *Martin Luther's Theology*, 209–10; Bayer, *Martin Luthers Theologie*, 188–89.

103. Bayer, *Martin Luther's Theology*, 205; Bayer, *Martin Luthers Theologie*, 185.

of Luther's teaching on the hidden God as a way to address the questions of double predestination and of the reality of evil in the world.[104]

Bayer claims that Luther is "radically serious in his opinion that there is no [God] outside-of-God."[105] Dualism, particularly in its Manichean, Gnostic, and Marcionite forms, says Bayer, actually posits that there are two gods or at least two equally powerful or equally ultimate entities, one responsible for good and the other for evil.[106] In contrast to this, Luther maintains that God is ultimately responsible for everything that happens, good and evil, life and death. Luther realizes, says Bayer, that if he were to deny this, he would deny the deity of God itself. If, says Bayer, one denies the "dark power" and "terrible hiddenness" of God, and all the evil entailed therein, God would cease to be God, for God would cease to be almighty and there would be some entity alongside God, whether another god, a demigod, or the human's "free will," effecting reality and events.[107]

According to Bayer, Luther states accurately that even the devil is under the omnipotent control of God. Bayer relates how the reformer saw the devil as an instrument used by the hidden God to accomplish evil indirectly.[108] Luther did not understand the devil as some figure on par with God effecting evil while God works good, but, rather, as a figure subject to doing the will of the hidden God. Bayer agrees with Luther that the devil is merely a mask of the hidden God, who works evil through the instrument of the devil.[109]

Dualism then, according to Bayer, fails to relieve the tension between the promise and the hiddenness of God, because both come from the same God.[110] Bayer rejects dualism because it resolves the tension by divesting God of God's hiddenness and attributing evil to another god. Luther did not adopt such an escape from the situation of tension between God's promise and God's hiddenness, and Bayer does not take it either.[111]

Bayer, "The Being of Christ in Faith," 147; Bayer, *Gott als Autor*, 126.

104. Bayer, *Martin Luther's Theology*, 198–199; Bayer, *Luthers Theologie*, 179. Bayer, "The Plurality of the One God," 342–343; 99–100.

105. Bayer, "God's Omnipotence," 91; Bayer, *Zugesagte Gegenwart*, 117.

106. Ibid. Bayer, *Martin Luther's Theology*, 205; Bayer, *Martin Luthers Theologie*, 185.

107. Bayer, *Martin Luther's Theology*, 205–7; Bayer, *Martin Luthers Theologie*, 185–86. Bayer, "God's Omnipotence," 91; Bayer, *Zugesagte Gegenwart*, 117.

108. Bayer, "God's Omnipotence," 92; Bayer, *Zugesagte Gegenwart*, 118. Bayer, *Martin Luther's Theology*, 204–5; Bayer, *Martin Luthers Theologie*, 184–85.

109. Bayer, *Martin Luther's Theology*, 205; Bayer, *Martin Luthers Theologie*, 185.

110. Ibid.

111. Bayer, *Martin Luther's Theology*, 205–6; Bayer, *Martin Luthers Theologie*,

Monism

Bayer also states that there is a very real tension within God's very self and that this tension must not be reduced to a monism by rationalistic speculations in philosophy and theology. Through the movements of the Enlightenment and its aftermath, says Bayer, philosophy tried to unite all truth, including conflicting experiences of God into a monistic whole. Such attempts at relieving the tension between God and God culminate in Hegelian idealism and its theological offspring in the Trinitarian renaissance.[112] These movements try to relieve the tension by rational, metaphysical speculations about the correspondence between self-consciousness and God-consciousness or about the interrelatedness of the persons of the Trinity in unity.[113]

Rationalist philosophy tries to relieve the tension by reasoning away the contradiction between God's promise and evil by means of some overall good that God works through what seems to be evil, an approach that Bayer labels "contemplative theodicy."[114] This is the sort of rationalist theodicy promulgated by Gottfried Wilhelm Leibniz, says Bayer, who held that God allows evil to happen so that good will come out of such evil.[115] Bayer states that G. F. W. Hegel also espouses a form of such contemplative theodicy when he argues that good, evil, and truth must be understood in the context of the whole of history and its eventual goal.[116]

Following this rationalist philosophical monism, contemporary Trinitarian theology has sought to utilize God's nature as Trinity to bridge the gap between the hidden God and the God of the justifying promise of the gospel revealed in Jesus Christ.[117] Moltmann's anthropologically centered, speculative view of the Trinity is an example of a "post-Christian, Hegelian" theology that has lost the evangelically centered understanding of God's triune nature.[118] Such Trinitarian efforts at resolution ultimately fail, however,

---

185-86.

112. Bayer, "The Being of Christ in Faith," 144-45; Bayer, *Gott als Autor*, 123-24. Bayer, *Theology the Lutheran Way*, 105; Bayer, *Theologie*, 416-17. Bayer, "The Plurality of the One God," 353; Bayer, *Zugesagte Gegenwart*, 109.

113. Bayer, *Theology the Lutheran Way*, 105: Bayer, *Theologie*, 416-17. Bayer, "The Plurality of the One God," 353; Bayer, *Zugesagte Gegenwart*, 109.

114. Bayer, *Living by Faith*, 11; Bayer, *Aus Glauben Leben*, 23.

115. Bayer, *Living by Faith*, 9-11; Bayer, *Aus Glauben Leben*, 21-23.

116. Bayer, *Living by Faith*, 11-12; Bayer, *Aus Glauben Leben*, 23-24.

117. Bayer, "The Plurality of the One God," 353; Bayer, *Zugesagte Gegenwart*, 109.

118. Bayer, "Poetological Theology," 165; Bayer, *Gott als Autor*, 15. Bayer, "Poetological Doctrine of the Trinity," 54-55; Bayer, "Poetologische Trinitätslehre," 78-79; Bayer, *Gott als Autor*, 145-46.

because they do not recognize that the hiddenness of God outside of revelation has nothing to do with God's triune nature.[119]

Ultimately the rationalist's monistic cure of a deeper truth is simply inadequate to the task of resolving the tension between the promise of God and the hiddenness of God experienced in *Anfechtung*. As Bayer states it, "One cannot reflect one's way out of the real-life situation of conflict and affliction, not even by means of Trinitarian theology."[120]

A Suffering God

The third false solution to the tension between the justifying promise of God in the gospel and the hiddenness of God experienced in *Anfechtung* is what Bayer terms "talk about a suffering God." This answer to the tension between God's promise and God's hiddenness is found in process theology and also especially in the philosophy of Hans Jonas.[121] In this approach, God is divested of all omnipotence, so that God is not only responsible for evil but also no longer accomplishes the task of salvation. For here, both the power to do evil and the power eradicate evil through both social change and salvation belongs to humanity alone.[122] In this scheme of resolution, says Bayer, God is reduced to "a postulate," symbolizing humanity's "unending responsibility to love" through a false theology of the cross in which God's is no longer the one who hides God's self under the sign of weakness and the cross, but in which God actually is weak and no longer almighty. Such a view proves itself unable to resolve the tension between the promise of God and the hiddenness of God without doing away with God altogether.[123]

Wrath and Evil as the Complement of Love

The fourth view that Bayer identifies as a false resolution to the tension between the promise of God and the hiddenness of God is that in which God's wrath and evil are understood to be merely the opposite side of God's love. To be sure, says Bayer, this view does seek to maintain the biblical notion that the God is love. In so doing, however, it universalizes this statement

---

119. Bayer, "The Plurality of the One God," 353; Bayer, *Zugesagte Gegenwart*, 109.

120. Ibid.

121. Bayer, *Martin Luther's Theology*, 206–207; Bayer, *Martin Luthers Theologie*, 186–87.

122. Ibid.

123. Bayer, *Martin Luther's Theology*, 207–8; Bayer, *Martin Luthers Theologie*, 187–88.

about God over all other aspects of God and God's work, so that evil and God's wrath through God's terrifying hiddenness have been essentially absorbed into the overarching love of God.[124]

Although Bayer sees Schleiermacher as a proponent of this view, he especially blames Karl Barth.[125] In Bayer's estimation, this view fails to provide a real solution because it ignores the fact that the tension exists. This is because, in this view, the world is seen as reconciled to God already and so God's wrath and evil have "been rendered impotent ever since Jesus' death," and because this view elevates the love of God to a substance that defines God.[126]

The problem with this view, says Bayer, is that it does not take the reality of evil seriously. Since it sees the resolution of God's promise and evil as something that has already taken place and God's love as now the only thing that characterizes theology, it does not find it necessary to address the situation of tension between God's promise and God's hiddenness. Yet, says Bayer, this does not square with the way things really are. Evil exists, the believer experiences it as the work of the hidden God through *Anfechtung*, and the pastoral care situation of the believer's comfort in the midst of the experience of the tension between God's promise and God's hiddenness is not satisfactorily addressed by this view.[127]

Calvin's Teaching on Double Predestination

The final false solution identified by Bayer is Calvin's teaching on double predestination. Like the Barthian universalization of God's love, the Calvinistic understanding of double predestination is anchored, at least to some extent in Scripture, says Bayer, particularly in Romans 9–11.[128] Yet, Bayer also judges this solution to be inadequate to the tension between the promise and the hiddenness of God.

According to Bayer, the Calvinistic doctrine of double predestination resolves the tension between God's promise and God's hiddenness through teaching that the double nature of God's decree in predestination means that God has determined already from all eternity all good and all evil as well as who will be saved and who will be damned. Like the Barthian view, this classic Calvinist view does not even really address the tension, because

124. Bayer, *Martin Luther's Theology*, 208; Bayer, *Martin Luthers Theologie*, 188.
125. Ibid.
126. Bayer, *Martin Luther's Theology*, 208–9; Bayer, *Martin Luthers Theologie*, 188.
127. Bayer, *Martin Luther's Theology*, 209; Bayer, *Martin Luthers Theologie*, 188.
128. Ibid.

it sees the problem already resolved in the past.[129] This view does not relieve the predicament in which the believer finds himself or herself in the midst of *Anfechtung* because it does not take the situation seriously.[130] Bayer also states here that he does not understand predestination itself as false but Calvin's teaching on it. Bayer recognizes that Luther too teaches predestination, but he shows that, contrary to Calvin, Luther does take the believer's situation of *Anfechtung* seriously and understands the proper role of predestination as comfort to the believer within the context of this situation.[131]

Like other approaches to resolving the existential tension experienced by the believer through *Anfechtung*, in Bayer's estimation, the Calvinistic teaching on double predestination fails to address and resolve the situation of this tension adequately. This is because Calvin's view that God has already ordained all good and evil and the salvation or damnation of each individual human.[132] Such a view does not solve the problem of the tension between the promise of God and the hiddenness of God, because it does not take seriously the existential struggle of *Anfechtung*, which believers, not reprobates, undergo in the present at the hand of the hidden God.[133]

Ultimately, Bayer finds all of these suggested resolutions of the tension formed by the hidden God's attack through *Anfechtung* on the believer's faith in the justifying promise of God to be wanting. Bayer argues that the tension cannot be relieved by dualism's absolving God for evil and crediting it to another God or by monism's rational sublimation of it. Bayer also rejects the way in which process theology and Jonas deal with the problem by divesting God of God's divinity. While Bayer does see a certain amount of truth in the Barthian affirmation of God's love and Calvinist doctrine of double predestination, he rejects how both of these views essentially dismiss the tension as non-existent on the account of what God has already done. Bayer rejects these two views, and indeed all of these false solutions to the tension, because they do not actually speak to and relieve the believer's real situation in *Anfechtung*. Though Bayer himself does not use the phrase, one is tempted to quote Luther's aphorism from *The Bondage of the Will* here to describe Bayer's rejection of these views: "The gouty foot laughs at your doctoring."[134]

---

129. Bayer, *Martin Luther's Theology*, 209; Bayer, *Martin Luthers Theologie*, 188–89.

130. Bayer, *Martin Luther's Theology*, 209; Bayer, *Martin Luthers Theologie*, 189.

131. Bayer, *Martin Luther's Theology*, 209–10; Bayer, *Martin Luthers Theologie*, 189.

132. Bayer, *Martin Luther's Theology*, 209; Bayer, *Martin Luthers Theologie*, 188.

133. Bayer, *Martin Luther's Theology*, 209–10; Bayer, *Martin Luthers Theologie*, 189.

134. *BOW*, 92; WA 626–27 . Cf. Forde, *Captivation of the Will*, 34, 44–45ff. In *The Bondage of the Will*, as Forde points out, Luther uses this phrase to compare the all-necessitating will of God with the impossible to cure ailment of gout. Luther argued

The Only Solution to the Hidden God's Contradiction of the Promise

While Bayer sees rationalist theodicy and speculative theology offering no real resolution to the tension, he asserts that there is a real resolution. Such a resolution, however, in Bayer's estimation, cannot come from any humanly manufactured arguments but from the action of God alone. According to Bayer, the only solution to the situation of God's hiddenness, in which the believer finds himself or herself, is God's ultimate eschatological complete fulfillment of the promise with the renewal of all creation. Ultimately Bayer argues that the relief from the attack of the hidden God on faith in the promise comes only eschatologically, saying that the tension between the hidden and revealed God will disappear in the eschaton, and though the believer still exist under this tension in the present, he or she lives by eschatological hope. The believer possesses the promise of God and uses that promise in the midst of *Anfechtung* to crying out to God in lament. Bayer maintains that there is real power in such crying out to God, for God has promised to answer the cry of the believer.

The Eschatological Resolution

According to Bayer, there can be no humanly constructed resolution to the tension between God's promise and God's hiddenness experienced by the believer through *Anfechtung*. The only one who can resolve the tension between God and God is God. Such resolution is part of God's eschatological future promised to believers in the present.[135] By interpreting Luther's doctrine of the hidden God through the reformer's discourse at the close of *The Bondage of the Will* regarding the three lights, Bayer argues that the only solution to the problem of God's hiddenness experienced by the believer through *Anfechtung* and the tension between such hiddenness and the promise is eschatological in nature.[136] Only in the eschaton, says Bayer, will the problem be solved and the tension relieved.[137] Until such time, the

---

that Erasmus' treatment of the all-necessitating will of God (i.e. that it should simply not be discussed) was like a doctor's ineffective treatment for gout; it simply does not cure the problem. The same could be said of Bayer's opinion of the false solutions to the tension brought about by the hidden God's attack on faith in *Anfechtung*.

135. Bayer, "God's Omnipotence," 91; Bayer, *Zugesagte Gegenwart*, 117.

136. Bayer, *Martin Luther's Theology*, 211–13; Bayer, *Martin Luthers Theologie*, 190–92.

137. Bayer, *Martin Luther's Theology*, 212–13; Bayer, *Martin Luthers Theologie*, 191–92. Bayer, "God's Omnipotence," 91; Bayer, *Zugesagte Gegenwart*, 117. Bayer,

believer must await the resolution to the tension in hope, holding to and doxologically confessing the truth of the promise and the unity of God in the midst of the contradiction of the gospel and God's unity in *Anfechtung*.[138]

The tension brought into being by the attack of the hidden God in *Anfechtung* between the justifying promise of God in the gospel of Jesus Christ and the terrifying hiddenness of God—the tension that forms two kinds of divine omnipotence and two doctrines of the nature of God—is not easily relieved. According to Bayer, no human philosophy or rationalistic theology can bring about such resolution, and, as I have delineated, Bayer decries some such philosophical and theological attempts at the resolution of this tension. Thus, the believer continues to live under this tension, under the assault of the hidden God, says Bayer, as long as the believer remains in this life, in the rupture of the ages, as a pilgrim before the eschaton, walking by faith and not yet by sight.[139]

Bayer here utilizes Luther's teaching on the three lights to elucidate the doctrine of the hidden God in the light of eschatology. In particular, Bayer uses this teaching to address the resolution of the question of theodicy. Luther articulates his teaching on the three lights at the conclusion of *The Bondage of the Will*. In this teaching, Luther uses the illustration of the three lights to describe how the human may understand God and God's work in the world: the light of nature, the light of grace, and the light of glory.[140] Luther states that by the light of nature (i.e. the enlightenment given to all humans through God's gift to them of reason), no one can understand why the righteous should be afflicted.[141] Consequently, the light of grace is still unable to enlighten the believer as to how God can damn the sinner who can do nothing but sin by nature and still be just. This, says Luther, will only

---

"Poetological Theology," 165; Bayer, *Gott als Autor*, 15–16.

138. Bayer, "Poetological Theology," 165; Bayer, *Gott als Autor*, 15–16. Bayer, "The Plurality of the One God," 352; Bayer, *Zugesagte Gegenwart*, 108. Bayer, "God's Omnipotence," 91; *Zugesagte Gegenwart*, 117–18.

139. Bayer, "Rupture of Times," 45; Bayer, *Gott als Autor*, 158. Bayer, *Martin Luther's Theology*, 11; Bayer, *Martin Luthers Theologie*, 10. Bayer, "Poetological Doctrine of the Trinity," 54; Bayer, "Poetologische Trinitätslehre," 78; Bayer, *Gott als Autor*, 146. Bayer, *Living by Faith*, 72–73; Bayer, *Aus Glauben Leben*, 79. Bayer, "Hermeneutical Theology," 141; Bayer, *Zugesagte Gegenwart*, 350. Bayer, "God's Omnipotence," 91; Bayer, *Zugesagte Gegenwart*, 117. Bayer, "The Plurality of the One God," 352; Bayer, *Zugesagte Gegenwart*, 108. Bayer, "Poetological Theology, 165; Bayer, *Gott als Autor*, 15. Bayer, *Schöpfung als Anrede*, 64. Bayer, *Gott als Autor*, 204.

140. BOW, 317; LW 18:785.

141. Ibid.

be understandable in the light of glory, with the complete revelation of all things regarding God in the eschaton.[142]

Bayer interprets and utilizes Luther's view of the three lights to argue that the resolution to the situation of the hidden God's attack in *Anfechtung* on faith in God's justifying promise. Bayer argues that by the light of nature, the human being can only ever guess at why evil exists and why the righteous suffer according to the laws of cause and effect, much like the conjectures made by Job's friends.[143] By the light of grace, says Bayer, the believer knowingly exists in the tension between the righteousness of God revealed in God's justifying promise and the terrible hidden God, who attacks the believer's trust in that promise in the experience of *Anfechtung*.[144] It is only in the eschatological light of glory that the believer's experience of the agonizing struggle of *Anfechtung*, with its tension between the promise of God and the hiddenness of God, will end. In the meantime, before the light of glory dawns, believers must still exist in the tension between the promise of God and the hiddenness of God, in the midst of *Anfechtung*, in the light of grace.[145]

At the consummation of the world and the dawning of the eschaton, however, says Bayer, there will be a complete resolution to the tension experienced by the believer in *Anfechtung*. Although believers currently live within the experience of the hidden God's contradiction of the justifying promise of God through *Anfechtung*, in the eschaton, such contradiction will be resolved.[146] Bayer does not, however, propose an ontological resolution to the eschatological conflict between God's promise and God's hiddenness along the lines of some kind of Hegelian dialectic, even one that presents itself in "Trinitarian" clothing.[147] He does not see there being some kind of eschatological *Aufhebung* wherein God's promise and God's hiddenness are reconciled and synthesized. To the contrary, the kind of resolution to the hidden God's contradiction of the promise that Bayer sees as being

---

142. Ibid.

143. Bayer, *Martin Luther's Theology*, 211; Bayer, *Martin Luthers Theologie*, 190–191. Cf. Job 4–31.

144. Bayer, *Martin Luther's Theology*, 212; Bayer, *Martin Luthers Theologie*, 191.

145. Bayer, *Martin Luther's Theology*, 212–13; Bayer, *Martin Luthers Theologie*, 191–192. Bayer, "Toward a Theology of Lament," 217–18; Bayer, "Zur Theologie der Klage," 298–99.

146. Bayer, *Martin Luther's Theology*, 213; Bayer, *Martin Luthers Theologie*, 192. Bayer "God's Omnipotence," 91; Bayer, *Zugesagte Gegenwart*, 117.

147. Bayer, "The Plurality of the One God," 353; Bayer, *Zugesagte Gegenwart*, 108–9. Bayer, "Poetological Doctrine of the Trinity," 55; Bayer, "Poetologische Trinitätslehre," 79; Bayer, *Gott als Autor*, 147.

realized in the eschaton is a resolution in which the hiddenness of God "no longer threatens us because it will be consumed by God's freeing, incomprehensible and revealed love."[148]

The true resolution to the hidden God's contradiction of the justifying promise of God, and the tension that such contradiction forms in the life of the believer through the experience of *Anfechtung* comes only by means of an eschatological reversal in which not only all of creation is renewed but in which God's wrath, the law, and evil are put away forever.[149] In this eschatological resolution and reversal, says Bayer, the promise of God will triumph against the hiddenness of God, and there will be no more contradiction between the hidden God and the revealed God, because the revealed God will "be all in all."[150] According to Bayer, such resolution also will bring with it the disappearance of the two contradictory forms of God's omnipotence as well as the distinction between the general knowledge of God and God's Triune nature, as the omnipotence of God in God's Word and the revelation of God as a God of grace and love in the Trinity win out in the end.[151] Even the contradiction of the promise evident in creation itself through all the evil occurring in nature and at the hands of human beings will be resolved, as God fully unfolds God's new creation through God's restoration of creation as God originally intended it.[152]

Yet, what is the believer to do in the meantime? What is the nature of the existence of the believer who is still living in the midst of *Anfechtung*, who is still encountered by the hidden God in the present, during the rupture of the ages? Bayer states that in the present, Christians are to wait patiently with faith in God's final promise and to confess such faith through doxology.

As pilgrims still on the way to the eschaton, says Bayer, the believer still lives in the present in faith and hope in the promise of God in Jesus Christ.[153] While still on the way, the believer must patiently wait in anticipa-

---

148. Bayer, "Poetological Doctrine of the Trinity," 55; Bayer, "Poetologische Trinitätslehre," 79; Bayer, *Gott als Autor*, 147.

149. Ibid. Bayer, "Does Evil Persist?," 143; Bayer, "Bleibt das Böse?" in *Freiheit als Anwort*, 297.

150. Bayer, "Poetological Doctrine of the Trinity," 55; Bayer, "Poetologische Trinitätslehre," 79; Bayer, *Gott als Autor*, 147.

151. Bayer, "God's Omnipotence," 91, 98–99; Bayer, *Zugesagte Gegenwart*, 117, 124–25. Bayer, "The Plurality of the One God," 352; Bayer, *Zugesagte Gegenwart*, 108. Bayer, "Poetological Theology," 165; Bayer, *Gott als Autor*," 15–16. Bayer, "Poetological Doctrine of the Trinity," 55; Bayer, "Poetologische Trinitätslehre," 79; Bayer, *Gott als Autor*, 146.

152. Bayer, *Martin Luther's Theology*, 116–17; Bayer, *Martin Luthers Theologie*, 106.

153. Bayer, *Theology the Lutheran Way*, 203; Bayer, *Theologie*, 522. Bayer, "Rupture

tion of the promised mercy and salvation of God to come in the eschaton, says Bayer.[154] In the midst of such anticipatory waiting, the believer walks by faith in the promise and not by sight. The believer will have sight added to faith one day, but not yet. At the moment, he or she is still on the way and so must live and walk by faith.[155]

While the believer is still on the path of pilgrimage before the eschaton, says Bayer, he or she will still have to endure the assault of the hidden God in *Anfechtung*; he or she will still have to wrestle with the questions of double predestination and evil in the world.[156] In the midst of such existence, the believer cannot prove the promised eschatological salvation; he or she can only confess it. Just as the believer walks by faith and not by sight during this present pilgrimage, so he or she lives not by thinking and reasoning about the promised future but by the confession of the Lord who promises.[157]

Such confession is a doxological one. It is a confession of the revealed Triune God in the midst of the experience of the terrifyingly hidden God. It is a confession of praise to the Triune God, who believers trust will return to complete the renewal of all creation begun in the resurrection. It is a doxological confession, in which the community of believers confesses that God is one, in the midst of the tension between the two kinds of God's omnipotence and between the two experiences of God. It is a confession that is able to praise and proclaim the Triune God revealed in Jesus Christ and the creative salvation of God that is presently only seen in the proclamation and doxology of the Church.[158] Thus, says Bayer, the form that the patient and expectant waiting of faith takes before the eschaton is not knowledge or speculative thinking but doxology and liturgy. For liturgy and poetry, which embody the doxological confession of faith in the midst of its contradiction in *Anfechtung*, have the power to hold the believer in the rupture of the times, between the beginning of the new age and its complete fulfillment in the passing away of the old. A liturgical and poetological perspective

---

of Times," 45; Bayer, *Gott als Autor*, 158. Bayer, *Martin Luther's Theology*, 11; Bayer, *Martin Luthers Theologie*, 10.

154. Bayer, "Toward a Theology of Lament," 217; Bayer, "Zur Theologie der Klage," 299.

155. Bayer, *Theology the Lutheran Way*, 203; Bayer, *Theologie*, 522.

156. Bayer, "Poetological Doctrine of the Trinity," 54; Bayer, "Poetologische Trinitätslehre," 78; Bayer, *Gott als Autor*, 146. Bayer, *Martin Luther's Theology*, 212–213; Bayer, *Martin Luthers Theologie*, 192.

157. Bayer, *Martin Luther's Theology*, 213; Bayer, *Martin Luthers Theologie*, 192.

158. Bayer, "The Plurality of the One God," 352–53; Bayer, *Zugesagte Gegenwart*, 108–109.

confesses faith in the promise in the midst of life, without trying to heal the open wound of *Anfechtung* with the false and ineffective medications of monism and Hegelian speculative Trinitarian theology. Instead, it encourages the believer in this life while recognizing the reality of the attack of the hidden God and the tension formed by that attack, which are still felt in the present.[159] As long as the believer is a pilgrim in this present age, he or she lives by the power of faith embodied in the corporate doxological confession of the people of God who trust in the promise in the midst of its contradiction.[160]

Bayer emphasizes that no human rationalization can bridge the tension between the promise of God and God's terrifying hiddenness experienced in *Anfechtung*. This tension will only be bridged eschatologically, when, at the consummation of the world, God will abolish the distinction between the promise and God's hiddenness, between the two kinds of divine foreknowledge, and between the two doctrines of God forever. Such eschatological action from God will not synthesize the contradiction between the promise of God and divine hiddenness; instead, it will bring an end to God's terrifying hiddenness as God becomes "all in all." Until such a time, however, believers are left in the rupture of the ages, in which they continue to feel the attack of the hidden God on faith through the experience of *Anfechtung*. As a pilgrim still on the way to the final realization of the promise in the eschaton, the believer hopes in faith, awaiting the eschatological fulfillment of the promise expectantly, confessing faith in the promise doxologically and liturgically together with the whole people of God. Such doxological and liturgical confession of God holds fast to God's promise, but it also recognizes the reality of God's hiddenness in *Anfechtung* in the present, a reality that cannot be brought to an end through and rational speculation. For such confession of God realizes that as long as believers are pilgrims walking by faith, then tension brought about by the hidden God's contradiction of the promise remains "existentially and theoretically irreducible."[161]

---

159. Ibid. Bayer, "Poetological Theology," 165–66; Bayer, *Gott als Autor*, 16–17. Bayer, "Poetological Doctrine of the Trinity," 55–56; Bayer, "Poetologische Trinitätslehre," 79; Bayer, *Gott als Autor*, 147–48.

160. Bayer, "The Plurality of the One God," 352–353; Bayer, *Zugesagte Gegenwart*, 108–9.

161. Bayer, "The Plurality of the One God," 343, 352–53; Bayer, *Zugesagte Gegenwart*, 100, 108–9. Bayer, "Poetological Theology," 165–66; Bayer, *Gott als Autor*, 16–17. Bayer, "Poetological Doctrine of the Trinity," 55–56; Bayer, "Poetologische Trinitätslehre," 79; Bayer, *Gott als Autor*, 147–48.

The Believer's Response of Lament

Bayer is clear that no human process of logical deduction, no amount of philosophical speculation, and no speculative Trinitarian theology can bring an end to the hidden God's contradiction of the promise through *Anfechtung*. That does not mean, however, that Bayer thinks the believer can do nothing in the face of the attack of the hidden God. Nor does Bayer advocate waiting in silence for the eschatological resolution to the hidden God's contradiction of the promise and the renewal of all creation. On the contrary, the experience of the hiddenness of God prompts the believer to "cry out" to God on the basis of the promise in the face of the attack of the hidden God. Drawing on the liturgical tradition of the Psalms, Bayer identifies this cry of the believer to the revealed God as "lament."[162]

According to Bayer, lament forms the *Sitz im Leben* of the believer who lives in the tension between the promise and the hiddenness of God in the rupture of the ages. It becomes the context for the believer's expectant waiting of God's final eschatological fulfillment of the promise.[163] Bayer describes lament as a response to the hiddenness of God based upon the promise that brings complaint and accusation against God. Lament has creational and Christological dimensions, and is at the same time based firmly on the eschatological hope that such lament will be answered.

"God against God": The Definition and Description of Lament

Bayer states that the lament uttered by the believer "does not happen all by itself," but that it is a very deep response to the promise, based upon the promise, and evoked by the promise, which only the believer who possesses and trusts the promise can utter. It is a cry from the depths of *Anfechtung*, which flows not from doubt but from faith, from faith in the promise in

---

162. Bayer, *Martin Luther's Theology*, 11; Bayer, *Martin Luthers Theologie*, 10. Bayer, "Rupture of Times," 46–47; Bayer, *Gott als Autor*, 157. The German term employed here by Bayer is "die Klage." This term could be interpreted either as "complaint" or as "lament." While Christine Helmer has translated it as "complaint," Thomas Trapp and Matthias Gockel have opted for "lament." I follow their lead here and employ "lament," because it seems to convey a broader range of meaning than complaint and because it is more commonly used in English translations of and commentaries on the Scriptures. Though Bayer's understanding of lament certainly entails the notion of complaint, it is also an understanding that takes on a more extensive description as a response to hiddenness based on the promise.

163. Bayer, *Martin Luther's Theology*, 11; Bayer, *Martin Luthers Theologie*, 10. Bayer, "Rupture of Times," 46–47; Bayer, *Gott als Autor*, 157. Bayer, *Living by Faith*, 71; Bayer, *Aus Glauben Leben*, 77.

spite of the experience of God's hiddenness in *Anfechtung*.[164] In fact, according to Bayer, it is the experience of the hidden God in *Anfechtung* that brings out lament. Lament is "wrung out from the agonizing struggle" of *Anfechtung* as a return to the promise in the midst of *Anfechtung*.[165]

In the experience of *Anfechtung*, lament is a return to the promise for the believer, who is driven back to the promise, as it is the only open escape from the hidden God. But lament is not simply an escape. In the midst of *Anfechtung*, lament is both an answer to and a defense against the assault of the hidden God. At the same time, it is an appeal to the revealed God for deliverance. It is the reminder to God how, before the coming of hiddenness in *Anfechtung*, God was the helper of the believer, the "one who promised to be true and faithful" to the believer. It is both a complaint of accusation against God that God is not honoring the promise as well as an appeal to God to do so.[166] For God is the one who has promised God's self to the believer, who has bound God's self to honor and fulfill the promise, and lament is the believer's challenge to God make good on God's promise.[167]

In this way, lament may be seen as a lawsuit brought by the believer against God. This is certainly the way that Bayer interprets the biblical story of Job.[168] Bayer argues that in his lament, Job complains against God. He knows God as a righteous God, and so he accuses God of being unjust, of being cruel, of becoming his enemy. Job thus turns to God's righteousness as an advocate against the hidden God; he turns to his redeemer, using God against God.[169]

In the same way, says Bayer, in lament, the believer uses the promise of God against the hiddenness of God, the revealed God against the hidden God. In lament, says Bayer, the believer calls to God against God.[170] In the highest sense then, theodicy is not discussion about God's goodness and evil

---

164. Bayer, *Living by Faith*, 71; Bayer, *Aus Glauben Leben*, 77.

165. Bayer, *Martin Luther's Theology*, 210; Bayer, *Martin Luthers Theologie*, 190.

166. Bayer, "God's Omnipotence," 90; Bayer, *Zugesagte Gegenwart*, 116. Bayer, *Martin Luther's Theology*, 213; Bayer, *Martin Luthers Theologie*, 192.

167. Bayer, "Preaching the Word," 260; Bayer, *Zugesagte Gegenwart*, 397. Bayer, "God's Omnipotence," 90; Bayer, *Zugesagte Gegenwart*, 116. Bayer, *Martin Luther's Theology*, 213; Bayer, *Martin Luthers Theologie*, 192.

168. Bayer, *Living by Faith*, 69; Bayer, *Aus Glauben Leben*, 76.

169. Bayer, *Theology the Lutheran Way*, 207; Bayer, *Theologie*, 526. Bayer, *Schöpfung als Anrede*, 182–183. Cf. Job 16:18–21, 19:25–27. The German word translated "lawsuit," which is used here by Bayer is "Rechtsstreit." Translated literally it means a fight over righteousness. This word communicates the sense of Job's argument against God as a struggle with God for righteousness.

170. Bayer, *Martin Luther's Theology*, 11; Bayer, *Martin Luthers Theologie*, 10. Bayer, "Rupture of Times," 46; Bayer, *Gott als Autor*, 159.

before the law court of human opinion and reasoning. It is not reflection on or dispute *about* God. It is, rather, a dispute *with* God and *against* God. It is a dispute in which the believer presses "God against God," summoning the gracious and merciful God revealed in Jesus Christ in the promise of the gospel against the terrifying hidden God of wrath experience in *Anfechtung*. It is summoning "God against God!" The lament uttered by the believer in the midst of the experience of the hidden God's contradiction of the promise is a case against the hidden God, made on the basis of God's own promise.[171] It is a call to God against God, reminding God of God's own beloved promise and the demand to honor it.[172]

The Creational Dimension of Lament

Although it is the calling out of the individual believer against the hidden God, the scope of lament also extends beyond the individual believer into the realm of creation. As I have discussed, Bayer understands God's speech act of justification through the promise of the gospel in Jesus Christ to include a renewal of creation. Bayer admits, however, that this renewal is an eschatological reality not fully realized in the present. In this context, lament takes on a creational dimension in Bayer's theology. The believer's cry out in lament is part of the groaning and crying out of all creation. By rebelling against God and sinning, the human dragged all of creation into decay and despair together with humankind. Because of this, now all creation, which acutely feels the effects of sin and the evil perpetrated by the hidden God, cries out in lament, groaning and yearning for the final act of God's redemption in the complete eschatological fulfillment of the promise.[173] The complaint of the believer in lament, says Bayer, does not give up faith in the goodness of creation and its promised renewal by the gospel but cries out

---

171. Bayer, *Martin Luther's Theology*, 213; Bayer, *Martin Luthers Theologie*, 192. Bayer, *Martin Luther's Theology*, 11; Bayer, *Martin Luthers Theologie*, 10. Bayer, "Rupture of Times," 46; Bayer, *Gott als Autor*, 159.

172. Bayer, "God's Omnipotence," 90; Bayer, *Zugesagte Gegenwart*, 116. Bayer, *Martin Luther's Theology*, 213; Bayer, *Martin Luthers Theologie*, 192.

173. Bayer, *Gott als Autor*, 187–89. Bayer, "Toward a Theology of Lament," 212; Bayer, "Zur Theologie der Klage," 291; Bayer, "Theologie der Klage, in *Zugesagte Gegenwart*, 62. Bayer, *Schöpfung als Anrede*, 177–78, 181–82. Bayer, "Erhörte Klage," 261, 267; Bayer, "Erhörte Klage," in *Leibliches Wort*, 337, 343. Bayer, *Martin Luther's Theology*, 113, 139, 183, 219; Bayer, *Martin Luthers Theologie*, 103, 127, 165, 198. Bayer, *Living by Faith*, 29–30; Bayer, *Aus Glauben Leben*, 37–38. Cf. Rom 8:18–25.

for that renewal: "How much longer?"[174] Bayer states that the answer to this cry lies in the Christological dimension of lament.

The Christological Dimension of Lament

God has not abandoned creation in its groaning and lament, says Bayer, but has become incarnate in human flesh in the person of Jesus Christ in answer to the sighing of creation. In such a "Christology of answered lament,"[175] Bayer describes God in Christ as having come to identify with the lamenting, groaning creation.[176] In Jesus Christ, says Bayer, God has come into the creation that groans in lament in order to identify with it. It is only in this sense, says Bayer, that one can truly see the full implication of Christ's word *"Ephatha!"* ("Be opened!"), for Jesus sighed when he uttered this word.[177] In sighing in conjunction with this word, which effects opening, God in Jesus Christ places God's self in solidarity with the groaning, fallen creation.[178] In the Christology of answered lament, Jesus Christ's identity and suffering can be understood afresh in the light of God's self-identification with the groaning creation. In Jesus Christ, "God sets God's self in opposition to God's own wrath against the human."[179]

Though the action of God against God occurs in time in space through the incarnation and death of Jesus Christ, Bayer argues that the Triune God eternally anticipated the lament of creation and that the persons of the Trinity conversed amongst themselves about the answering of this lament in the sending of the incarnate Christ. Once again, Bayer turns here to Luther's hymn *"Nun freut euch lieben Christen g'mein"* to explain the interaction amongst the persons of the Trinity related to human salvation.[180] Regard-

---

174. Bayer, "Rupture of Times," 46; Bayer, *Gott als Autor*, 159. Bayer, *Martin Luther's Theology*, 11; Bayer, *Martin Luthers Theologie*, 10. Bayer, "God's Omnipotence," 90; Bayer, *Zugesagte Gegenwart*, 116.

175. Bayer, *"Christologie der erhörten Klage."*

176. Bayer, "Toward a Theology of Lament," 211; Bayer, "Zur Theologie der Klage," 289–90; Bayer, *Zugesagte Gegenwart*, 61. Bayer, *Martin Luther's Theology*, 113; Bayer, *Martin Luthers Theologie*, 103. This brings to mind the words of the first verse of Daniel Schutte's popular hymn: "I the Lord of sea and sky, I have heard my people's cry. All who dwell in dark and sin, my hand will save." *ELW* 574.

177. Bayer, *Martin Luther's Theology*, 113; Bayer, *Martin Luthers Theologie*, 103. Mark 7:34.

178. Bayer, *Martin Luther's Theology*, 113; Bayer, *Martin Luthers Theologie*, 103.

179. Ibid. Bayer, "Barmherzigkeit," in *Zugesagte Gegenwart*, 55. Translation and gender-neutral language is my own.

180. Bayer, "Mercy from the Heart," 30; Bayer, *Zugesagte Gegenwart*, 55–56.

ing the second, third, and fourth stanzas of this hymn, Bayer states that "in eternity" the Triune God (i.e. the revealed God) anticipated and answered human lament before it occurred.[181] The response, in verses four and five, is a merciful turning of God towards humanity and a subsequent deliberation amongst the persons of the Triune Godhead, determining to turn God's self to the human being in mercy. The result in verse six is that the Father and the Holy Spirit send the Son into creation to become part of creation, to become a creature, in solidarity with creation and the human creature, for the purpose of redeeming the creation and the human creature.[182]

Such Trinitarian dialogue, the conversation amongst the persons of the Godhead, does not represent an attempt at some "speculative notion of Trinitarian philosophy" that seeks to probe into how God exists in God's self. On the contrary, the entire point to such a view of the Trinity's involvement in responding to lament Christologically is that the Triune God is revealed as a God of mercy and salvation in the person and work of Jesus Christ. Such a God, says Bayer, is no metaphysical monarch who remains unapproachable; for the Triune God revealed in Jesus Christ is a God who has humbled God's self to become part of creation in order to stand with the human being and creation in the solidarity of lament, in order to experience and suffer the wrath of God, and in so doing, to turn away God's wrath from humanity and the creation and to demonstrate to them God's mercy. The Triune God's answer to the anticipated lament of the believer and creation is an incarnational and Christological answer.[183]

The Christology of answered lament becomes tangible to the believer in the here and now through the word "Be Opened" in the preached promise and through the Word of promise connected to the created means of bread and wine that bear the infinite Triune God revealed in Jesus Christ. In the Sacrament of the Altar, says Bayer, Jesus Christ comes as the eternal Triune God who has come down from heaven to identify with human beings. Christ comes in the elements of Holy Communion as the God-human who has tasted death and returned to life and as the essence of God's mercy to sustain the believer in the midst of his or her *Sitz im Leben* of lament. Through these means in which the merciful God in Christ comes to humans, the believer is sustained in the midst of lament and *Anfechtung* by

---

181. Bayer, "Mercy from the Heart," 30; Bayer, *Zugesagte Gegenwart*, 55. I follow the original German text of both Luther and Bayer here, translating "in Ewigkeit" literally as "in eternity," as opposed to the more poetic translation "before the world's foundation" utilized in the *ELW* and the *LSB*. Cf. *EG*, 341; *ELW*, 594, *LSB*, 556.

182. Bayer, "Mercy from the Heart," 30; Bayer, *Zugesagte Gegenwart*, 55.

183. Bayer, "Mercy from the Heart," 30; Bayer, *Zugesagte Gegenwart*, 55–56. Bayer, *Martin Luther's Theology*, 113–14; Bayer, *Martin Luthers Theologie*, 103–4.

the one who has shown solidarity with the lamenting believer and has taken the wrath of the hidden God upon himself, and who sustains belief in the promise with the very words of promise on the words of institution, giving himself to the believer again as God for us.[184]

The Eschatology of Answered Lament

Even the activity by God in Christ, in which God stands in solidarity with the fallen creation, does not entirely put an end to lament. Indeed, it heightens the situation of the believer in lament, making him or her anxious for the final fulfillment of the promise and the end of *Anfechtung*.[185] The believer, says Bayer, still awaits the promised eschatological renewal of all things expectantly. Yet, it is this expectant eschatological hope that motivates the believer's lament in the present.[186]

The very fact that the believer appeals to the promise in lament, says Bayer, demonstrates that he or she expects the eschatological answer to lament to be answered.[187] In laments, then, the believer anticipates the ultimate eschatological fulfillment of the promise full of hope. Bayer describes the existence of lament in the context of such hope as "living and waiting in haste."[188] In this context, lament is nothing other than crying out to God, "*Maranatha!*" ("Come, oh Lord, with judgment!").[189] This eschatological cry to God, says Bayer, is motivated by a sure faith and hope that as the world is brought to an end, the Creator will renew all things and restore creation to its original goodness.[190] It demonstrates a confidence that the light of glory will dawn at the final judgment, ending the lawsuit with God, dispelling the

184. Bayer, "Rupture of Times," 47; Bayer, *Got als Autor*, 159–160. Bayer, *Martin Luther's Theology*, 11–12, 113–14; Bayer, *Martin Luthers Theologie*, 10–11; 103–4. Bayer, "Tod Gottes und Herrenmahl," 353–54; Bayer, "Tod Gottes und Herrenmahl," in *Leibliches Wort*, 296–97.

185. Bayer, "Mercy from the Heart," 31; Bayer, *Zugesagte Gegenwart*, 57.

186. Bayer, "Toward a Theology of Lament," 212; Bayer, "Zur Theologie der Klage," 291; Bayer, *Zugesagte Gegenwart*, 63 . Bayer, "What is Evangelical?" 11; Bayer, *Zugesagte Gegenwart*, 33.

187. Bayer, "Toward a Theology of Lament," 212; Bayer, "Zur Theologie der Klage," 291; Bayer, *Zugesagte Gegenwart*, 63. Bayer, "What is Evangelical?" 11; *Zugesagte Gegenwart*, 33. Bayer, "Mercy from the Heart, 31; Bayer, *Zugesagte Gegenwart*, 57.

188. Bayer, "Mercy from the Heart," 31; Bayer, *Zugesagte Gegenwart*, 57.

189. Ibid. Bayer, "Toward a Theology of Lament," 212; Bayer, "Zur Theologie der Klage," 291; Bayer, *Zugesagte Gegenwart*, 63. Bayer, "Lust am Wort," 796; Bayer, *Leibliches Wort*, 223.

190. Bayer, "Toward a Theology of Lament," 213; Bayer, "Zur Theologie der Klage," 292; Bayer, *Zugesagte Gegenwart*, 64.

hiddenness of God, and answering the lament of the believer and of creation forever. Lament itself thus evidences the trust and confidence that it will be answered.[191]

With this in mind, Bayer thus speaks of the second advent of Christ in terms of a particular kind of "eschatology of answered lament" ("*Eschatologie der erhörten Klage*").[192] The eschatological answer to the lament, "*Maranatha!*," is a particular kind of answer; it is the answer that fulfills the promise of a renewed creation. The lament "*Maranatha!*" is indeed a cry out for God's righteous judgment. Yet, says Bayer, the judgment that comes from God in response to such lament is not a retributive justice whereby God takes revenge upon sinful humans and a fallen creation, nor is it an analytic judgment wherein God renders a punishment for each and every misdeed. "God," says Bayer, "is not a bookkeeper."[193]

Instead, God's eschatological judgment, which comes in answer to lament, is a creative judgment, which is both healing and restorative. God is not interested in repaying every evil committed, but in putting away evil forever and restoring the broken creation.[194] To be sure, Bayer understands God's eschatological judgment to be purifying in some sense, but only to the extent that evil is destroyed, so that the restoration of creation may begin. Here, Bayer compares the eschatological judgment of God to the flood of Noah's day, recorded in Genesis. Like Noah, his family, and the animals in the ark, the creation itself will be saved and renewed through the judgment in which God does away with all evil, with injustice, and—yes, it must be said—with divine hiddenness forever.[195]

Of course, such creative, eschatological judgment is not a present reality, and the believer still lives in the present as a pilgrim, in the rupture of the ages, in the *Sitz im Leben* of lament. The believer still exists in the present, he or she continues to experience and lament against the hidden God, basing such lament upon the as yet unseen promise of ultimate deliverance and renewal, claiming the promise through faith and speaking it lament against the present reality of God's hiddenness.[196] In this way, the believer continues to live by faith and not by sight.[197]

191. Bayer, "Mercy from the Heart," 31; Bayer, *Zugesagte Gegenwart*, 58. Bayer, *Theology the Lutheran Way*, 208; Bayer, *Theologie*,

192. Bayer, "Toward a Theology of Lament," 213; Bayer, "Zur Theologie der Klage," 292; Bayer, *Zugesagte Gegenwart*, 63.

193. Ibid.

194. Ibid.

195. Ibid.

196. Bayer, "Erhörte Klage," 269; Bayer, *Leibliches Wort*, 345.

197. Bayer, "Rupture of Times," 45; Bayer, *Gott als Autor*, 158. Bayer, *Martin Luther's*

But God has not abandoned the believer to endure alone until the time of the eschaton. The Holy Spirit effects patience in the believer in the midst of ongoing *Anfechtung* at the hands of the hidden God and ongoing lament.[198] In the midst of the ongoing hidden work of God still experienced by the believer who laments, God gives God's self as a merciful God in Jesus Christ in the promise that is proclaimed through the preacher and that is given with the very body and blood of Jesus Christ in Holy Communion.[199] Furthermore, the believer does not stand alone, lamenting in the rupture of the ages, in face of the ongoing activity of the hidden God, but in solidarity with other pilgrim believers, united as one in the body of Christ.[200] For the believer exists in the community of believers, in the communion of lamenting saints, who together wait for the ultimate redemption in God's eschatological answer to lament and fulfillment of the promise. The pilgrim believer is not alone in his or her existence of lament in the rupture of the ages but laments together, liturgically, with the company of pilgrims, the community of lamenting brothers and sisters, in the Christian Church on earth.[201] The believer trusts in the promise and claims it against the hidden God through lament in the context of the community of believers and never alone. For, the whole of believers trusts in the promised eschatological redemption of the world in spite of the contradiction of the promise by the hidden God, confessing faith in the promise in the words of the creed, and the Church together cries out in lament to God "Lord have mercy!" in the Kyrie and "Thy Kingdom Come!" in the words of the Lord's Prayer, which form the corporate "*Maranatha!*" of the community of faith in the promise.[202]

Finally, the believer is not alone in lament, because through lament he or she is part of a groaning creation that awaits the eschatological reversal of sin and renewal of creation.[203] While presently, the believer suffers the hiddenness of God through evil in the world, he or she also lives in the hope of all creation for God's final destruction of evil and redemption of

---

Theology, 11; Bayer, *Martin Luthers Theologie*, 10. Bayer, *Living by Faith*, 72–73; Bayer, *Aus Glauben Leben*, 79. Bayer, *Schöpfung als Anrede*, 64. Bayer, *Gott als Autor*, 204. Bayer, *Theology the Lutheran Way*, 203; Bayer, *Theologie*, 522.

198. Bayer, "Toward a Theology of Lament," 217; Bayer, "Zur Theologie der Klage," 299.

199. Bayer, "Rupture of Times," 47; Bayer, *Got als Autor*, 159–60. Bayer, *Martin Luther's Theology*, 11–12, 113–14; Bayer, *Martin Luthers Theologie*, 10–11; 103–4. "

200. Bayer, "Erhörte Klage," 270; Bayer, *Leibliches Wort*, 346.

201. Bayer, "Erhörte Klage," 271; Bayer, *Leibliches Wort*, 347.

202. Bayer, "Erhörte Klage," 270–71; Bayer, *Leibliches Wort*, 346–48.

203. Bayer, *Gott als Autor*, 187–88.

creation.[204] In this way, it is not only the believer or the Church, but with the Church and the believer the whole creation, who long for God's eschatological fulfillment of the promise, crying out in lament "Lord, have mercy!" and "*Maranatha!*"[205]

According to Bayer, lament is the response of the believer, of one who has experienced the promise of God in the gospel of Jesus Christ, to the experience of the hidden God. This experience comes through *Anfechtung*, in which the hidden God assaults the believer's faith in the promise of God. All that the believer can in this situation is to cry out in anguish against this contradiction.[206] In doing so, the believer, says Bayer, the believer actually joins in the sigh of all creation, groaning under the weight of the rupture of the ages formed by the breaking of the promise of justification into the deterioration of the fallen creation under sin, death, and the wrath of God.[207] Yet, it is precisely here, in the crying out in anguish, groaning, and sighing, which occurs in the narrow straights of the desperate situation of the contradiction of the promise, that hope begins to dawn for the believer who is undergoing the attack of the hidden God in *Anfechtung*. For it is here, in crying out through lament, that the believer picks up the only weapon at hand that will function to defend himself or herself against the attack of the hidden God on belief in the promise of justification: the promise itself.[208]

In Bayer's estimation, lament is thus a cry out against the hidden God on the basis of the promise of the revealed God. It is using the promise of God against God, similar to Job's appeal God's righteousness against the assault of the hidden God. This appeal to the promise of God against the hidden God through lament has both creational and Christological dimensions, according to Bayer. The creational dimension of lament consists of the groaning that characterizes the present existence of creation in the rupture of the ages between the advent of the promise and the final fulfillment of the promise in the eschaton. Under the power of sin and decay, the creation itself has been subjected to the death and evil that characterizes the work of the hidden God and groans for eschatological redemption and renewal. Bayer's

---

204. Ibid., 188–91.

205. Ibid., 197.

206. Bayer, *Martin Luther's Theology*, 11; Bayer, *Martin Luthers Theologie*, 10. Bayer, "Rupture of Times," 45–46; Bayer, *Gott als Autor*, 158–59.

207. Bayer, *Martin Luther's Theology*, 113, 115–17; Bayer, *Martin Luthers Theology*, 103, 105–7. Bayer, *Martin Luther's Theology*, 9–10; Bayer, *Martin Luthers Theologie*, 8–9. Bayer, "Rupture of the Ages," 43–45; Bayer, *Gott als Autor*, 156–58. Bayer, *Theology the Lutheran Way*, 87; Bayer, *Theologie*, 396. Bayer, *Living by Faith*, 30; Bayer, *Aus Glauben Leben*, 38.

208. Bayer, *Martin Luther's Theology*, 113; Bayer, *Martin Luthers Theology*, 103.

understanding of the Christological dimension of lament incorporates his view of the Trinity as God's self-revelation as a God of mercy and grace in Christ into his discussion of lament. Sharpening his thoughts along the lines of Luther's hymn *Nun freut euch lieben Christen g'mein*, Bayer describes the conversation amongst the persons of the Trinity alluded to in this hymn as the Triune God's deliberation to be God for humanity and in solidarity with the fallen creation and sinful humanity in Jesus Christ against the wrath of the hidden God. This, says Bayer, is the Triune God's answer to the lament of the believer and the groaning of creation. Ultimately though, Bayer argues that this answer only comes fully eschatologically, outlining what he calls "an eschatology of answered lament," in which God hears and answers the cry of lament with a creational judgment against the present persistence of evil, decay of creation, and opposition of the hidden God to faith with the renewal of creation and the ending of the work of the hidden God.

The final end of the work of the hidden God, says Bayer, will come only in the eschaton with the complete renewal of creation and destruction of death and sin forever. According to Bayer, the human attempts to silence the hidden God—exemplified in dualism, the philosophical and theological forms of monism, the denial of God's omnipotence in process theology and the thought of Hans Jonas, the Barthian identification of God's wrath as a form of God's love, and the Calvinistic view of double predestination—simply do not work. The only thing that will ever silence the hidden God and bring an end to the hidden God's attack on faith through *Anfechtung* is God's own complete fulfillment of the promise in the eschaton. Until such a time, the believer is a pilgrim on the way. The only thing that the pilgrim has to go on in the meantime is the promise itself, and the only thing that can be done by such a pilgrim in response to the work of the hidden God is to cry out in lament in expectant hope in the eschatological fulfillment of that same promise.

It is the promise itself and alone that can deliver from the hidden God and that motivates the believer's lament against the hidden God. Were it not for the promise, the lament against the hidden God would have no power behind it. As it is, however, the believer has a firm faith in God's future fulfillment of the promise in the eschaton and the final ending of the hidden God's attack on faith, and this hope motivates the persistence of the believer in the *Sitz im Leben* of lament formed by the experience of *Anfechtung*. As Bayer states, "To dare to call upon God [i.e. through lament] whom this side of the grave we have to experience in ambiguous omnipotence—to dare to call upon him already now as a gracious and merciful Father is possible only in the light of the certainty of Romans 8:31–39, a certainty that overcomes the world. Faith that is certain of salvation will keep overcoming the attack

(*Anfechtung*)."[209] Such faith exists and is encouraged in the present in the community of believers through the continual proclamation of the Word of promise and the distribution of the revealed God in Christ through the bread and wine of Holy Communion.[210]

> Faith, that hears God's promise, awaits the abolition/resolution of the hiddenness of God. This happens not by sight or knowledge, but only in the hope of faith that God, whose righteousness is still incomprehensible, is just and will make God's righteousness manifest. (See Luther at the end of *The Bondage of the Will*).[211] This 'solution' to the question of theodicy does not settle [the contradicton of] lament, but it does slow it and brings a passionate hope for the consummation of the world, in which God God's self definitively brings justice, and this answer to lament will bring *Anfechtung* to an end.
>
> In the present—here and now—God's word of promise comes to me, God God's self comes to me, the God who says, 'I am the Lord, your God,' comes to me, the strong future of the advent of the Lord comes to me. This God comes to me in Holy Communion. So it is the same with all other suffering creatures stretched by waiting and pleading: 'Come, Lord Jesus.'[212]

Summary

Bayer's interpretation of Luther's doctrine of the hidden God and use of it in his own theology can only be understood in the context of Bayer's teaching on justification through the promise of God revealed in the gospel of Jesus Christ. From the basis of his understanding of justification as the center of all theology, Bayer defines the hiddenness of God as God's contradiction of the justifying promise of God in Jesus Christ. Bayer delineates that the hidden God assaults the believer with this contradiction of the promise and attacks faith in the promise through the experience of *Anfechtung*. Like Jacob on the banks of the Jabbok, the believer is assaulted by the hidden God who works evil, death, and all things.

---

209. Bayer, "What is Evangelical?" 11; Bayer, *Zugesagte Gegenwart*, 32.

210. Bayer, "Rupture of Times," 47; Bayer, *Got als Autor*, 159–60. Bayer, *Martin Luther's Theology*, 11–12; Bayer, *Martin Luthers Theologie*, 10–11.

211. WA 18:785.

212. Bayer, *Schöpfung als Anrede*, 2nd ed., "Aufhebung von Gottes Verborgenheit," 139. Translation is the authors own, with Oswald Bayer's approval.

Bayer argues that the activity of the hidden God in *Anfechtung*, leveled against the believer's faith in the promise, comes particularly through the question of double predestination and even more broadly through the reality of the problem of evil in the world, which call into question the validity of the promise. Bayer focuses in particularly on the second of these two venues for the experience of the hidden God's assault on faith and describes it as occurring through natural disasters, disease, death, war, and genocide. It is clear at this point that Bayer's understanding of justification through the promise directly effects how he understands the work of the hidden God.

Firstly, Bayer defines the hiddenness of God as God's attack on faith in the promise through *Anfechtung*. In his explanation of justification through the promise, Bayer argues that in the promise, God forgives sin, revealing God's self as a God of mercy in Christ, opening a new relationship of grace with the justified sinner. In Bayer's description of divine hiddenness, the hidden God contradicts all of this and undermines faith in God as a God of grace and mercy. The notion that the hidden God contradicts God's promise means that Bayer's understanding of hiddenness is dependent upon his understanding of justification as coming through God's promise. Furthermore, the question of double predestination through which God contradicts the promise is the inverse of the notion of God revealed as a God of grace and mercy, as God for the human.

Secondly, Bayer's understanding of the hidden God's work as the assault on faith in the promise relates directly to the idea that God's justification through the promise brings the believer assurance and confidence. In this way, Bayer defines God's hiddenness as the very opposite of what God does in justification. In justification, God brings the assurance of the forgiveness of sins and the confidence to live life. This is what the hidden God contradicts and attacks, and so, once again, Bayer defines God's hiddenness as the inverse of his description of God's justification.

Thirdly, Bayer's view of God's hiddenness being evident in the evil that takes place in the world is reliant upon his understanding of justification entailing the promised opening of creation and the renewal of all things. Bayer depicts the believer as one who is caught between the promise of the way creation should and will be, on the one hand, and the contradiction of this promise evident through the problem of evil, on the other hand. In delineating this aspect of God's hiddenness, Bayer very obviously relies upon his own view of the link between justification and creation and on his understanding of justification as the redemption of creation.

Finally, Bayer's argument that the believer can only be rid of the hidden God through the eschatological fulfillment of the promise and that before the eschaton the believer exists in lament is also formed by his understanding of justification through the promise. This makes Bayer's entire discussion of the hidden God ultimately dependent upon the promise. He began with the promise as the baseline and norm of Christian doctrine and experience (which the hidden God contradicts), and he ends with the promise as the only solution to the problem of the hidden God. It is the same promise that justifies the sinner, makes him or her a believer, brings him or her into a new relationship with God and other humans, and opens up and renews all of creation. It is the same promise that the hidden God attacks through *Anfechtung*, experienced through the question of double predestination and the problem of evil, which ultimately is the only thing that, one can use against the hidden God in lament. Finally, it is the same promise that God will one day fulfill at the consummation of history and the dawning of the eschaton, when the revealed God of the promise will complete renew all things and do away with the hiddenness of God forever.

Bayer's entire discussion of the hidden God depends on his view of justification. This discussion begins with justification by the promise as that which the hidden God contradicts, continues by contrasting the understanding and experience of God through the promise with the understanding and experience of the hidden God's contradiction of that promise in *Anfechtung*, moves to the cosmic dimensions of the contradiction of the promise in creation, presents lament as the believer's response to hiddenness that is based on the promise, and concludes with the promise as that which will bring an eschatological end to the hiddenness of God. Without exploring every teaching and contour in Bayer's theology, it is safe to say that with regard to his treatment of the doctrine of the hidden God, Bayer successfully demonstrates that his theology is centered on God's act of justifying sinners and renewing creation through the promise. In defining and describing the hidden God and the work of the hidden God, Bayer relies on his view of justification both with reference to its basic position in his theology and in regard to the content of his teaching that God justifies through the promise of God in the gospel of Jesus Christ.

Bayer utilizes Luther's notion of the hidden God in this, his own theology of justification, but is his view of God's hiddenness the same as Luther's? In the following chapter, I will take up this question and explore how Bayer adopts, interprets, and utilizes Luther's doctrine of the hidden God. In so doing, I will discuss how Bayer follows Luther in his view of divine hiddenness but also how Bayer diverges from and develops Luther's teaching concerning this theme. I will also compare Bayer's treatment of Luther's doctrine of the hidden God to the treatment that this teaching has received in the modern German Protestant tradition.

8

Bayer's Interpretation of Luther on the Hidden God

BAYER'S TEACHING ON THE hiddenness of God is formed by his overall approach to theology as well as by his particular theology of justification. In fact, Bayer's discussion of the hidden God is contained within these two greater aspects of his theological thought. In Bayer's approach to theology, the hiddenness of God features in the mode, method, and the data of theology.

In the mode of theology, the hiddenness of God forms part of the experience that makes a theologian. According to Bayer, the experience that makes a theologian is the experience of being addressed by God and passively suffering the experience of God. The fact that divine hiddenness is part of this experience means, for Bayer's theology, that the experience of being addressed by God that makes a theologian is not just a beneficial experience of God's grace but also entails the experience of God's wrath. Such experience, which forms part of the mode of theology, is then played out through the experiential theological method of Bayer. This method, which Bayer adopts from Luther, entails the experiences of prayer, meditation, and the agonizing struggle of *Anfechtung*. The hiddenness of God forms the content of the last of these three experiences, as the believer undergoes a spiritual attack from the hidden God in *Anfechtung*. In this attack, the hidden God undermines and contradicts the promise of salvation revealed in the gospel through a hidden work in the evil that occurs in creation, assaulting the believer's trust in the promise for the forgiveness of sins, a relationship with God as a gracious and merciful God of love, and the renewal of all creation. This experience of the hidden God in *Anfechtung* then serves as one of the three data of theology identified by Bayer. Bayer identifies the experience of the hidden God as a third datum of theology in addition to the law and the gospel—so essential is it to description of the forces that form a theology and to his approach to doing theology. What is unique about hiddenness, compared to the law and the gospel, is not only the radicality of the wrath contained therein but also the fact that hiddenness constitutes a form of divine address that is not heard *per se* but only experienced through the evil things that happen in creation. This presence of the hidden God in Bayer's experiential approach to theology means that the theologian who undergoes the address of God realizes that life is not always sweet with sugar but is, in the words of Döblin, "of sugar and dirt all mixed up."[1] The inclusion of the hiddenness of God in Bayer's approach to theology ensures that the content of his theology of justification will include a significant discussion the believer's experience of the hiddenness of God.

Bayer utilizes Luther's notion of the hidden God, but he makes this theme his own and interprets it along the contours of his theology of justification. Bayer's understanding of the hiddenness of God thus forms part of his own particular theology. It flows from his own approach to theology and his view of justification, and it makes up an integral part of his theology. Yet, Bayer adopts the concept of the hiddenness of God outside of revelation from Luther, who first expressed the doctrine as part of his argument against Erasmus in *The Bondage of the Will* and clarified it in his later biblical lectures. Moreover, as both a Luther scholar and a contemporary Lutheran theologian, Bayer endeavors to interpret and use Luther's views and insights in his own theology. This raises the question of whether or not Bayer is faithful to Luther in defining, describing, and utilizing Luther's doctrine of the hidden God.

Furthermore, there is nearly half a millennium of German Protestant theology between Luther and Bayer. As part of the modern German Protestant theological tradition, Bayer's discussion of the hiddenness of God stands, at least in part, as part of a more lengthy conversation in that tradition about Luther's doctrine of the hidden God. Though this is the case, Bayer interacts very little with fellow members of this tradition concerning the interpretation of Luther's doctrine of the hidden God. Even so, certain comparisons and contrasts may be drawn between Bayer's view of divine hiddenness and the treatments of this doctrine made by other figures of the German Protestant theological tradition.

In this chapter, I will compare Bayer's teaching on the hidden God first of all to Luther's articulation of the doctrine and secondly to the ideas of

---

1. Bayer, "Creation as History," 261; Bayer, *Zugesagte Gegenwart*, 229. Döblin, *Berlin Alexanderplatz*, 392.

divine hiddenness espoused by some of the important figures of the modern German Protestant theological tradition. In doing this, it is not my goal to subject Bayer to a litmus test of confessional Lutheranism, nor is it my desire simply to hold up Bayer as more preferable to every other figure in modern German Protestant theology. I simply wish to look at Bayer's teaching on the hidden God alongside that of Luther, in order to demonstrate where he adopts Luther's own thought and where he develops Luther's thought as a contemporary interpretation of the reformer's theology. I further seek to compare Bayer's teaching on the hidden God to other interpretations and treatments of Luther's doctrine of the hidden to discern if Bayer has captured something of the essence of this doctrine of the reformer's that others in the modern German Protestant theological tradition may have missed or rejected. Ultimately, these objectives of mine are motivated by a desire to utilize Bayer today as a figure whose thought might be able to help in a particular way those who, like Bayer, seek to do Lutheran theology today.

Comparison to Luther

Throughout his work, Bayer endeavors to be a truly Lutheran theologian and to do theology as a Lutheran. To this end, he utilizes insights from Luther in his approach to doing theology, in his positioning of justification at the center of the theological enterprise, in his view of the doctrine of justification, and in his views on various other points in theology, including in his view of the hiddenness of God. In describing and defining the hiddenness of God in his theology, Bayer displays both similarities with and some slight differences from the reformer concerning the doctrine of the hidden God.

While it is relatively clear that Bayer adopts the notion of God's hiddenness outside of revelation from Luther and essentially defines the work of the hidden God as does Luther, the comparison of Bayer's thought on hiddenness with that of Luther is more complex regarding the relationships between the hiddenness of God and the distinction between the law and the gospel as well as between the hiddenness of God and predestination. Although there is some similarity between Bayer and Luther concerning these relationships, Bayer also differs somewhat from Luther regarding the relationship of God's hiddenness to the law and the gospel and even somewhat reduces the reformer's connection between divine hiddenness and predestination. Moreover, Bayer's extensive use of God's hiddenness in his theology (i.e. *Anfechtung*) and his description of the believer experiencing of such hiddenness in *Anfechtung* specifically through the problem of evil constitutes a genuine development of Luther's doctrine of hidden God.

Nevertheless, despite the differences between Bayer's teaching of the hidden God and the reformer's own teaching, there is an overwhelming similarity between the two concerning the trajectory of the doctrine and its relationship to justification in Jesus Christ, which forms the center of theology for both theologians. For both Bayer and Luther, every point in theology, even divine hiddenness, is based upon and relates back to God's work of justifying sinners through faith in Jesus Christ. In this way, Bayer demonstrates that he is a theological follower of Luther both in the sense that his entire theology is based upon the doctrine of justification and the sense that he, like the reformer, relates God's hiddenness itself back to justification.

Bayer Adopts Luther's Doctrine of the Hidden God

Luther first articulates this definition in *The Bondage of the Will*, where he states that as well as existing inside of revelation as "God preached," God also exists hidden outside of revelation as "God not preached."[2] Here, Luther defines the hiddenness of the unpreached God outside of revelation as a hiddenness in which God is incomprehensible and in which God works wrath, death, damnation, and all things.[3] Bayer adopts this understanding of the hiddenness of the unpreached God and utilizes it in his own theology. Like Luther, Bayer defines this hiddenness of God outside of revelation as a hiddenness of God in which God is totally incomprehensible, clearly distinguishing it from the hiddenness of God in revelation and from the comprehensible voice of God's love and grace revealed in the gospel of Jesus Christ.[4] Bayer here also echoes Luther's prohibition against speculation concerning the incomprehensible hiddenness of God. Like Luther, Bayer states the hidden God should be left alone by inquisitive human minds and not explained away. Though one must recognize the existence of the hidden God, one cannot have dealings with the hidden God, call upon the hidden God in prayer, or believe in the hidden God. That is because, says Bayer, the promise of the revealed God in Christ is the only place where the human can have a relationship with God.[5]

As Bayer emulates Luther in his definition of the hiddenness of God, he also follows the reformer in delineating that the hiddenness of God outside of revelation is a hiddenness in which God exists as a God of wrath,

---

2. *BOW*, 169–170; WA 18:684–85.
3. *BOW*, 170; WA 18:685.
4. Bayer, *Martin Luther's Theology*, 198; Bayer, *Martin Luthers Theologie*, 178–79.
5. Bayer, *Martin Luther's Theology*, 39, 198; Bayer, *Martin Luthers Theologie*, 36, 178–79. *BOW*, 170; WA 18:685.

who is responsible for death, evil, and all things that happen.[6] For Bayer, as for Luther, the unpreached, hidden God appears as a God of terrifying hiddenness in wrath who cannot be understood or known by the human but is experienced as hostile to the human. While Luther does not outright state that this contradicts this gospel, at least not in those exact words, he does describe the hiddenness of the unpreached God as the contradiction of the gospel and contrasts this hiddenness with God's saving revelation in the Word.[7] As I have striven to demonstrate in the previous chapter of this thesis, Bayer essentially defines God's hiddenness as the contradiction of the promise of God revealed in the gospel.[8] This explanation of the hiddenness of God is thus in concert with Luther's definition of it as well.

Furthermore, Bayer follows Luther in identifying this hiddenness of God with the trials that God sends, experienced by believers in the agonizing struggle of *Anfechtung*. In some of his later writings, especially in his biblical lectures, Luther states that the hidden God sends trials upon all people, including believers, so that they will despair of their efforts at salvation and comfort and be turned instead to the salvation and comfort of God revealed in the gospel of Jesus Christ.[9] Luther identifies this aspect of the hiddenness of God as God's alien work, which is aimed ultimately at the fulfillment of God's proper work of justification in Christ.[10]

Bayer also identifies the work of the hidden God with God's work in *Anfechtung*.[11] Bayer states that through *Anfechtung* the hiddenness of God is experienced by the believer through an agonizing struggle in which the hidden God contradicts the believer's faith in the promise of God.[12] Bayer, like Luther, sees the ultimate outcome of this struggle with the hidden God as the believer's being driven anew to the merciful God of salvation revealed in Jesus Christ.[13]

From this basic definition of the hiddenness of God as God's incomprehensible hiddenness in wrath that assails the believer in *Anfechtung*,

---

6. Bayer, *Martin Luther's Theology*, 198; Bayer, *Martin Luthers Theologie*, 178–179.

7. *BOW*, 169–71; WA 18:684–86.

8. Bayer, *Martin Luther's Theology*, 39; Bayer, *Martin Luthers Theologie*, 36.

9. WA 50:660. LW 17:278–79; WA 31.2:476.

10. *LW* 16:233–35; WA 31–2:168–69.

11. Bayer, *Martin Luther's Theology*, 198–99; Bayer, *Martin Luthers Theologie*, 179. Bayer, *Living by Faith*, 71; Bayer, *Aus Glauben Leben*, 77.

12. Bayer, *Living by Faith*, 70–71; Bayer, *Aus Glauben Leben*, 77. Bayer, *Theology the Lutheran Way*, 102–4; Bayer, *Theologie*, 413–16. Bayer, *Martin Luther's Theology*, 20–21; Bayer, *Martin Luther s Theologie*, 19–20.

13. Bayer, *Martin Luther's Theology*, 20–21, 36–37; Bayer, *Martin Luthers Theologie*, 19–20, 33–34.

Bayer develops Luther's doctrine of the hidden God in his own theology that has both similarities and dissimilarities with Luther's own teaching on the hidden God. While there is some similarity between Bayer and Luther concerning the relationships between the hiddenness of God and the distinction between the law and the gospel and the hiddenness of God and double predestination, Bayer also makes a notable departure from the thought of the reformer on these points. It needs to be assessed how significant this departure is and whether or not Bayer remains faithful to the essence of Luther's doctrine of the hidden God in his own interpretation of this doctrine.

Hiddenness and the Distinction between the Law and the Gospel

In *The Bondage of the Will*, Luther actually first expresses his understanding of the hiddenness of God outside of revelation in the larger context of his argument concerning the distinction between the law and the gospel.[14] Furthermore, a certain parallelism may be observed, both in this work as well as elsewhere in Luther's theology, between the work of the hidden God and the work of God in the law. For Luther, both God's hiddenness and the law condemn the human sinner, killing the sinner's false belief in "free will" in order that the sinner might be saved by the revealed God in Christ through the gospel.[15]

While Luther articulates his doctrine of the hidden God within the context of his dialectic of law and gospel, Bayer places the work of the hidden God outside of this dialectic, identifying the hiddenness of God as something of a third word of God in addition to the law and the gospel.[16] Bayer draws a distinction not only between the hiddenness of God and the gospel, but also between the hiddenness of God and the law. This distinction between the law and hiddenness may be in part due to Barth's interaction with Elert's unequivocal identification of divine hiddenness with the law. Certainly Bayer rejects such the simple identification of hiddenness and the law that Elert makes, and I shall take up this rejection more fully below.

Bayer argues that the law constitutes God's understandable wrath, citing God's wrath against the rebellious Jonah in the storm as an example of this kind of wrath, while divine hiddenness constitutes God's

14. BOW, 169–71; WA 18:684–86. Cf. BOW, 151–89; WA 18:673–99.

15. BOW 157, 161–63, 165–67, 169–71, 287–88; WA 18:676, 679–86, 766–67.

16. Bayer, *Bayer, Theology the Lutheran Way*, 101–2; Bayer, *Theologie*, 413–14. Bayer, "The Plurality of the One God," 343; Bayer, *Zugesagte Gegenwart*, 100.

incomprehensible wrath.[17] While God's wrath in the law is a discernible, verbal wrath, the wrath of God in hiddenness is a non-verbal wrath that is not heard *per se* but only experienced as terror or primal dread.[18] Furthermore, this non-verbal wrath of God comes through creation itself and is experienced through nature rather than heard directly from God's address.[19]

Such a fine distinction between the law of God and the hiddenness of God as that which Bayer makes is not articulated in Luther's theology. It is true that Luther does not teach that God's work in the law exhausts the work of the hidden God, as such work encompasses all things that come to pass,[20] but Luther does draw a parallel between God's work in hiddenness and God's work in the law.[21] In Luther's writings, the hidden God's work of condemnation and the work of God in the law mirror one another to the extent that the reader could even identify them as interchangeable in Luther's thought. Bayer's identification of hiddenness as a third word goes beyond this.[22]

Moreover, Luther does not depict God's wrath against Jonah as being understandable wrath that comes through the law over and against incomprehensible wrath that comes through God's hiddenness. On the contrary, the description of God's wrath that Luther gives in his *Lectures on Jonah* weaves in and out of the categories of the law and God's hiddenness, so that it is nearly impossible to discern a difference between the two. In addressing the wrath of God experienced by Jonah and the sailors on the boat with him, Luther describes such wrath as a part of a natural knowledge of God that comes through creation and the conscience, outside of revelation.[23] Jonah is depicted by Luther as being driven by the wrath of the hidden God in creation to the mercy of the revealed God in the Word. Luther describes the wrath of God against Jonah as both coming through the natural order and damning Jonah in order to raise him up.[24] Such a description is representative both of Luther's view of the hiddenness of God outside of revelation as well as of the law of God, as Luther also describes the law as accomplishing

---

17. Bayer, *Bayer, Theology the Lutheran Way*, 87, 102; Bayer, *Theologie*, 396, 413. Bayer, *Martin Luther's Theology*, 196–198; Bayer, *Martin Luthers Theologe*, 177–79. Bayer, *Zugesagte Gegenwart*, 114–15.

18. Bayer, *Martin Luther's Theology*, 198; Bayer, *Martin Luthers Theologie*, 178–79.

19. Ibid. Bayer, *Gott als Autor*, 272.

20. *BOW*, 170; WA 18:684–85.

21. *BOW* 157, 161–63, 165–67, 169–71, 287–88; WA 18:676, 679–86, 766–67.

22. Bayer, *Bayer, Theology the Lutheran Way*, 101–2; Bayer, *Theologie*, 413–14. Bayer, "The Plurality of the One God," 343; Bayer, *Zugesagte Gegenwart*, 100.

23. *LW* 19:54–57; WA 19:206–8.

24. *LW* 19:18, 76; WA 13:250, 19:226–27.

such work and delineates that the condemning work of the law also comes through creation.[25] Luther does not make such a fine, direct distinction between the law and the hiddenness of God.

Bayer's distinction between the hiddenness of God and the law is motivated at least to some extent by his enumeration of the law, hiddenness, and the gospel as forming the three data of theology.[26] By identifying hiddenness as a datum for doing theology, Bayer brings God's hiddenness into his approach to theology. By doing this, Bayer ensures that the doctrine of the hidden God will have a prominent place in his theology.

One might be tempted to trace Bayer's identification of the hiddenness of God as a third word of God entirely to his use of Hamann's philosophy, particularly since he draws deeply from Hamann's notions of *Gott als Autor* and *Schöpfung als Anrede*. Hamann sees God as a poet who speaks to God's creatures through creation and creation itself as divine speech.[27] Yet, a large part of Bayer's use of Hamann in setting forth the data of theology is to define them in an anti-Kantian manner. Bayer uses Hamann in his discussion of the data of theology in order to argue that data of theology are not phenomena to be discovered and interpreted by the human mind but words from God that actually act upon the human. Bayer's point in using Hamann here is thus to put the word of God in the acting position and the human being in the passive position.[28] While Bayer may draw from Hamann in this way, Luther also certainly sees the human being as passive in the face of the work of God, whether it be in the law, the gospel, or hiddenness. Bayer may also draw from Hamann in portraying the hidden God's address coming to the human through creation itself, but once again, Luther does this as well. The reason that Bayer distinguishes so significantly between the law and God's hiddenness cannot be traced only to Hamann.

Bayer's real motivation in drawing this distinction is not entirely clear. Is it simply so that a difference can be portrayed between God's understandable and God's incomprehensible wrath? This appears to be the case. Yet, there is little to no damage done by Bayer's identification of God's hiddenness as a third word that constitutes a different kind of wrath than the wrath of God in the law. This is because, ultimately, Bayer describes the work accomplished by the hiddenness of God and the work accomplished by the

---

25. WA 39-1:361, 508–9, 515–17. *LW* 40:98; WA 18:81. Lohse, 273–74.

26. Bayer, *Bayer, Theology the Lutheran Way*, 102–6; Bayer, *Theologie*, 413–16.

27. Bayer, *Zeitgenosse im Widerspruch*, 75–83; Bayer, *A Contemporary in Dissent*, 54–62. Hamann, *Sämtliche Werke*, 2:140, 206. Bayer, *Gott als Autor*, 30–33. Bayer, *Autorität und Kritik*, 5–6.

28. Bayer, *Schöpfung als Anrede*, 13–18. Cf. Hamann, *Sämtliche Werke*, 2:195–217.

law of God as being identical. Bayer sees both driving the believer to the justifying promise of God revealed in the gospel of Jesus Christ.[29]

Furthermore, Bayer describes both the law and hiddenness as making up the doctrine of general knowledge of God, which is to be distinguished from the knowledge of God as Triune. According to Bayer, the knowledge of God as Trinity entails only the gospel. Bayer then lumps the law and hiddenness together as what gives humans a general knowledge of God. At this point, it is very difficult to see how Bayer maintains the distinction between the law and hiddenness.[30]

Bayer sets up a distinction between the law and God's hiddenness as two different kinds of divine wrath, but other than one being understandable and one being incomprehensible and God's work in hiddenness coming especially through creation, there seems to be no drastically significant difference between the two. Moreover, the effect of both is the same in Bayer's thought. Though he differs from Luther in that he draws a distinction between the law and the hiddenness of God, he ends up at essentially the same position as Luther, since he identifies both the law and hiddenness as driving the human to God revealed in the promise of the gospel of Christ. Bayer does draw too neat of a distinction between hiddenness and the law, whereas the two overlap in Luther's theology, but the effect for Bayer's theology is essentially the same as in Luther's theology: God's wrath comes through the law and hiddenness. If hiddenness were a venue for a positive natural theology in Bayer's thought, there might be more of a cause for concern about the relationship of the law and hiddenness in his theology, but this is not the case, since in his estimation, the law and hiddenness both convey God's wrath.

Hiddenness and Double Predestination

As in his description of the relationship between the hiddenness of God and the law, Bayer shows both similarity and some slight dissimilarity to Luther concerning the relationship between the hiddenness of God and double predestination. While Bayer does recognize that God's hiddenness outside

---

29. Bayer, *Martin Luther's Theology*, 61, 213; Bayer, *Martin Luthers Theologie*, 55–56, 192.

30. Bayer, *Martin Luther's Theology*, 337–40; Bayer, *Martin Luthers Theologie*, 306–9. Bayer, "Poetological Theology," 165; Bayer, *Gott als Autor*, 15. Bayer, *Zugesagte Gegenwart*, 177. Bayer, The Plurality of the One God," 350; Bayer, *Zugesagte Gegenwart*, 106.

of revelation is connected to the issue of double predestination,[31] he does not follow Luther into a robust view of God's double-willing in predestination. The result of this is that Bayer's teaching on the hidden God, though firmly grounded in Luther's, appears to take a somewhat new direction.

As I described in chapter two, when setting forth his teaching on the hidden God in *The Bondage of the Will*, Luther clearly delineates that the distinction between the revealed God and the hidden God extends to the will of God. Thus, Luther argues that God has two wills: a revealed will through which God wills the life and salvation of the sinner in Christ and a hidden will in which God wills the death and damnation of the sinner outside of Christ.[32] Though he did not articulate his full teaching on the hidden God until 1525, Luther expressed this understanding of double predestination in his *Lectures on Romans*, wherein he states that God damns the sinner and kills his or her false trust in "free will" through reprobation in order to save him or her through election in Jesus Christ.[33] Luther assumes this same argument in *The Bondage of the Will*, where he argues that God effects all things through God's immutable will.[34] In his treatise against Erasmus, Luther maintains that part of God's immutable will is God's damnation of sinners. From the broader context of his theological writings, it becomes apparent that this divine decree of reprobation is one in which God damns so that God may then save through God's gracious decree of election in Christ.[35] In his later writings, Luther clarifies that the hidden God's work of damnation comes through the trials of *Anfechtung* experienced by the believer.[36] According to Luther, the hidden God condemns through reprobation in order to save through election. Thus, for Luther, the two sides of double predestination—reprobation and election—make up the will of God hidden and God revealed and parallel God's respective condemning work in the law and saving work in the gospel.

Though Bayer recognizes to some extent that the hiddenness of God is connected to double predestination and sees the question of double predestination as part of the believer's experience of *Anfechtung*,[37] he does not ap-

---

31. Bayer, *Martin Luther's Theology*, 198–99, 209; Bayer, *Martin Luthers Theologie*, 179, 188–89. Bayer, "What Is Evangelical?" 4, 10; Bayer, *Zugesagte Gegenwart*, 25, 31–32.

32. *BOW*, 170–71; WA 18:685–86.

33. *LW* 25:371–72, 375, 377; WA 56:381–82, 385–87.

34. *BOW*, 170; WA 685.

35. *BOW*, 170–71; WA 18:685–86.

36. *LW* 16:24, 233–35; WA 31.2:16–17, 168–69. *LW* 5:49; WA 43:462. *LW* 6:151, 259; WA 44:112–13, 192. *LW* 7:175–76; WA 44:428–29. *LW* 8:7–8; WA 45:584–86.

37. Bayer, *Martin Luther's Theology*, 198–199, 209; Bayer, *Martin Luthers Theologie*,

pear to assume as a basis for his discussion Luther's view of the hidden God's condemning the sinner through reprobation in order that the revealed God in Christ may save through election. Instead, Bayer addresses the issue of double predestination only briefly and then leaves it out of his discussion of the relationship between the hiddenness of God and God's justification of the sinner through the promise in the gospel of Christ. Perhaps Bayer avoids discussing double predestination in order to avoid confusion with Reformed theology. This seems to be the case, given Bayer's strong rejection of Calvin's approach to double predestination.[38]

Bayer could address, utilize, and interpret the connection made between the hidden God and double predestination in Luther's theology. The terror the conscience experiences at double predestination, as Bayer himself notes, requires the establishment of this on the ground of God's almighty power and even God's hiddenness outside the law, otherwise one could simply use reason and the law to resolve the *Anfechtung*, not the gospel. He could even show how Luther views both reprobation and election from the standpoint of "the sinner" and how that contrasts with Calvin's view by demonstrating how Luther sees both of these works as befalling the same sinner instead of each work eternally categorizing and determining two different groups of people. Bayer, however, does not do this but only briefly mentions double predestination then moves on, focusing on the role of the problem of evil in *Anfechtung* as the work of the hidden God.

Neglect of the connection between the distinction between the hidden and revealed God and the two-fold doctrine of double predestination ignores the important aspect of Luther's doctrine of the hidden God regarding the two divine wills. Instead of addressing this aspect of the reformer's teaching, Bayer takes an alternative route than Luther's regarding the believer's experience of the hidden God. While Luther portrays the work of the hidden God in *Anfechtung* as embodying the damning will of God in reprobation, Bayer focuses instead on the hidden God's work in *Anfechtung* through the problem of evil. This focus represents a genuine development of Luther's doctrine of the hidden God.

179, 188–89. Bayer, "What Is Evangelical?" 4, 10; Bayer, *Zugesagte Gegenwart*, 25, 31–32. Bayer, "The Plurality of the One God," 342–43, 345–46, 353; Bayer, *Zugesagte Gegenwart*, 99–100, 102, 109.

38. Bayer, Martin Luther's Theology, 209–10; Bayer, *Martin Luthers Theologie*, 188–89.

Bayer's Development of Luther

Bayer functions as a true contemporary interpreter of Luther by developing, and not merely restating, the reformer's thought concerning divine hiddenness. Bayer begins and ends his understanding of divine hiddenness squarely in line with the thought of the reformer, but he also develops Luther's thought in two ways that the reformer did not. The first of these two ways consists of the significant position occupied by the doctrine of the hidden God in Bayer's theology. The second entails Bayer's inclusion of the problem of evil within the discussion about the work of the hidden God in *Anfechtung*, forming a creational dimension to that discussion. In neither of these ways in which Bayer develops Luther's doctrine of the hidden God, does Bayer radically depart from the trajectory of the teaching established by Luther. Bayer does, however, further Luther's teaching on the hidden God into areas not fully explored by the reformer, and in so doing does honor to the essence of Luther's teaching while, at the same time, actually pioneering new territory for this teaching.

The Place of the Hidden God in Theology

It is clear that the hiddenness of God plays a distinctly important role in Bayer's theology. It forms part of his understanding of the experiential mode of theology, one of the three aspects of the method of theology, and one of the three data divinely given for the doing of theology. It also serves in his overall theology as that work of God, which both contradicts God's justifying promise in the gospel of Christ and which ultimately leads back to that promise. Furthermore, Bayer uses this teaching of Luther's to address the apparent conflict between the promised eschatological opening and renewal of creation and the apparent contradiction of that opening and renewal in the present and to address this problem of contradiction with his teaching on the believer's lament amidst the work of the hidden God.

By assigning such a prominent systematic theological role for the hiddenness of God, Bayer builds upon Luther's doctrine of the hidden God while also developing this doctrine. It is not as if the doctrine of the hidden God is an unimportant or peripheral aspect of Luther's theological work. It is certainly a teaching that figures significantly in some of Luther's major writings from 1525 onward in the reformer's career. Even so, Luther's articulation of this doctrine, particularly in *The Bondage of the Will*, is set within a certain historical and rhetorical context, functioning as part of the reformer's overall argument against the Pelagianism of Erasmus.

Bayer has developed Luther's doctrine of the hidden God beyond what Luther does with the issue in *The Bondage of the Will* and the reformer's later writings and has used it as a systematic principle in the construction of his own theology. It is true, as I have demonstrated, that Luther speaks of the doctrine of the hidden God as a basic systematic feature for doing theology and that his doctrine of the hidden God is just that; it is a doctrine. It is a doctrine present throughout his writings and one that is interconnected with other themes in his theology. Yet, it is not as if Luther directly sets forth a way of doing theology wherein the hiddenness of God so specifically enters into the mode, method, and data of theology as does Bayer; nor does the reformer develop the theme of divine hiddenness along the same lines as Bayer does in his theology of lament.

Bayer, however, is not simply attempting to be a Luther scholar in the historical sense; he is also a Lutheran systematic theologian. Part of his task within that vocation is to interpret Luther's theology for people in today's world and to utilize it in a contemporary Lutheran theology. To be sure, Bayer reflects Luther's underlying concern that the true subject of theology is God's justification of sinners by faith in Jesus Christ through the preached gospel. Yet Bayer does not simply digest and regurgitate Luther's writings; instead, he takes into consideration the contemporary world of thought and experience, which stands nearly 500 years after the evangelical explosion of Luther's thought in the Reformation. In this way, Bayer does not merely summarize Luther's view of the hidden God but interprets and even develops it in his own theology, utilizing it as a core feature of how he approaches the very doing of theology itself to the extent that Bayer's theology would not be what it is without the pronounced theme of the hiddenness of God outside of revelation.

One might look at Bayer's use of the doctrine of the hidden God in his theology and raise the question of whether Bayer might have violated Luther's prohibition against speculating on the hidden God. After all, Luther argues that where God is hidden outside of creation, humans have no business dealing with God.[39] Bayer's use of the doctrine of the hidden God in his theology might be seen as going against Luther's teaching here in so much as he uses the doctrine epistemologically in his systematic theology. Yet, Luther himself is not silent about the hidden God, but expounds upon the work and will of the hidden God in contrast the work and will of the revealed God. Luther's main prohibition is not against saying anything about the hiddenness of God but against speculating concerning the hiddenness of God and seeking to comprehend the full breadth and depth of the hidden

---

39. *BOW*, 170; WA 18:685.

God, or to call upon or revere the hidden God in prayer or worship, or to view the hidden God as the object of belief.[40] Bayer may use the doctrine of the hidden God systematically, but he does not use the doctrine to construct a cataphatic description of God, at least not in the sense that Luther prohibits. On the contrary, Bayer voices essential agreement with Luther here, saying that humans cannot pray to, worship, or believe in the hidden God, since the only place where humans can pray to, worship, or believe in God is the promise of the revealed God in the gospel of Christ wherein God communicatively and graciously reveals God's self to humans.[41]

Moreover, Luther essentially invites the kind of use of his doctrine of the hidden God in which Bayer engages, when he states in *The Bondage of the Will* that theologians must always distinguish between the hidden God and the revealed God anytime they are discussing God.[42] Bayer, even more thorough and consistent in doing this than is the reformer himself, takes this distinction between the hidden and revealed God into the realm of prolegomena, uses it as one of the factors to define the mode, method, and data of theology, and utilizes this doctrine as way to approach the position of the believer between the advent of Christ and the eschaton. To be sure, Luther does not use the doctrine of the hidden God in these ways in his theology as does Bayer. Bayer's use of the hiddenness of God to describe the mode of theology, to identify one of the three aspects of the method of theology via *Anfechtung*, to set up a third datum of theology apart from the law and the gospel, and to explain the existence of the believer as a lamenting pilgrim before the eschaton constitutes a significant development of Luther's doctrine of the hidden God beyond its original setting. This does not mean, however, that Bayer's use of the doctrine constitutes a misuse of Luther's teaching on the hidden God, for Bayer communicates the essential definition of Luther's view of God's hiddenness and does not fall into the kind of speculation about the hidden God against which Luther warns.

The Hidden God's Work in Anfechtung as the Problem of Evil

Bayer follows Luther in describing the hiddenness of God as coming to the believer through the experience of *Anfechtung* and develops this notion into part of his approach to the doing of theology and description of the justified believer's existence before the eschaton. But Bayer's description of the way

---

40. BOW, 170-171; WA 18:685-86.

41. Bayer, Martin Luther's Theology, 39; 198; *Bayer, Martin Luthers Theologie*, 36, 178-79.

42. BOW, 170; WA 18:685.

in which the hidden God comes to the believer through *Anfechtung* appears also to differ somewhat from Luther's. Luther describes the hidden God's work of *Anfechtung* as taking place through God's decree in reprobation, which forms the negative side of double predestination. As I have already demonstrated, Luther portrays the hidden God as condemning and putting to death the sinner through reprobation in order to save and raise to life the sinner through the election of the revealed God in Christ. Though Bayer identifies the question of double predestination as one of the two ways in which the hidden God encounters the believer in *Anfechtung*, he does not follow Luther in describing how this takes place nor does he dwell long on the hidden God's work in double predestination. Instead, Bayer quickly moves on to the problem of evil as the second way in which the hidden God encounters the believer in *Anfechtung* and discusses it at length, making it a significant piece in his theology of justification by describing it as the main venue for the hidden God's contradiction of God's justifying promise.

There is no precise equivalent in Luther's theology for Bayer's discussion of the problem of evil as the main venue for the work of the hidden God. Instead, Bayer's description of the hidden God's work in *Anfechtung* coming to the believer through the problem of evil is influenced by streams of thought other than Luther's alone. Most significantly, Bayer's discussion of the hidden God and the problem of evil as the contradiction of the promise of the opening and renewal of creation demonstrates the influence of Hamann's thought upon Bayer. Such a theme, however, also exhibits the very modern concern in Bayer's theology of the problem of evil, significant in the currents of modern thought from Gottfried Wilhelm Leibniz (1646–1716) to more contemporary scholars such as John Hick (1922–).[43] Although Bayer may demonstrate that he is influenced by developments in thought since Luther, even his description of the problem of evil as the venue for the believer's experience of the hidden God in *Anfechtung* is ultimately rooted in Luther's teaching on the hidden God.

Bayer's focus on the hidden God's work of wrath in *Anfechtung* encountering the believer through creation itself as a contradiction of the promised opening and renewal of creation certainly demonstrates the extent to which Bayer has been influenced by Hamann's views of God as author, the world as text, and creation as address from God.[44] It is important to bear in mind, however, that Bayer—unlike the German idealists—does

---

43. Cf. Leibniz, *Theodicy*. Hick, *Evil and the God of Love*.

44. Bayer, *Zeitgenosse im Widerspruch*, 75–83; Bayer, *A Contemporary in Dissent*, 54–62. Hamann, *Sämtliche Werke*, 2:140, 206. Bayer, *Gott als Autor*, 30–33. Bayer, *Autorität und Kritik*, 5–6. Bayer, *Schöpfung als Anrede*, 13–18. Cf. Hamann, *Sämtliche Werke*, 2:195–217.

not follow Hamann into a romantic panentheism that understands every single thing in nature to be positive and beneficial revelation of God. On the contrary, Bayer may utilize Hamann to describe how the hiddenness of God as a datum of theology forms the theologian, but he does this precisely in a negative way, showing a deeper agreement with Luther that any encounter with God outside of the specific revelation of God in the promise is an encounter with the hiddenness of God in which the human only experiences the wrath of God.[45]

Similarly, though Bayer's specific focus on the problem of evil as the way in which the believer experiences the hidden God's contradiction of the promise reflects a very modern concern and demonstrates his chronological distance from Luther, he does not follow enlightenment modernity in seeking to establish some form of theodicy to exonerate God from doing evil. That was, after all, the effect on theology from Leibnitz through Kant up to the present, to turn theology into theodicy. On the contrary, Bayer decries the various different kinds of theodicy evident in philosophy and theology from the Enlightenment to today, and returns instead to Luther's reformational position that the hidden God is actually responsible for working evil[46] and commends Luther's view that the only escape from evil is to be found in the promise of the revealed God in the gospel of Christ.[47]

Furthermore, though there is no direct equivalent in Luther's theology for Bayer's view of the believer's experience of the hidden God's attack on faith in *Anfechtung* through the abstract problem of evil, and though Bayer's use of the motif of God's wrestling with Jacob could even be seen in this light as an existential-philosophical abstraction of Luther's interpretation of the biblical text, there are several similar factors present in Luther's discussion of the hiddenness of God. These factors are Luther's teaching that the hiddenness of God is experienced by all humans as a "natural knowledge" of God evident in creation, Luther's statement that the hidden God works all things, and Luther's teaching on the three lights. Though these factors in Luther's thought do not amount to a view in which the hidden God is perceived at being at work in the problem of evil, Bayer develops from them a view in which the hidden God is active in contradicting the justifying promise of God through the believer's experience of the problem of evil.

---

45. Bayer, Martin Luther's Theology, 39–40, 198; Bayer, *Bayer, Martin Luthers Theologie*, 36–37, 186–87.

46. Bayer, Martin Luther's Theology, 200–205; Bayer, *Martin Luthers Theologie*, 180–85.

47. Bayer, Martin Luther's Theology, 212–13; Bayer, *Martin Luthers Theologie*, 191–92.

Yet, the fact that Bayer utilizes Luther's imagery of Jacob wrestling with the hidden God actually safeguards Bayer's notion of hiddenness from being completely modern, in the sense that such imagery protects Bayer's view from seeming like a reiteration of Kantian transcendentalism. Kant taught that God was part of the *noumena* or "thing-in-itself," of which the empirical senses could know nothing but that reason recognized as real within the mind.[48] While it might be tempting simply to equate Bayer's idea of the hidden God with Kant's concept of the *noumena*, the two are not the same. For, while Kant maintains that one cannot truly experience the *noumenon*, Bayer asserts that the hidden God is experienced. While Kant holds that the *noumenon* is known to reason but not experienced, Bayer argues that the hidden God is experienced but incomprehensible to reason.[49]

Nevertheless, Bayer does develop several factors in Luther's doctrine of the hidden God. The first factor in Luther's discussion of the hiddenness of God used by Bayer in the development of his view of God's hiddenness experienced by the believer through the problem of evil is the reformer's description in his *Lectures on Jonah* of the experience of the hiddenness of God in *Anfechtung* through the natural order. While Bayer's depiction of the hidden God contradicting the promise through the problem of evil experienced through creation is definitely influenced by Hamann's understanding of creation as a vehicle for divine address, this theme in Bayer's thought also has its roots in Luther's idea that there is a certain kind of knowledge of God immanent in creation.[50] Such a knowledge of God, according to Luther, ultimately is only a knowledge of God's wrath.[51] Though the believer may better understand that the experience of this knowledge is the experience of God's wrath, even the unbeliever experiences this wrath of God.[52] One can certainly find an echo of this description of God's wrath experienced through the natural order in Bayer's understanding of the hiddenness of God experienced through *Anfechtung*, but at the same time, Bayer goes a step further than Luther by identifying such experience as occurring within the believer's wrestling with the question of the problem of evil in the context of the promise he or she has already received from God in Christ.

---

48. Kant, *Critique of Pure Reason*, 268–75.

49. Ibid. Bayer, Martin Luther's Theology, 198–99; Bayer, *Bayer, Martin Luthers Theologie*, 178–79.

50. *LW* 19:54–55; *WA* 19:206.

51. *LW* 19:66–67, 75; *WA* 19:217–18, 226.

52. *LW* 19:66–67; *WA* 19:217–18.

The second factor that Bayer develops is Luther's statement that the hidden God works all things and not merely death and damnation.[53] This statement obviously leaves the category of God's hiddenness open to a variety of interpretations, at least with regard to the content of the hidden God's work. Moreover, when this is coupled with Luther's teaching in *The Bondage of the Will* that God brings about all things that come to pass through God's immutable will, a picture emerges from Luther's writing of the hidden God effecting everything that happens outside of the realm of justification. If this is true, then obviously the hidden God is the one responsible for evil. As Bayer observes, elsewhere in *The Bondage of the Will* Luther readily admits that evil and the devil are but tools for God's work.[54] Though Luther may not state directly that part of God's hidden work is the doing of evil in the world, and though the reformer certainly does describe the problem of evil as the venue for the hidden God's attack on faith in the promise through *Anfechtung*, one can see how such a development is no great stretch, considering how Luther leaves his description of the work of the hidden God open to this possibility. By developing the reformer's thought in this direction, Bayer demonstrates a certain fidelity to Luther's theology.

The third factor in Luther's thought that serves as basis for Bayer's identification of the problem of evil as a venue for the work of the hidden God through *Anfechtung* is Luther's teaching at the conclusion of *The Bondage of the Will* concerning the three lights.[55] In particular, Luther's idea expressed here that there are some questions that are answered by the light of grace in the gospel and some questions that will only be resolved eschatologically in the light of glory, serves as the basis for his idea of the believer's existence in the *Sitz im Leben* of lament before the eschaton as one of pilgrimage.[56] Though it should be noted here that the particular question that Luther identifies in the teaching on the three lights as unanswerable this side of the eschaton is that of double predestination and not of the problem of evil;[57] Bayer's move to interpret the problem of evil and the hiddenness

---

53. *BOW*, 170; WA 18:685.

54. Bayer, *Martin Luther's Theology*, 200-201; Bayer, *Bayer, Martin Luthers Theologie*, 180-81. *BOW*, 202-3; WA 18:709. The immediate context for this claim is Luther's dispute with Erasmus over whether God hardened Pharaoh's heart or Pharaoh hardened his own heart. In the final analysis, Luther maintains that God is ultimately responsible for hardening God's heart. Cf. *BOW*, 203-12; WA 18:709-14.

55. *BOW*, 317; WA 18:786.

56. Ibid. Bayer, *Martin Luther's Theology*, 211-13; Bayer, *Bayer, Martin Luthers Theologie*, 190-92.

57. *BOW*, 317; WA 18:786. Nestingen, "Introduction," in Forde, *The Captivation of the Will*, xiii.

of God eschatologically does not contradict the central meaning of Luther's teaching on the three lights, which is that there are some things in the work of God that are simply incomprehensible on this side of eternity.[58] Bayer's use of the teaching on the three lights may differ somewhat in content from Luther's original expression of this teaching, but it hardly contradicts the essence of it.

Although Bayer's use of the problem of evil to describe how the believer is encountered by the hidden God constitutes an interpretation of the hidden God's work that is outside of the definition and description of that given by Luther, and though Bayer replaces Luther's preeminent concern of double predestination with this venue for the work of the hidden God; this innovation of Bayer's is not a departure from but a development of Luther's doctrine of the hidden God. As I have related above, Luther's claim that the hidden God works wrath through the created order, his statement that the hidden God works all things, and his teaching on the three lights all serve as factors in this thought that Bayer utilizes to develop his own interpretation of the hidden God's work through *Anfechtung* as coming to the believer particularly through the problem of evil. This development and interpretation of Luther's doctrine of the hidden God may indeed reflect the modern concern of theodicy over and against the reformational or late-medieval concern of double predestination, which was foremost in Luther's mind, but it does not conflict with the essence of Luther's thought on the hidden God. Moreover, Bayer's evangelical and eschatological solution to problem of evil, via the fulfillment of the promise and the anticipation of that fulfillment, constitutes a radical departure from modernity and the rationalistic solutions to the problem that it offers and a definite return to the theology of Luther anchored in justification.

Bayer's Faithfulness to Luther

Regardless of the various differences between Bayer's description of the hiddenness of God and that of Luther or of any development of the reformer's doctrine of the hidden God in Bayer's theology, Bayer's discussion and use of this teaching of Luther's is marked by an underlying faithfulness to Luther's expression of the doctrine. The essence of this faithfulness consists of the fact that Bayer demonstrates fundamental agreement and continuity with Luther concerning the relationship between the hiddenness of God and the justification brought about by the revealed God through the gospel of Jesus Christ. This continuity may be seen in how Bayer defines the

---

58. *BOW*, 317; WA 18:786.

hiddenness of God, how he contrasts between the hiddenness of God and God's saving revelation of God's self in Christ, how he describes the attack of the hidden God in *Anfechtung*, and how he ultimately returns to God's work of justification, demonstrating that this is the ultimate and true trajectory of the work of the hidden God.

Moreover, Bayer agrees with Luther concerning the relationship of the doctrine of the hidden God to the revealed God's justification of the sinner by faith in Christ through the Word. Bayer's overall theology is characterized by an essential agreement with Luther's thought in terms of how Bayer understands God's justification of the sinner by faith in Jesus Christ to be the central subject matter of theology.[59] Bayer follows Luther in defining the entirety of his theology with reference to the theological center of justification, and the doctrine of the hidden God is no exception to this rule. Bayer defines the hiddenness of God as the opposite and contradiction of the justifying promise of the revealed God in Jesus Christ.[60] This definition, though certainly nuanced by Bayer's contemporary explanation of the doctrine of justification in terms of speech act, essentially mirrors Luther's definition of the hiddenness of God as God's work that is contrary and alien God's proper work of justification in Jesus Christ through the Word.[61] Like Luther, Bayer describes the hidden God as existing outside God's Word and contrasts God's hidden existence as a God of wrath with the existence of God revealed in God's Word as a God of grace, mercy and love. Whereas in justification, God reveals and gives God's self to the human through forgiveness and mercy, in hiddenness God does not forgive and is not merciful but displays wrath and kills and condemns the human.[62] Bayer sees the gulf between these two existences of God as being so great that he argues that they present the theologian with two distinct doctrines of God, the general doctrine of God and the doctrine of God as Trinity.[63] While Luther may not say this exactly in so many words, Bayer's distinction between the two doctrines of God certainly flows from Luther's distinction between the

---

59. Bayer, *Theology the Lutheran Way*, 98; Bayer, *Theologie*, 408–9. Bayer, *Martin Luther's Theology*, 37–39; Bayer, *Martin Luthers Theologie*, 34–36. "Justification as the Basis and Boundary of Theology," 287; *Leibliches Wort*, 34. LW 12:311; WA 40.2:328.

60. Bayer, *Martin Luther's Theology*, 213; Bayer, *Martin Luthers Theologie*, 192. Bayer, *Theology the Lutheran Way*, 95, 102, 104–5; Bayer, *Theologie*, 406, 413, 415–417.

61. BOW, 169–70; WA 18:684–85.

62. Bayer, *Martin Luther's Theology*, 39, 198; Bayer, *Martin Luthers Theologie*, 36, 178–79.

63. Bayer, *Martin Luther's Theology*, 339; Bayer, *Martin Luthers Theologie*, 308–9. Bayer, "Poetological Doctrine of the Trinity," 52–53; Bayer "Poetologische Trinitätslehre," 76–77; Bayer, *Gott als Autor*, "144–45.

existence of God hidden outside of revelation and the existence of God in revelation, especially in so much as Bayer argues that the gospel only applies to God revealed as Trinity as a God of grace, mercy, and love for sinners.[64] Like Luther, Bayer fundamentally understands the concept of God's hiddenness to be an existence and experience of God that is categorically different from and contradictory to God's justifying Word of promise.

Like Luther, Bayer identifies this contradictory work of the hidden God as occurring through the hostile encounter between God and the believer in *Anfechtung*, in which even the believer is not exempt from experiencing the hiddenness of God that contradicts the revealed God's promise of justification in the gospel.[65] Bayer further emulates Luther by adopting the reformer's depiction of the hidden God's attack in *Anfechtung* coming upon the believer like God fell upon Jacob at the banks of the Jabbok,[66] claiming that the wrestling match between God and Jacob entails an argument over the validity of God's promise.[67] Like Luther, Bayer states that in the experience of this attack of the hidden God in *Anfechtung*, the believer cannot truly distinguish whether this attack is coming from God or the devil, because the hidden God cannot be distinguished from the devil.[68]

Finally, Bayer's teaching concerning the hidden God is in essential concord with Luther's because in it Bayer clearly teaches that the only escape from the hidden God and the only way to know God as a gracious and merciful God is as God has revealed God's self in the promise of the gospel of Jesus Christ through proclamation of the Word in preaching and the Sacraments. Bayer identifies the revelation of God in Christ through the Word as the only place wherein God and the human being can coexist peacefully.[69] While in hiddenness God comes in wrath and works death and damnation, wrestling with the believer and contradicting belief, in the

---

64. Ibid.

65. Bayer, *Gott als Autor*, 297. Bayer, *Theology the Lutheran Way*, 63; Bayer, *Theologie*, 101. Bayer, *Martin Luther's Theology*, 37; Bayer, *Martin Luthers Theologie*, 33–34.

66. Bayer, *Theology the Lutheran Way*, 18–19; Bayer, *Theologie*, 39. Bayer, *Martin Luther's Theology*, 4, 40, 202–4, 228; Bayer, *Martin Luthers Theologie*, 2, 36–37, 182–84, 206. LW 6:135–40; WA 44:100–104.

67. Bayer, *Martin Luther's Theology*, 40; Bayer, *Martin Luthers Theologie*, 36–37. LW 6:135; WA 44:100–101.

68. Bayer, *Martin Luther's Theology*, 2–4, 40, 204; Bayer, *Martin Luthers Theologie*, 2–4, 36–37, 184. Bayer, *Zugesagte Gegenwart*, 77. Bayer, "Rupture of Times," 37–38; Bayer, *Gott als Autor*, 150–52. LW 7:175–76; WA 44:428–29.

69. Bayer, *Martin Luther's Theology*, 39; Bayer, *Martin Luthers Theologie*, 36.

promise, God comes revealed in Christ through gracious address, speaking life to the believer and deliverinmg the believer from *Anfechtung*.⁷⁰

For Bayer as well as for Luther the ultimate trajectory of the hiddenness of God is the revealed God's justification of the sinner through the gospel of Jesus Christ. Although Bayer departs from Luther by not connecting the hidden work of God to God's killing and condemning alien work in the law and in reprobation and substitutes instead the hidden God's work of *Anfechtung* through the problem of evil for Luther's understanding of the hidden God's alien work of killing and condemning in order to raise to life and save, ultimately Bayer too portrays the revealed God's salvation in Christ through God's promise as the trajectory of his teaching on the hidden God and identifies God's hidden work through *Anfechtung* as the means by which God drives the believer anew to God revealed in Christ through the Word.⁷¹ While Luther demonstrates this as taking place through the alien work of God in the law and reprobation in service of God's proper work of salvation in Christ, Bayer depicts it as happening through the believer's return to the promise through lament, which is brought on by the promise and sustains the believer until the final eschatological fulfillment of the promise.⁷² For Bayer, as for Luther, the only escape from the hidden God is the revealed God of the promise in Jesus Christ, and for both of these theologians, the only ultimate trajectory of the doctrine of the hidden God—as it is for the entirety of theology—is precisely the subject of the saving revelation of God in Christ through the promise of the gospel preached and distributed in Word and Sacrament.

Comparison to the Tradition

I have related how Bayer's articulation of the doctrine of the hidden God compares to Luther's. Bayer's relationship to the overall modern German Protestant theological tradition is more difficult to assess, because he enters very little into any significant conversation with that tradition concerning

---

70. Bayer, *Martin Luther's Theology*, 40; Bayer, *Martin Luthers Theologie*, 37. Bayer, *Schöpfung als Anrede*, 138–39.

71. Bayer, Martin Luther's Theology, 36–37; Bayer, *Martin Luthers Theologie*, 33–34. BOW, 170–71; WA 18:685–686. LW 5:43–50; WA 43:458–63. LW 6:259, 354, 398; WA 44:192, 264–65, 297–98.

72. Bayer, *Martin Luther's Theology*, 213; Bayer, *Martin Luthers Theologie*, 192. Bayer, *Martin Luther's Theology*, 11; Bayer, *Martin Luthers Theologie*, 10. "Rupture of Times," 46; Bayer, *Gott als Autor*, 159. Bayer, "God's Omnipotence," 90; Bayer, *Zugesagte Gegenwart*, 116. BOW, 170–71; WA 18:685–86. LW 5:43–50; WA 43:458–63. LW 6:259, 354, 398; WA 44:192, 264–65, 297–98.

the doctrine of the hidden God. He does directly engage a few figures from this tradition, but on the whole, he simply presents his own view of God's hiddenness as it flows from Luther's teaching in the matter. Nevertheless, some significant observations may be made concerning how Bayer's handling of Luther's doctrine of the hidden God compares to how other figures within this tradition have approached Luther's doctrine of the hidden God, as well as concerning how Bayer compares to the tradition as a whole in how he utilizes Luther's doctrine of the hidden God in his own theology.

Bayer's Discussion of the Tradition on the Hidden God

As I outlined in chapter three of this thesis, there exists a particular history of interpretation of Luther's doctrine of the hidden God within the modern German Protestant theological tradition. Bayer, however, only directly references four representatives of the modern German Protestant theological tradition concerning this doctrine. These four figures are Rudolf Otto, Werner Elert, Karl Barth, and Eberhard Jüngel. While he alludes to an agreement on some level with Otto on Luther's doctrine of the hidden God, he voices a disagreement with Elert, Barth, and Jüngel concerning this doctrine. Investigating these particular figures will help clarify why Bayer develops Luther's discussion of hiddenness.

Rudolf Otto

In his essay entitled, "God's Omnipotence," ("*Gottes Allmacht*") contained within the collection *Zugesagte Gegenwart*, Bayer briefly references Rudolf Otto's discussion of Luther's doctrine of the hidden God. In the midst of outlining his position that the tension experienced by the believer caught between the terrible hidden God and the revealed God of the justifying promise entails a distinction between two kinds of divine omnipotence and two doctrines of God, Bayer expresses some approval of how Otto sees the hiddenness of God at work in world religions other than Christianity.[73] Bayer states: "It was no accident that Rudolf Otto made direct reference to Luther's *Bondage of the Will* in his classic in the history of religions, *The Idea of the Holy* (1917); some of the elements that he brought to bear in that work may now, for example, be integrated into a general understanding of God, as we hone in on a more specific definition."[74]

---

73. Bayer, "God's Omnipotence," 95; Bayer, *Zugesagte Gegenwart*, 121.
74. Bayer, "God's Omnipotence," 95–96; Bayer, *Zugesagte Gegenwart*, 121.

Such a statement by Bayer demonstrates a similarity between himself and Otto concerning the nature of the experience of the hiddenness of God. While Otto does not directly relate the hiddenness of God specifically to *Anfechtung* or contrast it with the experience of God in the promise as Bayer does, he does portray the hidden God as being experienced by the human through world religions.[75] Bayer affirms this idea in his essay "The Plurality of the One God," wherein he states that the thing that Christians and followers of other religions share most in common is the experience of the hiddenness of God, forming the non-specific general knowledge of God, which he then distinguishes from the specific revealed knowledge of God as Trinity.[76]

But that is where Bayer leaves this line of thought. He does not elaborate on specific experiences or doctrines connected to the hidden God in world religions. Furthermore, Bayer does not share Otto's opinion that such general knowledge of God through the experience of divine hiddenness is a positive, beneficial knowledge, nor is it simply a kind of wrath that is the obverse side of God's love.[77] Such a view of God truly would be dualistic on account of using hiddenness as a necessary negative side to God's love, as if God's love and grace could not be truly known without their obverse. Rather, Bayer explicitly denies this, teaching that the saving knowledge of God in the gospel is to be found only through the "more specific definition" of God wherein God graciously reveals God's self as Trinity and "God for us"[78] and argues instead that the hiddenness of God contradicts the saving knowledge of God in the promise of the Triune revealed in Jesus Christ.[79] Therfore, although he mentions Otto's view in relation to world religions somewhat favorably Bayer's overall view of the hiddenness of God contradicts Otto's because Bayer understands hiddenness as altogether different than the supposedly necessary contrast or shadow of love.

Werner Elert

Bayer's assessment of Elert's interpretation of Luther's doctrine of the hidden God is somewhat varied. On the one hand, Bayer commends Elert for

---

75. Otto, *The Idea of the Holy*, 38–39.

76. Bayer, "The Plurality of the One God," 349; Bayer, *Zugesagte Gegenwart*, 105.

77. Otto, *The Idea of the Holy*, 97–101. Bayer, *Martin Luther's Theology*, 208; Bayer, *Martin Luthers Theologie*, 188.

78. Bayer, "The Plurality of the One God," 350, 352; Bayer, *Zugesagte Gegenwart*, 108.

79. Bayer, "The Plurality of the One God," 345; Bayer, *Zugesagte Gegenwart*, 102–3. Bayer, *Theology the Lutheran Way*, 102; Bayer, *Theologie*, 413.

his teaching on the wrath of God, expressed particularly through the latter's understanding of the experience of *Urerlebnis* (primal fear) under the law. Yet, on the other hand, Bayer also criticizes Elert for not distinguishing between God's wrath in the law and God's wrath in hiddenness but speaking of the two as if they were the same thing.

In the untranslated portion of his work, *Theologie*, Bayer addresses the thought of several theologians since the time of Luther, and one of these individuals is Elert. Among the themes in Elert's theology addressed by Bayer is that of the wrath of God. Bayer relates how Elert understands the wrath of the hidden God to be revealed through the law and experienced by the unbeliever in terms of *Urerlebnis* and more directly by the believer as condemnation through the law.[80] Bayer applauds Elert for recovering the theme of God's wrath from the intentional neglect it received in the modern German Protestant theological tradition after Ritschl's rebuke of Theodosius Harnack's positive reception of Luther's teaching concerning the wrath of the hidden God.[81] Bayer also speaks well of Elert's understanding of the human experience of wrath as *Urerlebnis*, which is somewhat close to but not quite identical with his own understanding of the believer's experience of the wrath of the hidden God through *Anfechtung*.[82]

Though Bayer commends Elert for recognizing the connection between the hidden God and God's wrath experienced through *Urerlebnis*, he disagrees with Elert concerning the relationship between divine hiddenness and God's word in the law and voices his dissent. Working from the basis of his own understanding that the hiddenness of God constitutes a third datum of theology and a third divine address to the human in addition to both the law and the gospel, Bayer criticizes Elert's view of the hiddenness of God revealed through the law, arguing that Elert has confused the terrible hiddenness of God with the law.[83] For Bayer, there is a difference between the wrath of God in the law and the wrath of God in hiddenness. Bayer argues that God's wrath in the law is an understandable wrath that points out sin directly to the sinner, but that the wrath of God in hiddenness is an incomprehensible wrath, which comes not through a specific word like the law does but through the experience of *Anfechtung*.[84] Bayer later repeats this criticism in a side note of a discussion of the proper way to distinguish

---

80. Bayer, *Theologie*, 292, 299–300.
81. Ibid., 290–91.
82. Ibid., 290–92.
83. Ibid., 308–9.
84. Ibid., 290–92. Bayer, *Martin Luther's Theology*, 196–98; Bayer, *Martin Luthers Theologie*, 177–79. Bayer, *Theology the Lutheran Way*, 102–104; Bayer, *Theologie*, 413–15.

between law and gospel in his book *Zugesagte Gegenwart* and references his own discussion of the data of theology in *Theologie* as setting forth the correct way to distinguish between the law, the gospel, and divine hiddenness.[85]

Although he notes both his approval of Elert's focus on the wrath of God in Luther's theology and his criticism of Elert's "confusion" of the law and divine hiddenness, Bayer could expand his critique of Elert's view of the hiddenness of God. More specifically, Bayer could address how Elert's view of *Urerlebnis* differs from his own understanding of the hidden God's work through *Anfechtung*. Though Bayer does not here identify it, the main difference between Elert's understanding of *Urerlebnis* and Bayer's understanding of *Anfechtung* is that while Elert sees the wrath of the hidden God in *Urerlebnis* befalling the unbeliever, Bayer describes *Anfechtung* as an experience that more specifically befalls the believer. For Bayer, the *Sitz im Leben* of *Anfechtung* presumes faith in the promise, since *Anfechtung* is experienced by the believer as the contradiction of the promise.[86]

In addition, Bayer does not critique Elert for failing to distinguish between the two kinds of hiddenness in Luther's theology. Elert speaks of the hiddenness of God in wrath and the hiddenness of God under the sign of suffering and the cross as if they are the same kind of hiddenness, saying that the hiddenness of God in wrath can be seen by the believer as the hiddenness of God under the sign of God's opposite.[87] Although this certainly conflicts both with Luther's teaching concerning the hidden God and Bayer's interpretation of this teaching, Bayer does not appear to mention this contradiction. This seems odd both because Bayer does address what he sees as a conflation of hiddenness with the law in Elert's thought, and because Bayer does not himself suffer from the inability to distinguish between the terrible hiddenness of God in wrath and hiddenness of God in revelation under the sign of God's opposite. Instead, Bayer explicitly states that these two kinds of hiddenness are not the same and must not be confused, and his description of God's hiddenness in wrath reflects this basic distinction.[88] Bayer certainly does not think that the terrible hiddenness of God in wrath can become comprehensible and acceptable to the believer as something working in concert with God's revealed salvation in Christ. On the contrary, Bayer insists that the hiddenness of God in wrath cannot be understood, even by the believer, that it contradicts the revelation of God's

---

85. Bayer, *Zugesagte Gegenwart*, 310, including n. 13.

86. Bayer, *Theologie*, 290–92. Cf. Elert, 71–73, 211–13. Bayer, *Martin Luther's Theology*, 39–40, 198; Bayer, *Martin Luthers Theologie*, 36–37, 178–79.

87. Elert, 71–73, 211–13.

88. Bayer, *Martin Luther's Theology*, 198; Bayer, *Martin Luthers Theologie*, 178–79.

salvation in the promise of Christ, and that it will continue to contradict the promise until the eschaton.[89] Whether or not Bayer identifies it, his view of God's hiddenness differs significantly from Elert's in that he clearly distinguishes between the two kinds of hiddenness in Luther's theology while Elert conflates them. Consequently, God's wrath is viewed by Elert as something less than the terrible wrath of God's hiddenness discussed by both Luther and Bayer. This softened understanding of God's wrath appears in Elert's theology through the assertion that ultimately the human being, and not God is responsible for and the cause of God's wrath.[90] Certainly this notion is foreign to Bayer's thought entirely, for in his understanding of wrath, Bayer depicts the hidden God as actively attacking the human sinner and even the believer, as God fell upon Jacob on the banks of the Jabbok.[91]

Bayer's critique of Elert does not speak to the difference between Elert's view of *Urerlebnis* and Bayer's understanding of the work of the hidden God in *Anfechtung* or Elert's confusion of the two forms of hiddenness. He does, however, commend Elert for at least discussing Luther's understanding of the hidden God and God's wrath without rejecting the reformer's views out of hand, while at the same time criticizing his identification of God's wrath in hiddenness with the wrath of God in the law. At this juncture, the question should be raised as to whether or not Elert might actually be closer to Luther in what Bayer argues against as "confusing" God's hiddenness with the law. As I have observed above, Luther does not make so fine a distinction between the hiddenness of God and the law as does Bayer. Bayer's criticism of Elert on this point is motivated less by a detailed exposition of Luther's arguments in *The Bondage of the Will* concerning the law and the hiddenness of God than it is by the distinction between the law and hiddenness in his own description of the three data of theology.[92] Furthermore, when compared with Luther's discussion of God's hiddenness in the context of his discussion of the work of God in the law and his argument that God's wrath is revealed against humanity through the law, as the reformer expresses in *The Bondage of the Will*, Elert's identification of God's hiddenness in wrath

---

89. Bayer, *Martin Luther's Theology*, 198, 210–13; Bayer, *Martin Luthers Theologie*, 178–79, 189–92.

90. Elert, 35–37, 71.

91. Bayer, *Martin Luther's Theology*, 39–40; Bayer, *Martin Luthers Theologie*, 36–37

92. *Theologie*, 309. *Zugesagte Gegenwart*, 310, see especially n. 13 where by references his own articulation of the distinction between the hiddenness of God and the law in *Theologie*. Cf. Bayer, *Theology the Lutheran Way*, 102–104; *Theologie*, 413–15. Bayer, *Martin Luther's Theology*, 196–98; Bayer, *Martin Luthers Theologie*, 177–79.

with God's work of wrath in the law seems to have more merit than Bayer admits.[93]

Perhaps Bayer distinguishes between the law and hiddenness in order to correct what he sees to be an incorrect view of God's wrath in Elert's theology, a view in which God's wrath is always to be understood merely as the opposite of God's love. Certainly, this does appear to be the result of Elert's interpretation of Luther on divine hiddenness, since he does not distinguish between God's hiddenness in revelation and God's hiddenness outside of revelation. Yet, in spite of the differences between Bayer and Elert, there is certainly more agreement between these two theologians concerning the hiddenness of God than there is between Barth and Bayer on this matter.

Karl Barth

The third figure in the modern German Protestant theological tradition whose view of divine hiddenness is mentioned by Bayer is Karl Barth. Bayer can hardly ignore Barth as the greatest theologian of the twentieth century and as a thinker who directly engages with and specifically rejects Luther's doctrine of the hidden God. Given Barth's response to Luther regarding this teaching, it should not be surprising that Bayer's interaction with Barth on this issue, though brief, is entirely negative.

Bayer uses Barth to typify one of the false solutions to the tension formed by the hidden God's contradiction of the promise. Bayer identifies Barth as the key proponent of the view that seeks to relieve this tension by teaching that God is love in essence and that God's wrath is merely the converse of God's love.[94] Bayer goes on to say that Barth and the practitioners of this view see all evil as having been done away with completely through God's work in Christ on the cross. Bayer commends Barth and his followers for taking seriously the centrality of God's graciousness revealed in Christ and the teaching that God is love, but he argues that in articulating this view, they no longer take seriously the real existence of evil in the world. Through a "perfected Christology" in which Christ's work on the cross is seen to have brought about the restitution of the fallen creation already, says Bayer, Barth gives "all of theology a serene face," thereby denying the terrifying hiddenness of God in wrath.[95]

---

93. *BOW*, 151–89, 297–98; WA 18:673–99, 772–73. Cf. *LW* 25:39–40, 262, 279–81; WA 56:45–47, 274–75, 291–94.
94. Bayer, *Martin Luther's Theology*, 208; Bayer, *Martin Luthers Theologie*, 188.
95. Bayer, *Martin Luther's Theology*, 208–9; Bayer, *Martin Luthers Theologie*, 188.

Barth's theology contains what is probably the strongest and certainly the most Christological rejection of Luther's doctrine of the hidden God articulated by anyone in the modern German theological tradition. According to Barth, there is no hiddenness of God outside of revelation, because God has revealed God's self completely in Jesus Christ, so that any divine hiddenness identified in theology must be a hiddenness of God inside revelation.[96] Moreover, the notion that there is any contradiction within God's existence or dealing with humans is completely abhorrent to Barth, since he views God's being, God's Word, and God's activity to be at one with itself without any variance at all. Though God may veil God's self in the midst of God's revelation event in Christ, such veiling takes place only for the purpose of unveiling and is part of the broader category of God's revelation. Barth eschews any concept of a division or contradiction between God revealed and God hidden, because God is "one."[97] God is one, says Barth, and that means one in will, as God has decided to exist only in the gracious relationship of God's revelation to humanity.[98] There can be no talk of God against God. Because of this, Barth rejects Luther's doctrine of the hidden God,[99] the Lutheran dialectic between law and gospel,[100] and the idea that there is any general presence of God in nature or anywhere else outside of Jesus Christ.[101] In this stance Bayer observes a Christological monism that is at odds with his own Lutheran understanding of the data of theology, wherein the law and divine hiddenness diverge from and contradict the word of God in the gospel.[102]

Eberhard Jüngel

Much of Bayer's criticism of Barth concerning the latter's rejection of Luther's doctrine of the hidden God applies to Eberhard Jüngel's rejection of this same teaching. In fact, Bayer links Jüngel together with Barth concerning the Christological monism that leads both of these theologians to reject

96. *CD* II.1, 210–11.
97. Ibid., 234–35.
98. Ibid.
99. *CD* II.2, 210–11.
100. *CD* I.2 437–38. 498–99. *CD* II.1, 236. *CD*, II.2, 511–13. *CD* IV.1, 347. *CD* IV.2, 534–35. Barth, *Freie reformierte Synode zu Barmen-Gemarke*, 30; quoted in Sasse, *Here We Stand*, 163. Barth, *The Word of God and Theology*, 160. Barth, "Gospel and Law," 71–73, 80–84.
101. *CD* II.1:86–87, 175. Barth, *No!* 74–75.
102. Bayer, "The Plurality of the One God," 342–43; Bayer, *Zugesagte Gegenwart*, 99–100.

the distinction between the hidden and revealed God as well as the distinction between law and gospel. In his essay, "The Plurality of the One God and the Plurality of the Gods," Bayer decries the way in which both Barth and Jüngel portray the being and work of God as existing in essential unity, saying that this Christological monism in their theologies is a hangover from the metaphysical tradition, which presupposes the absolutely necessity of unity in theology.[103]

Like his criticism of Barth regarding divine hiddenness, Bayer's analysis of Jüngel's position and his association of Jüngel with Barth regarding the rejection of Luther's doctrine of the hidden God is on target. Bayer identifies that Jüngel voices his agreement with Barth concerning the essential unity of God as Bayer astutely recognizes.[104] Yet, Jüngel goes beyond mere agreement with Barth in his own discussion of divine hiddenness. He argues directly against Luther that "There is no *terrible Deus absconditus who incites terror*."[105]

Jüngel's rejection of Luther's doctrine of the hidden God and his agreement with Barth in this respect over and against Luther flows from his view that God's very nature is that of love itself. Jüngel identifies God's nature with love ontologically and says that the two should not be differentiated, arguing that in theology love must be exalted to the status of a substance.[106] Since God is love within God's very being, there can be no distinct existence of God outside of God's self-revelation as a God of love, for God does not contradict God's self.[107] In this context, as Steven Paulson identifies in his work, "Analogy and Proclamation," Jüngel rejects of Luther's teaching that there is a terrible hiddenness of God outside of revelation, an existence in which God is not merely love but also wrath, arguing instead that all divine hiddenness is a hiddenness of God within God's self revelation as a God of love.[108]

Although Bayer does not name Jüngel in his discussion of the false resolutions to the tension formed by the hidden God's contradiction of God's promise, it is almost as if he is responding to Jüngel directly in his

---

103. Bayer, "The Plurality of the One God," 342; Bayer, *Zugesagte Gegenwart*, 99.

104. *TE* II, 141. Here Jüngel states the foundational theme of Barth's *Church Dogmatics* is that "God corresponds to himself" and that "Theology does well not to turn from this insight of Barth." Bayer references this when he depicts Bayer and Jüngel together. Bayer, "The Plurality of the One God," 342n17; Bayer, *Zugesagte Gegenwart*, 99n17.

105. *TE* II, 137. Italics are Jüngel's not mine.

106. Jüngel, *God as the Mystery of the World*, 316.

107. Ibid., 316–317. *TE* II, 141. Reinhuber, *Kämfende Glaube*, 105.

108. *TE* II, 136–137. Paulson, "Analogy and Proclamation," 95–96.

discussion of the false resolution that seeks to identify God's wrath in hiddenness as a form of God's love.[109] Here Bayer identifies that this attempt at resolution works from the position that "God is love."[110] Though this can be said of Barth, it certainly is true about Jüngel's rejection of Luther's doctrine of the hidden God. Furthermore, Bayer's charge that this attempt misuses Christology to give "all of theology a serene face" seems to apply directly to Jüngel's rejection of the hiddenness of God outside of revelation as a terrible hiddenness of God in wrath.[111] Whether or not Bayer names Jüngel specifically here, he certainly recognizes that Jüngel shares the Barthian rejection of Luther's doctrine of the hidden God made on the basis that this doctrine is incompatible with the overarching unitary theme of God's revelation of God's self as a God of love in Christ.[112]

Bayer addresses Otto, Elert, Barth, and Jüngel directly regarding their views on Luther's doctrine of the hiddenness of God. While he voices some agreement with Otto concerning the hiddenness of God being experienced in other religions, he openly disagrees with Barth and Jüngel regarding their monistic view of God's existence, revelation, and work. This should come as no surprise, since one of the basic assumptions underlying Bayer's theology is that God is not experienced by humans, even by believers in a single, uniform way. Bayer can thus voice his agreement with Otto that the hidden God is experienced in world religions beyond Christianity, even though he does not think that such an experience is saving or even beneficial to humans. On the other hand, while Bayer shares with Barth and Jüngel a concern to anchor theology firmly in God's revelation in Jesus Christ, he does not share their view that God's revelation in Christ is the only thing that informs theology, and teaches that in addition to the saving experience of this revelation, the believer experiences the contradiction of this revelation as well.

One of the basic assertions of Bayer's approach to theology is that there is not one but three data of theology, and that the data known as the law and divine hiddenness contradict the datum known as the gospel. Through his definition and description of the data of theology, Bayer depicts the

109. Bayer, *Martin Luther's Theology*, 208–209; Bayer, *Martin Luthers Theologie*, 188.

110. Bayer, *Martin Luther's Theology*, 208; Bayer, *Martin Luthers Theologie*, 188.

111. Bayer, *Martin Luther's Theology*, 208–209; Bayer, *Martin Luthers Theologie*, 188. For a more in-depth refutation of Jüngel's rejection of Luther's doctrine of the hidden God, see Reinhuber, *Kämpfender Glaube*, 105–10, 136–38.

112. "The Plurality of the One God," 342; *Zugesagte Gegenwart*, 99. For a further treatment of Jüngel's rejection of Luther's doctrine of the hidden God, see Paulson, "Analogy and Proclamation," 95ff.

discussion of theology as conflicted regarding how God relates to human beings. Bayer describes God as displaying wrath against humans in the law and in divine hiddenness, while showing grace mercy to humans as a God of love in God's justifying promise in the gospel.[113] For Bayer, the hiddenness of God outside of revelation and the notion that it contradicts the justifying promise of God in the gospel of Christ is so important to the theological enterprise, that he describes the experience of it as forming part of the mode of theology[114] and adopts this experience, which he categorizes as *Anfechtung*, as part of his theological method.[115] Because of his insistence that God is not experienced uniformly by believers but diversely and even in contradictory ways,[116] Bayer disagrees with the Christological monism of Barth and Jüngel. In fact, this disagreement makes Bayer's theology antithetical to theirs concerning the doctrine of the hidden God.

Bayer only briefly alludes to this antithesis, and he could certainly make more of it. Bayer could, for instance, discuss more how Barth and Jüngel's disagreement with Luther is in concert with the Barthian rejection of the distinction between the law and the gospel.[117] He could then relate his critique of Barth and Jüngel to Ebeling's critique of Barth concerning the relationship between the law and the gospel while articulating a contemporary Lutheran view of the dialectical data of theology over and against the monistic Barthian approach to the data of theology. Bayer could also be more specific concerning how Barth and Jüngel reflect the metaphysical tradition in their concern to preserve the unity of God at all costs. He might also discuss how sharing in this tradition, at least at this point, might display similarities between Barthian theology and Thomism or Barthian theology and the "Trinitarian Renaissance."

Much more could be said by Bayer concerning Barth and Jüngel's Christological monism, their rejections of Luther's doctrine of the hidden God, and the Barthian unitary approach to the law and the gospel. Bayer, however, simply points out their disagreement with the doctrine of the

---

113. Bayer, *Theology the Lutheran Way*, 102–4; Bayer, *Theologie*, 413–416. Bayer, *Martin Luther's Theology*, 196–199; Bayer, *Martin Luthers Theologie*, 177–79.

114. Bayer, *Martin Luther's Theology*, 11, 39–40; Bayer, *Martin Luthers Theologie*, 10, 36–37. Bayer, *Theology the Lutheran Way*, 113–14; Bayer, *Theologie*, 425–26. Bayer, "Rupture of the Times," 46; Bayer, *Gott als Autor*, 158–59.

115. Bayer, *Martin Luther's Theology*, 20–21, 35–37; Bayer, *Martin Luthers Theologie*, 19–20, 33–34. Bayer, *Theology the Lutheran Way*, 59–65; Bayer, *Theologie*, 96–105.

116. Bayer, "The Plurality of the One God," 343–44; Bayer, *Zugesagte Gegenwart*, 100–101.

117. As it is, he only mentions this connection once. Bayer, "The Plurality of the One God," 341; Bayer, *Zugesagte Gegenwart*, 99.

hidden God, illustrates that this is due to a Christological monism motivated by the view that God's nature is love and is so unitarily, and disagrees with them. Perhaps the small amount of attention that Bayer pays to Barth and Jüngel's rejection of the doctrine of the hidden God is because he ultimately shares with them a desire to center theology on the work of God's salvation of humanity in Jesus Christ. Certainly Bayer shares something with Barth and Jüngel in this regard that he does not share with a figure such as Wolfhart Pannenberg, who sees part of the mission of theology as providing humanity with a unified truth that encompasses and addresses all of reality.[118] Whether this implied agreement concerning the subject of theology motivates Bayer to limit his discussion of Barth and Jüngel's rejection of Luther's doctrine of the hidden God or not, he does identify their rejection, singling it out in particular amongst the various rejections of the doctrine articulated by figures within the modern German theological tradition.

Comparing Bayer to Others in the Tradition

Although Bayer only directly addresses Otto, Elert, Barth, and Jüngel concerning their views on Luther's doctrine of the hidden God, Bayer's articulation of this doctrine may also be compared to the views of others in the modern German Protestant theological tradition, especially those of Theodosius Harnack, Ritschl, Holl, Althaus, and Ebeling. Bayer demonstrates some continuity with Harnack, but also develops his own line of thinking concerning Luther's doctrine of the hidden God. While there are some similarities between Bayer and some of these figures, a comparison of Bayer's view of the doctrine of the hidden God with their views also demonstrates some significant differences.

Theodosius Harnack

Although he only cites Harnack's reception of Luther's doctrine of the hidden God and does not engage in direct discussion with him, it is clear that Bayer's view of this teaching of Luther's is close to Harnack's. Like Harnack, Bayer observes that God's hiddenness outside of revelation is a hiddenness of God in wrath.[119] Moreover, in continuity with Harnack, Bayer recognizes

118. Cf. Bayer, *Theology the Lutheran Way*, 98; Bayer, *Theologie*, 408–9. Bayer, *Martin Luther's Theology*, 37–38; Bayer, *Martin Luthers Theologie*, 34–35. Pannenberg, *Theology and Philosophy of Science*, 297–99.

119. T. Harnack, 93–97. Bayer, *Martin Luther's Theology*, 198; Bayer, *Martin Luthers Theologie*, 178–79.

that in his discussion in *The Bondage of the Will* of the distinction between the hiddenness and the revelation of God Luther posits two different and even conflicting ways in which God deals with human beings. Bayer agrees with Harnack that God reveals God's self as a God of grace, mercy, and love in Jesus Christ through the promise of the gospel in the Word, but that outside of God in Christ revealed in the Word, in the hiddenness of wrath, God encounters humans as the one who works all things who wills condemnation towards humans.[120]

Bayer does not engage directly with Harnack but merely references his work in conjunction with this doctrine.[121] Nevertheless, it may be seen how his own interpretation of Luther's doctrine of the hidden God is close to Luther's and how he, like Harnack but unlike others such as Barth and Jüngel, actually views this doctrine of the reformer as a positive contribution to theology and not as an embarrassment to be avoided or decried. Yet, Bayer also goes beyond Harnack in dealing with this doctrine. Bayer is not content merely to comment on how it features in Luther's thought as a Luther scholar, but, rather, he is intent upon using it in his own contemporary theology as a Lutheran systematic theologian.[122] In this way, Bayer develops Luther's doctrine of the hidden God in a way that Harnack does not.

Ritschl and Holl

Although Holl is part of the Ritschlian tradition in theology, as I have identified in chapter three of this thesis, he accepts Luther's doctrine of the hidden God as being in concert with the overall flow of the reformer's theology, while Ritschl rejects it altogether. In Ritschl's analysis, Luther's doctrine of the hidden God presents God as a God of wrath, and such an understanding of God contradicts what Ritschl perceives as the core teaching of Luther's theology, that God is a God of love.[123] Holl, on the other hand, sees Luther's doctrine of the hidden God as presenting a kind of divine wrath that is a wrath of God's mercy, which does not contradict God's love and which ultimately aims at salvation by driving the sinner to God revealed as a God

---

120. T. Harnack, 87–89. Bayer, *Martin Luther's Theology*, 39–40, 198; Bayer, *Martin Luthers Theologie*, 36–37, 178–79. Bayer, *Theology the Lutheran Way*, 104; Bayer, *Theologie*, 415–16.

121. Bayer, *Theologie*, 291, 299. Bayer, *Martin Luther's Theology*, 208; Bayer, *Martin Luthers Theologie*, 188.

122. Bayer, *Theology the Lutheran Way*, 93–94, 102–5; Bayer, *Theologie*, 403–4, 413–16.

123. Ritschl, *Geschichtliche Studien zur christlichen Lehre von Gott*, 84. *JR* 1:201.

of love in Christ, and identifies this wrath with Luther's view of reprobation in double predestination.[124]

Bayer and Ritschl

Bayer's reception of Luther's doctrine of the hidden God differs greatly from that of Ritschl. Ritschl completely rejects the doctrine because he finds it incompatible with Luther's doctrine of God revealed as a God of love in Jesus Christ as well as with his own theology centered on the idea of the given togetherness of humans and God because of this revelation.[125] Bayer, on the other hand, adopts this doctrine of the reformer, utilizing it as an indispensable feature in his approach to theology and in his theology of justification through the promise.[126]

The difference between Ritschl's and Bayer's interactions with Luther's doctrine of the hidden God is stark, but both Ritschl and Bayer do share one important common point. Both see the wrath of the hidden God as contradicting God revealed as a God of love in Jesus Christ.[127] The difference between the two is that, while Ritschl then rejects the doctrine of the hidden God, Bayer holds onto it in spite of the fact that it contradicts God's revelation as a God of love in Jesus Christ and addresses this very contradiction in his theology. Perhaps this is due in part to the fact that Ritschl's theology of given togetherness between God and humanity is based on neo-Kantian philosophy, but Bayer shows no loyalty to Kantian thought of any kind. Whether or not that is the case, the result of the difference between Ritschl and Bayer concerning how each views Luther's doctrine of the hidden God is shown in how Ritschl sacrifices this doctrine of Luther's for the sake of the unity of his theology around its theme of God revealed as a God of love, while Bayer's theology holds the wrath of God and the love of God in a dialectical tension. In Bayer's estimation, this tension will only be relieved eschatologically and cannot be so easily removed by false attempts at resolution.[128]

124. Holl, *What did Luther Understand by Religion*, 44, 54–55.

125. Ritschl, *Geschichtliche Studien zur christlichen Lehre von Gott*, 84. JR 1:201.

126. Bayer, *Martin Luther's Theology*, 11; Bayer, *Martin Luthers Theologie*, 10. Bayer, "Rupture of the Times," 46; Bayer, *Gott als Autor*, 158–159. Bayer, *Martin Luther's Theology*, 39–40; Bayer, *Martin Luthers Theologie*, 36–37. Bayer, *Theology the Lutheran Way*, 102, 104–5, 113–14; Bayer, *Theologie*, 413, 415–17, 425–26.

127. Ritschl, *Geschichtliche Studien zur christlichen Lehre von Gott*, 84. JR 1:201. Bayer, *Martin Luther's Theology*, 39; Bayer, *Martin Luthers Theologie*, 36. Bayer, *Theology the Lutheran Way*, 102, 104–5; Bayer, *Theologie*, 413, 415–17.

128. Bayer, "The Plurality of the One God," 343–44, 352–53; Bayer, *Zugesagte*

Although he briefly references Ritschl in a footnote when dealing with the Barthian attempt to resolve then tension, Bayer does not critique or even really address Ritschl's view of Luther's doctrine of the hidden God.[129] This is surprising given Ritschl's significance as a seminal thinker in the modern German Protestant theological tradition. Although Bayer implicates Ritschl by association with the Barthian attempt to resolve the tension between God's hiddenness and God's revelation of God's self as a God of love in Jesus Christ through the elimination of the hiddenness of God in wrath, Bayer does not hold Ritschl responsible for this view.[130] Bayer could develop a critique of Ritschl based on this association, especially since his criticism of Barth and Jüngel for rejecting the hiddenness of God for the sake of the unity of God as a God of love revealed in Christ fits Ritschl exactly. Bayer does not do this, however, but merely references Ritschl in passing, leaving the reader to connect the dots between him and the Barthian tradition concerning their common rejection of Luther's doctrine of the hidden God on the account that it contradicts the revelation of God as a God of love in Christ.

Bayer and Holl

The comparison of Bayer and Holl is the exact converse of the comparison of Bayer and Ritschl concerning this doctrine. While Bayer agrees with Ritschl that the hiddenness of God contradicts the love of God revealed in Jesus Christ, Holl does not see the hiddenness of God as contradicting God's revelation of God's self as a God of love. On the other hand, while Ritschl rejects this doctrine, Holl does not.

Bayer is then similar to Holl in that he does not reject Luther's doctrine of the hidden God out of hand, but he differs from Holl in terms of whether or not he sees any contradiction between the hiddenness of God outside revelation and the revelation of God as a God of love in Jesus Christ. While Bayer embraces the contradiction between the hiddenness of God and God's self-revelation as a God of love in Christ, utilizing this contradiction prominently in his theology, Holl rejects the idea that God's hiddenness contradicts God's revelation as a God of love in Christ.[131] In fact, Holl goes to great

---

Gegenwart, 100, 108–9. Bayer, "God's Omnipotence," 99; Bayer, *Zugesagte Gegenwart*, 125. Bayer, *Martin Luther's Theology*, 212–13; Bayer, *Martin Luthers Theologie*, 191–92.

129. Bayer, *Martin Luther's Theology*, 208, n. 40; Bayer, *Martin Luthers Theologie*, 188, n. 40.

130. Ibid.

131. Bayer, *Martin Luther's Theology*, 11, 39–40; Bayer, *Martin Luthers Theologie*,

lengths to demonstrate through Luther's teaching in his *Lectures on Romans* on double predestination that God's wrath in hiddenness is the alien work of God, which ultimately serves the proper work of God's salvation revealed in the gospel of Christ.[132] Yet, in doing so, Holl inevitably confuses Luther's notion of God's hiddenness outside of revelation with God's hiddenness in revelation, so that when Holl speaks of the hiddenness of God as God's alien work, it is unclear if he means the hiddenness of God outside of revelation, the hiddenness of God in revelation, or some amalgamation of the two.[133]

In the final analysis, although Bayer like Holl portrays God's wrath in hiddenness driving the sinner to the revealed God in Christ, he also insists that there is a real contradiction between God's wrath in hiddenness and God's revelation of God's self as a God of love in the justifying promise in the gospel of Jesus Christ.[134] Bayer argues that this real contradiction will never fully be resolved until the eschaton, and that, until then, believers exist as pilgrims and sojourners in the present age, caught between the promise and its contradiction in divine hiddenness.[135] Furthermore, as I delineated above, Bayer does not discuss the connection between God's wrath in hiddenness and reprobation that exists in Luther's theology. Perhaps it is partially an account of the neglect of this connection that Bayer sees the hiddenness of God as contradicting the revelation of God as a God of love in Christ while Holl does not.

In comparison to Ritshl and Holl, Bayer's view of divine hiddenness stands out from the views of these two theologians as one that sees the wrath of the hidden God as a real contradiction of God's self-revelation as a God of love in Jesus Christ but that does not exclude this doctrine from the discipline of theology on that basis. In contrast to both Ritschl and Holl, Bayer adopts Luther's understanding of God's hiddenness outside of revelation, even while admitting that this kind of hiddenness contradicts the love of God revealed in Christ. The result is that Bayer expresses a theology that is far more dynamic and dialectical than either of these two nineteenth-century theologians.

10, 36–37. Bayer, "Rupture of the Times," 46; Bayer, *Gott als Autor*, 158–59. Bayer, *Theology the Lutheran Way*, 102, 104–5, 113–14; Bayer, *Theologie*, 413, 415–17, 425–26.

132. Holl, *What did Luther Understand by Religion?*, 54.

133. Ibid., 44, 54–55.

134. Bayer, *Martin Luther's Theology*, 213; Bayer, *Martin Luthers Theologie*, 192.

135. Bayer, "The Plurality of the One God," 343–44, 352–53; *Zugesagte Gegenwart*, 100, 108–9. "God's Omnipotence," 99; *Zugesagte Gegenwart*, 125. Bayer, *Martin Luther's Theology*, 212–13; Bayer, *Martin Luthers Theologie*, 191–92.

Paul Althaus

The comparison between Bayer and Althaus follows the same general structure of that between Bayer and Ritschl. Althaus maintains that Luther's doctrine of the hidden God presents God as a God of wrath and thus differs from the hiddenness of God in revelation and contradicts the teaching that God reveals God's self as a gracious, merciful, and loving God in Jesus Christ. Althaus then rejects Luther's doctrine of the hidden God on this basis.[136]

Although Bayer does not engage with or even mention Althaus directly in regard to Luther's doctrine of the hidden God, it is possible to draw up a basic comparison of their respective views on the hiddenness of God. Bayer and Althaus essentially agree that Luther understands the hiddenness of God outside of revelation as a hiddenness of God that is different from God's hiddenness in revelation and that this hiddenness outside of revelation is a hiddenness of God in wrath that contradicts God's revelation of God's self as a God of grace, mercy, and love in the gospel of Christ.[137] Like Althaus, Bayer also fails to observe the connection in Luther's thought—particularly in *The Bondage of the Will*—between the condemnation of God in the law and the wrath of God in hiddenness, and perhaps the neglect of this connection causes both to fail to see how Luther sees part of the hidden God's work as consisting of killing in order to raise up and damning in order to save.[138] Yet, unlike Althaus, Bayer does not articulate a radically altered view of the law and the gospel in which the law (or the command) has the positive use of serving as the original basis of the relationship between God and humanity and in which the gospel is a mere interruption in this law-based relationship. Instead, even Bayer's notion that hiddenness constitutes a third datum of theology that is distinct from the law still ultimately serves the fundamental theme of God's justification of the sinner and renewal of all creation through the promise of God in the gospel alone.

In spite of their agreement on the fact that God's hiddenness outside of revelation contradicts God's self-revelation as a God of grace, mercy, and love in Christ through the Word, Bayer and Althaus diverge in their responses to this teaching of Luther's. Althaus utterly rejects Luther's doctrine of the hidden God, saying that it constitutes a teaching in which the reformer advocates knowing God outside of God's revelation in Christ and

---

136. Althaus, *The Theology of Martin Luther*, 278–79.

137. Ibid. Bayer, *Martin Luther's Theology*, 39–40, 198; Bayer, *Martin Luthers Theologie*, 36–37, 178–79.

138. Bayer, *Martin Luther's Theology*, 196–97; Bayer, *Martin Luthers Theologie*, 177–78. Bayer, *Theology the Lutheran Way*, 102–4; Bayer, *Theologie*, 413–15.

outside of the Word.[139] Bayer neither rejects this doctrine nor does he see in it Luther advocating that humans know God outside of Christ and the Word. On the contrary, Bayer recognizes that Luther teaches exactly the opposite: that humans cannot know God in hiddenness, for they can only know God in Christ and through God's gracious speech of promise in the Word.[140]

While there is a great similarity between Bayer and Althaus in that both see God's wrath in God's hiddenness outside of revelation as contradicting the revelation of God in Christ as a God of grace, mercy, and love, the difference between how each react to this teaching of Luther's could hardly be greater. Althaus rejects this teaching, but Bayer utilizes it as an essential feature of his theology. The significance of this difference should not be underestimated. Althaus stands as one of the greatest twentieth-century Luther scholars, whose work has been utilized by students and scholars throughout the world. Now, however, Bayer—an equally important Luther scholar of a more recent generation—has recovered Luther's important doctrine of the hidden God, which Althaus had previously discarded, and uses it prominently in his theology. Certainly, Bayer has not been the only figure in the modern German Protestant tradition in theology since Althaus to accept Luther's doctrine of the hidden God. As I relate below, Gerhard Ebeling has done so as well. Yet, Ebeling has not adopted the hiddenness of God as an integral and even foundational part of his theology as Bayer has done.

Gerhard Ebeling

Bayer thanks Ebeling in the foreword of his published dissertation, *Promissio*, and he can be seen as extending some of Ebeling's thought, especially his linguistic approach to theology through Luther's teaching concerning the Word.[141] Bayer, somewhat understandably, does not enter into a direct critique of Ebeling, but we can note several differences that develop.

First, like Elert, Ebeling does not clearly distinguish between the two kinds of hiddenness in Luther's theology. While Bayer does distinguish between the hiddenness of God in revelation and the terrible hiddenness of God outside of revelation in wrath, Ebeling speaks simply of God's hiddenness. Instead, Ebeling speaks both of God's hiddenness in suffering and the cross and the incomprehensible hiddenness of God who works all things,

---

139. Althaus, *The Theology of Martin Luther*, 277.
140. Bayer, *Martin Luther's Theology*, 39; Bayer, *Martin Luthers Theologie*, 36.
141. Bayer, *Promissio*, 8.

including wrath and damnation both under the same generic title of "the hiddenness of God."[142]

A second difference between Bayer and Ebeling regarding the interpretation of Luther's doctrine of the hidden God is that, like Elert, but unlike Bayer, Ebeling identifies the work of the hidden God as God's alien work, wherein God damns in order to save and kills in order to raise to life. He even links Luther's teaching on the hidden God in *The Bondage of the Will* to the alien work of God as described in the reformer's earlier writings.[143] Ebeling does not identify this condemning, alien work of the hidden God with God's decree of reprobation in double predestination. He does, however, come very close to the identification of double predestination with the alien and proper works of God hidden and revealed and certainly comes closer to Luther than does Bayer in this respect.

The third difference between Bayer's interpretation of Luther's doctrine of the hidden God and Ebeling's interpretation of this teaching is that, while Bayer describes the work of the hidden God as coming through *Anfechtung*, Ebeling does not.[144] It is not as if Ebeling denies this or as if there is anything in his thought that contradicts this. In fact, his understanding of the hidden God working an alien and hidden work to condemn the sinner in order to save the sinner could even be read in harmony with the idea that the hidden God does this specifically through *Anfechtung*. Yet, Ebeling does not state this, and in this way, Bayer seems to identify something in Luther's teaching concerning the hiddenness of God—especially as contained in some of the reformer's later works—that Ebeling does not articulate.

Although Bayer's interpretation of Luther's doctrine of the hidden God conflicts with Ebeling's interpretation of this doctrine on these points, there are also some noteworthy congruities between these two theologians concerning this doctrine. The first of these similarities regards how each of these two defines the hiddenness of God. Although Bayer distinguishes between the hiddenness of God in revelation from the terrible hiddenness of God outside of revelation and Ebeling does not, Bayer's definition of the hiddenness of God as God's incomprehensible wrath is almost exactly the same as Ebeling's definition of this hiddenness of God.[145]

The second similarity is that neither one identifies the connection between the hiddenness of God and God's work of condemnation in the law.

---

142. Ebeling, *Luther*, 226–28, 240.

143. Ibid., 236–37.

144. Bayer, "Rupture of Times," 46; Bayer, *Gott als Autor*, 159. Bayer, *Martin Luther's Theology*, 11, 210–14; Bayer, *Martin Luthers Theologie*, 10, 189–92.

145. Bayer, *Martin Luther's Theology*, 198; Bayer, *Martin Luthers Theologie*, 178–79. Ebeling, *Luther*, 240.

While Ebeling comes close, but does not finally point out this connection,[146] Bayer denies the connection outright.[147] Yet, neither sufficiently addresses how Luther's *The Bondage of the Will* frames the discussion of God's hiddenness within a larger discussion of God's work in the law. In this way, both Ebeling and Bayer fail to relate an important part of Luther's doctrine of the hidden God in its original context.[148]

The third similarity between Bayer's view of the hidden God and that of Ebeling regards how both interpret Luther as attributing evil and the work of the devil to the hidden God. Both of these theologians are essentially correct in their understanding that that, for Luther, nothing is outside of God's will. According to both of them, for the reformer, this means that in addition to God's condemning work, the hiddenness of God, which encompasses "all things," includes the evil that occurs in the world and even the devil's work, since nothing is outside of the will of the hidden God.[149]

The final and most important similarity lies in how both of these theologians define the relationship between the terrible hidden God of wrath and the revealed God of grace, mercy, and love in Jesus Christ. Both Bayer and Ebeling describe the terrible hiddenness of God as standing in radical contradiction to God's revealed salvation through the promise of God in Jesus Christ.[150] Both also argue that although there may be a human experience of the hidden God in the natural order, such an experience of God can never be considered a true knowledge of God and certainly in no way a knowledge of God as a merciful God, since this comes only through God's revelation in Jesus Christ through God's saving Word of the promise in the gospel.[151]

Bayer, however, goes beyond Ebeling even in these points concerning the hiddenness of God upon which they agree. In fact, it is not unreasonable to think that Bayer adopts these aspects of his teacher's interpretation of Luther's doctrine of the hidden God and develops them further. Bayer embodies Ebeling's understanding of the hiddenness of God in wrath as God's incomprehensible working of the human's condemnation and of all things,

---

146. Ebeling, *Luther*, 137, 236–37.

147. Bayer, *Theology the Lutheran Way*, 101–2; Bayer, *Theologie*, 413–14. Bayer, "The Plurality of the One God," 343; Bayer, *Zugesagte Gegenwart*, 100.

148. *BOW*, 151–89; WA 18:673–99.

149. Bayer, *Martin Luther's Theology*, 202–6; Bayer, *Martin Luthers Theologie*, 182–86. Ebeling, *Luther*, 240–41. Cf. *BOW*, 202–3; WA 18:709.

150. Ebeling, *Luther*, 270–72. Bayer, *Martin Luther's Theology*, 39–40; Bayer, *Martin Luthers Theologie*, 36–37.

151. Ebeling, *Luther*, 270–72. Bayer, *Martin Luther's Theology*, 39–40; Bayer, *Martin Luthers Theologie*, 36–37.

and that this hiddenness of God stands in radical contradiction to God's salvation given in the promise of Jesus Christ. Bayer, like Ebeling, also fails to connect this hidden work of God to God's work in the law. Furthermore, Bayer maintains with Ebeling that this hiddenness encompasses even evil and the work of the devil and is experienced through the natural order.

Bayer develops these aspects of Ebeling's interpretation of Luther's doctrine of the hidden God into a systematic view of the hiddenness of God in which the hiddenness of God in wrath is so distinguished from the revelation of God that it is even distinguished from the hiddenness of God in revelation,[152] and in which the distinction between the hiddenness and revelation of God runs so deep that it constitutes a distinction in the doctrine of God between a general knowledge of God as the hidden God and the Christian knowledge of God as Triune.[153] In this view developed by Bayer, the hidden God works evil particularly through the believer's experience of *Anfechtung*, which comes inescapably through the problem of evil so perceptible by the believer through the created order.[154] Above all, Bayer's development of Ebeling's interpretation of Luther's doctrine of the hidden God can be seen in how Bayer utilizes this doctrine systematically as an essential building block of his approach to doing theology and to his theology of justification by the promise. While Bayer may agree significantly with Ebeling concerning the historical-theological task of establishing what exactly Luther's doctrine of the hidden God was, he goes beyond Ebeling in using this doctrine systematically.

Summary

Throughout his theological works, Bayer demonstrates a deep desire to undertake the task of systematic theology from a decidedly Lutheran perspective. Bayer develops his approach to doing theology from Luther, utilizing insights from the reformer to define the mode, method, data, and subject matter of theology. Like Luther, Bayer centers his theology on the teaching of justification by faith alone, and has brought new focus to how Luther

---

152. Bayer, *Martin Luther's Theology*, 198; Bayer, *Martin Luthers Theologie*, 178–79.

153. Bayer, *Martin Luther's Theology*, 337–340; Bayer, *Martin Luthers Theologie*, 306–9. Bayer, "Poetological Theology," 165; Bayer, *Gott als Autor*, 15. Bayer, *Zugesagte Gegenwart*, 177. Bayer, The Plurality of the One God," 350; Bayer, *Zugesagte Gegenwart*, 106. Bayer, *Schöpfung als Anrede*, 161. Bayer, "Der neue Mensch," 126–27; Bayer, *Zugesagte Gegenwart*, 244–45. Bayer, "Der Glanze der Gnade," 80. Bayer, *Gott als Autor*, 272.

154. Bayer, *Martin Luther's Theology*, 202; Bayer, *Martin Luthers Theologie*, 182. Bayer, "Creation as History," 261; Bayer, *Zugesagte Gegenwart*, 229. Bayer, "God's Omnipotence," 92–93; Bayer, *Zugesagte Gegenwart*, 119.

sees justification flowing from God's active word of promise. Bayer remains faithful to Luther's essential of justification and to the reformer's notion that justification is the center of all theology, even as he interprets this doctrine in a contemporary manner through the linguistic philosophies of J. L. Austin and Johann Georg Hamann. Moreover, Bayer develops the connection between justification and creation in the reformer's thought into a robust creational theology of justification, wherein justification and creation are inseparable and mutually define one another.

In faithfulness to Luther and with an eye toward using Luther to construct a contemporary Lutheran theology, Bayer anchors all of his theological teachings firmly within the central doctrine of justification by the promise. Bayer's interpretation and use of Luther's doctrine of the hidden God is no exception to this general rule. Although he differs from the reformer regarding the relationships between the law/gospel dialectic and the double-willing of God in predestination to the hiddenness of God, Bayer largely adopts the reformer's precise teaching on divine hiddenness and uses it in his own theology of justification.

Bayer adopts Luther's definition of the hiddenness of God outside of revelation as a human experience of the divine in which God's dealing with the human is ultimately incomprehensible and in which God wills the death and damnation of the human and wills all things that happen. Like Luther, Bayer delineates that this hiddenness of God is not the hiddenness of God in revelation, wherein God reveals God's self under the sign of suffering and the cross. Bayer reflects Luther's view that the hiddenness of God outside of revelation is a terrifying hiddenness of God, which radically contradicts the saving revelation of God in the gospel of Jesus Christ through the Word, and in which the human cannot truly know God and cannot coexist with God. Bayer further reflects Luther's own view that the hidden God contradicts and attacks faith in the promise of God in the gospel through trials sent to the believer through the experience of *Anfechtung*.

Bayer does not, however, share Luther's view that the hidden God's work condemnation parallels the condemning work of God in the law. Instead, Bayer argues that the hiddenness of God is not to be identified with the work of God in the law, but that divine hiddenness constitutes a third address of God in addition to and in distinction from the law and the gospel. Similarly, Bayer does not address the parallel between Luther's teaching concerning double predestination, that God damns the sinner through reprobation in order that the sinner may be saved as parallel to the condemning work of the hidden God, but rather Bayer briefly identifies the question of double predestination, which arises in the mind of the believer, as one of the forms of the hidden God's attack through *Anfechtung* on faith in the promise.

Bayer does not simply reconstruct his understanding of what Luther meant by the hiddenness of God but also develops the reformer's understanding of divine hiddenness for use in his own theology. More specifically, Bayer broadens the space that the hiddenness of God occupies in theology beyond its original place as an aspect of Luther's theology to a factor that determines Bayer's very approach to theology and the *Sitz im Leben* of the justified sinner who exists in the rupture of the ages between the cross and the eschaton, which forms the starting point for his theology of lament. Furthermore, Bayer develops the scope of the believer's experience of *Anfechtung* to include the existential question of the problem of evil. Though these features of Bayer's thought on divine hiddenness are certainly developments and not mere extrapolations of the reformer's teachings, they are developments from possibilities left open by Luther himself, including the reformer's statements in *The Bondage of the Will* that one must always distinguish between the hidden God and the revealed God anytime one is speaking of "God" and that the hidden God wills all things.

Ultimately, Bayer is essentially faithful to the basic thrust of Luther's doctrine of the hidden God and indeed to the core of his theology. This is demonstrated in how Bayer defines hiddenness from the statement of its relationship to the gospel (i.e. that it radically contradicts God's justifying promise in Christ) but that it ultimately also drives the believer back to that same gospel through the experience of *Anfechtung* and the believer's response of lament. This level of interaction with Luther's doctrine of the hidden God, with its grounding in the core teaching of God's justification of the sinner and with its existential dimension in *Anfechtung* that appears in the work of Bayer is without equal in the modern German Protestant theological tradition.

Bayer stands out amongst his fellow members of this tradition not only because he actually addresses Luther's doctrine of the hiddenness of God in wrath—from which many figures in this tradition shy away completely—but also because he understands the relationship between the heart of Luther's theology and this doctrine as embodied through *Anfechtung*, and because he positively develops this teaching of Luther through his own theology of lament. Bayer stands apart from Ritschl, Althaus, Barth, and Jüngel because he does not immediately dismiss the doctrine of the hidden God from Luther's theology on the notion that it is utterly incompatible with salvation in Christ. Instead, Bayer's reception of Luther's doctrine and his use of it in his own theology is characterized by a dialectical tension between the hiddenness of God in wrath and God's work of justification in Christ, which divine hiddenness radically contradicts.

Although he also agrees with each of them to a certain extent, Bayer also differs from Elert and Ebeling in that he depicts the tension between God's hiddenness and God's gracious revelation in the gospel of Christ as being greater than they do. This is perhaps most readily apparent in how Bayer distinguishes between the hiddenness of God in revelation and the terrible hiddenness of God in wrath outside of revelation, while Elert and Ebeling fail to make this distinction. This, however, can also be observed in how, unlike Elert and Ebeling, Bayer insists that the law and God's hiddenness are two different data of theology and two different human encounters with the divine.

Bayer differs even from Theodosius Harnack regarding Luther's doctrine of the hidden God. Bayer agrees with Harnack's interpretation of the hiddenness of God to a great extent, and Bayer is perhaps the best interpreter of this doctrine since Harnack. Nevertheless, he goes beyond Harnack in that he uses this doctrine systematically in his theology instead of merely interpreting it.

While it is true that in some sense it could be said that Otto uses Luther's doctrine of the hidden God systematically, but Bayer's use of this doctrine may still be seen to be an original contribution. This is because Bayer, unlike Otto, actually understands, preserves, communicates, and develops the essential thrust of the doctrine of the hidden God as Luther expresses it, while Otto does not. Otto argues that the human's true knowledge of God begins with the hidden God of wrath and prescribes this knowledge. Bayer in no way advocates this but to the contrary maintains in concert with Luther that one cannot know the hidden God but that one can only know God as God is revealed in Christ through the Word.

Bayer differs from and goes beyond the figures before him in the modern German Protestant theological tradition who address Luther's doctrine of the hidden God. While his predecessors neglected this theme in their discussions of this teaching of Luther's, Bayer discerns how Luther sees the hidden God at work, contradicting faith in the promise through the trials the hidden God sends upon the believer in *Anfechtung*. Moreover, the way in which Bayer describes this as taking place constitutes an original contribution to this tradition. In elucidating how the hidden God encounters the believer through *Anfechtung*, Bayer functions as a Lutheran theologian who not only interprets Luther's doctrine of the hidden God in the context of centering all theology in justification as Luther did, but also as one who utilizes and even develops Luther's doctrine of the hidden God. This development is shaped by Bayer's own theological concern of justification as coming through God's speech act of promise, which opens and renews creation and consists of Bayer's description of divine hiddenness as God's radical contradiction of God's justifying promise in the gospel of Jesus Christ.

Building on Luther's description of this hiddenness of God in wrath and also expounding his own thoughts, Bayer characterizes the hidden God's contradiction of the promise as encountering the believer in the experience of *Anfechtung* particularly through the problem of evil and forming a tension in the believer's experience of God's omnipotence and knowledge of God that will not be relieved until God's final, eschatological fulfillment of the promise. Bayer then constructs a theology of lament to describe the pilgrim existence of the believer in faith in the midst of such contradiction before the eschaton. This exploration and development of Luther's doctrine of the hidden God in Bayer's theology, while firmly rooted in Luther's thought and in the central reformational teaching of justification by faith in Christ alone, constitutes something genuinely new in the modern German Protestant tradition in general and in Lutheran theology more specifically. In the following chapter, as I conclude this thesis, I will discuss the possibilities Bayer's teaching on hiddenness may evoke for those undertaking systematic theology as Lutherans today.

9

Review, Assessment, and Possibilities

OSWALD BAYER HAS MADE notable contributions to the field of Luther studies as well as to the study of theology within the modern German Protestant tradition. Bayer's contributions to these fields consist of his unique, Lutheran approach to theology and especially his theology of justification by the promise. Part of that theology is Bayer's teaching on the hidden God. Both Bayer's interpretation of Luther's doctrine of the hidden God and his own discussion of hiddenness in his theology are formed by his understanding of the prominence and nature of justification, making Bayer perhaps the most faithful interpreter of Luther's doctrine of the hidden God within the modern German Protestant theological tradition.

In this final chapter of my thesis, I will summarize the view of hiddenness that emerges from Bayer's Lutheran approach to doing theology and his contemporary Lutheran theology of justification and discuss how this view might be helpful in constructive theology today. In addressing the constructive potential of Bayer's view of the hidden God I will relate the criticisms his view has received as well as my own assessment of his view. Finally, I will address the value of engaging with Bayer's unique understanding of the hiddenness of God for the constructive task of systematic theology, including a few possibilities for how Bayer's view of hiddenness and the study of it could be further developed, as well as how Bayer's teaching on the hidden God and the theology in which he expresses it might be relevant and useful for Lutheran theologians and Christians in today's world.

Review

According to Luther, the hiddenness of God outside of God's revelation in Jesus Christ consists of the unpreached God's working of death, damnation, and all things. In Luther's theology, the hidden God's work of death and condemnation parallels God's condemning work in the law, and the reformer actually delineates his doctrine of the hidden God in the context of his description of God's work in the law. Luther's description of the hidden God's will and work also parallels his understanding of God's damning the sinner in order to save the sinner, expressed not only in his later works but also prominently in his early *Lectures on Romans*.

Ultimately, Luther's definition of the hiddenness of God outside of revelation is determined by the center of his theology: God's justification of the human sinner in Jesus Christ. In *The Bondage of the Will*, Luther defines the will and the work of the hidden God as the opposite of God's will and work of justifying the sinner as God is revealed in Jesus Christ. Furthermore, in some of his later works, Luther describes the work of the hidden God as coming through the trials sent to the believer through *Anfechtung*, making clear that such contradiction of the revealed God's work of justification in Christ is not limited to those outside of faith but includes those within it. In the final analysis, however, the work of the hidden God, according to Luther, is one that drives the sinner (including the justified sinner) to despair of self-efforts and false belief in "free will" in order that the grace of God revealed in the gospel of Jesus Christ might save and comfort the sinner through faith.

After a time of neglect, interest in Luther's doctrine of the hidden God was piqued in the modern German Protestant theological tradition during the nineteenth century by Theodosius Harnack, who correctly identified this teaching of the reformer's as a teaching of God's wrath. Since Harnack, figures within this tradition have addressed this doctrine of Luther's but have tended either to reject it categorically, to conflate it with God's hiddenness in revelation, or—in the case of Otto—to radically reinterpret it in such a way that it no longer resembles Luther's actual teaching but contradicts it. Bayer does not, however, embody any of these tendencies. On the contrary, in the context of how Luther's doctrine of the hidden God has been interpreted in the modern German Protestant tradition, Bayer's discussion of this teaching appears as something genuinely new and even refreshing.

Bayer does not reject Luther's doctrine of the hidden God but embraces it and even seeks to use it in his own theology. Bayer excels other figures in the tradition in that he not only correctly understands that God's hiddenness outside of revelation is different from God's hiddenness in revelation and that the terrifying hiddenness of God outside of revelation is incomprehensible and condemns the sinner in wrath, but also in that he, unlike others in the tradition, observes that Luther sees the work of the hidden God as being played out through *Anfechtung*. Above all, however, Bayer supersedes others in the tradition in that he correctly sees Luther as defining the hiddenness of God in opposition to God's justification of the sinner and then utilizes this in his own theology.

For Luther, even the notion of the hiddenness of the unpreached God ultimately is governed by his central teaching of God's justification of the sinner in Jesus Christ, even if the relationship of hiddenness to justification is a negative one. Bayer's discussion of divine hiddenness echoes the theological concern of the reformer that all aspects of theology be centered on justification. Bayer's view of the hidden God resonates with Luther's teaching on hiddenness in that it also ultimately defines God's hiddenness outside of revelation through its relationship to justification, even if Bayer does not follow Luther's exact teaching concerning the hiddenness of God at every point. Bayer does not adopt Luther's teaching on hiddenness with reference to the parallels between the hiddenness of God and God's work in the law and between the hiddenness of God and God's decree of damnation, but he does follow Luther in the more basic definition of God's hiddenness outside of revelation as God's work that contradicts God's justification of the sinner through God's Word of the gospel in Christ.

Furthermore, Bayer adopts Luther's view of the hiddenness of God as the opposite of the revealed God's salvation of the sinner in Christ and develops it into a significant feature in his own theology. For Bayer, the hiddenness of God functions in a formative role in the doing of theology. Bayer utilizes Luther's notion of the terrible hiddenness of the unpreached God in his explanation of the mode, method, and data of theology. For Bayer, the mode of theology is determined by the human's experience of the living God, and part of this experience is the experience of God hidden outside of God's address of law and gospel.[1] Bayer proceeds to incorporate the hiddenness of God further into his approach to theology by giving it a place in his theological method via the specific experience of the believer in the agonizing struggle of *Anfechtung*.[2] Bayer further uses the hiddenness of God in his approach to theology by assigning it the role, alongside the law and the gospel, of one of the three data for doing theology. In stating this last piece, Bayer is very clear that the hidden God is experienced as a God of wrath,

---

1. Bayer, *Martin Luther's Theology*, 11; Bayer, *Martin Luthers Theologie*, 10. Bayer, "Rupture of the Ages," 46; Bayer, *Gott als Autor*, 158–59.

2. Bayer, *Theology the Lutheran Way*, 53–54; Bayer, *Theologie*, 86–88. Bayer, *Martin Luther's Theology*, 36–37; Bayer, *Martin Luthers Theologie*, 33–34.

and that this wrath goes beyond the condemnation of the law and radically contradicts the gospel.[3] The result of this is that the way in which Bayer does theology is impossible without the hiddenness of God. Unlike any before him in the modern German Protestant theological tradition, and even unlike Luther himself, Bayer brings God's hiddenness into the very way in which he approaches theology. Consequently, Bayer's theology is shaped in part by the notion that humans experience God outside of God's Word in a way that radically contradicts God's justifying work in Jesus Christ.

In this theology, Bayer articulates his own view of God's hiddenness defined as the opposite and contradiction of God's justification of the sinner in Christ from the basis of his Lutheran theology of justification.[4] Following Luther, Bayer defines justification as the only true subject matter of all theology and in keeping with this central tenet, forms his teaching on divine hiddenness along the contours of his view of justification. According to Bayer, God's justification of the sinner occurs through the active address of God's promise to the sinner in the gospel of Jesus Christ.[5] Bayer utilizes the linguistic philosophy of Austin to describe this justifying speech act of God, but his understanding of justification is firmly rooted in Luther's understanding of the promise.[6] Building on Luther, Bayer argues that part of God's justifying work in the promise is the opening and renewing of all creation. Bayer's view of God's hiddenness cannot be understood apart from this understanding of justification.

Bayer describes God's hiddenness as the contradiction of God's justification experienced by the believer through *Anfechtung*.[7] In this vein, Bayer significantly develops Luther's doctrine of the hidden God by focusing on how hiddenness affects the believer. Bayer clearly begins with the reformer's description of this, illustrating the hidden God's contradiction of God's justifying promise through the description of the hidden God as

---

3. Bayer, *Theology the Lutheran Way*, 17, 102, 104; Bayer, *Theologie*, 36–37, 413, 415. Bayer, "The Plurality of the One God," 343; Bayer, *Zugesagte Gegenwart*, 100. Bayer, *Martin Luther's Theology*, 196–98; Bayer, *Martin Luthers Theologe*, 177–79. Bayer, *Zugesagte Gegenwart*, 114–15.

4. Bayer, *Martin Luther's Theology*, 213; Bayer, *Martin Luthers Theologie*, 192. Bayer, *Theology the Lutheran Way*, 95, 102, 104–5; Bayer, *Theologie*, 406, 413, 415–17.

5. Bayer, *Promissio*, 11–14, 163. Bayer, *Martin Luther's Theology*, 46–47; Bayer, *Martin Luthers Theologie*, 44–46. Bayer, "Die reformatorische Wende in Luthers Theologie," 98–101.

6. Bayer, *Theology the Lutheran Way*, 127–28; Bayer, *Theologie*, 441–42. Bayer, *Martin Luther's Theology*, 50–51; Bayer, *Martin Luthers Theologie*, 46–47. Bayer, "Preaching the Word," 255; Bayer, *Zugesagte Gegenwart*, 392–393.

7. Bayer, *Martin Luther's Theology*, 39–40, 228; Bayer, *Martin Luthers Theologie*, 36–37, 206.

one who attacks and wrestles with the believer as God wrestled with Jacob on the banks of the Jabbok, and saying that in the midst of the struggle of *Anfechtung* God is indistinguishable from the devil.[8] Bayer then states that the believer is faced with this kind of encounter with the hidden God through the questions of double predestination and the problem of evil.[9] Although he mentions double predestination,[10] Bayer focuses much more on the believer's encounter with the hidden God in *Anfechtung*. Bayer addresses the problem of evil as the main venue for the believer's experience of *Anfechtung* and thus develops the doctrine of the hidden God so that the hidden God's contradiction of the promise has a cosmic dimension as well as a personal one. This development is based upon Bayer's understanding of justification, which includes God's opening and renewing of the creation by speech act.[11]

According to Bayer, the believer does not see the promised opening and renewing of creation taking place in the present and thus experiences a great contradiction between the promise of God and experienced reality in the world, living in "the rupture of the ages" between the advent of the promise and its eschatological fulfillment.[12] Bayer states that in the midst of this contradiction, the believer experiences two omnipotences of God and, indeed, two different doctrines of who God is. While the believer experiences God in God's Word as the God whose omnipotence saves the sinner, God's omnipotence experienced by the believer in life outside of God's Word tells a very different story. Outside the Word of God, God's omnipotence is experienced through all of the evil things that occur in nature and in human affairs, with God being responsible for everything from natural disasters to genocide.[13] Through God's Word, the believer experiences God's existence as the Trinity whose sole relationship to humanity is one of grace revealed through the death and resurrection of Jesus Christ. Outside of God's Word, however, the believer experiences the general doctrine of God, which consists entirely of the hidden God's activity outside of revelation, an activity

---

8. Bayer, *Martin Luther's Theology*, 39–40; Bayer, *Martin Luthers Theologie*, 36–37.

9. Bayer, *Martin Luther's Theology*, 198–99; Bayer, *Martin Luthers Theologie*, 179.

10. Ibid.

11. Ibid. Bayer, "The Plurality of the One God," 345; *Zugesagte Gegenwart*, 102.

12. Bayer, *Martin Luther's Theology*, 11; Bayer, *Martin Luthers Theologie*, 10. Bayer, "Rupture of Times," 45–46; *Gott als Autor*, 158–59. Bayer, *Martin Luther's Theology*, 113; Bayer, *Martin Luthers Theologie*, 103.

13 Bayer, "The Plurality of the One God," 345–46; Bayer, *Zugesagte Gegenwart*, 102. Bayer, "God's Omnipotence," 86–87; Bayer, *Zugesagte Gegenwart*, 112–13.

hostile to humans, wherein God wills and effects all things that come to pass.[14]

Before the eschatological resolution of this contradiction between the revealed God of promise and the hidden God of wrath, says Bayer, the believer lives a pilgrim existence in the rupture of the ages, between the promise and its fulfillment.[15] Bayer then comes full circle through hiddenness as the contradiction of the justifying promise of God back to that promise itself. Bayer states that, although not yet apparent, the promise will be fulfilled and the tension between God's promise and God's hiddenness relieved, not by a reconciliation between these two contradictory works of God but by the complete ending of God's hiddenness, as the promise of God triumphs over God's wrath and the gospel over the law.[16] The only hope for the believer in the meantime, says Bayer, is that same promise. The *Sitz im Leben* of the pilgrim believer caught under the contradiction between promise and hiddenness during the rupture of the ages is that of lament.[17] The only thing that the believer can do under this contradiction is to cry out to God on the basis of the promise in the midst of the experience of hiddenness.[18] In doing so, says Bayer, the believer gives voice to the groaning of all creation in anticipation of the eschatological fulfillment of the promise and renewal of all creation.[19]

---

14. Bayer, "Poetological Doctrine of the Trinity," 52–53; Bayer, "Poetologische Trinitätslehre," 76–77; Bayer, *Gott als Autor*, 144–45. Bayer, *Martin Luther's Theology*, 339; Bayer, *Martin Luthers Theologie*, 308–9. Bayer, *Zugesagte Gegenwart*, 175–77.

15. Bayer, *Theology the Lutheran Way*, 203; Bayer, *Theologie*, 522. Bayer, "Rupture of Times," 45; Bayer, *Gott als Autor*, 158. Bayer, *Martin Luther's Theology*, 11; Bayer, *Martin Luthers Theologie*, 10.

16. Bayer, "Poetological Doctrine of the Trinity," 55; Bayer, "Poetologische Trinitätslehre," 79; Bayer, *Gott als Autor*, 147. Bayer, "Does Evil Persist?," 143, Bayer, *Freiheit als Anwort*, 297.

17. Bayer, *Martin Luther's Theology*, 11; Bayer, *Martin Luthers Theologie*, 10. Bayer, "Rupture of Times," 46–47; Bayer, *Gott als Autor*, 157. Bayer, *Living by Faith*, 71; Bayer, *Aus Glauben Leben*, 77.

18. Bayer, *Martin Luther's Theology*, 213; Bayer, *Martin Luthers Theologie*, 192. Bayer, *Martin Luther's Theology*, 11; Bayer, *Martin Luthers Theologie*, 10. Bayer, "Rupture of Times," 46; Bayer, *Gott als Autor*, 159. Bayer, "God's Omnipotence," 90; Bayer, *Zugesagte Gegenwart*, 116.

19. Bayer, *Gott als Autor*, 187–89. Bayer, "Toward a Theology of Lament," 212; Bayer, "Zur Theologie der Klage," 291; Bayer, *Zugesagte Gegenwart*, 62. Bayer, *Schöpfung als Anrede*, 177–78, 181–82. Bayer, "Erhörte Klage," 261, 267; Bayer, *Leibliches Wort*, 337, 343. Bayer, *Martin Luther's Theology*, 113, 139, 183, 219; Bayer, *Martin Luthers Theologie*, 103, 127, 165, 198. Bayer, *Living by Faith*, 29–30; Bayer, *Aus Glauben Leben*, 37–38.

Assessing Bayer's View of the Hidden God

In the last chapter, I compared Bayer's understanding and use of the doctrine of the hidden God to Luther's own articulation of this teaching. Here, I now turn to evaluating Bayer's view of hiddenness for myself. I approach this task of assessing Bayer's view of the hidden God from the perspective of Lutheran systematic theology. This perspective might be termed "confessional" in the sense that it takes the Lutheran teaching on justification, as articulated by Luther and interpreted in the Lutheran confessions to be the central doctrine of theology, as that which is the core of the Christian faith from which all areas of doctrine and faith proceed. Such perspective on theology also embodies traditional Lutheran categories such as the living and creative Word of God (the *viva vox evangelii*), God's forgiveness in Christ coming to humans through Word and Sacrament, and the ubiquity of Jesus Christ. This is not to say that my standpoint is one that sees no possibility for the contemporary confession, nuancing, interpretation, and development of the classic Lutheran theological themes, as if it is necessary simply to return to the sixteenth century and repeat its wisdom verbatim. Certainly the twentieth century was rich with modern Lutheran systematic enterprises and, if Bayer's theology is any indication of things to come, the twenty-first century holds great promise for Lutheran theology as well. I believe that it is fair to evaluate Bayer's view of hiddenness from such a vantage point, because he himself works out his theology from such an approach. To this end, I seek here briefly to outline my own appreciative thoughts on Bayer's expression of the doctrine of the hiddenness of God, but before entering into this in earnest, I will first relate the criticisms of two contemporary Lutheran scholars who have entered into written conversation with Bayer's view of the hidden God, which may be helpful in assessing Bayer's view.

The Reception of Bayer's View of the Hidden God

As I outlined in the introduction of this thesis, a handful of scholars have addressed the theme of the hidden God in Bayer's theology, namely Christine Helmer, Mark Mattes, Reinhard Hutter, Hans Schaeffer, Gerhard Sauter, Thomas Reinhuber, Paul Hinlicky, and Klaas Zwanepol. While Mattes, Hutter, Schaeffer, Sauter, and Reinhuber merely describe Bayer's view of hiddenness, Hinlicky, Helmer, and Zwanepol actually enter into critical appraisals of Bayer's view of divine hiddenness. These three scholars are Lutheran theologians and both reject Bayer's understanding of the hidden God, though they do so to different extents and by different criteria. Hinlicky explicitly and Helmer implicitly rejects entirely Bayer's interpretation and use of the doctrine of the hidden God, but Zwanepol's criticisms are more limited and more focused. This is likely due to the fact that Zwanepol's approach to theology and interpretation of Luther is closer to Bayer's own, while Hinlicky attacks Bayer from the basis of his own understanding of the task of Lutheran theology today. I will here briefly relate these critiques of Bayer's understanding of the hidden God and respond to them before continuing to my own analysis of Bayer's teaching on the hidden God.

Paul Hinlicky

According to Hinlicky, the task of Lutheran theology today is to engage in "a postmodern critical dogmatics 'after Christendom'" through a "complex of anthropological ideas that I [Hinlicky] have designated by the terminology of the somatic, the centered, and the ecstatic self."[20] In the wake of the collapse of Christendom, this task is to be accomplished within the Church, which is the "Beloved Community," over and against the world.[21] It is clear that by his use of the anthropological motif of the "somatic, the centered, and the ecstatic self," Hinlicky intends to reinstate a kind metaphysics as foundational for the doing of theology and understands the nature of faith in Christ ecclesiologically rather than eschatologically.[22]

Though Hinlicky believes that Luther supports him in these views, his arguments evidence that his project is also characterized by a reaction against modernism in some of its various forms and especially against modern "representations" of Luther's thought.[23] Hinlicky believes that Luther is a catholic figure, a purveyor of the *fides catholica*,[24] and a figure whose thought must be understood "within the broader stream of the Pauline-Augustinian tradition."[25] Hinlicky seeks to probe Luther's work "to ask whether Luther can provide help for a creedal Christian theology in Euro-America today that looks to the social salvation of the beloved community, and from that perspective asks centrally about the moral burden of the individual and the atoning work of Christ."[26] It is not my goal to engage here with Hinlicky regarding the veracity of his reading and use of Luther or his theological

20. Hinlicky, *Luther and the Beloved Community*, 360.
21. Ibid.
22. Ibid., 67, 141–49, 155, 259–62, 360.
23. Ibid., 5–6, 221–24.
24. Ibid., 61.
25. Ibid., 6.
26. Ibid, 364.

project, but merely to note it, since it colors entirely his reception of Bayer's teaching on the hidden God.

Hinlicky addresses Bayer's understanding of the hidden God in the midst of his own discussion of Luther's theology of the cross. Hinlicky sees the theology of the cross and the hiddenness of God as epistemological symbols, as forms of a new wisdom, and as paradoxical possibilities for the inclusion of the needy sinner into the Beloved Community.[27] In discussing these motifs in Luther's theology and relating them to his own project, Hinlicky does not explicitly distinguish between the hiddenness of God in revelation under the sign of God's opposite (i.e. the theology of the cross) and the terrible hiddenness of God outside of revelation.[28] In fact, Hinlicky criticizes Luther's discussion of the terrible hiddenness of God in *The Bondage of the Will*, as something that "presses" a heretical, dualistic view of God existing "unbound by His Word."[29] Hinlicky states that, in his estimation, Luther softens his view of the hiddenness of God at the conclusion of *The Bondage of the Will* through his teaching that what is not revealed in the light of grace will be revealed in the light of glory. He expresses, however, that it would be better theologically if Luther would say instead that God is hidden to the fallen human but intelligibly revealed to the believer. In my analysis, this amounts to saying that it would be better to understand the hidden God as becoming the revealed God in the light of faith rather than saying that the hidden God remains hidden even to the believer.[30]

Hinlicky's dislike for Luther's doctrine of the hidden God as expressed in *The Bondage of the Will* is reflected in how he deals with Bayer's interpretation and use of this doctrine. Hinlicky rejects Bayer's teaching on the hidden God on account of its portrayal of divine hiddenness as radically contradictory to God's revelation and on account of its reliance upon eschatology. In my opinion, Hinlicky's treatment of Bayer's view of hiddenness is something of a caricature. Although he falls just short of accusing Bayer of heresy and dualism, as he also does with Luther, Hinlicky implies that on this matter Bayer stands outside "the broader stream of the Pauline-Augustinian tradition." Hinlicky states that Bayer comes "very close to dualism, though he [Bayer] denies that his position entails it."[31] Furthermore,[32]

27. Ibid., 359–60.

28. Ibid., 360–61, 368–71.

29. Ibid., 162.

30. Ibid. Such an understanding of the hiddenness of God is reminiscent of Elert's interpretation of Luther on this point.

31. Hinlicky, 369. Cf. Bayer, *Martin Luther's Theology*, 213; Bayer, *Martin Luthers Theologie*, 192.

32. Hinlicky, 161–62.

Hinlicky believes Luther and Bayer border on espousing Trinitarian heresy in saying God is not bound by his Word (that is, according to an eternal, universal law).[33]

In addition to suspecting that Bayer's understanding of the doctrine of the hidden God is dualistic, Hinlicky rejects Bayer's eschatological explanation of the revealed God's resolution of the tension brought about by the hidden God. Hinlicky correctly estimates that Bayer sees God's eschatological fulfillment of the promise and renewal of all things as the only solution to the situation formed by the hidden God's contradiction of the promise of the revealed God. According to Bayer, the hiddenness of God will one day be done away with forever but that, until such a time, believers live as pilgrims by faith in the promise and not by sight.[34] Hinlicky disagrees with this solution proposed by Bayer because resolution comes only in a future, leaving the believer presently with faith alone, not sight.[35]

These reactions against Bayer's interpretation and explanation of the doctrine of the hidden God reflect Hinlicky's own concern for metaphysics and ecclesiology in theology that are available to sight. His concern for metaphysics can be detected in how he rejects Bayer's description of the hiddenness of God as incomprehensible and as being outside of and contrary to God's activity in Christ.[36] His concern for ecclesiology, on the other hand, can be sensed in his rejection of Bayer's eschatological resolution to the hidden God's contradiction of the promise.[37] For Hinlicky, such a robust eschatology is undesirable, because he finds the fulfillment of faith to be present ecclesiologically in the Beloved Community rather than only in some unseen eschatological reality that is present through the promise but not fully "realized" or ontologically present.[38]

Hinlicky then attempts to turn his critique into a counterintuitive description of Bayer's hidden God as a "theology of glory" and so associates Bayer with glory's dualism and heresy.[39] Hinlicky then applies a grave charge: Bayer's teaching on the eschatological solution to hiddenness is a form of "gnosis."[40] Hinlicky does not discuss how Bayer's notion of the hid-

33. Ibid., 162, 369.
34. Ibid., 369–70.
35. Ibid., 370.
36. Ibid., 369.
37. Ibid., 369–70.
38. Ibid., 360, 364, 370.
39. Ibid., 368–69.
40. Ibid., 371. Hinlicky is not unique in articulating the notion that Lutheran theologians of a Word-event orientation are "gnostic." This is a rather common critique of such theologians in evangelical catholic theological circles. The classic expression

den God is defined by and relates to his understanding of justification by God's promise. Hinlicky must set his entire project against Bayer, since his assumed ontology of God means that God cannot really be hidden from faith without by definition being a gnostic secret in a dualistic universe. Yet, they do both find Luther's three lights as crucial for the discussion of hiddenness in the bondage of the Will. Bayer sees it as the appropriate conclusion to the argument about God hidden in majesty, outside the word, and Hinlicky takes it to be some kind of corrective or abandonment of what preceded it. But what the eschatological light is, and how it resolves the tension of the preached and unpreached God differs radically in an eschatological versus an ecclesiological approach.

Christine Helmer

Helmer treats Bayer's view of hiddenness similarly to the way in which Hinlicky treats it. Helmer fails to describe fully Bayer's view due to the fact that she limits her discussion of it to an example utilized in order to prove a point. Her use of Bayer's view of hiddenness comes in an essay in which she argues that Lutheran theologians interpret Luther according to their own historical and philosophical contexts and perspectives.[41] While such a charge may arguably be valid in and of itself, her categorization of Bayer's view of hiddenness together along with Ritschl's view of hiddenness as "Neo-Kantian," fails to appreciate fully some of the nuances of Bayer's theology and falls short of actually adequately comparing it to Luther's own view.[42]

Certainly, Helmer accurately describes a portion of Bayer's view of the hidden God, when she states that Bayer contrasts God's hiddenness with God's revelation and with the speech act of God's promise in the justifying gospel of Jesus Christ; when she says that Bayer views the hidden God as the "referent" for human experiences of evil and suffering; and when she identifies that Bayer contrasts between God's revelation of God's self as Trinity and the "general doctrine" of God as God's hiddenness.[43] Yet, Helmer also

---

of this critique is to be found in David Yeago's essay, "Gnosticism, Antinomianism, and Reformation Theology." Here, Yeago castigates Word-event oriented confessional Lutherans, particularly Elert, as gnositc for emphasizing the proclamation of God's Word in law and gospel at the expense of a dogmatics focused on the teaching on an ontological Christology. Yeago, "Gnosticism, Antinomianism, and Reformation Theology," 41–43.

41. Helmer, "Does Luther Have a 'Waxen Nose'?" 26.
42. Ibid., 27.
43. Ibid., 27–28.

makes several incorrect statements about Bayer's view of hiddenness. In comparing Bayer's views of the hiddenness of God and God's verbal promise of the gospel, Helmer purports that Bayer describes hiddenness in this context as "God's silence."[44] While this is true to an extent, Bayer does not maintain that God remains silent in the face of the believer's experience of hiddenness and the believer's corresponding lament, as Helmer argues he does.[45] Bayer understands the incarnation and passion of Jesus Christ as the revealed God's direct answer to this lament. Moreover, Bayer proclaims that God will actually deliver creation itself from God's hiddenness, and that there will indeed be an eschatological reckoning in which God's hiddenness and silence will be put to an end forever.

Furthermore, the castigation of Bayer as a neo-Kantian contextualization of Luther's theology in his view of hiddenness on account of its concern with God's word-event in Christ is amiss. In the first place, Helmer does not here deal with the fact the Bayer goes to great lengths to demonstrate his differences with Kant and his use of Hamann over and against Kant. Secondly, such an inaccurate categorization of Bayer prevents an actual comparison of Bayer's thought with that of Luther's on hiddenness. A more a extensive discussion of Bayer's view of hiddenness, his use of linguistic philosophy, and his interpretation of Luther is needed than that which Helmer provides.

Like Hinlicky's, Helmer's depiction of Bayer's teaching on the hidden God appears as something of a caricature. Moreover, like Hinlicky, Helmer is motivated by her own concerns when she addresses Bayer's view of hiddenness. Her entire point in describing Bayer's teaching on the hidden God is to illustrate that Lutheran theologians contextualize Luther according to their own historical and philosophical concerns. While it is certainly true that theologians do this, unavoidably so, it is not representative of Bayer's full teaching on hiddenness, his overall theology of justification by the promise, or his scholarship on Hamann to categorize him as "neo-Kantian" without qualification.

Finally, whatever the case may be about theologians contextualizing Luther, Helmer tips her hand by showing the reader her own contextualization of Lutheran theology when she expresses her regret that Bayer identifies Luther's distinction between the hidden and revealed God as a distinction between God outside of Christ and God revealed in Christ during, and thereby between God experienced in world religions and the God revealed in Christ through the Word during "an age of religious pluralism."[46]

---

44. Ibid., 28.
45. Ibid., 28–29.
46. Ibid., 209n9.

Like Hinlicky's, Helmer's review of Bayer's teaching on the hidden God is incomplete and thus unrepresentative of Bayer's actual view.

Klaas Zwanepol

While Hinlicky and Helmer reject Bayer's discussion of hiddenness, Zwanepol engages in more of a *sic et non* approach to this theme in Bayer's theology. Zwanepol's article, "Zur Diskussion um Gottes Verborgenheit," is probably the best secondary resource on Bayer's understanding of the hiddenness of God. In this article, Zwanepol approaches Bayer's discussion of the hidden God from the perspective of Lutheran theology. Zwanepol is a Lutheran theologian of the *Protestantse Kerk in Nederland*. As he explains in this article, Zwanepol agrees with Bayer that the subject of theology is God's justification of the sinner as both the center of theology from which all doctrines proceed and as the teaching representative of the whole of theology, the article of faith "upon which the Church stands or falls."[47] While his theology is influenced heavily by Jüngel and indirectly by Barth—as is apparent in this article—this concern for justification demonstrates that Zwanepol shares a common theological concern with Bayer, even though he is somewhat critical of Bayer's understanding and use of the hiddenness of God.[48]

Approaching the theme of the hidden God in Bayer's theology from the shared basis of the doctrine of God's justification of the sinner by faith in Christ, Zwanepol both commends Bayer and critiques him concerning this theme. Zwanepol follows Bayer up to a certain point in delineating the difference between the hiddenness of God in revelation under the sign of God's opposite and the terrible hiddenness of God. Yet, Zwanepol thinks that Bayer has gone too far in separating these two kinds of hiddenness.[49]

Zwanepol does not essentially disagree with Bayer that these two forms of divine hiddenness exist in Luther's theology, nor does he argue that they are essentially the same kind of hiddenness.[50] He even admits that Bayer is correct in saying that God hidden outside of revelation is indistinguishable from the devil and that the believer must "appeal to God against God."[51] Zwanepol does not, however, agree with Bayer that the tension between the hiddenness of God and God's gracious revelation in Christ constitutes

---

47. Zwanepol, "Zur Diskussion um Gottes Verborgenheit," 51.
48. Ibid., 53.
49. Ibid., 52–53.
50. Ibid.
51. Ibid., 55.

two different human experiences and, therefore, two different doctrines of God. Though he agrees with Bayer that the hiddenness of God outside of revelation exists and comes from Luther's thought, he disagrees with Bayer when the latter states that the general doctrine of God concerns only God's hiddenness and wrath and that the doctrine of God as Trinity concerns only the gospel. For Zwanepol, this move by Bayer drives too great a wedge between God's hiddenness in wrath and God's gracious revelation in Christ.[52]

Against Bayer's teaching concerning the hiddenness of God and the impossibility of beholding complete divine unity on this side of the eschaton, Zwanepol maintains that both the hiddenness of God in revelation and the hiddenness of God outside of revelation serve the revelation of God in Christ, just as the distinction between the law and the gospel is "fully integrated in God's revelation in the gospel."[53] Zwanepol argues that a distinction implies not only a contradiction but also an agreement, and that this is the case with Luther's distinction between God's terrible hiddenness and God's revelation in Christ.[54] According to Zwanepol then, the distinction between the law and the gospel and the difference between the hiddenness and revelation of God are encapsulated in the greater, overarching unity of the Triune God and God's revelation in the gospel of Jesus Christ.[55]

Although he articulates this disagreement with some of the features of Bayer's teaching concerning the hidden God, Zwanepol nevertheless finds the trajectory of this teaching to pose some helpful topics for further discussion, including Bayer's notion that the tension between the hiddenness of God and the revelation of God remains "until the last day."[56] It is thus clear that, while Zwanepol disagrees with Bayer, he does not write off the latter's teaching on the hidden God but appreciates it to a certain extent. This is not surprising given the basis of the centrality of God's justification of the sinner in Christ shared by Zwanepol and Bayer.

There is, however, another factor affecting Zwanepol's reception of Bayer. Within Zwanepol's interaction with Bayer, a certain influence from Barth and Jüngel regarding the hiddenness of God and the relationship between the law and the gospel may be detected. Zwanepol argues against what he sees as Bayer's overly broad distinction between the hidden and revealed God, saying that the dialectic between the hidden and revealed God and the distinction between the law and the gospel must be seen as

52. Ibid., 56–57.
53. Ibid., 55.
54. Ibid., 57.
55. Ibid., 57–58.
56. Ibid., 58.

fully integrated within the broader context of the gospel. Accordingly, even the terrible hiddenness of the incomprehensible unpreached God must be understood in the service of the revealed God of the gospel, just as the hiddenness of God under God's opposite is understood this way in the theology of the cross.[57]

Zwanepol may have some basis in Luther's thought for arguing this point against Bayer, since Bayer categorizes the hiddenness of God as existing outside of the dialectic of law and gospel as a third divine-human encounter in addition to the law and the gospel. Furthermore, Zwanepol is correct to some extent that even the hiddenness of God ultimately serves the revealed God's justification of the sinner through the gospel. As I argued in the last chapter, it is true that Luther ultimately demonstrates that the terrible hiddenness of God drives the sinner to desperation, while the revealed God saves the same desperate sinner. Yet, as I also articulated, Bayer ultimately reaches this conclusion as well, through his eschatological qualification of the hiddenness of God and his subsequent theology of lament, wherein the believing sinner is driven by the hiddenness of God experienced through *Anfechtung* to claim the promise of the revealed God against the hidden God. Moreover, Bayer's entire discussion of the hidden God is framed within the context of justification by God's Word of promise as the sole subject for theology, and, as I have argued throughout this thesis, Bayer's definition of the hiddenness of God is dependent upon and formed by his understanding of justification.

When he says that the law and the hiddenness of God function within the more overarching context of the gospel, Zwanepol seems to have something in mind beyond the ultimate service of the purpose of the revealed God rendered by the hiddenness of God that Luther and Bayer teach. He seems to embody the kind of Lutheran-Barthian view evident in Jüngel's understanding that the law and the gospel are ultimately encapsulated by and overarching Word of God characterized as gospel, and although he affirms the existence of the terrible hiddenness of the unpreached God alongside the hiddenness of the revealed God under God's opposite, his discussion of divine hiddenness belies this distinction. In both of these cases, Zwanepol seems to take up Jüngel's argument against Luther's doctrine of the hidden God in his own criticism of Bayer.[58] For Bayer, there is no unity between the

---

57. Ibid., 55. "Genauso wie die Verborgenheit Gottes unter dem Gegenteil – als Grundgedanke von Luthers Kreuztheologie – vom deus revelatus in Dienst genommen wird, so kann auch die Verborgenheit Gottes in der Unbegreiflichkeit des deus nudus letzendlich nicht umhin, in den Dienst des deus revelatus zu treten."

58. Ibid, 55–57. Cf. *TE* II, 125–27, 135–37, 143–44. Paulson, "Analogy and Proclamation," 95–96.

terrible hiddenness and the gracious revelation of God or between the law in the gospel in a more overarching Word. Instead, there is a completion and ending of hiddenness in revelation and of the law in the gospel that comes by faith in the moment through the promise and by sight eschatologically through the fulfillment of the promise.[59]

Zwanepol's rejection of Bayer's understanding of hiddenness is made at least in part by an approach to theology that differs slightly from Bayer's. Ultimately, Zwanepol disagrees with Bayer because he sees a greater unity existing between the law and the gospel and the hiddenness and revelation of God in the present than Bayer or even Luther does. This does not immediately disqualify Zwanepol's critique, but it limits the extent to which someone with a less Barthian understanding of law and gospel can use his critique in assessing Bayer's view of hiddenness.

The question that I am able to form from the critiques by Hinlicky and Zwanepol is: "Does Bayer leave the resolution of the tension brought about by the hidden God to the future?" This question forms part of Hinlicky's concern that the present ecclesiological existence of the unity of God is compromised by the eschatological nature of Bayer's understanding of the unity of God revealed in the fulfillment of the promise. This concern of leaving too much to the future is also what Zwanepol is implicitly expressing in his critique of Bayer, for Zwanepol operates from the premise that there is an evangelical unity of hiddenness and revelation as well as the law and the gospel discernable in the present. In both cases the position of present unity is taken against Bayer's position of future resolution of present tension, due perhaps to an underlying Calvinistic concern for the unity of God's being and will from all eternity.

Evaluation of Bayer's View on the Hidden God

For myself, I do not find the objections of Hinlicky, Helmer, and Zwanepol convincing against Bayer. Moreover—as a confessional theologian seeking to do theology in the present as a Lutheran, seeking to speak the good news of Christ to sinners and believers in their present existence and context, seeking to express faithfully the gospel of justification by faith in Christ as a present reality in terms of the present, and seeking to articulate a contemporary Lutheran theology anchored in the message of God's justification of the sinner in Christ—I find Bayer's theology with its center of justification

---

59. Bayer, "Twenty-Four Theses," 73; Bayer, *Zugesagte Gegenwart*, 34. Bayer, "Poetological Doctrine of the Trinity," 55; Bayer, "Poetologische Trinitätslehre," 79; Bayer, *Gott als Autor*, 147.

through the promise and its teaching on hiddenness to be faithful to Luther's theology and capable of addressing the contemporary context of the human. I find Bayer's interpretation and use of Luther's doctrine of the hidden God to be useful for me as a contemporary, confessional, Lutheran theologian in view of its faithfulness to Luther, consistency with the central doctrine of justification by faith alone and the preaching of the gospel, and taking into account the real experience of the believer.

Faithfulness to Luther

Although there may be some genuine inconsistencies between Bayer and Luther concerning the hiddenness of God, particularly regarding the connections between hiddenness and the law and hiddenness and reprobation, as I have outlined in the previous chapter, Bayer largely demonstrates fidelity to the essential thrust of Luther's teaching concerning the hidden God. Bayer's definition of hiddenness as the experience of the hidden God's contradiction of the revealed God's promise in the gospel, his description of how the believer's experience of such hiddenness takes place through *Anfechtung*, his illustration of the intensely personal nature of the hidden God's attack on the believer, and his use of the imagery of God's assault upon Jacob on the banks of the Jabbok all flow from the reformer's articulation of the doctrine of the hidden God. Furthermore Bayer's contention that the promise of the revealed God is the only solution to the tension formed by the hidden God's contradiction of the promise reflects both Luther's own teaching on the hiddenness of God as well as Luther's utmost concern that all theology be anchored in the good news of God's justification of the sinner.

While Bayer certainly develops this doctrine of Luther's along his own lines of thought, even this development is consistent with Luther's views. Bayer's development of the reformer's understanding of the hiddenness of God in maximizing the role of the idea of the hidden God in theology through utilizing it in his own articulation of the mode, method, and data of theology, is essentially invited by Luther himself in *The Bondage of the Will*, where the reformer states that when one speaks of God, one must differentiate if one is speaking of God revealed in God's Word or of God hidden outside and above God's Word. Such differentiation is precisely what Bayer does in bringing the distinction between the hidden and revealed God into his very approach to doing theology. Similarly, Bayer's broadening of Luther's understanding of the hidden God's attack upon the believer in *Anfechtung* does not contradict Luther's description of the work of the hidden God, since, in addition to condemning in order to save, the hidden

God effects all things that come to pass. Bayer's approach to the work of the hidden God through the experience of the question of the problem of evil is faithful to Luther's teaching on the hidden God, because through his theology of lament and eschatological qualification of God's hiddenness, Bayer ultimately finishes his discourse on the hidden God with the revealed God's salvation in Christ.

Consistency with Justification by Faith and the Preaching of the Gospel

By ending his discussion of the hidden God in the good news of God's salvation of the sinner in Christ through God's Word of promise, Bayer grounds his interpretation and development of Luther's doctrine of the hidden God in the central, reformational teaching of justification by faith in Christ and the preaching of the gospel. As a contemporary, confessional Lutheran systematic theologian, I understand such grounding of one's theology as being essential to articulating a specifically Lutheran theology. The way in which one does this may vary and differ in form and approach across generational, ethnic, and geographical contexts, but the essential meaning of the Lutheran understanding of the Christian faith in these terms, articulated in the fifth and sixth articles of the Augsburg Confession, serves as a basis for undertaking the task of theology as a Lutheran.

Bayer's entire theological enterprise is centered on the doctrine of justification, and, as I have consistently emphasized throughout this work, his understanding of the hidden God flows from and returns to his understanding of justification by God's promise in the gospel of Christ. Bayer's understanding of justification is intrinsically related to the preaching of the gospel. For Bayer, the doctrine of justification, which functions as the center, basis, and boundary of all theology, is defined by the preaching of the gospel. As Bayer explains it, justification is the speech-act of God's Word of promise. It is an alien righteousness of God in Christ that is spoken to the sinner. It is a verbal act of God, wherein the sinner is spoken righteous through the proclaimed gospel in the bodily Word (*Leibliches Wort*) of preaching, absolution, and the Sacraments. It is a view in which justification is defined by the preaching of the gospel.

Bayer's understanding of the hiddenness of God, flowing from this view of justification, is thus also defined by the preaching of the gospel, though in a paradoxical way. For Bayer defines the activity of the hidden God as the opposite and contradiction of justification, the opposite and contradiction of the preaching of the gospel. As justification is the salvation-event that takes place through preaching of the gospel, hiddenness is God's contradiction of that event by a non-verbal divine-human encounter, which throws doubt upon the veracity of the justifying preaching of the gospel. Even though the definitive relationship between the hiddenness of God and the preaching of the gospel is a negative one (after all, such hiddenness is the hiddenness of the unpreached God), Bayer still defines the hiddenness of God by the preaching of the gospel. Furthermore, Bayer's description of the Christian's response to the hiddenness of God through lament based upon the preached promise of the gospel as well as his explanation of the eschatological end of hiddenness in the complete fulfillment of the promise demonstrates the essential importance of the preached gospel to his approach to the doctrine of the hidden God.

Congruence with the Experience of the Believer

Bayer's definition of the hiddenness of God as the activity of God that contradicts God's act of justification through the preached gospel seems to me to be congruous with the ongoing experience of believers in a fallen creation. Bayer's description of how the hidden God encounters believers with this contradiction through *Anfechtung* and the tension formed by the hidden God's contradiction of justification and the gospel provides a unique understanding of the believer's existence between being encountered by God in the preached gospel and the eschaton. Talk of the hidden God always runs the risk of taking flight into worlds of speculation far above the reality of the day-to-day real life of the believer, but the dialectical definition and existential depth of Bayer's description of hiddenness rule this error out of Bayer's view.

Far from being disengaged with human experience, Bayer's discussion of divine hiddenness enters into the mire of the believer's existence. In my estimation, Bayer's description of reality experience by the believer rings true. The believer has been given the promise of God's forgiveness and salvation and of the opening and restoration of all creation through the preached gospel, which states that "in Christ God was reconciling the world to himself,"[60] that "creation itself will be set free from its bondage to decay,"[61] and that "death will be no more."[62] Yet, the believer lives in a present situation in which such a promise is not only unrealized but also blatantly and daily contradicted. Bayer's description of the hiddenness of God encounter-

60. 2 Corinthians 5:19 (NRSV).
61. Rom 8:21(NRSV).
62. Rev 21:4 (NRSV).

ing the human through the question of the problem of evil in the world and his characterization of the believer's existence in the tension between the hiddenness of God and the promise of God in the rupture of the ages does justice to the present experience of the believer.

While some may charge Bayer as being a dualist and a heretic because of his teaching on hiddenness, I believe that he is not. Only the most rigorous anti-dualist could possibly hold that one being, God alone, is responsible for all that takes place, including even the disastrous and evil, and in this position, Bayer stands shoulder to shoulder with Luther. Moreover, Bayer's eschatological qualification of the activity of the hidden God precludes the accusation of Marcionism or Manichaeism. Indeed, Bayer does believe that there is a unity to God, but that such a unity is an eschatological one which must be believed by faith. On this side of the eschaton, however, believers experience a confused reality to say the least, and I believe that Bayer's theology does more justice to the reality of the perplexing and agonizing situation of believers in the midst of life than the monism of other theologians who follow in the train of Plato and Hegel.

Bayer does not cheapen the contradictory experience of the believer who is caught between the promise and the hiddenness of God by appealing to Platonic dualism or Hegelian idealism in which such experience is written off as something less than true reality or by exonerating God of responsibility for the contradiction of the promise. Instead, Bayer takes both the situation and God's responsibility for it seriously. In my estimation, there could hardly be a better response to the situation than the one offered by Bayer—that of lament. In the context of the contradiction of God's promise through natural disasters, starvation, human conflict, terror, and oppression, it seems to me that crying out to God from the depths of the experience of such contradiction really is the only response that the theologian—and ultimately the Christian—can make on the basis of the promise before the eschaton.

While Christians certainly are called to serve others in the midst of their sufferings and to identify with the oppressed, what can one do to halt the seemingly unending cycles of violence in the world? One can render as much aid as possible in the event of a natural disaster, but what can one do to control the chaos so often unleashed in nature? What can a believer do when confronted with the realities of human-caused starvation in Somalia and genocide in former Yugoslavia, Rwanda, and the Sudan? Certainly, the believer hopes for the fulfillment of God's salvation in the eschaton when all things are renewed and God becomes all in all, but what about right now? What else can a believer do, but cry out, "God, you promised! What now? How long?"

Bayer's view of the hidden God does not satiate the anguish of the believer in the face of evil here in this life other than by offering the eschatological hope of the promised renewal of all creation, but it does takes the horror of the present situation seriously, and it does so without sacrificing the Christian understanding of the almighty God, unlike so many contemporary attempts at making the situation more tolerable. What Bayer's view of the hidden God offers to the real situation of the believer in a world of evil and contradiction is both a future hope of redemption and a present gospel-empowered response to the God who does not presently make an end to evil. Bayer's view does this in the form of the cry that is simultaneously a cry of desperation and faith: "Maranatha!" It is a cry based firmly on God's justifying promise in the preached gospel, and it is a cry that is rooted in the prayer, "Thy kingdom come," a prayer that is sure to be heard and answered by God, "for he himself commanded us to pray like this and has promised to hear us."[63]

As a confessional Lutheran theologian, I find Bayer's view of the hidden God to be helpful for the doing of theology as a Lutheran today. In my estimation, Bayer's view is faithful both to Luther's own articulation of the doctrine of the hidden God and to the reformer's stipulation that all theology be centered on the teaching concerning God's justification of the sinner by faith in Jesus Christ. Furthermore, Bayer's interpretation of Luther's doctrine of the hidden God and use of it in his theology is consistent with the doctrine of justification by faith and with the preaching of the gospel in that Bayer defines the hiddenness of God through justification and the preaching of the gospel. Finally, Bayer's understanding of the work of the hidden God, as portrayed in his theology, takes seriously and addresses the incongruity between the promise given to believers in proclamation and the experience of its contradiction in existence in the present life with all of its sorrows and horrors. Moreover, in addressing the tension between the gift of the promise and the experience of the contradiction of that promise in the believer's present existence, Bayer holds forth the promise as both a present comfort and the basis of future hope in God's all-encompassing and renewing work of salvation. Certainly not all theologians, not even all Lutheran theologians, will share my appreciative view of Bayer's understanding of the hidden God, but I believe that Bayer's teaching on the hidden God is one that evidences a deep commitment to the center of Lutheran theology and that offers a genuinely helpful contribution to those seeking to do systematic theology from a reformational standpoint.

---

63. SC, "The Lord's Prayer," in *BC*, 358; *BSLK*, 550.

Possibilities for Bayer's View of the Hidden God in Constructive Theology

Having outlined my own assessment Bayer's view of the hidden God, I will now turn to addressing how this view might be used in the constructive task in systematic theology today. It is my contention that Bayer's teaching on the hidden God is a resource that contemporary theology, especially contemporary Lutheran theology, would do well to take up and advance. In furtherance of this contention, I will now suggest some possibilities for future study opened up by Bayer's view of the hidden God as well as how the task of doing evangelical and reformational theology in the twenty-first century could benefit from this teaching of Bayer's.

Possibilities for Future Development in Scholarship

Some development of Bayer's teaching on the hidden God has already been made by Bayer's student Thomas Reinhuber. In his book, *Kampfende Glaube*, Reinhuber adopts and furthers Bayer's interpretation of Luther's doctrine of the hidden God, especially with reference to the hidden God's contradiction of the gospel, the personal nature of the assault of the hidden God on faith through *Anfechtung*, and God's hiddenness experienced through the problem of evil understood from the perspective of the three lights.[64] From this basis in Bayer's thought combined with his own careful and articulate study of Luther's theology in *The Bondage of the Will*, Reinhuber constructs the notion that he calls a *"kampfende Glaube"* (fighting faith). According to Reinhuber, a fighting faith is a faith that holds fast to God's promise in the midst of the experience of divine opposition in *Anfechtung*.[65] It is a faith that categorizes a certain epoch in time, known as "the time of faith" or "the time of fight," a time in which the existence of the believer is marked by the fight between the devil and God and between the hidden God and the revealed God. It is a time in which the believer is caught in the middle of a fight and has his or her existence characterized by this fight.[66]

To be sure, Reinhuber develops his view of a fighting faith from Bayer's understanding of the believer's experience of the hidden God through *Anfechtung*. Reinhuber has stayed relatively close to Bayer's interpretation of the hiddenness of God and has formed his own view of Luther's message in *The Bondage of the Will* from Bayer's understanding of Luther's doctrine of

---

64. Reinhuber, *Kämpfende Glaube*, 106–10, 197–98.
65. Ibid., 109–10.
66. Ibid., 110–12.

the hidden God. Yet, the scholarship that could be developed from Bayer's understanding of the hidden God is not exhausted by Reinhuber's study. In my opinion there are other areas of scholarship related to Bayer's view of hiddenness that await investigation. Some future approaches to such scholarship might including a deeper engagement of Bayer's thought with social-Trinitarian views, an interaction with Swedish Lutheran theologies such as those of Gustaf Wingren and Bo Giertz,[67] a comparison of Bayer's view of hiddenness with that of the American Lutheran theologian Gerhard Forde,[68] a response to the essentialist theologians and those such as Hinlicky who seek a concrete ecclesiological ground of faith rather than an eschatological one, a dialogue between the modern German Protestant theological tradition and the Anglo-American vein of philosophy,[69] a dialogue between Bayer's view of hiddenness experienced through a fallen creation and ecological theologies, and a more international appropriation of Bayer's understanding of hiddenness, particularly in the global south. As the history of Christianity progresses and with it the interpretation of Luther's doctrine of the hidden God, it is inevitable that this teaching of the reformer will come into dialogue with global, post-colonial, and liberating theology. Lutheran theologians Paul Chung, Ulrich Duchrow, and Craig Nessan have already opened the conversation between Lutheran systematic theology and global liberation theology.[70] The addition of new voices and new themes in that discussion could enrich the overall task of Lutheran theology in a global context.

In my opinion though, it would be especially interesting to put Bayer's understanding of hiddenness in conversation with liberation theology. While there are significant differences in how Bayer and liberation

67. In particular, one could explore the similarities and differences between Bayer's view of the human encountered by the hidden God and the human being's existence under God's law of condemnation, both in conjunction with the preached gospel of the revealed God in Christ. Cf. Wingren, *The Living Word*, 137–47. Giertz's novel, *The Hammer of God*, wherein he describes the effects of the law, could also provide an interesting opportunity for comparison with Bayer's understanding of God's incomprehensible wrath in hiddenness. Cf. Giertz, *The Hammer of God*.

68. One could compare the views of God's hiddenness in espoused by each of these confessional Lutheran theologians as well as how Bayer, more than Forde, nuances his view of hiddenness through his doctrine of creation. Cf. Forde, *The Captivation of the Will*, 40–45. Forde, *On Being a Theologian of the Cross*, 74–81. Forde, *The Preached God*, 33–54.

69. Bayer's use of Austin constitutes an interesting and unusual interaction of a German theologian with a philosopher of the Anglo-American tradition. Such interaction is not generally characteristic of the modern German Protestant theological tradition, which tends to interact primarily with German thinkers.

70. Cf. Chung, Duchrow, and Nessan, *Liberating Lutheran Theology*.

theologians approach theology—especially regarding Bayer's rejection of the dialectic of theory and praxis—I believe that there are points of contact between Bayer and liberation that could be explored. One of these areas is the theological concept of lament. Here, Bayer shares a common theme with both black theology represented in the figure of James Cone, and with Latin American liberation theology represented by Gustavo Gutiérrez. Investigating the commonalities and contrasts between Bayer and these two thinkers could be helpful for Lutherans seeking to engage theologically across contexts as well as for reading Bayer's view of hiddenness in the light of theological traditions other than confessional Lutheranism.[71] Bayer has made such an endeavor possible by already stepping into a context broader than confessional Lutheranism or German Protestantism by engaging in the discussion of theodicy.

Bayer's View of the Hidden God and Theology in the Twenty-First Century

In addition to raising possibilities for future scholarship, Bayer's teaching on the hidden God also presents a promising approach to engaging in the constructive aspect of systematic theology in the twenty-first century. Bayer's view of hiddenness provides those seeking to do theology today in a way that is both faithful to the gospel and that takes seriously the concrete reality in which the gospel must be confessed and proclaimed with a unique opportunity to undertake this constructive task. In particular, Bayer's understanding of hiddenness as the opposite and contradiction of the gospel, which encounters believers in *Anfechtung* through the problem of evil, speaks both to the contemporary interest in language and to unparalleled suffering that characterizes the current state of affairs in the world.

In contemporary philosophy and theology, there has been a dramatic shift away from foundationalism and rationalistic metaphysics[72] and a con-

---

71. Gutiérrez addresses the themes of God's wrath, the problem of evil, suffering, and lament in his book *On Job*. Gutiérrez, *On Job*, 14, 58–62. Perhaps the most interesting comparative study would be one between the thought of Bayer and that of James Cone. Cone discusses God's identifying with those suffering and taking evil upon God's self. Cone, *God of the Oppressed*, 160–64. Cone also discusses the believer's response to suffering and evil through lament and identifies the African-American spirituals and the music of the blues as a particular kind of lament uttered in response to a particular kind of evil and suffering. Cone, *God of the Oppressed*, 169–78. Cone, *The Spiritual and the Blues*, 115. Cone, *The Cross and the Lynching Tree*, 12–26. Cone even brings the story of Jacob's wrestling with God into his discussion of lament in the context of the African American Christian community. Cone, *The Cross and the Lynching Tree*, 23–25.

72. Taylor, 8. Bowie, *Introduction to German Philosophy from Kant to Habermas*,

sequent turn towards linguistics—particularly towards the preeminence of language and the ability of speech and words to accomplish things.[73] In this intellectual context, Bayer's definition of the gospel as God's speech act of promise that accomplishes salvation, while perhaps not forming the basis of a new apologetic form of theology, can at the very least perhaps provide a frame of reference whereby the contemporary person can envision God's speaking a person into a series of new relationships in justification. Furthermore, this understanding of justification combined with Bayer's description of divine hiddenness as God's non-verbal opposition to faith in such a promise provides a way in which contemporary Lutherans might be enabled to enter into the discussion of these central themes of Martin Luther's theology in terminology that resonates with contemporary people.

Yet the relevance of Bayer's view of hiddenness to the constructive task of contemporary theology is hardly relegated to a discussion that could be deemed arcane and irrelevant for all but the intellectual elite. On the contrary, Bayer's understanding of the activity of the hidden God in *Anfechtung* has the potential to connect with contemporary people at a very deep and very personal level. For today, perhaps more than ever, the question of why suffering and evil seem to persist is a concern of many Christians and unbelievers alike who cannot reconcile what they see in reality with the message of the gospel.

In an age of mass communication and instant information, the reality of evil in the world, of the contradiction of God's goodness and of the promised renewal of creation, is omnipresent. While the theologian must be faithful to the gospel, he or she must be faithful to it in this present reality. This means that he or she must address the contradiction of the good news of Jesus Christ, which is so apparent to anyone who is conscious of the world around them and is not satisfied with the spiritualistic escapism preached by many Christians. Proclamation of the gospel and catechesis today must take seriously this context.

Bayer's understanding of the hidden God, and especially his understanding of the response of faith to the hidden God through lament, within the context of his theology of justification can be helpful for those of us trying to do evangelical theology today because it takes seriously the existence and human experience of the hidden God. In today's secular, pluralistic, and post-Christian society many have no contact with the church's proclamation of the condemning law of God, but few if any are untouched by evil and suffering in life. Bayer's understanding of hiddenness provides the

---

222ff.

73. Ibid., 156ff.

theologian with an entry into this context, because it recognizes that God's condemnation of the sinner is evident not only through the preached law but also through the evil and suffering that continue to plague humans in this world.

Yet, Bayer's view of hiddenness can be helpful even more to theologians of the Church today as they seek to encourage believers in the midst of the present evil and suffering evident in the world. Bayer's view can be helpful in this task because it does not try to make sense of such ongoing evil and suffering, but it takes seriously the existence of evil in the world, which is all too apparent through the human's experience of natural ills such hurricanes, tornadoes, earthquakes, floods and tsunamis, malnourishment and famine, pandemics, infant death, and global climate change, as well as through humanly wrought evils such as murder, theft, the hoarding of wealth and resources, genocide, and the recognition of the ever present reality that "Political power grows out of the barrel of a gun."[74]

Bayer's view does not dismiss these manifestations of evil as Platonic, Kantian, Hegelian, or even Augustinian shades of a higher, more spiritual or more rational reality. Nor does it, on the other hand, eviscerate God's deity by denying God's omnipotence, omniscience, responsibility for world events and so-called "free moral agents,"[75] or God's capability to cope with reality.[76] Nor does Bayer satisfy the question of the existence of evil and the truthfulness of God's promise with some a non-Christian answer via dualism. Instead, Bayer takes the reality of evil, God's responsibility for it, and God's ultimate unity and love for humans seriously. Bayer's answer to the problem of evil is that evil will eventually come to an end, even the evil for which God is responsible, and that God's promise of the renewal of all things will be fulfilled. Moreover, Bayer's way of dealing with the present and real experience of the contradiction of that promise is no escapist way out of a serious and difficult conversation about evil and God. Instead, Bayer provides evangelical theologians today with a view of God and evil in which the believer is caught between the promise of God and its contradiction evident through evil and suffering. In this view, the question "Why?" is not

---

74. Mao, "Problems of War and Strategy" (1938), in *Selected Works of Mao Tse-tung*, Vol. 2, 224.

75. The term "free moral agents" is a term used by proponents of the so-called "free will defense" approach to theodicy to describe the identity of the human being in regard to good and evil. In order to exonerate God from the responsibility for evil, this view blames evil on the inherent and inviolable "free will" of the human being. Cf. Stephen T. Davis, "Free Will and Evil," in *Encountering Evil: Live Options in Theodicy*, A New Edition, ed. Steven T. Davis (Louisville, KY: Westminster John Knox Press, 2001), 73–82.

76. E.g. The view of process theology summarized well by David Ray Griffith. David Ray Griffith, "Creation and the Problem of Evil," in *Encountering Evil*, 119–31.

dismissed as impiety or rationalized away but encouraged to be expressed. Through Bayer's view of lament, the "Why?" is understood as a cry of faith that is not given a cheap answer. For Bayer's view recognizes that the situation is too real and too desperate for cheap answers and that the only answer that will suffice is God's own eschatological answer through the complete fulfillment of the promise made in justification.

Thus, although Bayer's view of the hiddenness of God presents opportunities for further scholarship today and even for dialogue of reformational Lutheran theology with other theological traditions, the greatest opportunity that Bayer's view offers is that of a serious, meaningful, and evangelical discussion of the good news of the gospel in spite of the experience of its contradiction in the present reality. Even greater than the opportunity to discuss justification and hiddenness in our contemporary intellectual context is the opportunity it brings to actually preach and teach the gospel of justification by faith in Christ in the contemporary context of the experience of evil and suffering.

The great value of Bayer's theology with its understanding of justification by the promise, the hidden God's contradiction of that promise, and the revealed God's eschatological fulfillment of that promise, for theology today is that it preaches hope in the creative and redeeming God's work of reconciling humans and, indeed, the whole world to God's self in Jesus Christ. In the hell of sin, death, and decay evident presently in reality, Bayer's theology—though it is rooted deeply in the Reformation—preaches not a reactionary retreat into a new Christendom but the outward-looking hope of a new creation. Into the present context, it preaches the eschatological message that God will deliver the believer, God's people, and creation itself from their present misery into a renewed creation in which everything is reconciled to God in Christ.

While he is perhaps not as acclaimed as some contemporary theologians, Oswald Bayer has given the discipline of systematic theology and the Christian Church of today a great gift through his contemporary Lutheran theology that is both anchored in the thought of Martin Luther and addresses the present context of contemporary theology. In concert with Luther, Bayer insists that God's justification is the only true subject for all of theology, and his interpretation and use of Luther's doctrine of the hidden God is faithful to this qualification of what makes theology evangelical, reformational, and Lutheran. At the same time, Bayer describes the hiddenness of God in such a way that it reflects the reality that appears so contrary to the good news proclaimed in the promise of God in justification. It is my great hope for and challenge to those of us undertaking the task of systematic theology today not merely to take up, read, study, and further

Bayer's theology, but to engage in the kind of theology that Bayer does, with justification at the center, that does theology in the real world, taking the hidden God's contradiction of the gospel of justification seriously, and that is unafraid to preach the liberating gospel of God's promise in Jesus Christ, while we await anxiously for the eschatological fulfillment of that promise, praying, "Marantha! Amen, come Lord Jesus."

Bibliography

Works by Oswald Bayer

Bayer, Oswald. "A priori willkurlich, a posteriori notwendig: Die sprachphilosophische Verschränkung von Ästhetik und Logik in Hamanns Metakritik Kants." *NZSTh* 42 (2000) 117–139.

———. "Angels Are Interpreters." Translated by Christine Helmer. *LQ* 13 (1999) 271–84.

———. *Aus Glauben Leben: Über Rechtfertigung und Heiligung*. Stuttgart: Calwer, 1990.

———. *Autorität und Kritik: Zu Hermeneutik und Wissenschaftstheorie*. Tübingen: Mohr Siebeck, 1991.

———. *Barmen zwischen Barth und Luther*. In *Luther und Barth: Veröffentlichungen der Luther-Akademie e.V. Ratzeburg*, vol. 13, ed. Joachim Heubach, 21–36. Erlangen: Martin-Luther-Verlag, 1989.

———. "Barmherzigkeit." In *Dass Gott eine grosse Barherzigkeit habe*, ed. Doris Hiller and Christine Kress, 77–84. Leipzig: Evangelische Verlagsanstalt, 2001.

———. "The Being of Christ in Faith." Translated by Christine Helmer. *LQ* 10 (1996) 135–50.

———. "Creation as History." Translated by Martin Abraham. In *The Gift of Grace: The Future of Lutheran Theology*, edited by Niels Henrik Gregersen et al., 253–63. Minneapolis: Fortress, 2005.

———. "Das Problem der natürlichen Theologie." In *Einfach von Gott redden: Ein theologischer Diskurs: Festschrift fur Friedrich Mildenberger zum 65. Geburtstag*, edited by Jürgen Roloff and Hans G. Ulrich, 151–58. Stuttgart: Kohlhammer, 1994.

———. "Das Wort ward Fleisch: Luthers Christologie als Lehre von der Idiomenkommunikation." In *Veröffentlichungen der Luther-Akademie Ratzeburg*, vol. 34: *Jesus Christus—Gott für uns*, ed. Friedrich-Otto Scharbau, 58–101. Erlangen: Martin-Luther-Verlag, 2003.

———. "Das Wort ward Fleisch: Luthers Christologie als Lehre von der Idiomenkommunikation" (abbreviated version). In *Creator est Creatura*, edited by Oswald Bayer and Benjamin Gleede. Berlin: de Gruyter, 2007.

———. "Der Glanz der Gnade: Dimensionen eines weiten Begriffs." *K&D* 56 (2010) 69–82.

———. "Der neue Mensch." In *Gottes Offenbarung in der Welt: Horst Georg Pöhlmann zum 65. Geburtstag*, edited by Friedhelm Krüger, 117–28. Gütersloh: Kaiser, 1998.

———. "The Doctrine of Justification and Ontology." Translated by Christine Helmer. *NZSTh* 43 (2001) 44–53.

———. "Does Evil Persist?" Translated by Christine Helmer. *LQ* 11 (1997) 143–50. Also in *Freedom in Response*, 239–44.

———. "Die Ehe zwischen Evangelium und Gesetz." *Neue Zeitschrift für evangelische Ethik* 25 (1981) 164–80.

———. "Die Ganze Luthers Theologie." *K&D* 47 (2001) 254–74.

———. "'Die grösste Lust zu haben / allein in deinem Wort.'" In *Jesus Christus als die Mitte der Schrift*, edited by Christof Landmesser et al., 793–804. Beihefte zur Zeitschrift für die neutestamentliche Wissenschaft 86. Berlin: de Gruyter, 1997.

———. "'Eia, vere sic est!' cor per verbum veritatis verificatur." In *Befreiende Wahrheit*, 159–170. Marburg: Elwert, 2000.

———. "Endgültig: die erste Liebe." In *Caritas Dei: Beiträge zum Verständnis Luthers und der gegenwärtigen Ökumene. Feschrift für Tuomo Mannermaa zum 60. Geburtstag*, edited by Oswald Bayer et al., 58–65. Helsinki: Luther-Agricola Gesellschaft, 1997.

———. "Entmythologisierung: Christliche Theologie zwischen Metaphysik und Mythologie im Blick auf Rudolf Bultmann." *NZSTh* 34 (1992) 109–24.

———. "Erhörte Klage." *NZSTh* 25(1983) 259–72.

———. "Erzählung und Erklärung: eine Bestimmung des Verhältnisses von Theologie und Naturwissenschaften." *NZSTh* 39 (1997) 1–14.

———. "The Ethics of Gift." Translated by Mark A. Seifrid. *LQ* 24 (2010) 447–68.

———. "Freedom? The Anthropological Concepts of Luther and Melanchthon Compared." Translated by Christine Helmer. *Harvard Theological Review* 91 (1998) 373–87.

———. *Freedom in Response: Lutheran Ethics: Sources and Controversies*. Translated by Jeffrey E. Cayzer. Oxford: Oxford University Press, 2007.

———. *Freiheit als Antwort: Zur theologsiche Ethik*. Tübingen: Mohr Siebeck, 1999.

———. "Für eine bessere Weltlichkeit: Ernst Steinbach zum Gedenken." *ZThK* 83 (1986) 238–60.

———. "Gegen Gott für den Menschen: zu Feuerbachs Lutherrezeption." *ZThK* 69 (1972) 34–71.

———. "Gegen System und Struktur: die theologische Aktualität Johann Georg Hamanns." In *Johann Georg Hamann: Acta des Internationalen Hamann-Colloquiums in Lüneburg 1976*, ed. Bernhard Gajek, 40–50. Frankfurt: Klostermann, 1979.

———. "Gegenwart: Schöpfung als Anrede und Anspruch." *Luther: Zeitschrift der Luther-Gesellschaft* 59 (1988) 131–44.

———. "Gesetz und Evangelium." In *Bekenntnis und Einheit der Kirche: Studien zum Konkordienbuch*, edited by Martin Brecht and Reinhard Schwartz, 155–74. Stuttgart: Calwer, 1980.

———. "God's Omnipotence." Translated by Jonathan Mumme. *LQ* 23 (2009) 85–102.

———. "God as Author of My Life-history." *LQ* 2 (1988) 437–56.

———. *Gott als Autor: Zu einer poietologischen Theologie*. Tübingen: Mohr Siebeck, 1999.

———. "Grundzüge der Theologie Paul Tillichs, kritisch dargestellt." *NZSTh* 49 (2007) 325–48.

———. "Hermeneutical Theology." *SJT* 56 (2003) 131–47.

———. "'I Believe That God Has Created Me with All That Exists'": An Example of Catechetical-Systematics." Translated by Christine Helmer and edited by Richard Bliese. *LQ* 8 (1994) 129–61.

———. *Johann Georg Hamann: Der hellste Kopf seiner Zeit*. Tübingen: Attempto, 1998.

———. "Justification." *LQ* 24 (2010) 337–40.

———. "Justification as the Basis and Boundary of Theology: Monotony or Concentration." Translated by Christine Helmer. *LQ* 15 (2001) 273–92.

———. "Law and Morality." Translated by Christine Helmer. *LQ* 17 (2003) 63–76.

———. "Leibliches Wort: Öffentlichkeit des Glaubens und Freiheit des Lebens." *K&D* 27 (1981) 82–95.

———. *Leibliches Wort: Reformation und Neuzeit im Konflict*. Tübingen: Mohr Siebeck, 1991.

———. *Living by Faith: Justification and Sanctification*. Translated by Geoffrey W. Bromiley. Grand Rapids: Lutheran Quarterly Books, Eerdmans, 2003.

———. "Lutheran Pietism, or *Oratio, Meditatio, Tentatio*, in August Hermann Francke." *LQ* 25 (2011) 383–97.

———. "Lutherischer Pietismus: *Oratio, Meditatio, Tentatio* bei August Hermann Francke." In *Religiöse Erfahrung und wissentschaftliche Theologie: Festschrift für Ulrich Köpf zum 70. Geburtstag*, edited by Albrecht Beutel and Reinhold Rieger, 1–12. Tübingen: Mohr Siebeck, 2011.

———. "Macht, Recht, Gerechtigkeit." *K&D* 30 (1984) 200–212.

———. "Martin Luther." *The Reformation Theologians: An Introduction to Theology in the Early Modern Period*, edited by Carter Lindberg, 51–66. Oxford: Blackwell, 2002.

———. "Martin Luther as Interpreter of Holy Scripture." Translated by Mark Mattes. In *The Cambridge Companion to Martin Luther*, edited by Donald K. McKim, 73–85. Grand Rapids: Eerdmans, 2003.

———. *Martin Luthers Theologie: Eine Vergegenwärtigung*, 3. Rev. ed. Tübingen: Mohr Siebeck, 2007.

———. *Martin Luther's Theology: A Contemporary Interpretation*. Translated by Thomas H. Trapp. Grand Rapids: Eerdmans, 2008.

———. "Mercy from the Heart." Translated by Jonathan Mumme. *Logia* 19 (2010) 29–32.

———. "Metakritik in nuce: Hamanns Antwort auf Kants Kritik der reinen Vernunft." *NZSTh* 30 (1988) 305–14.

———. "The Modern Narcissus." Translated by Christine Helmer. *LQ* 9 (1995) 301–13.

———. "Nature and Institution: Luther's Doctrine of the Three Orders." Translated by Luis Dreher. *LQ* 12 (1998) 125–59. Also in *Freedom in Response*, 90–118.

———. "Der neuzeitliche Narziß." *Evangelische Kommentare* 3 (1993) 158–62.

———. "Notae ecclesiae," (with new introduction). In *Lutherische Beiträge zur Missio Dei: Veröffentlichungen der Luther-Akademie e.V. Ratzeburg*, vol. 3: 75–90. Erlangen: Martin-Luther-Verlag, 1982. First printed as "Leibliches Wort," in *K&D*.

———. "Paradox: Eine Skizze." In *The Theological Paradox: Interdisciplinary Reflections on the Centre of Paul Tillich's Thought*, edited by Gert Hummel, 3–8. Berlin: de Gruyter, 1995.

———. "Passion und Wissen: Kreuzestheologie und Universitätswissenschaft." *K&D* 39 (1993) 112–22.

———. "The Plurality of the One God and the Plurality of the Gods." Translated by John A. Betz. *Pro Ecclesia* 15 (2006) 338–56.

———. "Poetological Doctrine of the Trinity." Translated by Christine Helmer. *LQ* 15 (2001) 43–58.

———. "Poetological Theology: New Horizons for Systematic Theology." *IJST* 1 (1999) 153–67.

———. "Poetologische Trinitätslehre." In *Lutherische Beiträge zur Missio Dei: Veröffentlichungen der Luther-Akademie e.V. Ratzeburg*, vol. 26: 67–79. Erlangen: Martin-Luther-Verlag, 1996.

———. "Preaching the Word." Translated by Jeffrey G. Silcock. *LQ* 23 (2009) 249–69.

———. *Promissio: Geschichte der reformatorischen Wende in Luthers Theologie*. Göttingen: Vandenhöck & Ruprecht, 1971.

———. "Promissio und Gebet nach Luthers Rogatepredigt von 1520." In *Studien zur Geschichte und Theolgie der Reformation: Feschrift für Ernst Bizer*, edited by Luise Abramowski and J. F. Gerhard Goeters, 121–39. Neukirchen-Vluyn: Neukirchener, 1969. Also in *Promissio: Geschichte der reformatorischen Wende in Luthers Theologie*, 319–38.

———. "Dei reformatorische Wende in Luthers Theologie." In *Der Durchbruch der reformatorischen Erkenntnis bei Luther: Neuere Untersuchungen*, ed. Bernhard Lohse, 98–133. Stuttgart: Steiner, 1988. Also in *Promissio: Geschichte der reformatorischen Wende in Luthers Theologie*, 319–38.

———. "Rückblick." In *Der Durchbruch der reformatorischen Erkenntnis bei Luther: Neuere Untersuchungen*, edited by Bernhard Lohse, 154–166. Stuttgart: Steiner, 1988. Also in *Promissio: Geschichte der reformatorischen Wende in Luthers Theologie*, 319–38.

———. *Rechtfertigung*. Neuendettelsau: Freimund, 1991.

———. "Rupture of Times: Luther's Relevance for Today." Translated by Christine Helmer. *LQ* 13 (1999) 35–50.

———. "Schleiermacher und Luther." In *Internationaler Schleiermacher-Kongress Berlin 1984*, 2, edited by Kurt-Viktor Selge, 1005–16. Berlin: de Gruyter, 1985.

———. *Schöpfung als Anrede: Zu einer Hermeneutik der Schöpfung*. Tübingen: Mohr Siebeck, 1986.

———. *Schöpfung als Anrede: Zu einer Hermeneutik der Schöpfung*. 2nd ed. Tübingen: Mohr Siebeck, 1990.

———. "Schöpfung als Anrede und Anspruch." *Zeitschrift der Luther-Gesellschaft* 59 (1988) 131–44.

———. "Schöpfung als 'Rede an die Kreatur durch die Kreatur': Die Frage nach dem Schlüssel zum Buch der Natur und Geschichte." *Evangelische Theologie* 40 (1980) 316–33.

———. "Schöpfung und Verantwortung." *Lutherjahrbuch* 57 (1990) 192–206.

———. "Schriftautorität und Vernunft—Ein ekklesiologisches Problem." In *Schrift und Auslegung: Veröffentlichungen der Luther-Akademie e.V. Ratzeburg*, vol. 10: 69–87. Erlangen: Martin-Luther-Verlag, 1987.

———. "Selbstschöpfung? Von der Würde des Menschen. In *Schöpfungsglaube: Veroffentlichungen der Luther-Akademie e.V. Ratzeburg*, vol. 32: 179–99. Erlangen: Martin-Luther-Verlag, 2001.

———. "Self Creation? On the Dignity of Human Beings." Translated by Martin Abraham, Tim Beech, and Jeffrey Cayzer. *Modern Theology* 20 (2004) 275–90.

———. "Selbstdarstellung." In *Systematische Theologe der Gegenwart in Selbstdarstellungen*, edited by Christian Henning and Karsten Lehmkühler, 300-315 Tübingen: Mohr Siebeck, 1998.

———. "Selbstverschuldete Vormundschaft: Hamanns Kontroverse mit Kant um wahre Aufklärung." *Wirklichkeitsanspruch von Theologie und Religion. Herausforderung: Ernst Steinbach zum 70. Geburtstag*, 3-34. Tübingen: Mohr Siebeck, 1976.

———. "Staunen, Seufzen, Schauen: Affekte der Wahrnehmung des Schöpfers." In *JBT*, vol. 5: *Schöpfung und Neuschöpfung*, ed. Ingo Baldermann et al., 191-204. Neukirchen-Vluyn: Neukirchener, 1990.

———. "Systematische Theologie als Wissenschaft der Geschichte." *Verifikationen: Feschrift für Gerhard Ebeling zum 70. Geburtstag*, edited by Eberhard Jüngel, Johannes Wallmann, Wilfrid Werbeck, 341-361. Tübingen: Mohr Siebeck, 1982.

———. "Tempus creatura verbi." In *Eschatologie in der Dogmatik der Gegenwart: Veroffentlichungen der Luther-Akademie e.V. Ratzeburg*, vol. 11: 91-102. Erlangen: Martin-Luther-Verlag, 1988.

———. *Theologie*. Gütersloh: Gütersloher, 1994.

———. "Theologie, Glaube und Bildung." *ZThK* 72 (1975) 225-239.

———. "Theologie und Philosophie in produktivem Konflikt." *NZSTh* 32 (1990) 226-36.

———. *Theology the Lutheran Way*. Translated and edited by Jeffrey G. Silcock and Mark C. Mattes. Grand Rapids: Lutheran Quarterly Books, Eerdmans, 2007.

———. "Tillich as a Systematic Theologian." In *The Cambridge Companion to Paul Tillich*, ed. Russell Re Manning, 18-36. Cambridge: Cambridge University Press, 2009.

———. "Tod Gottes und Herrenmahl." *ZThK* 70 (1973) 346-63. From *Leibliches Wort*, 289-305.

———. "Toward a Theology of Lament." Translated by Matthias Gockel. In *Caritas et Reformatio*, edited by Carter Lindberg and David Whitford, 211-20. St. Louis: Concordia, 2002.

———. "Twenty-Four Theses on the Renewal of Lutheranism by Concentrating on the Doctrine of Justification." *LQ* 5 (1991) 73-75.

———. *Umstrittene Freiheit: Theologische-philosophische Kontroversen*. Tübingen: Mohr Siebeck, 1981.

———. "Unsere Hoffnungen und das Reich Gottes." In *Reich Gottes und Kirche: Veröffentlichungen der Luther-Akademie e.V. Ratzeburg*, vol. 12: 53-76. Erlangen: Martin-Luther-Verlag, 1988.

———. *Vernunft ist Sprache: Hamanns Metakritik Kants*. Stuttgart-Bad Connstatt: Frommann, 2002.

———. *Was ist das: Theologie? Eine Skizze*. Stuttgart: Calwer, 1973.

———. "What is Evangelical? The Continuing Validity of the Reformation." Translated by Jeffrey G. Silcock. *LQ* 25 (2011) 1-15.

———. "With Luther in the Present. The Present: Delivered from the Past to the Present." Translated by Mark A Seifred. *LQ* 21 (2007) 1-16.

———. "The Word of the Cross." Translated by John R. Betz. *LQ* 9 (1995) 47-55. English translation of "Das Wort vom Kreuz" in *Autorität und Kritik*, 117-24.

———. *Zeitgenosse im Widerspruch: Johann Georg Hamann als radikaler Aufklärer*. Munich: Piper, 1988.

———. *Zugesagte Gegenwart*. Tübingen: Mohr Siebeck, 2007.

———. "Zur Theologie der Klage." *JBT* 16 (2002) 289–301.
Bayer, Oswald, and Christian Knudsen; Johann Georg Hamann. *Kreuz und Kritik: Johann Georg Hammans Letztes Blatt, Text und Interpretation*. Tübingen: Mohr Siebeck, 1983.
Bayer, Oswald, and Robert Kremer. "L'héritage paulinien chez Luther." *Recherches de science religieuse* 94 (2006) 381–94.

Secondary Literature Addressing Bayer's Theology

Grube, Dirk Martin. "Luthers reformatorischer Durchbruch: zur Auseinandersetzung mit Oswald Bayers Promissio-Verständnis." *NZSTh* 48 (2006) 33–50.
Helmer, Christine M. "Does Luther Have a 'Waxen Nose'?: Historical and Philosophical Contextualizations of Luther." In *The Devil's Whore: Reason and Philosophy in the Lutheran Tradition*, edited by Jennifer Hockenbery Dragseth, 23–29. Studies in Lutheran History and Theology. Minneapolis: Fortress, 2011.
———. "The Subject of Theology in the Thought of Oswald Bayer." *LQ* 14 (2000) 21–52.
Herrmann, Erik. "Writing a Theology of Luther: A Review Essay on Contributons New and Old." *Concordia Journal* 35 (2009) 380–89.
Hütter, Reinhard. *Suffering Divine Things: Theology as Church Practice*. Translated by Doug Stott. Grand Rapids: Eerdmans, 2000.
Jonkers, Peter. "Theologie und (Post)modernität: philosophische Fragen zu Oswald Bayers Luther-Buch." *NZSTh* 48 (2006) 4–17.
Link, Christian. *Schöpfung: Schöpfungstheologie angesichts der Herausforderungen des 20. Jahrhunderts*. 2 vols. Gütersloh: Gütersloher, 1991.
Lüpke, Johannes von, and Edgar Thaidigsmann, eds. *Denkraum Katechismus: Festgabe für Oswald Bayer zum 70. Geburtstag*. Tübingen: Mohr Siebeck, 2009.
Mattes, Mark C. *The Role of Justification in Contemporary Theology*. Grand Rapids: Lutheran Quarterly Books, Eerdmans, 2004.
Sauter, Gerhard. "Katechismus-Grammatik: Kateschismusunterricht als Pendant des Theologiestudiums," in *Denkraum Katechismus: Festgabe für Oswald Bayer zum 70. Geburtstag*. Edited by Johannes von Lüpke und Edgar Thaidigsmann. Tübingen: Mohr Siebeck, 2009.
Schaeffer, Hans. *Createdness and Ethics: The Doctrine of Creation and Theological Ethics in the Theology of Colin E. Gunton and Oswald Bayer*. Berlin: de Gruyter, 2006.
Rikhof, Herwi. "Luther und die Trinitätstheologie zu Oswald Bayer: Martin Luthers Theologie. Eine Vergegenwärtigung." *NZSTh* 48 (2006) 74–82.
Wyller, Trygve. *Glaube und Autonome Welt: Diskussion eines Grundproblems derneueren systematischen Theologie mit Blicki auf Dietrich Bonhoeffer, Oswald Bayer und K. E. Løgstrup*. Berlin: de Gruyter, 1998.
Zwanepol, Klaas. "Zur Diskussion um Gottes Verborgenheit." *NZSTh* 48 (2006) 51–59.

Works by Figures Who Have Influenced Bayer, Secondary Material on Bayer's Infleunces, Works by Luther, Secondary Material on Luther's Theology, and Works Tangential to Bayer's Theology

Althaus, Paul. *Die Christliche Wahrheit: Lehrbuch der Dogmatik*. Gütersloh: Gütersloher, 1972.

———. *The Divine Command: A New Perspective on Law and Gospel*. Translated by Franklin Sherman. Philadelphia: Fortress, 1966.

———. *Grundriss der Dogmatik, I*. Gütersloh: Bertelsmann, 1947.

———. *The Theology of Martin Luther*. Translated by Robert C. Schultz. Philadelphia: Fortress, 1966.

Asendorf, Ulrich. *Lectura in Biblia: Luthers Genesisvorlesung (1535–1545)*. Göttingen: Vandenheok & Ruprecht, 1998.

Austin, J. L. *How to Do Things with Words*. Cambridge: Harvard University Press, 1962.

Barth, Hans-Martin. *Die Theologie Martin Luthers: Eine kritische Würdigung*. Gütersloh: Gütersloher, 2009.

———. *The Theology of Martin Luther: A Critical Assessment*. Translated by Linda M. Maloney. Minneapolis: Fortress, 2013.

Barth, Karl. *The Christian Life: Church Dogmatics IV, 4 Lecture Fragments*. Edited by Eberhard Jüngel. Translated by Geoffrey W. Bromiley. Grand Rapids: Eerdmans, 1981.

———. *Church Dogmatics*. Translated and edited by Geoffrey W. Bromiley and T. F. Torrance. Edinburgh: T. & T. Clark, 1936–69; rev. ed., 1975, reprinted 2004.

———. *The Epistle to the Romans*. Translated by Edwyn C. Hoskyns. Oxford: Oxford University Press, 1968.

———. *Evangelical Theology: An Introduction*. Translated by Grover Foley. Grand Rapids: Eerdmans, 1979.

———. *Freie reformierte Synode zu Barmen-Gemarke: am 3. und 4. Januar 1934*. Barmen: Müller, 1934.

———. "Gospel and Law." In *Community, State and Church: Three Essays*. Edited by Will Herberg. Translated by A. M. Hall. Garden City, NY: Anchor Doubleday, 1960.

———. *The Göttingen Dogmatics: Instruction in the Christian Religion, Volume I*. Translated by Geoffrey W. Bromiley. Edited by Hannelotte Reiffen. Grand Rapids: Eerdmans, 1991.

———. *No! A Reply to Emil Brunner*. In *Natural Theology*. Translated by Peter Fraenkel. Edited by John Baillie. 1946. Reprinted, Eugene, OR: Wipf & Stock, 2002.

———. *The Word of God and Theology*, trans. Amy Marga. London: T. & T. Clark, 2011.

Die Bekenntnisschriften der evangelisch-lutherischen Kirche. 2. Auflage. Edited by Horst Georg Pöhlmann. Gütersloh: Gütersloher, 1987.

Berlin, Isaiah. *J. G. Hamann and the Origins of Modern Irrationalism*. Edited by Henry Hardy. New York: Farrar, Straus & Giroux, 1993.

———. *Three Critics of the Enlightenment: Vico, Hamann, Herder*. Edited by Henry Hardy. Princeton: Princeton University Press, 2000.

Betz, John R. "Enlightenment Revisited: Hamann as the First and Best Critic of Kant's Philosophy." *Modern Theology* 20 (2004) 291–301.

Beutel, Albrecht. *Aufklärung in Deutschland*. Göttingen: Vandenhoeck & Ruprecht, 2006.
Biel, Gabrielis. *Collectorium crica quattor libros Sententiarum*. Vol. 1. Edited by Wilfrid Werbeck and Udo Hoffman. Tübingen: Mohr Siebeck, 1973.
Bizer, Ernst. *Fides ex auditu: Eine Unterschung über die Entdeckung der Gerechtigkeit Gottes durch Martin Luther*. 3rd ed. Neukirchen-Vluyn: Neukirchener, 1966.
The Book of Concord: The Confessions of the Evangelical Lutheran Church. Edited by Robert Kolb and Timothy J. Wengert. Translated by Charles Arand, Eric Gritsch, Robert Kolb, William Russell, James Schaaf, Jane Strol, and Timothy J. Wengert. Minneapolis: Fortress, 2000.
Bonhoffer, Dietrich. *Dietrich Bonhoeffers Werke*, vol. 5: *Geimeinsames Leben; Das Gebetbuch der Bibel*. Edited by Gerhard Ludwig Müller and Albrecht Schönherr. Munich: Kaiser, 1987.
———. *Dietrich Bonhoeffers Werke*, vol. 8: *Widerstand und Ergebung: Briefe und Aufzeizchungen aus der Haft*. Edited by Christian Gremmels, Eberhard Bethge, and Ilse Tödt. Munich: Kaiser, 1998.
———. *Dietrich Bonhoeffer Works*, vol. 5: *Life Together and Prayerbook of the Bible*. Translated by Daniel W. Bloesch and James H. Burtness. Edited by Geffrey B. Kelly. Minneapolis: Fortress, 1996.
———. *Deitrich Bonhoeffer Works*, vol. 8: *Letters and Papers from Prison*. Translated by Isabel Best, Lisa E. Dahill, Reinhard Krauss, and Nancy Lukens. Edited by John W. De Gruchy. Minneapolis: Fortress, 2010.
Bowie, Andrew. *Introduction to German Philosophy from Kant to Habermas*. Oxford: Blackwell, 2003.
Braaten, Carl E., and Robert W. Jenson, eds. *Union with Christ: The New Finnish Interpretation of Luther*. Grand Rapids: Eerdmans, 1998.
Brecht, Martin. *Martin Luther, Vols. I, II, and III*. Translated by James L. Schaaf. Minneapolis: Fortress, 1985–1993.
Busch, Eberhard. *The Barmen Theses Then and Now*. Translated by Darrell and Judith Guder. Grand Rapids: Eerdmans, 2010.
———. *The Great Passion: An Introduction to Karl Barth's Theology*. Translated by Geoffrey W. Bromiley. Grand Rapids: Eerdmans, 2004.
The Cambridge Companion to Immanuel Kant. Edited by Paul Guyer. Cambridge: Cambridge University Press, 1999.
The Cambridge Companion to Martin Luther. Edited by Donald K. McKim. Cambridge: Cambridge University Press, 2003.
Cajetan, Cardinal. *Augsburg Theses* (1518). In *Cajetan Responds: A Reader in Reformation Controversy*. Washington, DC: Catholic University of America Press, 1978.
Calvin, John. *Articles concerning Predestiantion*. In *Calvin: Theological Treatises*. Translated and edited by J. K. S. Reid. Philadelphia: Westminster, 1954.
Chemnitz, Martin. *Loci Theologici*. Translated by J. A. O. Preus. St. Louis: Concordia, 1989.
Chung, Paul. *Karl Barth: God's Word in Action*. Eugene, OR: Cascade Books, 2008.
Chung, Paul, Ulrich Duchrow, and Craig L. Nessan. *Liberating Lutheran Theology: Freedom for Justice and Solidarity in a Global Context*. Minneapolis: Fortress, 2011.
Cone, James H. *The Cross and the Lynching Tree*. Maryknoll, NY: Orbis, 2011.
———. *God of the Oppressed*. Rev. ed. Maryknoll, NY: Orbis, 1997.
———. *The Spirituals and the Blues: An Interpretation*. Maryknoll, NY: Orbis, 1991.

Croghan, Christopher. "Melanchthon's *Der Ordinanden Examen* and *Examen Eorum*: A Case Study in Pedagogical Method." Ph.D. diss., Luther Seminary, 2007.

Davis, Stephen T., ed. *Encountering Evil: Live Options in Theodicy*. New ed. Louisville: Westminster John Knox, 2001.

Dillenberger, John. *God Hidden and Revealed: The Interpretation of Luther's Deus Absconditus And Its Significance for Religious Thought*. Philadelphia: Muhlenberg, 1953.

Döblin, Alfred. *Berlin Alexanderplatz: Die Geschichte vom Franz Biberkopf*. Munich: Deutscher Taschenbuchverlag, 1972.

Dragseth, Jennifer Hockenberry, ed. *The Devil's Whore: Reason and Philosophy in the Lutheran Tradition*. Studies in Lutheran History and Theology. Minneapolis: Fortress, 2011.

Dunn, James D. G. *The Theology of Paul the Apostle*. Grand Rapids: Eerdmans, 2006.

Ebeling, Gerhard. *Dogmatik des Christlichen Glaubens*. 3 vols. Tübingen: Mohr Siebeck, 1979.

———. *Evangelische Evangelienauslegung: Eine Untersuchung zu Luthers Heremneutik*. 3rd ed. Tübingen: Mohr Siebeck, 1991.

———. *God and Word*. Translated by James W. Leitch. Philadelphia: Fortress, 1967.

———. *Luther: An Introduction to His Thought*. Translated by R. A. Wilson. Philadelphia: Fortress, 2007.

———. *Lutherstudien*. Tübingen: Mohr Siebeck, 1971–1985.

———. "Uber die Reformation hinaus? Zur Luther-Kritik Karl Barths." In *Luther und Barth: Veröffentlichungen der Luther-Akademie e.V. Ratzeburg*, vol. 13, edited by Joachim Heubach, 85–125. Erlangen: Martin-Luther-Verlag, 1989.

———. *Word and Faith*. Translated by James W. Leitch. Philadelphia: Fortress, 1963.

———. *Wort und Glaube*. Tübingen: Mohr Siebeck, 1960.

Elert, Werner. *The Structure of Lutheranism, Volume One: The Theology and Philosophy of Life of Lutheranism, Especially in the Sixteenth and Seventeenth Centuries*. Translated by Walter A. Hansen. St. Louis: Concordia, 1962.

Erasmus of Rotterdam, Desiderius. *On the Freedom of the Will: A Diatribe or Discourse*. Translated by Gordon E. Rupp. In Luther and Erasmus: Free Will And Salvation. Philadelphia: Westminster, 1969.

Erikson, Erik H. *Young Man Luther: A Study in Psychoanalysis and History*. New York: Norton, 1962.

Feuerbach, Ludwig. *The Essence of Christianity*. Translated by George Eliot. New York: Harper, 1957.

Francke, August Hermann. *A Letter to a Friend Concerning the Most Useful Way of Preaching* (1725). Translated by David Jennings. In *Pietists: Selected Writings*, edited by Peter C. Erb, 117–27. New York: Paulist, 1983.

———. *Simple Instruction, or How One Should Read Holy Scripture for One's True Edification*. Introduced and Translated by Jonathan Strom. *LQ* 25 (2011) 373–82.

———. *On Christian Perfection* (1690). Translated by Gustav Kramer. In *Pietists: Selected Writings*. Edited by Peter C. Erb, 114–116. New York: Paulist, 1983.

Forde, Gerhard O. *The Captivation of the Will: Luther vs. Erasmus on Freedom and Bondage*. Grand Rapids: Lutheran Quarterly Books, Eerdmans, 2004.

———. *The Law-Gospel Debate: An Interpretation of Its Historical Development*. Minneapolis: Augsburg, 1969.

———. *A More Radical Gospel: Essays on Eschatology, Authority, Atonement, and Ecumenism*. Edited by Mark C. Mattes and Steven D. Paulson, 137–155. Grand Rapids: Lutheran Quarterly Books, Eerdmans, 2004.

———. *On Being a Theologian of the Cross: Reflections on Luther's Heidelberg Disputation, 1518*. Grand Rapids: Eerdmans, 1997.

———. *The Preached God: Proclamation in Word and Sacrament*. Edited by Mark C. Mattes and Steven D. Paulson. Lutheran Quarterly Books, Eerdmans, 2007.

Gerhard, Johann. *Theological Commonplaces: Exegesis, or A More Copious Explanation of Certain Articles of the Christian Religion (1625), Volume 1: On the Nature of God and on the Most Holy Mystery of the Trinity*. Translated by Richard J. Dinda. Edited by Benjamin T. G. Mayes. St. Louis: Concordia, 2007.

Gerrish, B. A. "'To the Unknown God:' Luther and Calvin on the Hiddenness of God." *Journal of Religion* 53 (1973) 263–92.

Giertz, Bo. *The Hammer of God*. Minneapolis: Augsburg, 1960.

Goethe, Johann Wolfgang von. *Selected Poetry*. Translated by David Luke. London: Penguin, 2005.

Gorman, Michael J. *Inhabiting the Cruciform God: Kenosis, Justification, and Theosis in Paul's Narrative Soteriology*. Grand Rapids: Eerdmans, 2009.

Graybill, Gregory G. *Evangelical Free Will: Philipp Melanchthon's Doctrinal Journey on the Origins of Faith*. Oxford: Oxford University Press, 2010.

Gutiérrez, Gustavo. *On Job: God-Talk and the Suffering of the Innocent*. Translated by Matthew J. O'Connell. Maryknoll, NY: Orbis, 1986.

Hamann, Johann Georg. *Entkleidung und Verklärung: Eine Auswahl aus Schriften und Briefen des "Magnus im Norden"*. Edited by Martin Seils. Berlin: Union, 1963.

———. *Sämtliche Werke*. Vienna: Herder, 1949–1957.

Harnack, Adolf von. *History of Dogma*. Vol. 7. Translated by Neil Buchanan. Boston: Little, Brown, 1900.

Harnack, Theodosius. *Luthers Theologie mit besonderer Beziehung auf seine Versöhnungs- und Erlösungslehre, Erste Abteilung: Luthers theologische Grundanschauungen*, New ed. Munich: Kaiser, 1927.

Hays, Richard B. *The Faith of Jesus Christ: The Narrative Structure of Galatians 3:1— 4:11*. 2nd ed. Grand Rapids: Eerdmans, 2002.

———. *A Moral Vision of the New Testament: A Contemporary Introduction to New Testament Ethics*. San Francisco: HarperCollins, 1996.

Hegel, Georg Wilhelm Friedrich. *Faith and Knoweldge*. Translated by Walter Cerf and H. S. Harris. Albany: SUNY Press, 1977.

Hick, John. *Evil and the God of Love*. Glasgow: Collins, 1977.

Hinlicky, Paul R. *Luther and the Beloved Community: A Path for Christian Theology after Christendom*. Grand Rapids: Eerdmans, 2010.

———. *Paths not Taken: Fates of Theology from Luther to Leibniz*. Grand Rapids: Eerdmans, 2009.

Holl, Karl. *Die Rechtfertigungslehre in Luthers Vorlesung über den Römerbrief mit besonderer Rucksicht auf die Frage der Heilsgewissheit*. In *Gesammelte Aufsätze zur Kirchengeschichte*, vol. 1: *Luther*. Tübingen: Mohr Siebeck, 1932.

———. *What Did Luther Understand by Religion?* Edited by James Luther Adams and Walter F. Bense. Translated by Fred W. Meuser and Walter R. Wietzke. Philadelphia: Fortress, 1977.

Holy Bible: New Revised Standard Version. Iowa Falls, IA: World Publishers, National Council Of Churches in Christ in the United States of America, 1997

Hunsinger, George. "What Karl Barth Learned from Martin Luther." In *Disruptive Grace: Studies in the Theology of Karl Barth*, 279–304. Grand Rapids: Eerdmans, 2000.

Iwand, Hans Joachim. *Glaubensgerechtigkeit: Lutherstudien*. Edited by Gerhard Sauter. Munich: Kaiser, 1991.

———. *Um den Rechten Glauben*. Edited by Karl Gerhard Steck. Munich: Kaiser, 1959.

Jodock, Darrell, ed. *Ritschl in Retrospect: History, Community, and Science*. Minneapolis: Fortress, 1995.

The *Joint Declaration on the Doctrine of Justification*. The Lutheran World Federation, The Pontifical Council for Promoting Christian Unity of the Roman Catholic Church. Grand Rapids: Eerdmans, 2000.

Jüngel, Eberhard. "Anthropomorphismus als Grundproblem neuzeitlich Hermeneutik." In *Verifikationen Feschrift für Gerhard Ebeling zum 70. Geburtstag*, edited by Eberhard Jüngel, Johannes Wallmann, Wilfrid Werbeck, 499–522. Tübingen: Mohr Siebeck, 1982.

———. *God as the Mystery of the World: On the Foundation of the Theology of the Crucified One in the Dispute between Theism and Atheism*. Translated by Darrell L. Guder. Grand Rapids: Eerdmans, 1983.

———. *Justification: The Heart of the Christian Faith*. Translated by Jeffrey F. Cayzer. London: T. & T. Clark, 2001.

———. "The Revelation of the Hiddenness of God. " In *Theological Essays II*. Translated by Arnold Neufeldt-Fast and J. B. Webster. Edited by J. B., 120–144. Webster. Edinburgh: T. & T. Clark, 1995.

Kafka, Franz. *Der Prozeß*. Berlin: Aufbau Taschenbuch, 2003.

———. *The Trial*. Translated by Willa and Edwin Muir. New York: Schocken, 1974.

Kant, Immanuel. *Basic Writings of Kant*. Edited by Allen W. Wood. New York: Modern Library, 2001.

———. *Critique of Judgment*. Translated by James Creed Meredith. In *The Critique of Pure Reason, the Critique of Practical Reason, and the Critique of Judgment*, by Immanuel Kant. Chicago: Encyclopedia Britannica, Inc., University of Chicago Press, 1988.

———. *Critique of Practical Reason*. Translated by Thomas Kingsmill Abbott. In *The Critique of Pure Reason, the Critique of Practical Reason,* and the *Critique of Judgment*, by Immanuel Kant. Chicago: Encyclopedia Britannica, Inc., University of Chicago Press, 1988.

———. *Critique of Pure Reason*. Translated by Norman Kemp Smith. New York: St. Martin's, 1965.

———. *Foundations of the Metaphysics of Morals*. Translated by Thomas K. Abbott. New York: Modern Library, 2003.

———. *Lectures on Philosophical Theology*. Translated by Allen W. Wood and Gertrude M. Clark. Ithaca, NY: Cornell University Press, 1978.

———. *Religion within the Limits of Reason Alone*. Translated by Theodore M. Greene and Hoyt H. Hudson. New York: Harper & Row, 1960.

Kattenbusch, Ferdinand. *Deus Absconditus bei Luther*. Tübingen: Mohr Siebeck, 1920.

Kittelson, James M. *Luther the Reformer: The Story of the Man and His Career*. Minneapolis: Fortress, 2003.

Kolb, Robert. *Bound Choice, Election, and Wittenberg Theological Method: From Luther to the Bondage of the Will to the Formula of Concord.* Grand Rapids: Eerdmans, 2005.

Kolb, Robert, and Charles P. Arand. *The Genius of Luther's Theology: A Wittenberg Way of Thinking for the Contemporary Church.* Grand Rapids: Baker Academic, 2008.

Kuropka, Nicole. "Melanchthon and Aristotle." Translated by Timothy J. Wengert. *LQ* 25 (2011) 16–27.

———. *Philipp Melanchthon: Wissenschaft und Gesellschaft. Ein Geleherter im Dienst der Kirche.* Tübingen: Mohr Siebeck, 2002.

Leibniz, Gottfried Wilhelm. *Theodicy: Essays on the Goodness of God, the Freedom of Man, and the Origin of Evil.* Translated by E. M. Huggard. London: Routledge & Kegan Paul, 1952.

Leibrecht, Walter. *God and Man in the Thought of Hamann.* Translated by James H. Stam and Martin H. Bertram. Philadelphia: Fortress, 1966.

Lohse, Bernhard. *Martin Luther's Theology: Its Historical and Systematic Development.* Translated by Roy A. Harrisville. Minneapolis: Fortress, 1999.

Lotz, David W. *Ritschl and Luther: A Fresh Perspective on Albrecht Ritschl's Theology in the Light of His Luther Study.* Nashville: Abingdon, 1974.

Löwenich, Walther von. *Luther's Theology of the Cross.* Translated by Herbert J. A. Bouman. Minneapolis: Augsburg, 1976.

Lowrie, Walter. *Johann Georg Hamann: An Existentialist.* Princeton Pamphlets 6. Princeton, NJ: Princeton Theological Seminary, Princeton Univeruisty Press, 1950.

Luther Handbuch. Edited by Albrecht Beutel. Tübingen: Mohr Siebeck, 2005.

Luther, Martin. *The Bondage of the Will* (1525). Translated by J. I. Packer and O. R. Johnston. Grand Rapids: Revell, 2000.

———. *D. Martin Luthers Werke. Kritische Gesamtausgabe.* Weimar: Böhlaus, 1883–.

———. *First Sunday in Advent.* In *The Complete Sermons of Martin Luther Vol. 1.1–2.* Translated and edited by John Nicholas Lenker. Grand Rapids: Baker Book House, 2000.

———. *Luther's Works.* Edited by Jaroslav Pelikan and Helmut T. Lehmann. 56 vols. Philadelphia: Fortress Press; St. Louis: Concordia, 1955–86.

Luther und Barth: Veröffentlichungen der Luther-Akademie Ratzeburg, vol. 13. Edited by Oswald Bayer. Erlangen: Martin-Luther-Verlag, 1989.

Mackintosh, Hugh Ross. *Types of Modern Theology: Schleiermacher to Barth.* London: Nisbet, 1947.

Mahlmann, Theodor. "Die Interpretation von Luthers *De servo Arbitrio* bei orthodoxen lutherischen Theologen, vor allem Sebastian Schmidt (1617–1696)." In *Luthers Erben: Festschrift für Jörg Baur sum 75. Geburtstag.* Edited by Notger Slenczka and Walter Sparn, 73–136. Tübingen: Mohr Siebeck, 2005.

Mannermaa, Tuomo. *Christ Present in Faith: Luther's View of Justification.* Translated and edited by Kirsi Stjerna. Mineapolis: Fortress, 2005.

Manschreck, Clyde Leonard. *Melanchthon: The Quiet Reformer.* New York: Abingdon, 1963.

Mao Tse-Tung (Zedong). *Selected Works of Mao Tse-tung.* Peking (Beijing): Foreign Languages Press, 1967–1969.

Marquardt, Friedrich-Wilhelm. *Theologie und Sozialismus: Das Beispiel Karl Barths.* Munich: Kaiser, 1972.

Martens, Gottfried. "Inconsequential Signatures? The Decade after the Signing of the *Joint Declaration on the Doctrine of Justification*." Translated Mark D. Menacher. *LQ* 24 (2010) 310–36.

Markschies, Christoph, and Michael Trowitzsch, eds. *Luther, zwischen den Zeiten: Eine Jenaer Ringvorlesung*. Tübingen: Mohr Siebeck, 1999.

Marx, Karl. *Critique of Hegel's 'Philosophy of Right'*. Translated by Annette Jolin and Joseph O'Malley. Edited by Joseph O'Malley. Cambridge: Cambridge University Press, 1970.

Marx, Karl, and Friedrich Engels. *Karl Marx-Friedrich Engels Werke*, vol. 1. Berlin: Dietz Verlag, Institut für Marxismus-Leninismus beim Zentralkomitee der Sozialistische Enheitspartei Deutschlands, 1972.

———. *Karl Marx-Friedrich Engels Werke*. Vol. 20. Berlin: Dietz Verlag, Institut für Marxismus-Leninismus beim Zentralkomitee der Sozialistische Enheitspartei Deutschlands, 1962.

———. *Marx-Engels Gesamtausgabe*. Vol. 2. Berlin: Dietz, 1982.

Matz, Wolfgang. *Der befreite Mensch: Die Willenslehre in der Theologie Philipp Melanchthons*. Forschungen zur Kirchen- und Dogmengeschichte 81. Göttingen: Vandenhoeck & Ruprecht, 2001.

Maxfield, John A. *Luther's Lectures on Genesis and the Formation of Evangelical Identity*. Sixteenth Century Essays & Studies 80. Kirksville, MO: Truman State University Press, 2008.

McCormack, Bruce. *Karl Barth's Critically Realistic Dialectical Theology*. Oxford: Clarendon, 1995.

———. *Orthodox and Modern: Studies in the Theology of Karl Barth*. Grand Rapids: Baker Academic, 2008.

McDonald, Suzanne, "Barth's 'Other' Doctrine of Election." *IJST* 9 (2007) 134–147.

McGrath, Alister. *Luther's Theology of the Cross*. Oxford: Blackwell, 1990.

Melanchthon, Philipp. *Philippi Melanthonis Opera*. Corpus Reformatorum 1–28. Halle: Schwetschke, 1834–1860.

———. *Excerpts from the Writings of Philip Melanchthon (1519–1557)*. Selected and translated by Michael Rogness. Howard Lake, MN.

———. *The Loci Communes of Philip Melanchthon (1521)*. Translated by Charles Leander Hill. 1944. Reprinted, Eugene, OR: Wipf & Stock, 2005.

———. *Loci Communes (1543)*. Translated by J. A. O. Preus. St. Louis: Concordia, 1994.

———. *Loci Communes (1555)*. Translated and edited by Clyde L. Manschreck. Oxford: Oxford University Press, 1965.

———. *Melanchthon: Selected Writings*. Edited by Elmer Flack and Lowell Satre. Minneapolis: Augsburg, 1962.

———. *Studienausgabe—Melanchthons Werke*. Edited by Robert Stupperich. Gütersloh: Gerd Mohn, 1952–.

Menacher, Mark. "Gerhard Ebeling in Retrospective." *LQ* 21 (2007) 163–196.

Moltmann, Jürgen. *Trinität und Reich Gottes: Zur Gotteslehre*. Munich: Kaiser, 1980.

———. *The Trinity and the Kingdom*. Translated by Margaret Kohl. Minneapolis: Fortress, 1993.

Nestingen, James Arne. "Luther's Heidelberg Disputation: An Analysis of the Argument." In *All Things New Essays in Honor of Roy A. Harrisville*. Word & World Supplement

Series 1. St. Paul: Word & World, Luther Northwestern Theological Seminary, 1992.

Nürnberger, Klaus. *Martin Luther's Message for Us Today: A Perspective from the South*. Pietermaritzburg: Cluster, 2005.

Oberman, Heiko. *The Dawn of the Reformation: Essays in Late Medieval and Early Reformational Thought*. Grand Rapids: Eerdmans, 1992.

———. *The Harvest of Medieval Theology: Gabriel Biel and Late Medieval Nominalism*. Grand Rapids: Baker Academic, 2000.

———. *Luther: Man between God and the Devil*. Translated by Eileen Walliser-Schwarzbart. New York: Doubleday, 1992.

Otto, Rudolf. *The Idea of the Holy*. Translated by John W. Harvey. Oxford: Oxford University Press, 1958.

———. *The Kingdom of God and the Son of Man: A Study in the History of Religion*. Translated by Floyd V. Filson and Bertram Lee Woolf. Rev. ed. 1957. Reprinted, Grand Rapids: Zondervan, n.d.

Pannenberg, Wolfhart. *Systematic Theology, Volume 1*. Translated by Geoffrey W. Bromiley. Grand Rapids: Eerdmans, 1991.

———. *Systematic Theology, Volume 2*. Translated by Geoffrey W. Bromiley. Grand Rapids: Eerdmans, 1994.

———. *Systematic Theology, Volume 3*. Translated by Geoffrey W. Bromiley. Grand Rapids: Eerdmans, 1998.

———. *Theology and Philosophy of Science*. Translated by Francis McDonagh. London: Dartman, Longman & Todd, 1976.

Paulson, Steven D. "Analogy and Proclamation: The Struggle over God's Hiddenness in the Theology of Martin Luther and Eberhard Juengel." Th.D. diss. The Lutheran School of Theology in Chicago, 1992.

———. "Luther on the Hidden God." *Word & World* 19 (1999) 363–71.

———. *Lutheran Theology*. London: T. & T. Clark, 2011.

Pinomaa, Lennart. *Faith Victorious: An Introduction to Luther's Theology*. Translated by Walter J. Kukkonen. Lima, OH: Academic Renewal, 2001.

Reinhuber, Thomas. *Kämpfende Glaube: Studien zum Luthers Bekenntnis am Ende von De servo arbitrio*. Berlin: de Gruyter, 2000.

Ritschl, Albrecht. *The Christian Doctrine of Justification and Reconciliation: The Positive Development of the Doctrine*. Translated by H. R. Mackintosh and A. B. Macauly. Edinburgh: T. & T. Clark, 1900.

———. *A Critical History of the Doctrine of Justification and Reconciliation*. Translated by John S. Black. Edinburgh: Edmonston & Douglas, 1872.

———. *Drei Akademische Reden*. Bonn: Marcus, 1887.

———. *Gesammelte Aufsätze*, Neue Folge. Freiburg: Akademische Verlagsbuchhandlung von J. C. B. Mohr, 1896.

———. *Three Essays: Theology and Metaphysics, "Prolegomena" to the History of Pietism, Instruction in the Christian Religion*. Translated by Philip Hefner. Philadelphia: Fortress, 1972.

Rogness, Michael. *Melanchthon: Reformer without Honor*. Minneapolis: Augsburg, 1969.

Saarinen, Risto. "The Language of Gift in Theology." *NZSTh* 52 (2010) 268–301.

Saarnivaara, Uuras. *Luther Discovers the Gospel: New Light upon Luther's Way from Medieval Catholicism to Evangelical Faith*. 1951. Reprinted, Eugene, OR: Wipf & Stock, 2003.

Sanders, E. P. *Paul and Palestinian Judaism*. Philadelphia: Fortress, 1997.

Sasse, Hermann. *Here We Stand: Nature and Character of the Lutheran Church*. 2nd ed. Translated and edited by Theodore G. Tappert. New York: Harper, 1938.

Scheel, Otto. *Martin Luther: Vom Katholizmus zur Reformation*. Vol. 2: *Im Kloster*. Tübingen: Mohr Siebeck, 1930.

Schleiermacher, Friedrich. *The Christian Faith*, Volume 1. Translated by H. R. Mackintosh and J. S. Stewart. New York: Harper & Row, 1963.

Schlink, Edmund. *Theology of the Lutheran Confessions*. 3rd ed. Translated by Paul F. Koehneke and Herbert J. A. Bouman. Philadelphia: Muhlenberg, 1961.

Schwanke, Johannes. *Creatio ex Nihilo: Luthers Lehre von der Schöpfung aus dem Nichts in der Grossen Genesisvorlesung (1535–1545)*. Berlin: de Grutyer, 2004.

―――. "Luther on Creation." Translated by John R. Betz. *LQ* 16 (2002) 1–20.

Schwarzwäller, Klaus. *Sibboleth: Die Interpretation von Luthers Schrift De servo arbitrio seit Theodosius von Harnack, Ein systematisch-kritischer Überblick*. Munich: Kaiser, 1969.

―――. *Theologia Crucis: Luthers Lehre von Prädestination nach De servo arbitrio, 1525*. Munich: Kaiser, 1970.

Scruton, Roger. *Kant: A Very Short Introduction*. Oxford: Oxford University Press, 2001.

Seils, Martin. "Hamann und Luther." In *Luther, zwischen den Zeiten: Eine Jenaer Ringvorlesung*, edited by Christoph Markschies and Michael Trowitzsch, 159–84. Tübingen: Mohr Siebeck, 1999.

Slenczka, Notger. "Neuzeitliche Freiheit oder ursprüngliche Bindung? Zu einem Paradigmenwechsel in der Reformations- und Lutherdeutung." In *Luthers Erben: Festschrift für Jörg Baur sum 75. Geburtstag*. Edited by Notger Slenczka and Walter Sparn, 205–44. Tübingen: Mohr Siebeck, 2005.

Sources and Contexts of the Book of Concord. Edited by Robert Kolb and James A. Nestingen. Minneapolis: Fortress, 2001.

Stein, K. James. "Philip Jakob Spener." In *The Pietist Theologians: An Introduction to Theology in the Seventeenth and Eighteenth Centuries*, edited by Carter Lindberg, 84–99. Oxford: Blackwell, 2005.

Smith, Ronald Gregor. *J. G. Hamann: A Study in Christian Existence: With Selections from His Writings*. New York: Harper, 1960.

Spener, Philip Jakob. *Der Hochwichtige Articul von der Widergeburt*. Frankfurt: Zunner, 1696.

Stayer, James M. *Martin Luther, German Saviour: German Evangelical Theological Factions and the Interpretation of Luther, 1917–1933*. Montreal: McGill-Queens University, 2000.

Steinmetz, David C. *Luther in Context*. 2nd ed. Grand Rapids: Baker Academic, 2002.

Taylor, Charles. *A Secular Age*. Cambridge, MA: Belknap, 2007.

Theologische Realenzyklopädie. Vol. 2. Edited by Gerhard Krause and Gerhard Müller. Berlin: de Gruyter, 1977–2004.

Tillich, Paul. *Systematic Theology, Volume I: Reason and Revelation, Being and God*. Chicago: University of Chicago Press, 1951.

―――. *Systematic Theology, Volume II: Existence and the Christ*. Chicago: University of Chicago Press, 1965.

———. *Systematic Theology, Volume III: Life and the Spirit, History and the Kingdom of God*. Chicago: University of Chicago Press, 1963.

Troeltsch, Ernst. *Protestantism and Progress: The Significance of Protestantism for the Rise of the Modern World*. Translated by W. Montgommery. Edited by B. A. Gerrish. Philadelphia: Fortress, 1986.

Vercruysse, Joseph. *Fedelis populous*. Wiesbaden: Steiner, 1968.

Wainwright, Geoffrey. "Recent Continental Theology." *Expository Times* 104 (1993) 362–66.

Wengert, Timothy J. *A Formula for Parish Practice: Using the Formula of Concord in Congregations*. Grand Rapids: Lutheran Quarterly Books, Eerdmans, 2006.

———. *Human Freedom, Christian Righteousness*. Oxford: Oxford University Press, 1998.

Walter, Gregory. "Karl Holl (1866–1926) and the Recovery of Promise in Luther." *LQ* 25 (2011) 398–413.

Wilson, John E. *Introduction to Modern Theology: Trajectories in the German Tradition*. Louisville: Westminster John Knox, 2007.

Wingren, Gustaf. *The Living Word: A Theological Study of Preaching and the Church*. Translated by Victor C. Pogue. Philadelphia: Fortress, 1960.

Yeago, David. "Gnosticism, Antinomianism, and Reformation Theology: Reflections on the Costs of a Construal." *Pro Ecclesia* 2 (1993) 37–49.

Name Index

Abraham, 27
Althaus, Paul, 10n41, 67, 72, 75–80, 96, 98, 100, 107, 111–12, 114, 289, 294–95, 300
Aristotle, 117
Aquinas, Thomas, 82, 115, 124, 126–27, 131
Austin, J. L., xi, 150, 154–56, 158, 172, 299, 306, 325n69

Barth, Karl, x, 11, 67, 80–90, 93–94, 96, 100, 107–8, 111–12, 114, 142, 151, 166, 190–91, 191n78, 201, 229, 232, 236–37, 253, 262, 279, 284–90, 292, 300, 315–18
Biel, Gabriel, 118–20, 127
Bizer, Ernst, 2, 5, 2n27, 151–53
Bonhoeffer, Dietrich, 97, 125n38, 127n50
Brunner, Emil, 67, 80, 83, 90–94, 96, 97, 111–13
Bultmann, Rudolf, 97, 117, 124

Cajetan, Cardinal, 4, 4n20, 5n27, 128–29, 151, 153
Calvin, John, 36, 45, 81, 84n161, 93, 148, 218, 236–37, 267
Chemnitz, Martin, 42, 44, 44–45n13, 45n16
Chung, Paul 83–86, 84n161, 325
Concordists. *See Formula of Concord*
Cone, James, 326, 326n71

Döblin, Alfred, 179, 258

Ebeling, Gerhard, 5, 5n27, 67, 97–101, 111, 113–14, 151–52, 288–89, 295–98, 301
Elert, Werener, 10n41, 67–68, 71–75, 79–80, 98, 100, 111, 113–14, 262, 279–84, 287, 289, 295–96, 301, 311n30, 312–13n40
Engels, Friedrich, 135n95

Feuerbach, Ludwig, 108, 108n251,
Francke, August Hermann, 46
Forde, Gerhard, 193n309, 237n134, 325, 325n68

Gerhard, Johann, 46–47
Giertz, Bo, 325, 325n76
Gnesio-Lutherans, 41–46
Goethe, Johann Wolfgang von, 167, 178n24
Gorman, Michael J., 149, 149n12
Gutiérrez, Gustavo, 326, 326n71

Hamann, Johann Georg, xi, 1, 3, 5–7, 11, 118–23, 134, 137–41, 144, 162, 166–68, 168n100, 172, 188–89, 202–4, 264, 271–73, 299, 314
Harnack, Theodosius, xiii, 47–50, 53, 73, 80, 93, 100, 110, 113–14, 281, 289–90, 301, 304
Harnack, Adolf von, 57
Hegel, Georg, Friedrich, Wilhelm, 50, 104n237, 134, 234, 322

NAME INDEX

Helmer, Christine, 8n36, 9–11, 244n162, 309–10, 313–15, 318
Herbst, Georg, 44
Herder, Johann Gottfried, 6, 134, 167
Hick, John, 271
Hinlicky, Paul, 9–11, 156n39, 309–15, 318, 325
Hitler, Adolf, 220
Holl, Karl, 49, 57–63, 66–67, 73, 111–14, 148, 289–93
Hutter, Reinhard, 9–10, 309

Jacob, x, 27, 30, 32, 159, 177, 200, 205, 211, 214–16, 222, 254, 272–73, 277, 283, 307, 319, 326n71
Jonah, 20–22, 262–63
Jüngel, Eberhard, xiii, 11, 57–58n63, 67, 83, 89, 101, 107–14, 279, 285–90, 292, 300, 315–17

Kafka, Franz, 135
Kant, Immanuel, xi, 1, 6–7, 49–51, 51n35, 117, 120–21, 132–134, 138–140, 166, 272–73, 314
Käsemann, Ernst, 2, 97
Kattenbusch, Ferdinand, 57
Kolb, Robert, xv, 28n59, 44

Leibniz, Gottfried Wilhelm, 234, 271
Loewenich, Walter von, 67–72, 74–75, 79–80, 98, 100, 110–12
Lohse, Bernhard, 75
Lombard, Peter, 119
Lotze, Rudolf Hermann, 50, 51n35

Mannermaa, Tuomo, 57n63, 149n11
Mao Zedong, 328n74
Marx, Karl, 123, 134, 169
Mattes, Mark, 6n28, 8n36, 9–10, 104n237, 124n36, 309

Melanchthon, Philipp, 41–43, 42n2, 45, 57–58n63, 148
Moltmann, Jürgen, 3, 67, 101, 105–7, 111–12, 181, 198n116, 234

Novalis, 134

Otto, Rudolf, 49, 62–67, 111–14, 279–80, 287, 289, 301, 304

Pannenberg, Wolfhart, 67, 101–6, 111–12, 117, 124, 126–27, 149, 289
Paul, 58–61, 68, 70, 91, 149, 152
Paulson, Steven D., xv, 286, 287n112
Philipists, 41–46, 45n16
Pinomaa, Lennart, 38

Ritschl, Albrecht, 49–58, 60, 62–67, 72, 80, 100, 110–12, 114, 148, 281, 289–94, 200, 313

Saarnivaara, Uuras, 59–60n72
Sasse, Hermann, 191n78, 285n100
Sauter, Gerhard, 3, 9–10, 10n41, 309
Schaeffer, Hans, 9–10, 142n124, 309
Schwarzwäller, Klaus, 37, 48
Schiller, Friedrich, 167
Schleiermacher, Friedrich, xi, 47, 50, 63, 117, 125, 134–35, 135n91, 137–38, 176–77, 236
Spangenberg, Cyriacus, 44
Stuhlmacher, Peter, 3
Swedenborg, Emanuel, 130

Tillich, Paul, 67, 80, 93–97, 111–13
Trapp, Thomas, xv, 124n36, 244n162
Troeltsch, Ernst, 57

Yeago, David, 312–13n40

Zwanepol, Klaas, 9–11, 309–10, 315–18

Subject Index

absolution, ix, 31, 155, 158–59, 166, 320
Anfechtung (tentatio), x, 20–24, 29, 46, 62, 74, 92, 100, 113, 124–26, 124n36, 181–88, 186n59, 200–208, 210–24, 219n38, 231–32, 235–61, 237–38n134, 266–85, 288, 296–307, 317, 319, 321, 324, 326–27
Apology to the Augsburg Confession, 147n1, 148n2, 190n77
Aristotelianism, 42, 42n2, 99, 117–18, 122–24, 131–32
Augsburg Confession, 42n4, 148n2, 166n87, 190n76, 320
Augustinianism, 152, 156n39, 310–11, 328

the Bible. *See* Scripture.
Baptism, 28, 30–31, 155–57, 165–66

Calvinism, 45, 74–75n129, 232, 236–37, 253, 318
capitalism, 169
catechesis, 327
Christendom, 310, 329
Christology, 84, 84n161, 247–48, 284, 287, 312–13n40
creation, xi, 2, 4, 7, 10–11, 84–87, 85n163, 130, 133–34, 134n87–88, 140–43, 143n130, 150–51, 156, 160–72, 178, 178n24, 179n25, 189, 192, 202–6, 209, 211, 214, 217–23, 220n46, 238, 241–44, 246–58, 263–65, 268– 69, 271–73, 284, 294, 299, 302, 306–8, 314, 321–329, 328n76

death, xiii, 13–23, 14n3, 30–36, 68, 76–78, 85, 95, 116, 144, 169–70, 174–75, 178, 178n24, 186, 192, 198–99, 204–205, 208, 211, 213, 220, 225, 227, 229–30, 233, 236, 247–48, 252–55, 260–61, 266, 271, 274, 277, 299, 304, 307, 321, 328–29
cross, x, 13–14, 14n3, 71, 85–89, 91, 94, 98, 102–10, 104n237, 121–22, 200, 203, 235, 282, 284, 295, 299–300
dualism, x, 65, 88, 216, 232–33, 237, 253, 311–12, 322, 328

Enlightenment, the, xi, 1, 6–7, 51, 118–20, 201, 234, 239, 272
eschatology, 19, 29, 57–58n63, 102, 111, 130, 142–45, 161, 170–73, 193, 193n91, 201, 218, 226, 231, 238–44, 246, 249–56, 268, 274–75, 278, 291, 302, 307–8, 310–14, 317–18, 320–23, 325, 329–30
escapism, 327
ethics, 2, 8, 51–55, 64, 120–21, 133, 139–42, 142n124, 148, 172–73, 180, 191n78, 191–92
Eucharist. *See* Holy Communion.
evil. *See* problem of evil.

Formula of Concord, 42, 45, 45n16, 74, 74n129, 76, 147n1, 190n76–n77, 192, 192n85

God, alien work of, 24–26, 37–40, 58, 61–62, 73–75, 80, 85–86, 89, 91–92, 98–100, 108–10, 112–13, 135, 261, 276–78, 293, 296, 320

God, as author, 7, 121, 138–41, 167–68, 168n100, 271

God, as poet, 136–45, 168, 264

God, freedom of, 55, 58, 81–83

God, love of, 34, 53, 59–65, 108, 236, 291–93

God, preached, 13, 15, 17–19, 34–35, 38–39, 53, 55–58, 60–62, 66–70, 93–94, 96, 108, 110, 151, 168, 197, 260, 269, 278, 313

God, proper work of, 25, 36–40, 58, 60–61, 73, 75, 79, 86, 92, 114, 127, 141–43, 161, 163, 183, 206, 231, 237, 261, 276–78, 293, 296

God, suffering of, 106–7, 122, 200, 232, 235

God, Triune. *See* Trinity.

God, unpreached, x, 13–21, 18, 34–35, 37–39, 45, 48–49, 53–71, 74, 76–77, 79–80, 85, 93–4, 96, 107–10, 260–61, 304–5, 313, 317, 321

God, wrath of, xiii, 15, 18–23, 25, 28, 30–31, 34–35, 40, 42, 48–49, 52–67, 72–75, 80, 85–96, 98–101, 104, 108–11, 113, 144–45, 152, 159, 174–78, 180, 189, 194–96, 198–99, 201, 207, 212, 221–22, 230, 232, 235–36, 241, 246–49, 252–53, 257–58, 260–65, 271–77, 280–84, 286–308, 316, 325–26

God, wrestling of, x, 30–32, 159, 205, 213–17, 221, 272–73, 277, 326n71

the gospel, justifying and life-giving promise of God, x, xiii, 1, 5, 11, 15, 17–18, 24, 29–31, 34–35, 38, 64, 69–70, 79, 88, 89n182, 97–100, 116, 137–38, 147–50, 152, 154–60, 164–65, 168, 171–73, 175, 177, 180–81, 183–89, 188n71, 191, 193, 256, 260, 262, 265–70, 272, 274–75, 277–78, 280, 288, 290, 293–94, 297, 319–30

the gospel, as the eschatological end of the law, 141–47, 193n91, 193–94

the gospel, as the eschatological end of hiddenness. *See* hiddenness, eschatological end of.

the gospel, in conflict with divine hiddenness. *See* hiddenness, as the contradiction of the justifying gospel.

Hegelianism, 50, 104n237, 198, 228, 232, 234, 240, 243, 322, 328

hermeneutics, 2, 7, 97n213, 122, 136–46, 152

hiddenness of God, and the problem of evil. *See* the problem of evil.

hiddenness of God, as the contradiction of the justifying gospel, 10, 196–214, 223–32, 234–35, 239, 246, 252, 254, 257, 261, 277–78, 285, 299–307, 313–14, 316–19, 323, 330

hiddenness, eschatological end of, 201, 218, 223, 226, 231, 238–44, 246, 249–56, 308, 321

hiddenness of God, in revelation. *See* theology of the cross.

hiddenness of God, relationship to law and gospel, 15–20, 25–26, 33–35, 37–39, 49, 62, 69–80, 90–92, 97–98, 100, 109, 111–13, 115, 137, 144–45, 158–59, 188–201, 212, 262–65

History of Religions School, 48–49, 62–67, 111, 279–80

Holy Communion, 1, 154–55, 158–59, 165–67, 248–51, 254

Holy Spirit, 43, 65, 81, 83, 87, 166, 193, 227–28, 248, 251

Joint Declaration on the Doctrine of Justification, 131, 136, 149, 149n9

justification, and hiddenness. *See* hiddenness of God, as the

SUBJECT INDEX

contradiction of the justifying gospel.
justification, by faith in the Lutheran tradition, ix,, xiii, 2–5, 8–12, 8n36, 37–38, 49, 57, 57–58n63, 59–60n72, 60–62, 111, 114ff.
justification, by God's active word of promise, 116, 126–37, 141–46, 147–74, 176, 191, 193, 205ff.

Kantianism, 49–50, 57, 111, 133–34, 139, 144, 192, 264, 273, 291, 328

lament, x, 63, 170, 183, 206, 210, 231, 238, 244–56, 268–70, 274, 278, 300, 302, 308, 314, 317, 320–22, 326–27, 326n71, 329
the law, condemning or killing word of God, x, 14n3, 16–20, 25–26, 34–35, 37, 55, 59–60, 62, 69, 72–80, 88, 90–92, 97–98, 100, 112–13, 140–41, 150, 158–59, 167, 188–99, 188n71, 207, 212, 226–27, 229, 262–67, 278, 281–84, 283n92, 288, 294, 296–99, 301, 304–6, 308, 319, 325n67, 327–28
the law, eschatological end of, 141–143, 145, 193, 193n91, 241
the law, Kantian view of, 120–21, 133
law and gospel, ix–xiii, 4, 15–18, 33–38, 69–70, 76, 79, 88, 92, 109–12, 137, 140–45, 152, 189–91, 190n76, 191n78, 191n79, 194–99, 201–3, 212, 258–59, 262, 270, 281–82, 285–88, 294, 299, 305, 312–13n40, 316–18
life, given by God, x, 14, 18–19, 26, 33, 35–37, 43, 54, 76, 79, 99, 116, 140–142, 161, 166, 169, 185–186, 199, 211, 213, 225, 227, 233, 266, 271, 278, 296
linguistics, 327
liturgy, 242–244, 251
Lord's Supper. *See* Holy Communion.
Lutheran orthodoxy, 41, 46, 124, 147
Lutheran pietism, 41, 46, 50, 124
Lutheranism, 11, 74n129, 124, 142, 166, 191, 259, 326

Marxism, 169
meditation, *meditatio*, xii, 125–26, 176, 182–84, 188, 206–7
monasticism, 122–23
monism, 234–35
mythology, 117, 121, 179

Nazism, 220
Neo-Kantianism, 49–51, 51n35, 56–57, 62, 67, 72, 111, 291, 313, 314
New Finnish interpretation of Luther, 149
New Perspective on Paul, 149, 149n7

poetry, 242
prayer, *oratio*, xii, 22, 97, 125, 170, 182–84, 188, 206–7, 251, 260, 270, 323
preaching, ix–x, 5n27, 83–84, 86, 148, 154–59, 167–68, 172, 180, 209, 214, 222, 242, 254, 277, 312–13n40, 319–31, 323, 327
predestination, x, 28, 32, 42, 45n16, 52–54, 60–62, 65, 74, 74n129, 76, 82, 88, 90, 97, 259
predestination, double, 29, 33, 36–37, 39, 42–43, 45–46, 45n16, 74, 74n129, 76, 87–88, 92–93, 100, 112–13, 184–85, 210–11, 217–19, 219n38, 221–23, 229–33, 236–37, 242, 253, 255–56, 262, 265–67, 271, 274–75, 291–99, 307
predestination, election, 28–29, 36–40, 45, 45n16, 87–89, 92–93, 217–218, 266–67, 271
predestination, reprobation, 36–40, 46, 65, 74–75, 87–89, 92–93, 98, 100, 112–13, 184–85, 217–18, 266–67, 271, 278, 291–99, 319
problem of evil, x, 11, 19, 40, 94–95, 99, 109, 161, 169, 178–80, 178–79n24, 184–87, 196, 200, 202–8, 210–11, 216–25, 229–59, 261, 267–68, 270–78, 284, 297–98, 300, 302, 307–8, 313, 320, 322–24, 326–30, 326n71, 328n75–76

proclamation. *See* preaching.
Promise. *See* justification, by God's active word of promise.

the Reformation, 1, 16, 93, 116, 122, 124, 128–32, 152–53, 175, 269, 275, 329
the Ritchlian tradition, 48–50, 56–57, 60–62, 64–66, 72, 89, 111, 290–93
romanticism, 134, 167, 272
rupture of the ages, 161, 169–72, 223, 231, 239, 241–44, 250–52, 300, 307–8, 322

Sacraments, 5n27, 28–29, 31–33, 37–39, 123, 154–60, 165–68, 172, 189, 197, 209, 214, 248, 277–78, 309, 320. *See also* baptism, absolution, Holy Communion.
Sacrament of the Altar. *See* Holy Communion.
Scripture xi–xii, 4, 17, 46n20, 81, 140, 162, 167–68, 177, 181–84, 187, 207, 232, 236, 244n162
socialism, 169
Small Catechism, 106n245, 323n63
speech act, xi, 150–61, 164, 167, 172–73, 191, 193, 206, 209, 211, 214, 246, 276, 302, 306–7, 313, 320, 327
suffering, 13–14, 14n3, 71, 77, 91, 98, 106, 144, 179–80, 185, 200, 219
suffering of God. *See* God, suffering of.
suffering, undergoing divine address and the experience of hiddenness, xi, 7, 118, 120–22, 140

tentatio. *See* Anfechtung.
theology, data of. *See* law and gospel.
theology, Erlangen, 67–80
theology, Marburg, 67, 97–101, 111
theology, method of, *oratio, meditatio, tentatio* xii, xiv, 2, 4, 46n20, 115–16, 122–26, 137, 145, 173, 176–77, 181–88, 206–7, 209, 228, 257, 268–70, 288, 298, 305, 319

theology, mode of, experiential wisdom, 4, 116–26, 138, 145, 176–82, 206, 257, 268, 270, 288, 305
theology, Neo-Orthodox, 72, 80–97, 111
theology of the cross, the hiddenness of God in revelation, ix, x, 13–15, 14n3, 62, 68–76, 80–81, 86, 91, 93, 98, 101, 103–7, 111–12, 121–22, 152, 200, 235, 282, 284, 293–94, 299, 304, 311, 315, 317–18
theology, Roman Catholic, 117, 127, 131–32, 136, 154
theology, subject matter of theology, justification as, xiv, 4–5, 8, 37–38, 115–16, 119, 126–38, 145, 157, 173, 176, 188, 205–6, 208–9, 212, 214, 269, 276, 289, 298, 306, 315
theology, Trinitarian, 67, 101–109, 111, 181, 194, 197–201, 198n116, 232, 234–35, 240–44, 248, 288, 325
the three lights, 17–20, 29, 238–40, 272, 274–75, 311, 313, 324
Trinity, 8, 82–83, 87, 89, 101–2, 104, 104n237, 181, 193–94, 196–97, 201, 226–31, 234, 241, 247–48, 253, 265, 276–77, 280, 307, 313, 316
Trinity, poetological doctrine of, 226–31

vita passiva, the passive life, 118–25, 125n38

will bound, 4, 16–19, 28, 33, 38, 42–46, 80, 92–93, 100, 150, 162, 197, 219, 313
will, free, x, 14n3, 16–19, 34–38, 43, 68–69, 74, 78, 90, 92, 97, 99, 112, 185, 225, 233, 262, 266, 304, 328n75
Word of God, effectual nature, ix–xii, 3–5, 5n27, 9, 11, 25, 30, 38–39, 125, 140–43, 148–73, 192, 209, 211, 214
Word of God, *Leibliches Wort*, bodily Word, xi, 142n124, 157–58, 165–69, 172, 188, 188n71, 222, 320

Scripture Index

Genesis
11:1–9	203
26	27
32	30, 215

Deuteronomy
30:11–19	17

Psalms
51	27n49, 212
119	124

Isaiah
1	25
1:19–20	17
18:11	25n48
45:6	219n43
45:7	219n42
45:15	24
46:8	17
57:17	25

Jeremiah
26:3–4	17

Ezekiel
18:23	16, 18, 34, 68–69
18:31	17
33:11	34

Joel
2:12	17

Jonah
1:5	20
3:8	17

Mark
7	171
7:31–37	164n74
7:34	164n75

John
1:18	103

Romans
8:18–25	247n173
8:21	321n61
8:31–39	253
9–11	236

2 Corinthians
5:19 — 321n60

Galatians
3:19 — 143

2 Thessalonians
2:4 — 68, 70

Revelation
21:4 — 321n62